SACRED AND PROFANE BEAUTY

The Holy in Art

SACRED AND PROFANE BEAUTY

The Holy in Art

BY GERARDUS VAN DER LEEUW

Preface by Mircea Eliade

Translated by David E. Green

HOLT, RINEHART AND WINSTON

New York · Chicago · San Francisco

Library of Congress Catalog Card Number: 63-11867

First Edition

Designer: Ernst Reichl
88961-0113
Printed in the United States of America

PREFACE

Gerardus van der Leeuw was a versatile genius and a prolific writer. It is even probable that this versatility prevented him from becoming a world-renowned figure, like Karl Barth, Rudolf Bultmann, or Nikolai Berdyaev. Of course he was, and still is, extremely popular in his native Holland, and he is well known outside his country as the author of the only existing large and complete treatise on the phenomenology of religion. He was acknowledged as one of the outstanding historians of religion in the world. He organized and presided over the first International Congress for History of Religions, held after the war, in Amsterdam (1950). Nevertheless, his works do not enjoy the popularity which they deserve.

One of the reasons is doubtless his many-sided activities and the appalling diversity of his production. Gerardus van der Leeuw was a theologian and a philosopher, and he taught History of Religions at the University of Groningen. Though as a young man he studied Oriental languages and obtained his doctorate with a thesis on Egyptian religion, he later published two excellent books on primitive religion and innumerable articles on various other religions, the problem of *Urmono theismus* and the psychology of religion. In addition, he is the author of *Phänomenologie der Religion* (1935), preceded by *Einführung in die Phänomenologie der Religion* (1925). And besides all this, he was a poet, a musician, a man of the Church, and after the liberation of Holland, for some time served his country as Minister of Education.

I do not know to what extent van der Leeuw realized that his multilateral creativity exemplified an enduring European cultural model: the "Encyclopedic" or "Universal" man, personified by such

v

figures as Leonardo da Vinci, Michelangelo, Leibnitz, and Goethe. All cultures have their saints, their poets, and their sages; but a Leonardo da Vinci could appear only in Europe. At a certain moment during the nineteenth century, however, owing to the rapidly increasing fragmentation and specialization of knowledge, the Renaissance tradition seemed definitely concluded. The isolation of the different branches of knowledge became almost absolute. The immense domain of the arts was ignored or neglected by scientists and philosophers, as well as by historians. It is difficult to imagine a philosopher or a professor of philosophy at the end of the nineteenth century seriously discussing a poet, a painter, or a musician.

Things have changed in the last thirty to forty years, and van der Leeuw is one of the authors who best exemplifies this change. The tremendous success of Nietzsche and the discovery of Kierkegaard, the triumph of depth psychology and existential philosophy, together with other factors, have contributed to break down the walls between intellectual disciplines. Today, Heidegger comments laboriously on Hölderlin; professors at the Sorbonne and the Collège de France—such as Jean Wahl, Baruzi, Etiemble—publish poetry or novels; and the author of *L'être et le néant* writes short stories, novels, plays, literary criticism, and is passionately involved in the political life of his country.

Gerardus van der Leeuw was among the precursors of this movement. In his books, and particularly in his *Phänomenologie der Religion*, one finds copious quotations from poets and prose writers, and references to all the other arts. Ultimately, however, his inexhaustible curiosity and his many-sided interests did not serve van der Leeuw's work. There are still a great number of people who take for granted the old French proverb: *qui trop embrasse, mal étreint*. Moreover, van der Leeuw was an extremely gifted writer. He wrote beautifully and always with crystalline clarity. His books are easily understood; they do not need elaborate commentaries. In an epoch when dry, difficult, enigmatic writing has become almost a fashion in philosophical circles, clarity and artistic excellence are in danger of being confused with superficiality, dilettantism, or lack of original thinking.

Besides, van der Leeuw was not a systematic writer. Not that his books are without structure or are clumsily articulated, but they do not have the didactic heaviness which characterizes the majority of scholarly works. He writes with grace and elegance, almost impressionistically. He may even seem superficial or paradoxical. He had a wonderful sense of humor, and he delighted in quoting Chesterton or his four-year-old daughter while discussing primitive beliefs or the theology of the sacraments. He never took his enormous learning too seriously, nor his academic or social positions; he did not behave like a "Herr Professor." He was at heart an artist and a religious man. He knew that taking oneself too seriously is the product of a sinful pride, or, as he put it, "a fatal, morbid pride, which tempts man to take himself so seriously that he forgets that human life has the nature of a game. And at the same time he forgets God."

For van der Leeuw, human life had the nature of a game, but a game in which God was somehow involved. He begins the present work, *Vom Heiligen in der Kunst*, undoubtedly the masterpiece of his maturity, with a study of "Beautiful Motion," a presentation of the primordial unity of the dance and religion. Van der Leeuw believed that the dance is the original art. "All arts are found within it in its undivided unity. The image, made dynamic through movement and countermovement, sings and speaks simultaneously, forms a circle and then a house. From the unity, the arts free themselves by turning to the image: undanced drama and rhetoric, painting, sculpture, and architecture" (p. 303). This "split" of the original unity of art is followed, in more recent times, by a separation of each art into *sacred* and *profane* forms. Drama, for instance, grew out of the primitive liturgy and finally split into spiritual and profane drama. "One might say that the drama emerged from the church to the church square, from the temple into the market place. The history of the drama is a history of secularization" (p. 80).

Van der Leeuw describes this process of secularization with each of the arts: dance, drama, music, architecture, sculpture, and painting. He points out the original sacredness of an art, then the tension and conflict between art and religion, and finally their complete separation, *i.e.*, the secularization of the art and its absolute autonomy. But this process is not as simple as it seems at first sight. The religious life, even in a modern society, continues to utilize artistic forms. Art is better able to convey the holy than the pure idea, for "its point of departure is the whole man, body and soul, an indivisible unity. The holy, too, is concerned with the whole man, not an abstract 'spirit' which might be hindered by a material body" (p. 180). Religion needs the arts because it cannot live without forms and figures. But the arts must also come to religion, "as to the broader and deeper stream into which its floods can pour" (p. 189). The holy, says van der Leeuw, is not afraid of

reality, but of naturalness. The ancient Greeks did not place Phidias'
masterpieces in their temples, but rather the somewhat awkward,
archaic statues, or the xoanon.

At the end of each chapter, van der Leeuw indicates briefly the
theological significance of the art in question. But the problem of
"theological aesthetics" is most amply discussed in the last part of the
book, where van der Leeuw tries to summarize the results of his previous analysis.

> The dance reflects the movement of God, which also moves us
> upon the earth. The drama presupposes the holy play between God
> and man. Verbal art is the hymn of praise in which the Eternal and
> his works are represented. Architecture reveals to us the lines of the
> well-built city of God's creation. Music is the echo of the eternal
> *Gloria*. In the pictorial arts, we found images. . . . [p. 265]

And yet, he goes on, the questions, How can we make art religious?
or, When or how does art become religious? are meaningless.

> This would be too external, as though holiness and beauty were
> two ingredients which can be mixed together according to certain
> principles. We ask only: when and how is the unity revealed to us
> which was self-evident to primitive man, but which we can only per-
> ceive with effort? In other words, there is no particular art which
> can be designated religious. Still less is there a religion which we
> could call aesthetic. There is only a single art, and it is first of all art.
> There is only a single religion, and it is always and everywhere re-
> ligion [p. 266].

The complete unity of religion and art cannot be conceived, nor
should it be desired, for both need to be absolute.

> Religion and art are parallel lines, which intersect only at infinity
> and meet in God. If in spite of this we continue to speak of a renewed
> unity, of influences by which holiness and beauty can meet, of a
> point at which religion and art meet in our world, actually we
> always mean a direction, a striving, a recognition, which ultimately
> must destroy itself [p. 333].

In this learned and highly provocative book, Gerardus van der Leeuw does not pretend to show where the two paths, those of beauty and holiness, cross. But he says:

> Climb up upon this height and you will see how the paths of beauty and of holiness approach each other, growing distant, until finally in the far distance, they can no longer be held apart. Thus we shall view this study, to use Kierkegaard's phrase, as "preliminary." We erect no ultimate truths, but remain modestly to one side. We believe we have noticed something there, and so we point it out [pp. 335, 336].

One might disagree with van der Leeuw's conclusions or might even challenge his theological approach; but it is difficult to imagine a better-equipped author for a phenomenologically and historically grounded theology of art. By the breadth of its learning, by the audacity of its purpose, by the gracefulness of its style, his is a unique book.

MIRCEA ELIADE
UNIVERSITY OF CHICAGO

FOREWORD

Whoever writes about religion and art comes into contact with two sorts of people: Christians of the most varied stamp, and connoisseurs of art. Both are rather difficult to get along with.

There are Christians who are delighted to discover that although a picture by Rembrandt may be very beautiful, it is still just as transitory as the rest of the world. In their hearts they think that something might exist which could be assumed to escape this general impermanence. The thought that this is not true pleases them. Their love of art is like resentment, and is brought forth by their ostensible grief at their own impermanence. Because they see no possibility of changing this, they make a dogma of it. If I must perish, at least I shall drag everything down with me when I go.

On the other hand, there are connoisseurs who devote themselves with equal pleasure to the blessed self-assurance which the enjoyment of beauty can furnish; who imagine that they have a monopoly on art; for whom the practice of art is synonymous with piety and culture and science and similar worth-while pursuits. These are the literati and aesthetes, the melomaniacs and company managers of beauty, who do not want to join the rest of the world in perdition, but want to enter this world in its glorification through beauty.

Their position, too, is based on resentment.

There are Christians who value art, or even love it, but who at the same time want to put it at the service of their "persuasion"; they will allow art entrance into their lives only when they have consecrated it. They have become so accustomed to kneeling that they force everything to its knees with them, but they have forgotten how to rise up again. And they are often capable of kneeling only on the backs of others.

There are connoisseurs who view this "consecration" as the worst idolatry. For them there is nothing higher than beauty; there is nothing, indeed, other than beauty. It is impossible for them to find the connection between art and life, and certainly not between art and life's boundary. They stand, proud and straight, unable to kneel, and have actually forgotten even how to sit down.

There are Christians for whom the question of the relationship between the beautiful and the holy is exhausted by the question of the moral and pedagogical demands which must be made of a work of art. For them, a "Christian" book is a book in which there is no swearing, but preaching; "Christian" music is composition free from the blemishes which infect opera and dance; a "Christian" picture is a work of art in which everyone is decently dressed, preferably representing biblical figures.

There are, on the other hand, connoisseurs for whom art is exhausted in a purely formal game of colors and sounds, of lines and forms. When God proclaims his law from Sinai with thunder and lightning, they have eyes only for the glow and depth of the landscape.

There are many, many more. To all of them this study will not have much to say.

But I hope that there are still a few Christians and men of art who think differently. Perhaps there are a few for whom the problems are not so hopelessly simple, and who have learned reflection and modesty from the modern study of art and religion. Perhaps there are a few generous, humane Christians and a few reflective, reverent servants of art, Christians who have learned, through the manifestation of their Lord, to love the whole manifest world. Perhaps there are servants of beauty who are conscious that their love is directed toward him who is beauty itself, indeed more than beauty. Perhaps there are men on both sides who have not bent their knees before Baal, the Baal of a self-made Christianity or a self-made art, but who can kneel before God, always and everywhere.

In Bach's *Mass in B Minor*, the Credo is a glorious piece of music, an expression of beauty and an expression of holiness. All the voices speak, one after another: "Credo . . ." It is as though all the stops of human piety and human sense of beauty were released. We fear a letdown immediately. Then the violins begin, high and radiant, the old intona-

tion of the liturgy. Now it is as though the mystery were revealed;
here God speaks.

Within this study I have tried to find paths and boundaries for anyone who says he understands something of the way God speaks
through beauty, anyone who thinks that God's word could never be
without the highest beauty. It is a first and very incomplete attempt.
No one has dared more than a first step in this field, in this country or
elsewhere. But if a few will let themselves be stimulated to reflection
by this attempt, I shall be satisfied.[1]

GERARDUS VAN DER LEEUW

CONTENTS

Preface   V
Foreword   XI

INTRODUCTION   3

    Rivalry or Ultimate Unity?   3
    What Is the Holy?   4
    Methodology   5
    Can Art Be a Holy Act?   6
    "Primitive" and "Modern"   7
    Organization   7

PART ONE: *Beautiful Motion*   9

  1 The Unity of Dance and Religion   11
    Circles and Planes   11
    Dance and Culture   12
    Prayer, Work, and Dance   16
    Pantomime   17
    Ecstasy   24
    The Dance as the Movement of God   29
    The Dance and Contemporary Culture   32
  2 The Breakup of Unity   36
    The Dance in the Diversity of Life   36
    Profane Dance   38
    Procession   39
    The Dance of Death   44
    Labyrinth Dances   44
    Love Dances   48

3 Enmity Between Dance and Religion   50
     Hostility   50
     Dance and Theater   53
     The Body Cult or Culture?   54
4 Religious Dance: Influences   57
     The Ancient   57
     Apollonian Movement   59
     Dionysiac Movement   61
     The Human   66
5 Religious Dance: Harmony   67
     The Heavenly Dance   67
6 The Theological Aesthetics of the Dance   73

PART TWO: *Movements and Countermovements*   75

1 Holy Play   77
     Dance and Drama   77
     Drama   78
     Sacer Ludus   80
     The Mask   84
2 The Breakup of Unity   86
     Art Is Not Imitation   86
     Tipi Fissi (Fixed Types)   88
     Secularization   90
     Liturgy   92
3 The Enmity Between Religion and Theater   97
     The Enmity   97
     The Nature of the Enmity   100
4 Influences: Harmony   104
     The Broadening and Deepening of Life   104
     The Human   108
5 The Theological Aesthetics of the Drama   110
     Liturgy   110

PART THREE: *Beautiful Words*   113

1 Holy Words   115
     The Work Song   115
     Rhythm   117
     The Image   118
     The Poet   122

Word and Gesture 124

". . . A God Gave Words to Tell My Suffering" 125

2 The Breakup of Unity 127

From Carmen to Literature 127

Rain Magic Becomes Poetry 127

Poetry Becomes Prose 128

The Fairy Tale Becomes the Short Story 129

3 The Rejection of the Word by Religion 132

The Forbidden Image 132

The Forbidden Word 136

4 Influences Toward Harmony 139

The Sublime 139

Light 140

Silence and Near Silence 141

The Human 142

Harmony 142

5 The Theological Aesthetics of the Word 145

Poet and Prophet 145

Inspiration 147

The Divine Word 149

PART FOUR: *The Pictorial Arts* 153

1 The Fixation of an Idea as a Holy Image 155

The Art of Movement and Pictorial Art 155

Image Is Not Likeness 156

Ornament 157

Representation 157

Imagination and Representation 160

Freezing Motion 161

The Image of God 162

Complete Stasis 165

The Living Image 167

2 Unhindered Pictorial Representation 169

Real and Decorative Nakedness 169

Expression of the Holy Becomes Expression of Holy
Feelings 171

Transferences 172

Opposition Between Image and Likeness 173

Transition 176

3 The Prohibition of Images and the Iconoclastic Controversy   177
   The Prohibition of Images   177
   Iconomachy   182
4 The Holy Image: Influences   189
   Paths and Boundaries   189
   Fascination   190
   The Awe-Inspiring   190
   The Ghostly   190
   Darkness and Semidarkness   190
   The Human   191
   Harmony   192
   The Theological Aesthetics of the Image   192

PART FIVE: *The House of God and the House of Man*   193

1 The Building of the House of God   195
   The House of God   195
   Building   196
2 The House of God Becomes a Human House: Alienation
   and Conflict   199
   The House Can No Longer Be a Temple   199
   The Temple Becomes a House   201
   God Needs a House   202
   Man Needs a House   204
   No One Needs a House   204
3 Influences Toward Harmony   206
   The Massive and Monumental   206
   Profusion   207
   Emptiness   207
4 The Theological Aesthetics of Building   209

PART SIX: *Music and Religion*   211

1 Holy Sound   213
   Powerful Sound   213
2 The Transitional Structure   217
   Liturgical Music Becomes "Church Music"   217
   Passion and Oratorio   218
   Words and Music   220
   Refrain   221
   Da Capo   222
   Imitation   223
   The Decline of Church Music   223
   Music and Religion   223

3 Discord   225
    No Conflict?   225
    Music, not Tonal Art   226
    Silence, neither Speaking nor Singing   227
    Altercations   227
4 Influences   230
    The Last Defense of External Continuity   230
    The Sublime   231
    Light   232
    Suspension   233
    The Heavenly   234
    The Transition   234
    Darkness and Semidarkness   236
    Silence and Near Silence   236
    The Endless   238
    Objectivity   238
5 Harmony   243
6 The Theological Aesthetics of Music   245
    Music, the "Telephone of the Beyond"?   245
    Music Which Leads to the Depths   248
    Program Music   254
    In Praise of Opera   256
    Music as a Game   258
    The Theology of Music   259
    Eschatological Music   261

PART SEVEN: *Theological Aesthetics*   263

1 Paths and Boundaries   265
    To Seek, Not to Construct   265
    "Religious Art"   267
    The Antithetical Structure   271
    "Artists"   271
    Style   273
    L'Art pour l'Art   275
    Service   276
    The World of Art   280
    Absolutism   282
    Psychological Parallels   283
    Resistances   284
2 The Republic of the Arts   288
    Words   289
    Music   293

Conflict   295
The Holy Word   299
Holy Sound   300
Unity of Word and Music   300
The Hierarchy of the Arts   302
3   The Image of God   304
Phenomenological Component   305
Exegetical-Historical Component   307
Dogmatic Component   317
4   The Theology of the Arts   328
Independence and Interdependence   332
Point of Intersection   333
Harmony as the Creation of God   334
A Metaphysics of Art?   336
A Worship of Beauty?   337
Incarnation   339
Bibliography   341
Index   353

SACRED AND PROFANE BEAUTY

The Holy in Art

INTRODUCTION

RIVALRY OR ULTIMATE UNITY? The relationship between religion on the one hand and art, moral philosophy, and science on the other, raises great difficulties for human thought and comprehension. Pious men of strict observance can hardly see in art an obedient maidservant. Artists of *l'art pour l'art* look down on religion with distrust and often with contempt. Independent moral philosophy demands freedom from religious restrictions. Imperialistic religion condemns "works" and glorifies faith. Science and religion have been at war with each other for centuries. Many believers consider science dangerous; many scientists see in religion a passing phenomenon, already almost past.

Thus rivalry reigns: first, in general, rivalry between the religious spirit and the aesthetically, ethically, or scientifically oriented man; second, a much sharper and more implacable rivalry between the Christian religion and these manifestations of the intellectual world. Religion is always imperialistic. No matter how vague or general it may be, it always demands everything for itself. It can tolerate, at most, the claims made by art, ethics, and science, but it can never recognize their independent justification.

True as this was, for example, of the romantic pantheism of the young Schleiermacher, how much more true it is for the specific historical form which religion found in Christianity. Naturally, most of those who see in Christ the complete and final revelation of God will not want to deny that God also reveals himself in other ways in the world: in nature, in art, in history, and in science. But this is not true revelation. Fine names are invented for it. One speaks of *gratia communis* and "general revelation"; but no essential connection is seen

3

between God's revelation in Christ and the formless revelations in the rest of the world. One hesitates to say, with John, that the world is evil, but a path from the revelation in Christ to art, ethics, and science is not known, and, usually, is not sought.

Christ is thought of as the Holy One of God. Beauty, goodness, and truth are not denied, but they are not sought in Him; nor does one often find in Him the beautiful, the good, and the true. The relationship between religion on the one hand and art, ethics, and science on the other, is (to use an example from the history of the Netherlands) like the relationship of the seven provinces to the States-General at the time of the Republic. They indeed belong to it, primarily to obey, but they have no voice in it. It is not simple to see the situation in a different light. In Christ, God's fullness has been revealed; there is really nothing more to be added.

On the other hand, science, art, and ethics are also imperialistic, each in its own right and also in combination with the others. Each claims all of life. Just as it is not possible to serve both God and Mammon, thus the possibility of serving any master other than the strict master art seems to be excluded. Nor is it necessary:

> Who has art and science both,
> He also has religion;
> Whoever does not have them both,
> Let him have religion.

And yet the paths of religion, art, ethics, and science not only cross, they also join. There is a religious art. A close connection exists between religion and ethics. There is even a point at which science seems to lose itself in religion. How does this come about? Is rivalry the final word? Or is there ultimately a unity? Where and how can we find it?

WHAT IS THE HOLY?   If we want to discover paths which join and boundaries which separate the holy and the beautiful, we must first have a clear idea of what the holy is. At this time we have a great advantage. The nature of the religious consciousness and its object, the holy, has been examined in the past decades from two completely different, complementary points of view, in the works of Rudolf Otto and Eduard Spranger.

Otto[2] has shown us the holy as the "wholly other," that forces itself upon us as being of wholly other form, other origin, and other effect than everything else that is known to us. It is, in the phrase of the ancient Roman, a *nobis sepositum*, separated from us and from our world. We respond to this intrusion with mixed feeling. The awe which the completely other awakens in us breaks down at once into feelings of fear, of dread, of reverence, of smallness, indeed of nothingness, and at the same time a feeling of being drawn in, of joyous astonishment, of love. The holy, as Otto has taught us to see, both attracts and repels. It allows us to become aware of infinite distance and feel a never-suspected nearness. If we succeed in finding paths from the holy to the beautiful, then the beautiful will also have to call forth this consciousness within us, and will have to lead us to the wholly other.

All this refers to the content, the substance, of the holy. The studies by Spranger[3] have elucidated its form for us. According to him, the peculiarity of the religious activity of the human spirit is characterized by the fact that the object of consideration is never a specific value or a sense limited to a single point of view, but, rather, is final value and the ultimate sense. An act can be evaluated from different points of view: ethically, aesthetically, economically, etc. The religious man evaluates in regard to total value, utlimate meaning. Religion demands totality, its judgments recognizing no others after or besides themselves. The values which it recognizes are not conditioned by a particular point of view, but are values before God. Therefore, religion is not concerned with what is beautiful, true, or useful, but with what is eternal. Religion gives to culture again and again the command Jesus gave the rich young man: "Sell all that thou hast." We shall have to decide whether aesthetic, scientific, or moral culture can assume that sort of value and express it, if need be, by denying their own essence. Then we shall discover to what degree their own essence blocks this process.

METHODOLOGY We shall see how, in the course of history, paths have been laid and boundaries drawn. Nevertheless, we do not want to engage in historical analysis. We shall see ourselves confronted with the question of the ultimate value of the holy, the beautiful, the good, and the true, independently and in relation to one another. But our analysis is not philosophic or dogmatic. It is phenomenological. The use of the phenomenological method has, recently, been widespread. In this context, of course, we cannot give a more detailed statement of its aims.[4] Let this be indicative: Where history asks, "How did it happen?", phenomenology asks, "How do I understand it?"; where philosophy examines truth and reality, phenomenology contents itself with the data without examining them further with respect to their content of truth or reality. We do not intend to pursue causal relationships, but rather to search for comprehensible associations. Further, we do not intend to investigate the truth behind the appearance, but we shall try to understand the phenomena themselves in their simple existence.

We are fully convinced that this method has its limitations. That it is nevertheless unavoidable for all historical as well as systematic analyses we shall show by our practical experiment, rather than by theoretical disputations.

CAN ART BE A HOLY ACT? It is in this formulation that the problem concerning the paths and boundaries between holiness and beauty confront the phenomenologist most clearly. This means that we shall not attempt to give a philosophical definition of the beautiful, nor shall we immerse ourselves in the question of whether nature is beautiful in its own essence or whether the intellect carries over its own beauty into nature. These are questions of the absolute value of the beautiful; that is to say, questions that belong to the metaphysics of the beautiful.

We are not concerned with the beautiful per se, but with how the beautiful influences our spirit and finds expression through it. The impression and expression of the beautiful we usually call art. Of course we are not using the word in a technical sense, and are not even concerned with the practice of art. Whoever sees the beauty of a landscape experiences the beautiful. Whoever, above and beyond that, is capable of saying that it is beautiful and in what way it is beautiful; that is, he who can express his experience, is an artist. If he is not capable of this, then he experiences the beauty of nature in the same way in which he perceives the beauty of a work of art. In both cases he is concerned not with beauty as such, but rather with his experience of beauty; that is, with art, whether it is potential (impressionistic), or actual (expressionistic).

We limit the question of the relationship between beauty and holiness to the analysis of the relationship between beauty and holiness as man experiences them; that is to say, to the holy act and the beautiful act, or art.

Thus we see from our periphrase of the holy that the relationship can only be grasped by the question, "Can art be a holy act?" The reverse question, "Can religion be art or resolve itself into art?" becomes inadmissible on the ground of our definition of the holy as the "wholly other" and the "absolutely valid."

What, of course, can be asked easily, and must be asked, is to what degree the consciousness and the realization of the holy can be art. This formulation of the question implies the possibility of a very complicated modern art which coalesces into a unity with religion in a way which we shall examine more closely later. We shall consider the primitive artistic expression that stands in just as close a connection, though of a different sort, to the holy act of a magico-religious nature.

Depending on whether we are concerned with a primitive or a modern intellectual context, this connection assumes such different guises that we shall divide our object according to its relationship to the primitive mentality.

"PRIMITIVE" AND "MODERN"   This is not the place to propose at length what is meant by "primitive" and "modern." I have done that in another place.[5] From what follows, usage will become apparent automatically. One remark only should be made in this regard: "primitive" never means the intellectual situation of earlier times or other lands, and "modern" never that of here and now. Neither is a description of a stage in the evolution of the human spirit; rather, both are structures. We find them both realized today just as much as three thousand years ago, both in Amsterdam and in Tierra del Fuego. Of course, a more complete realization of the primitive intellectual structure is evidenced by the ancient and so-called uncivilized peoples than by the West Europeans of today. But as the primitive is never completely lacking even in the most modern cities, so the modern is present in the least-educated native of Surinam.

ORGANIZATION   This book is so constructed that the different arts are treated one after the other in six chapters: the dance, drama, rhetoric, the fine arts, architecture, and music. The discussion is according to a fixed plan, which is repeated six times.

Thus one will find in each chapter the following points taken up: first, primitive expressions of art, which are nothing more than religious acts, are described and analyzed. A review of the development of the art in question follows, in which it is ascertained how the art frees itself from religion and makes itself independent. From this, the conflict between religion and art inevitably arises. On the basis of facts which arise with the beginnings of a *rapprochement*, we continue by describing a few impulses which prove to be necessary for the reactivation of the original unity, that is, for religious art.

Each chapter ends with a theological aesthetic. In it, the search is pursued for the connection between what we have found on the one hand to be the essential core of the art in question, and God's revelation on the other hand.

A seventh chapter is devoted to a general theological aesthetic. This chapter contains, first, a comprehensive review of the arts in their organization, their unity, and their dependence on each other, and then a fundamental theological treatment of the connection between art and religion. We believe we have found this unity of essence in the fact that both are answers of man to the call of God. Here the "image of God," that is to say Christ, forms the central idea.

In the discussion of the various arts, as in nature, the boundaries are not sharply drawn, for, in reality, also, their domains coalesce.

PART ONE

Beautiful Motion

1   THE UNITY OF

DANCE AND RELIGION

CIRCLES AND PLANES   There was a period—and for the so-called primitive peoples this period still exists—when art and religion stood so close to each other that they could almost be equated. Song was prayer; drama was divine performance; dance was cult. Every act of primitive man is, by its very nature, a magical act. All action, not merely the wonderful and inexplicable, takes place through "power," even though it is only in unusual cases that it is worth while expressly to emphasize this power and to designate the act as magical, holy. In practice, primitive man proceeds empirically. That "otherness," which reveals itself in an act, he speaks of only when it intrudes upon him as something remarkable; when it places itself in his way. He does not generalize and he does not theorize. Therefore, only exceptionally will he explain as holy his own actions or those of others, as well as natural phenomena, and events in society. But our dichotomy between super-natural and natural is not his criterion. To kill an enemy at some dis-tance by means of an incantation demands holy power; the killing of a strong, well-armed enemy by means of a simple club also demands this "power." The natural and supernatural—to our minds two strictly separated realms—lie for the primitive man in one plane, like two con-centric circles, which he calls the usual and the unusual. There is no absolute line of demarcation.

Thus between religion and art, and between other domains, there is no actual contrast. What for us is a series of neatly separated planes, the primitive man sees as concentric circles. Life, for him, is still a unity. In our system of language, every act, every happening, can be judged scientifically, logically, aesthetically, religiously, or ethically. By primitive criteria, it can possess all these characteristics at the same

11

time, one merging into another. Even if we do not always hold ourselves to this separation, we have learned at least to avoid setting up ethical criteria in an economic situation. For the primitive mind there are, of course, various motives and criteria as well; but one does not purposely differentiate them. A person performing a religious act can *eo ipso* act aesthetically. For example, one who dances acts through motives and pursues goals which, to our minds, are at once recreational, economic, aesthetic, and religious. One of these motives or goals can predominate. Then, to retain our metaphor, one of the concentric circles is larger than the others. Nevertheless, they all exist at the same time and have the same center. This center is the single, unbroken life itself. There do not yet exist an "earth" and a "heaven"; there is neither the concept "religious" nor the concept "aesthetic." In other words, the problem we are considering does not yet exist for the primitive mind. We do not need to search for paths and boundaries when there are no boundaries and therefore also no paths. All primitive art is religious, but not in the sense that it is purposely dedicated to religious goals. It is, rather, religious in itself, even when specifically religious objectives are lacking.

DANCE AND CULTURE   "Dance is one of the purest and most perfect forms of game," says Johan Huizinga in his study of man at play.[6]

In writing about the dance, I discovered that, even more than in the other arts, participation is necessary if it is to be understood.[7] With the spoken or written word, little can be explained when the point is to appreciate the rhythm and imitate it. And yet the word is able to follow the dance, at a distance; for the word itself is only one of the many forms of human expression (like music) which, though they have their independent life and rules, cannot be separated from the dance, and in comparison to it are less broad, less comprehensive, less totalitarian.

The dance is the most universal of the arts, since, as Goethe justly said, it could destroy all the fine arts.[8] It is an expression of all the emotions of the spirit, from the lowest to the highest. It accompanies and stimulates all the processes of life, from hunting and farming to war and fertility, from love to death. It enables, in turn, other arts to come into being: music, song, drama. Despite all this richness, the dance is no formless complex, but a simple unity. To dance, one needs nothing, not paint, nor stone, nor wood, nor musical instrument; nothing at all except one's own body. Man can produce for himself the rhythm which induces the body to dance (though, of course, others may do this); it is marked out by the stamping of feet and the clapping of hands. Verbal art has just as little need of material or instruments, but it needs thought which is articulated in an image. The dance is its own articulation. In the greatest simplicity it remains constant, century after century.

In this respect, too, the dance occupies a special place among the arts. "Since the stone age the dance has assumed neither new forms nor new content. The history of creative dance is completed in prehistory," says the greatest expert on the history of the dance.[9] Its motifs have remained the same since antiquity, as the round dance, the spinning dance, the masked dance, the forest ring, etc. All have their origin in the fertility magic of the most ancient times.

The art of beautiful motion is far and away the oldest. Before man learned how to use any instruments at all, he moved the most perfect instrument of all, his body. He did this with such abandon that the cultural history of prehistoric and ancient man is, for the most part, nothing but the history of the dance. We must understand this literally. Not only is prehistory mostly dance history, but dance history is mostly prehistory. Like a giant monolith, the dance stands in the midst of the changing forms of human expression. Not only as an art, but also as a form of life and culture, the dance has been grievously wounded by the general disappearance of culture. In the European culture of today the dance plays only a very small and often inferior role. Only in recent times have changes in its character become noticeable. Since there have existed men who write about it, like myself, for example, and who, like the "audience" at an afternoon ball, would rather look on than dance themselves, since the couple dance has pushed aside all other forms of dance and eroticism has laid claim to the dance for itself alone, the monolith seems to totter. This tottering is connected with the general and much more serious tottering of our culture. The revivification of genuine dance in the folk-dance movement, the pantomime (Ballet Jooss), and the religious dance (The Maidens of the Grail) justifies the hope that balance will gradually be restored.

It is already clear from this that the influence of the dance on culture is exceptionally great. "*Beschaving*" (Dutch; literally something like "grinding to a finish") is a beautiful word. "Culture" has become an ugly word. But I believe that we can see in them this common ground. Both mean the domain of what is properly human, of the man who does not simply accept the world as he finds it, but rather transforms it into his own world. He makes of the steppes a farmland, of the forest a clearing in which he erects his house; he rides upon the waters; he makes of the music of the birds a song, of the movements of the animals a dance. Culture (*beschaving*) is the movement of man through nature. In the process, three main possibilities are realized: man overcomes the world and masters it, succeeding with the help of his magic and his science, which are related to each other and coincide to a degree with each other; or he controls his dependence on the powers of this world, either by subjecting himself to them or allowing himself to be ruled, doing this in a state of enthusiasm or ecstasy; or he seeks for himself a place outside the course of the world, which allows him to observe, and this he does in art, in science, and in contemplation.

Let us further complete this picture of the movement of man through nature. Man tries to stride, heavily and emphatically, to hover, light and high, or to move along calmly and more or less conscious of responsibility. Obviously he fulfills all three functions in every hour of his life, and none of the three is completely lacking in a single one of his actions.

Now what meaning do we attach to the dance within the totality of human culture? The dance is indeed the movement of man in the literal sense, but it is not his natural movement, being rather the specifically human movement created by him. It is ordered movement. The dance is a movement of the self in a purposeful, definite manner. It is walking the way we walked as children, with one foot on the sidewalk and the other in the street; or three steps forward on the right foot, then one on the left. In the dance, man discovers the rhythm of the motion that surrounds him, just as it surrounds another man or an animal or a star. He discovers the rhythm and invents a response, but it is a response that has its own forms, that is stylized and ordered. He does with motion the same thing that he does with a shape when he carves or chisels, draws or paints. He places his own movements and those of the creatures which surround him into an ordered whole.

> Like the other animals born in the mud, only man refused to remain stuck in it. So he dances through life as though he wanted to dance until he collapsed, and thereby discovers that he is able, through his rhythmic dancing, to develop at the same time a second spirit.[10]

This characteristic of the dance appears clearly in the custom described by Curt Sachs, observable both among many primitives and also among cultured peoples, of raising those who are unable to dance up onto the shoulders of the dancers: children, those who are exhausted, menstruating women, etc.[9] Thus they are "danced," and although they do not move, they participate in the rhythm which orders life. Many rituals in which, for example, a child is carried in procession about the hearth (like the Amphidromia in Greece and Rome) are nothing other than such passive dances.

Alongside a river in Australian New Guinea an old man sits and stares at the water. A tree trunk drifts past: at certain intervals it rises to the surface and then sinks again, always with the same motion. The old man reaches for his drum and softly takes up the rhythm that he has discovered. While he beats the drum, the image of a dance takes form in his mind. So the Orokaiva-Papuas express the process among themselves.[9] The rhythm must be discovered; then the dance arises, which imposes it on the environment, thereby drawing the environment into the movement as well. This is what is meant when the dance is spoken of as a "motion-magic." This is not a beautiful word, but it makes the situation clear. Man perceives the motion of the surrounding environment, and then, in his turn, forces it upon the world after his own fashion.

This is very clear in those dances which imitate the motions of animals. The animals, too, dance. In the zoo we see, for example, how the cranes dance. The anthropoid apes, with which the psychologist Wolfgang Köhler experimented in Tenerife, engaged in round dances. Moor hens dance, and likewise other animals. Sachs has determined that the following dance forms are present in the animal world: the round dance and ellipse dance about a post, stepping together and apart, rhythmical stamping of feet, and the whirling dance about an axis. Now here lies a problem. If culture means the manner in which man transforms the world into his human world, then it might appear that we stand confronted by two alternatives: either the dance is not a part of culture, or the animals also possess culture. The one is as nonsensical as the other. The dance of the animals is an instinctive, almost automatic, movement, and is therefore not a dance at all. Ethelreda Lewis has recorded "Trader" Horn's description of the movement of elephants within a stockade:[11]

Mr. Horn told me once of elephants which, after they were captured, walked for two uninterrupted days mechanically in a circle along the stockade, which they could have trampled down with ease.

This is reminiscent of Fabre's procession of caterpillars, except that the wild banana accidentally seemed to break the spell.

There is something compulsive, something completely certain, about the dance movement of animals, which impresses man. For this reason he imitates the motions of animals. Innumerable dances, throughout the whole world, are imitations of animal dances: the crane and bear dances in Greece and China;[12] the ram and monkey dances in Greece; the buffalo dances of the North American Indians;[13] the fox dance of the Basques, and our fox trot; the pavan or peacock dance, and many, many more. By dancing the movements of the animals, man becomes master of the animal rhythm. He subjects to himself the order of the animals, he adds the power of the animals to his own. He compels them to flee so that they fall into his trap or come within range of his weapons; he makes them mate in order to multiply and provide him with domestic animals and food. And with this we come to the actual meaning of the dance.

PRAYER, WORK, AND DANCE   The dance is neither an "art" in a present-day, one-sided aesthetic sense, nor an entertainment. It is half ritual, half work, and both together. Movement is ordered firmly and ceremonially in a dance, but for a useful purpose. In primitive cultures, prayer, work, and dance—for us strictly separate concepts with fully different modes of expression—belong together, indeed so closely that they can scarcely be differentiated. Dance is not only relaxation, sport, and art, but at the same time a holy and also useful action. "Throughout the whole world, the primitive man in the magico-religious stage danced where we would pray or worship," says Jane Harrison. Actually the art of the dance is even more primitive than verbal art. Here rhythm is all powerful; it rules the whole man and the whole world. It gives expression to all emotions, loosing all forces and compelling them to follow the right path. This is not to say that primitive man does not also know the dance as an entertainment or bodily exercise, but this never exhausts it. In Mexico the Indians have a single word for dancing and working. A strenuous dance lasting for many days is considered indispensable for the success of the harvest. While all the others are at work in the fields, one remains at home whose job it is to dance throughout the entire day. If he neglects to do so, he harms the entire work. It is obvious that in such circumstances we can, at most, conceive how a member of the family might remain at home in order to pray for the success of the work. Among the Kagaba Indians, festival time is called "time of work," and consists of many days of continuous, very strenuous dancing, which is prepared in year-long practice.[14] Feasts and dances here are by no means "recreation" or "free time." In New Caledonia, a chieftain with leanings toward Christianity decided to do away with the dances, and so he buried the objects which were invariably used at the dances, or gave them to the evangelist. When this was discovered, a great sadness came over the whole people: "Sorrow overcomes them, they raise their arms and let them drop again. Alas, the god of dance has been robbed. We cannot dance any more. Our legs have been broken off."[15]

That the dance has religious meaning does not mean that it can express only religious feelings. On the contrary, all feelings, from the most solemn to the most frivolous, find their expression in the dance. The religious is not a particular sensation alongside other sensations, but the summation of them all. Thus the dance can also serve a purpose which we, too, would call religious. An old inhabitant of Halmahera, who did not want simply to give up the feasts for the dead of his people, said, in his defense, to the missionary: "My dancing, drinking, and singing weave me the mat on which my soul will sleep in the world of the spirits." But even when the dance stands in the service of what to our mind is a purely secular matter, it is by its very nature religious, for through it holy power is freed. The primitive man dances for everything, from his wife to eternal life, from a hunting trophy to a profit in trading. The dance not only accompanies all the actions of his life, but also leads it, supports it, and brings it to a good end. To the accompaniment of a dance, one exhibits his wares in New Caledonia; looks for lice in North Queensland; divorces his wife among many Indian tribes, and, in the Cameroons, goes to the gallows.

PANTOMIME   The religious character of the dance is shown most clearly in the dance pantomime. Here the dance approaches the drama. An action is imitated, and the dancers appear as actors. Through imitation, the power of the original act is transferred to a new act. For the primitive mind, the representation of an action is realistically bound up with what is represented. The war dance, accordingly, is a kind of war, and its movement influences the outcome. Similarly, the hunting dance is a kind of hunt. Many primitive peoples know how to imitate, with extreme artistry, the movements of the kinds of animals they are hunting for. To these pantomime dances the love dance belongs also, which in our eyes, accordingly, quickly becomes obscene.

But the case is no different with the religious in the narrow sense than it is with these—again, in our eyes—secular things. There are countless ritual dances in which the participants, mostly priests, represent the holy powers of the spirits or the gods. The Greek writer Lucian says that the dance represents an important element in the religious mysteries of his time. It is important in every primitive and classic ritual. The great movement of death and life is imitated and made dependable in the dance.

The pantomime is ancient. It already is present in the cultural fund of the Stone Age. The rock sketches of the Bushmen of South Africa picture all kinds of magical dances, including phallic ones. A Bushman explains the nature of the pantomime very clearly in the following words: "I believe that someone who has killed an antelope becomes like it, together with his companions."[16] The dancers assume the character of animals, spirits, gods, or other beings which in ancient times possessed power. Through personification, this power is continued into the present.

In Japan, every Shinto temple has a dance room. There virgins dance and perform pantomimes at the feasts.[17] A very widespread form of pantomime is the phallic dance, in which the male and female dancers tie on a large artificial phallus. This is the case, for example, at the Greek Korythalia, and among the primitives in Asia, Africa, and America.[9] The dancers are thus wearing the power of reproduction.

In order, however, to be able to take on all the powers which move through these processes of life, and to put them into one's own order, one must identify himself with them. To imitate animals in a dance, one must be an animal. Everywhere in the world, men assume the nature of animals, the dead, or the gods, in order to make sure, by means of the dance, that whatever is desired of them will be performed. "Mortals clothe themselves with the 'flesh' of the immortal; that is, with the paint and masks proper to the gods, whereby the gods are compelled to grant their blessings," it is said of the dances of the Zuñi Indians.[18] Herein lies the great importance of the mask for the dance.

Naturally, primitive men take just as much pleasure in disguising themselves as do our children, and presumably we ourselves. We must not think that the primitive mentality is capable only of seriousness.

The difference between us lies in the fact that we are serious in the morning and amuse ourselves in the evening. In the morning we put on judge's robes, and in the evening, perhaps, a suit of armor, because we have been talked into taking part in an "entertainment" at the wedding of our niece. We dress up wonderfully in the evening for a masked ball, and the next morning, with bored expressions, put on our lieutenant's uniform in order to perform our "service" in it. For the primitive man, "entertainment" and court session, ball and "service," coincide. He amuses himself delightfully and yet sustains a serious purpose within his play. He dances with weighty seriousness, dancing for his gods, indeed, dancing in pantomime the deeds of his gods. This brings us by a new path to the *other*, the holy: the depersonification that lies in the playing of a role, the turning away from everyday life that is involved in putting on a mask. The mask unites the dancer with the being that is represented by him, whether animal, god, or spirit of the dead.

Thus, the dogs and the dead dance also. The Indian god Krishna dances for the shepherd girls, and Indra dances to the octosyllabic meter of the Veddas.[19] In the imagination of many peoples, the stars dance. The dead dance not only the Dance of Death of the Middle Ages and Holbein; in ancient Egypt (*danse macabre*, from Arabian *makabr*, cemetery[20]) the souls of the dead kings dance, too. Wanting to personify animals, the dead, or the gods, and to reproduce their dance, one puts on a mask.

The masked dances are among the most widespread of human cultural phenomena. They are met with in Africa, America, Australia, and in the most distant parts of Asia. Many remains can still be found in Europe.[21] The mask represents the identity of the dancer and what is danced. It is, indeed, a holy object which is carefully preserved and even worshiped.[22] A sick dancing girl in Siam or Cambodia directs her prayer to the dance mask.[9] Through the mask, as long as the dance lasts, the dancers *are* animals, spirits, gods.[23] What demonic power can issue from the mask is shown especially in Melanesia, the land of the dance masks. Sachs has described this superbly:

What a world! Unchained, free of all organic restraints, the creative fantasy shapes into new forms what nature has distributed into strict classes and orders. From the almost human face juts the mighty beak of the frigate bird; from the gaping mouth of the giant shoots, not a tongue, but an insect more than a yard long;

in place of a tail rises a greedy goose neck, or grows a cobra snake. In addition, the individual parts blur into unreality. Goggling shell eyes bug out; a neckless head is fastened to the body, or a headless neck rises up, tips forward, and seems to open its interior like a mouth; or, where neck and head should rest, a sharp cone juts into the air. . . . All restraint is gone; the headdresses tower a hundred feet into the air.

Even in a museum, freed from the dancer and their natural environment, standing on display behind panes of glass, they preserve a little of their weird, demonic nature. But outside, in their own world, worn and feared by believers and the hypersensitive, breaking threateningly out of the forest and jerking closer with rhythmic, superhuman steps, bows, and totters, accompanied by incorporeal, ghostly sounds—what a terrifying drama![9]

Thus one attains the power that resides in the surrounding world by dancing. Ruth Benedict, who knows how to formulate these matters so wonderfully, describes a Zuñi dance: "There is nothing at all wild about them; what makes them work on us is the power of the rhythm and the unified movements of forty dancers." The corn is danced out of the ground; wild animals are danced into range; rain is danced from the clouds.[18] For this reason the Kagaba Indians call the time of festivals and dances the "time of work." The dances, which may last for many days, are in fact really strenuous.[14] Harvest and hunt, say the mountain Damas in South Africa, need a good dance; the dance needs a good fire; the fire needs a good fire maker.[23] They expressly insert the dance into the process of production. The dancing master in *The Would-be Gentleman* speaks better than he knows:

> Man needs nothing so much as the dance. . . . A man who does not dance is good for nothing. . . . All human unhappiness, all blows of fortune which history reports to us, all mistakes of politics, all defeats of the great commanders result solely from the fact that the dance is not understood.[24]

This practical import of the dance is best known to us in the function that it retains, even today, in the game of love. Dance and love are indissolubly bound. The ball at which, in our youth, the marriageable daughter was presented, and the dance hall of today demonstrate this to an unhappy degree. In all of courtship, from the first date to marriage, the dance is indispensable. But it does not stop with the arousing of the senses (the only function, by the way, that the dance has retained in our impoverished culture). The dance unchains the natural drives, but it also enchains them. Ultimately, it makes possible the game of exploding and controlled passion. Our fathers understood how one danced "the bride to bed." The *Bettleite* is an old dance known in Germany.[25] In ancient times, in Venice, the bride was introduced to the groom in a dance.[9]

If we trace cultural history back further, to older and more primitive times, the erotic dances have a character no less erotic, but less direct. These dances are independent activities which make the game of love possible, but they are not the game itself. They are more like rituals. For this reason, the erotic couple-dance is rare among the primitives; and when it occurs, it is "open,"[9, 13] that is, the partners do not touch. They approach each other with gestures which are very often clearly erotic. Sometimes two men stand opposite one woman, or two women opposite one man (remains of this can be found in the Ukrainian *hopak* and the *écossaise*),[9] very often a group of men opposite a group of women. But in the approach the separation is still preserved. It remains a game. Even in the fourteenth, fifteenth, and sixteenth centuries, the couple-dances, even such a popular one as the *lavolta*, were often forbidden.[25] The simple erotic dance of the primitive and classical world, still found among the common people today, is either a solo-dance, of exhibitionistic nature (like the belly dance), or a free dance in which either the girl stands still while the man (or men) dances around her, or the man, standing still, has the women dance around him. The latter type has as its oldest example the miolithic rock drawings at Cogulin Lérida in Spain, in which nine women dance around a naked ithyphallic man. "From this group of nine women the view ranges through the millennia to the ceremonial ring of the nine shepherd girls around Krishna and the nine Muses around Apollo."[9]

Huizinga is therefore completely correct when he says that the displacement of group-pattern dances by closed couple-dances indicates a weakening and an impoverishment.[6] The nature of the game is lost, and the dance, the oldest and most universal art, loses its claim to this designation.

The erotic function of the dance borders on its more inclusive function as the awakener of fertility. Imitation of the gestures of coitus insures fertilization and birth, not only in the ones concerned, but in all of nature. Peasant dances, such as Sebald Beham drew and Nithard sang of, with their wild leaps, their "hem-grabbing," and their throwing of the girls into the air or onto the ground, represent the remains of this primeval fertility ritual.[9] The Greek vases, with their satyr and Sileni dances, bring us even closer. Among completely primitive peoples, the entire process of coition is realistically represented. The examples can be referred to in Sachs.[9]

A large number of dances have as their goal the awakening or main-tenance of fertility. Thus the round dances (*rondes*) arose out of the magic circle which the dancers described around a holy object, tree, post, or well, and, on occasion, around the coveted woman or the coveted man, or around the field which is to yield the crop. The country-dance (*contredanse*), the snake dance (like the *vlöggelen*, which can still be observed in Twente, a region of Holland), was origi-nally conceived as a dance procession around the land.[26] The phallic dances among the primitives and on Greek vases speak for themselves, but even innocent social dances like the quadrille and the *Zevensprong* were once fertility dances.[9, 13] As Preuss has ascertained, there are no fixed boundaries between the imagination, exhibition, and magical ac-tion. Representation has the nature of compulsion.[13] The symbol is at the same time an effective cause, as in sacramental theology. But the dance is separate from the action itself. After the dance comes the sow-ing and plowing, and, not rarely, mating.[27] But the dance itself stands alone. It is game, art, ritual. It contains reality, but it is not reality.

Hunting dances are no less widespread than love and fertility dances. Usually they represent, in pantomime, the wild animal or its prey. The mountain Damas have no fewer than twenty-two dances with animal names: the dance of the springbok, the jackal, the leopard, etc.[23] Equally widespread are war and weapon dances, which repre-sent battle. The transition between so-called shadowboxing and the weapon dance is fluid.[9] All of this is fairly familiar to us. Dances which imitate the motion of the stars are further removed. These, too, have the purpose of securing the regular paths of the heavenly bodies, and thereby of earthly events. Man interpolates, so to speak, the path of the stars into his own path. The *Chebi* is the prototype of a very old dance of the planets.[28] Lucian says that the dance originated at creation, and is as old as Eros: "In the dance of the heavenly bodies, in the complicated movements by which the planets are brought into harmonious relation with the fixed stars, you see an example of this art in its infancy."[29] In Dante's *Paradiso* the stars dance.[30] And Joost van den Vondel, a Dutch poet (1587–1679), has Adam sing:

Learn to dance the festive measure
        Which the Lord
God invented in his leisure;
Imitate with knowing pleasure
        Heaven's chord.

If you'd change to form supernal
        Fields of earth,
Follow heaven's course diurnal:
Stars obey the role eternal
        Of their birth.

Some stand fixed; yet always spinning
        Seven dance,
Dancers who the prize are winning,
Ringing in since time's beginning
        Sky's expanse.

Bride, begin! For I am taking
        Every day
The journey which the suns are making.
Thou, like moonlight fresh awaking,
        Lead the way!

The dance can achieve still another advantage: new life. An Indian tribe marches from the interior of Brazil, dancing and fasting, to the coast. They think they will become so light through their dancing that they will reach the land across the ocean dry-shod, where everything, fruit and animals, can be had without work, and eternal youth will be granted them.[14]

This land on the other side of the ocean is the land of the dead. And, as we have seen, the dead also dance. This can be observed in Euripides:

The music that lieth hid in lamentation,
The song that is heard in the deep hearts of the dead,
That the lord of dead men 'mid his dancing singeth,
And never joy-cry, never joy it bringeth.[32]

For those who do not view religion as a kind of pious entertainment, but as the daily bread of the believer—as his constant confrontation with the powers which rule all life—it is obvious that even the approach to God or to the gods can, indeed must be a dance.

The essential role that sacral dances play in the cultures of different peoples is general knowledge. Among the Greeks, disapproval of the dance was considered blasphemy. No wonder, since the mystery cults could not take place without the dance, and the man who disclosed the secret rites was said to "dance them out."[29]

ECSTASY Up to now we have been considering the energetic steps in which the dance wins for itself certain portions of life, and, like an occupying power, takes possession as it advances.

But it is not only mask and pantomime which bring the *other* nearer, but also the movement itself. Among the primitives and in antiquity, the games and contests were always religious, since they were held in order to win life. The Greek contests and the labyrinth dances of antiquity and the Middle Ages meant a freeing from the bonds of death. But there is another kind of freeing, which we can understand today, that which comes through frenzy or ecstasy. With this, we have come to the second kind of movement, that of hovering. In the ecstatic dance, too, one dances for the good things of life. The two sorts cannot be separated; only the rhythm is different. We are no longer concerned with the round dance and its well-defined center, but with the whirl of the leaves. Here man does not subjugate the world by mastering a rhythm, but by being himself caught up in and ruled by this rhythm. The following description of an ecstatic dance of the secret society of the Waieie, among the Wanyamwezi of East Africa, speaks more plainly than all our theorizing:

> The members form a closed circle, in which between three and five drummers and a few agile dancers take up positions. The drummers crouch in a row, and play tirelessly on their instruments with a sharp rhythm. The leaders of the dance make a few circuits around the ring, as they accompany the beat of the drums with a hard stamping of their heels. The drummers keep their eyes glued on the dancers. Suddenly the dancers spring to life. A shudder runs through the whole body, all the muscles work, the shoulder-blades roll as though they no longer belonged to the body. Louder and louder play the drums. Madder and bolder become the motions of the dancers. The body is completely bathed in sweat. Suddenly they stand as though changed to statues; only the weird jerking of the muscles over the entire body continues. Then, when the excitement has reached its highest pitch, they crumple suddenly, as though struck by lightning, and remain lying for a time

as though unconscious. After a short interval, the game begins anew.[9]

Here the dance is a compulsion which assumes control of the man, a madness sweeping him along. The dancer does not move actively, but floats or hovers passively. Even that is strenuous enough. The California medicine man dances before the fire in the sweathouse every night for months on end. In the first instance, the tension brought about by the power of the rhythm—represented by the dance itself—issues in even, flowing movements; here the same thing happens in jolts and explosions. The man "is danced."

There is a certain sense in which all dance is ecstatic. "The adult who places his arm around his partner in the ballroom and the child who skips in a ring out in the street both forget themselves; they lose the heaviness of being bound to earth, the stiffness of everyday life."[9] But in addition, the ecstatic dance is always a kind of taking possession. B. A. van Groningen has shown how in Greece the *molpe* originally formed a unity of poetry, song, and dance. When the dance was dropped, surrender and ecstasy vanished. When song vanishes, too, there remains what we call poetry, metrical and melodic words. But then we have a purely derivative art.[33]

The intoxication of the ecstatic dance is vividly brought to life in the Dionysiac art of the Greeks, in the vase paintings as well as in the choruses of the tragedies. But even Apollo dances:

> To the dance, to the dance!
> Now I whirl, now I leap
> As once at my father's
> Triumphs I danced.
> Ho, holla, ho!
> In dance the gods are worshiped best—
> Apollo, lead the dance.

Upon these words of Cassandra, Apollo's wretched prophetess, the chorus warns:

> You must restrain her, Queen, lest madness' dance
> Progress and fall upon the Greeks encamped.[34]

Intoxication is contagious. It is transmitted from one man to the next, until finally the entire world is swept along.

The noblest incarnation of this dance is the Hindu god Siva, also called Nataraja, the king of the dancers. He is the one who always "dances, full of yearning," the one who, "like the hidden fire in firewood, pours his power into spirit and material, and sets each in turn to dancing." His dance is the ceaseless rhythm of the universe, destruction and creation together.[19] In Siva, who is pictured as dancing within a circle of flame, the whole world, completely caught up, dances to the same compelling rhythm of life and death.

The dance of the dervishes is also a typical form of the ecstatic dance. The motion of the dervishes, says Sachs, is not active, but passive, ". . . open to the generative power that takes possession of him . . . the spinning dance is the purest form of the dancer's surrender."[9] This ecstatic whirling dance, together with the wailing cry *Allah-hu*, is at the same time, though perhaps secondarily, a representational dance, a pantomime. It represents the emanations of the godhead, according to the doctrine of the Sufi. In any case, this dance, too, sucks everything into its vortex.[35]

Among the Indians on the northwest coast of America, the leader of the dance must be beside himself, foam with rage, tremble, and do terrible things. Often it is even necessary to bind him with cords. At the same time, the following song is sung: "Great is the wrath of the great spirit. He will press men in his arms and torture them. He will devour them, skin and hair, chew them to bits, skin and bones, with his teeth." The neighboring Kwakiutl Indians actually ate human flesh during their dances. They did this, not for pleasure, but with awful disgust. While the cannibal trembles in the dance in the presence of the flesh which he must eat, the chorus sings a song which represents his feelings: "Now I am about to eat; my face is pale like that of a ghost." Often the ecstatic dancer is given emetics; often he simply cannot swallow the human flesh. The compulsive transition to the other, to the nonhuman, is very apparent here. The sharp rhythm, the monotonous movement, the furious tempo, all put the dancer beside himself. And at all times man has believed that the negation of self has brought him closer to a higher life. Whoever has lost his self has room for God.

In the *Laude* of the Franciscan ecstatic Jacopone da Todi, there lives something of the same ecstatic yearning for union with God through and in the dance. Presumably they were originally dance songs: "Everyone who loves the Lord, come to the dance and sing of love. May he come to the dance, completely caught up by love."[36]

To understand the psychology of the dance and to see at the same time its connection with religion, we must look upon its rhythm as motion and response, the seizing of life and the discarding of life. The rhythm unfolds in a double manner. By constraining life, seizing it and limiting it, rhythm gives strength to life. One can rise from the trivial to the most exalted by saying that rhythm moves the feet, the spirit, and the gods. It is the pulse of animal life, the heartbeat of our spiritual life, the movement of the world and the course of the gods. The cosmic meaning of the dance is not a secondary speculation, but has existed from the beginning. For this reason, the psychology of the dance brings us, with no abrupt transition, to its metaphysics. The cosmic meaning of the dance is beautifully felt and expressed in a song of the German poet, Paul Fleming, of the seventeenth century:

> *Lasst uns tanzen, lasst uns springen!*
> *Denn die Sterne, gleich den Freiern,*
> *Prangen in die lichten Schleiern.*
> *Was die lauten Zirkel klingen,*
> *Darnach tanzen sie am Himmel*
> *Mit unsäglichem Getümmel.*
>
> *Lasst uns tanzen, lasst uns springen!*
> *Denn der Wolken schneller Lauf*
> *Steht mit dunklem Morgen auf.*
> *Ob sie gleich sind schwarz und trübe,*
> *Dennoch tanzen sie mit Liebe*
> *Nach der lauen Lüfte Singen.*
>
> *Lasst uns tanzen, lasst uns springen!*
> *Denn der bunten Blumen Schar,*
> *Wenn auf ihr betautes Haar*
> *Die verliebten Weste dringen,*
> *Geben einen lieben Schein,*
> *Gleich als solltens Tänze sein.*
>
> *Lasst uns tanzen, lasst uns springen!*
> *Lasst uns laufen für und für!*
> *Denn durch Tanzen lernen wir*
> *Eine Kunst von schönen Dingen.*

Let us dance, let us spring!
For the stars, like heavenly lovers,
Glitter through their filmy covers.

As the spheres loudly ring,
Through the heavens they go spinning
Without end, without beginning.

Let us dance, let us spring!
For the clouds in their course
From the darkness take their source.
Though with storm they may be roaring,
They dance loving and adoring
To the song which they sing.

Let us dance, let us spring!
For bright flowers everywhere
With the dew upon their hair,
That the soft west winds bring,
Yield a beauty to the glance
Which is sweet and like a dance.

Let us dance, let us spring!
Let us run our course forever!
For the dance can teach us clever
Art in every lovely thing.

Movement reaches out and overpowers all things, until the stars, the clouds, and the flowers join the dance and become a roundelay which includes the entire world. This, too, can be expressed psychologically. Rhythm literally sweeps everything along, and transfers itself to everything that comes under its influence. We have already spoken of the epidemic character of the dance. We are reminded of the fairy tale about the boy condemned to hang, who makes everyone, from the hangman to the king, dance again, and finally is pardoned. In the thirteenth and fifteenth centuries, the dancers of the Rhineland were put in motion by a similar infection, and carried their strange piety and their bittersweet frenzy from town to town. Saint Vitus, the patron saint of the dance, knew how to cure them.

The dance overpowers whatever it finds in its path. Thus movement finally becomes universal. Everything spins and circles; everything leaps to the rhythm of the universe. The Hebrew poet sees how the floods clap their hands, the mountains rejoice and spring like goats, the hills skip like lambs. Every movement of the world is rhythmically ordered; the same principle reigns in the dance as in the cosmos. Every movement can be derived from a primal movement, the *primum movens*.

Thus the rhythm of the dance reaches out and conquers the world. But contemporaneously with the outreaching movement and constantly alternating with it, there unfolds the contrary movement which discards life. The dance, by its very nature, is ecstatic. It makes man beside himself, lifts him above life and the world, and lets his whole earthly existence perish in the maelstrom.

"*Nemo fere saltet sobrius, nisi forte insanit*," said Cicero. (No one dances soberly unless he has lost his senses.) That is a hostile formulation of an indisputable truth. Intoxication and the dance belong together. When dance is genuine, one can no longer speak of an action which one performs, but of a dance which sweeps one away. Of course, the dance, like every other art, demands practice and knowledge. But the dancer who gives the impression that he is executing a well-thought-out plan, instead of surrendering to a power which uses his limbs as willing instruments, is not a true dancer.

THE DANCE AS THE MOVEMENT OF GOD   Finally, we must consider briefly the third kind of ordered progress, that of wandering, or pacing. Here the dance has lost its immediate, concrete goal, and in addition, the exuberance of ecstasy is lacking. The dance becomes contemplative and reflects the highest form of movement, the movement of God. The most eloquent example of such a dance of mystic contemplation is the image of the dancing Christ, which was current in Gnostic circles during the early centuries of our era. The movement of God's love in Christ is apprehended as a dance which Christ performs with his twelve disciples.[37] Here the classic idea is still preeminent, as we found in Lucian: "Whoever does not dance does not know what will happen."[9]

Medieval mysticism takes up this theme and describes the whole life of the Lord in the form of a dance:

> Tomorrow shall be my dancing day;
> I would my true love did so chance
> To see the legend of my play,
> To call my true love to my dance.
> Sing, oh! my love, my love, my love,
> This have I done for my true love.
>
> Then I was born of a Virgin pure,
> Of her I took fleshy substance;
> Then I was knit to man's nature,
> To call my true love to my dance.[38, 39]

Or in the Shrove Tuesday song of the fifteenth century:

> Jesus, he must dance the lead,
> And the Virgin Mary;
> All must pay his rhythm heed
> To reach God's sanctuary.

Or in Bernardine mysticism:

> Jesus the dancers' master is,
> A great skill at the dance is his,
> He turns to right, he turns to left;
> All must follow his teaching deft.

The whole Christian life is thought of as a dance, again first by the Gnostic heretics.[41] But St. Gregory Nazianzus and St. Basil also knew the mystery of the dance. The latter viewed all of life as a dance of the angels about God, as *tripidium angelorum*.[39, 42] Even the saints in heaven cannot avoid the dance. Virgins, patriarchs, prophets, Apostles, martyrs, priests, confessors, and doctors dance in heaven with Christ and Mary. There indeed, in the words of the old Flemish song,[39] "all is dance." Dante saw this dance of the blessed in Paradise:

> When those bright suns so gloriously singing
> Had circled three times 'round about us turning,
> Like stars which closely 'round the pole go swinging,
>
> They seemed like women who are not yet willing
> To dance, but to the melody stand clinging
> While the new rhythm mind and ear is filling.[30]

And Vondel:

> . . . for the guests so merry
>   At the wedding, must not rest,
> Since their dance is necessary.
>   Heaven holds no ghost nor guest
> Who with holy dance and singing
>   Does not spend eternity. . . .[31]

But life on earth, too, resembles a dance when it is filled with the joy of the divine incarnation. Mystical rapture discovers for itself the image of the dance, according to the exquisite song attributed to Sister Bertke, the hermitess of Utrecht. It may seem amazing that a recluse, who cannot move three steps within her cell, finds no other image for the movement of her soul than the dance. But if physical dancing is impossible, one takes refuge in the inner dance.

> Love wears roses' elegance,
> The lilies move themselves to dance,
> Their beauty lies within them.
> They take their place, and dance with grace,
> When love comes in between them.
>
> Who understands the exalted dance,
> The bowing, bending, waiting stance,
> The spinning round forever?
> The mincing pace, the whirling space,
> The flight that ceases never?
>
> For love may stop, and love may hop,
> And love may sing, and love may spring,
> And love may rest in loving,
> And love may sleep, and love may leap;
> What mind can follow, proving?[43]

This is rapturous mysticism, and a dance can be reconstructed from the directions in the song. But the dance is also a superb mode of expression for the more self-possessed delights which life with God brings. Thus Vondel sees how the Church dances with God:

> As air through many organ-pipes is guided,
> One spirit is to many tongues divided,
> In equal time through field of equal sound,
> Where Church and God together dance the round.
> The angel hosts from heaven's height descending
> Dance deeply down, our sacrifice attending,
> About Christ's body on His altar-stone. . . .[44]

To this category we must finally add the ceremonial dance which, although by no means contemplative, is still a dance of the third kind, pacing. Bright, bubbling life is poured out into the calm watercourse, joining itself, in the old forms and gestures, to the calm progress. The holy dances, with their ancient melodies belonging to the court ceremonial, worshipped in Djokjakarta and Solo as *pusaka*, relics, do not

yet fall into this category. There is still too much ritual in them, too
little pure ceremony. The ceremonial dance is secularized, the old
forms receiving a new, this-worldly content, like the ballet which
Leonardo da Vinci composed, in which the whole solar system appears,
dancing.[9] The great mythological court ballets were similar, in which
Louis XIV himself danced the divine parts and of which Sachs ap-
propriately says: "He is not possessed by God, for he does not dance
the god in whom he believes. The dance of the Sun King is the idle
ticking of complete self-possession."[9] Here we have come into the
world of the theater and the ballet, of the "grace" and somewhat
empty ceremonial of the eighteenth century, in which fashion reigns
supreme:

> The minuet is declining;
> We see how the end is approaching
> Of the Courante and Sarabande:
> Now we have nobler pleasures to move us,
> Let us cherish and honor forever
> That divine dance, the Allemande.[45]

Although the dance has not quite lost its vital function, it has
become purely ceremonial.

THE DANCE AND CONTEMPORARY CULTURE   Around 1700,
it was still the custom in Germany at the presentation of a degree
by the theological faculty, for the dean and professors to perform
a dance around the *Doctor Theologiae*.[9] Is it accidental that it
was the theological faculty which retained the dance as a ritual—the
dance which, by its very nature, is itself ritual? Or must we ascribe it
only to their conservatism, their sense of solemnity?

We have lost the dance as an element of culture almost completely,
and so the graduation dance may strike us as somewhat ridiculous. It
is true, thank heavens, that the dance was rescued in music. The
superannuated courante and saraband, which, as dances, were only
"gracious," stimulated music to new delights and a new ordering of
the depths of life. The amazing vitality of music since the days of Bach
and Handel is, to a great extent, only the power of the dance, which
was temporarily lost as an independent art and mode of expression
for the feeling of life.

Profane dance is an outgrowth of the original dance. Dance as an art form, as pure entertainment, is a fossil of the living dance, which once had its own, much more inclusive, social function.

"There is little hope of a Europe which . . . will not have a more exalted form of the dance than it does at present." This pronouncement of the Dutch poet and writer J. W. F. Werumeus Buning[46] may sound too Cassandra-like, but beyond doubt it contains a good measure of truth. Chesterton said the same thing once many years ago, in his own unpretentious style: "The odd thing about the dance is not that there is an Alhambra Ballet, and that serious people are annoyed at it, but that these serious people do not themselves participate in the Alhambra Ballet." The great difficulty, indeed the tragedy of our modern life, lies in the fact that we differentiate between the things which concern us and things which do not concern us. We are musical or we are not; we are religious or we are not; we are concerned with economic affairs or we are not. We have our "job" and our "free time"; we drive off on our vacations and stare at the natives who work at the resort; and the natives come to us and cannot imagine what these people are about in all their buildings. We are concerned with politics or we despise all politics as a sordid business. We dance at the ball while wondering at the evolution of the ballet; or we do not dance at all and are annoyed by the crazy acrobatics that claim to be art or entertainment. Chesterton is right in that we would not wonder or be annoyed if the dance formed a part of our education. In a word, we have lost the unity of life. We know the dance as a form of entertainment, the acrobatic dance which we can watch on television. We know the artistic dances which ladies and gentlemen perform before our eyes, with or without tights. We know spontaneous dance, or at least our children know it. Every single one of these forms demands different dancers and a different audience. Likewise, we have a music for students of the art or for the dance hall, for devotional assemblies or for fanfares, or for the radio, just as we hold services for the Protestant rural congregation or for the youth movement, for the young people, or for the liberal businessmen; we have a music for distant county seats, or for the congregation of fishermen, concerned for the strict tradition of their denomination; there is music for services to have us buried as Catholics, or to overcome ethical problems, or to show how *avant-garde* we are. We have built dance halls and concert halls, churches and all sorts of other halls. But just as we have no cathedrals, we also have no spaces where everyone dances, sings, and makes music. And yet we must not complain, for through the differentiation of modern culture we have learned, much better than ever before, to grasp the nature and depth of the various human activities. But we must be aware of the one fact that under the weight of our modern culture the unity of human life has been lost beyond retrieve. Science, art, religion, each has been specialized by its own circle for its own circle. Again we are forced to think of those circles and planes. Among us, it is true, the planes border on each other; but they have little in common, least of all a mid-point. We must continually shift from one domain to another, while the primitive man finds himself in several at once. When we dance, we do not pray; when we pray, we do not dance. And when we work, we can neither dance nor pray. We go to church in the morning, to a concert in the afternoon, and to a dance in the evening. At least this is what mankind as a whole does; for possibly those who go to church do not dance, and perhaps also do not go to the concert, and vice versa. The culture of primitive man is at the same time sport, dance, concert, and much more. In other words, we consider the question of religious dance, because after a few decades we have once again recognized the value of the dance as an expression of art and of life, and because we recognize that all values must have a connection with the highest and most comprehensive value known to religion. This problem does not occur to the primitive, because for him every expression of life is an expression of all of life, relevant to the whole.

For us, with the exception of our children, the dance is a problem. We still understand the effect, the magical power, of the dance best when we are dealing with the erotic dance. Whoever listens to Weber's "Invitation to the Dance" and does not at once feel something of the compulsive force of the rhythm, has probably removed himself quite far from his primitive humanity.* We find the erotic dance in the most varied guises, among all peoples, and at all periods, ranging from coarse sensuality and indecency to the utmost sophistication. Even among animals the dance often has an erotic meaning. What a range we perceive among men (about whose intentions we are more certain), from the obscene and exhibitionistic dances of the primitives to the village dance in Faust, "the peasant dressed for the dance"; and from the peasant dances such as Breughel or Beham picture, to the Vienna waltz. An earlier generation of mothers could still talk about the good

* Music is needed by the dance only for its rhythm. For this reason, among all primitive peoples, the percussion instruments are most important: everything depends on the rhythm. The religious instruments, even in classical culture, are the drum and tambourine.

effects of the dance. Ours knows only too well the by-no-means purely aesthetic or gymnastic purposes of the dance hall.

As we have seen, primitive man views the dance as a most serious affair, with religious significance. It sets into motion powers which are holy to man; it touches on all of life and raises it to a higher level. All other meanings are included in the religious: the gymnastic, the aesthetic, the social, the military, the erotic. And so we must not say that the primitives are more "religious" than we are. What the domain of religion gains among them in breadth, it loses in depth. But where we would speak of a religious dance in opposition to an erotic or other sort of dance, the primitive man, because of this breadth, does not recognize this opposition. It is therefore just as wrong to speak of a "religious origin" of the dance (as is occasionally done) as it is to seek the origin of the dance in eroticism alone. The dance is an independent quantity, bound up with all domains of life, and since these domains cannot be separated sharply from one another, the dance, by its very nature, is religious.

At times the dance, as an independent art form, has been lost. But only at times, for it cannot die. The more one becomes conscious of the unity of body and soul, the more the dance will again achieve its rightful position as a function of life. It will not be the first time that it has vanished, only to reappear. Even in ancient Egypt, the consciousness of the unbroken unity of life was so weakened that only the children danced spontaneously. The Egyptian himself did not dance, but watched the professional dancers who appeared at all important events, both happy and sad.[28] But the dance is truly alive only when one not merely stages dance productions, but dances himself; when the dance is the natural expression of the man who is just as conscious of his body as he is of his soul.[47] In the dance, the boundaries between body and soul are effaced. The body moves itself spiritually, the spirit bodily.

Chesterton says somewhere that since the Middle Ages the dance has turned into a race, and that the religion of the dance has become a race-track religion; order has become "progress."[48] The scientific historian will be inclined to see this transition beginning somewhat earlier and ending somewhat later. It is even more probable that he would discard any idea of an ending, not only in the hope of a better period of genuine culture, but also because history is never finished with anything. Before the *lavolta* is finished, the movement of the dance reverses.

2 THE BREAKUP OF

UNITY

THE DANCE IN THE DIVERSITY OF LIFE   For the time being, dance as an all-inclusive function of life has vanished. Within the foreseeable future, the critics of the dance will probably not dance in the Alhambra, as Chesterton hoped. The unity between dance and the rest of life seems irretrievably destroyed. Today neither poetry, nor music, nor dance is a common form of expression for man's feelings and thoughts; rather, the dance, like the other arts, is the talent of a small group and the pleasure of a somewhat larger one. Even purely as a form of entertainment, it gives expression—again like music —only to specific feelings, and those not exactly the most noble. In connection with religion, with work, it is scarcely alive, or not at all.

The opinion is therefore defensible that the structure of the transition from unity to diversity of life, as far as the art of dance is concerned, has already been completely realized; that in this case the transition is not something with eternal meaning, but only points to a period that is over and gone. That is, it would be a defensible opinion if it were not for the fact that the most recent developments in the art of dance, and above all the flourishing of the folk dance, have reopened to us unimagined perspectives and long-lost possibilities.

Yet the religious dance in our time is certainly nothing more than a reflection of the past and a hesitant awaiting of the future. The dance, once *the* religious art in the strictest sense of the word, is today scarcely conceivable as an expression of the holy. The Church speaks, sings, paints, and builds, but it does not dance; or at least it does so no longer. Once it did dance (see page 30), and occasionally, in some hidden corner, it still does. But its dance is a "relic" and reminds us of the fact that the Christian Church is not only a church, but also a superb museum.

36

Our profane life is also a museum, housing more or less hallowed relics. I am thinking particularly of the parade. The need to make life rhythmical has been powerfully felt at all times, especially by the military. Granted, the need for order is also a powerful factor, and perhaps also the awareness that life must reach its greatest possible intensity when it is in danger. But the pleasure of uniforms, military music, parade marches, and harmonious movement far overwhelms the needed measure of regularity and order. We have learned this to our disaster, having lived in the age of German boots. A tribe of men without roots, who would "live dangerously," puts on boots and discovers, since all other purposes in life have vanished, a meaning in marching per se. "The S.A. will march," even into hell. It is a long way from the goose step to our "junior commandos" (*Jeugdstormertjes*), but in both cases there is the assurance that something "matters." When something matters in life, one feels festive; the expression of life becomes stylized into a fixed, rhythmical form. We still cannot tear ourselves loose from the compulsive fascination of a squad of marching soldiers, even without music. It awakens in us a vague feeling of the rhythm of life, the festively moving background of all existence. Every event needs a rhythm. We do not race at a funeral, but walk with measured step. The preacher does not run to his pulpit, but goes with a grave pace. In the commencement processions at their universities, professors try to reflect the rhythm of the cosmos and history. All this is a kind of petrified dance, in which, unfortunately, the style is determined more by the funeral parlor than by life itself. As soon as we are involved in those ceremonious moments in which we approach the depths of life's background, the undertaker replaces the thyrsus-bearer. That, too, must be counted among the prices we have had to pay for our culture.

It is less well known that Synagogue and Church retain elements of the dance; the former, for example, in the Kaddish recited twice daily, on the word "holy . . ." •

In the year 1271, the residents of Appenzell held dances along the entire way as they returned from the burial of Abbot Berthold of St. Gall. In Switzerland and in Dresden, dances were performed upon the graves on the day of a burial. Traces can be found of sword dances, performed naked on the graves. In many places, after the celebration of his first Mass, the priest danced in the church, often with his mother.[49] In spite of the powerful resistance which the Church offered

---

• Oral report of Dr. J. Premsela (cf. [9]).

to the dance, it has continued to exist for a long time within the Church, or close to it.

Three times a year at the Cathedral in Seville, * a dance called *los seises* is performed before the high altar. [26, 50, 51] Papal intervention has been unable to banish this honorable relic. The famous procession at Echternach still continues to progress to the ancient rhythm of five steps ahead, three steps back, to the accompaniment of a remarkable, equally ancient melody. But in general our culture no longer knows the dance as an expression of the holy.

PROFANE DANCE   The dance has become profane. But, as we have seen, this does not detract from its religious origin or its essentially religious character. We should consider this development in more detail. All the dances we have today bear the stamp of their origin, and indicate it even in their names. Our fox trot is an old pantomime dance which imitates the fox, just like the Basque *acideranza*. The pavan is a peacock dance. We, too, give our dances the names of animals, just like the mountain Damas of South Africa.[9] In China, the girls dance the pheasant dance in the spring as a summons to the young men.[12] The old German stream dances are based on an ancient magical dance which brings rain.[25] In connection with the ancient fertility dances we have already mentioned the French quadrille (*changez les dames!*), as well as the cotillion and country dance.[9] The dances which are characteristically performed in a squatting position —hornpipe, rigadoon, jig, the Russian *hopak*, etc.—are fertility dances with a different structure. The tarantella is an ecstatic dance of compulsive nature. This Italian dance, which remains even today ecstatic, albeit innocent, was a contagiously compulsive dance in the fourteenth century, an expression of life breaking forth from the depths of the soul, like St. Vitus' dance in Germany, which is described in a Strasbourg chronicle of 1518:

> *Ein seltsam sucht ist zu der zeit*
> *Under dem Volck umbgangen,*
> *Dan viel Leut ausz Unsinnigkeit*
> *Zu Dantzen angefangen.*
>
> *Welchs sie allzeit Tag und Nacht*
> *Ohn unter lass getrieben,*

* In Toledo and Valencia, also, cultic dances were, or are, performed on feast days.

Bisz das sie fielen in ohnmacht,
Viel sind Todt drüber blieben.

About that time a strange disease
Did seize the population,
For many folk of all degrees
Did dance without cessation.

They kept at dancing night and day
And never left their leaping
Until their strength had ebbed away
And death came on them creeping.

The dances of the professional dancers in the Middle Ages, like many folk dances (the morris dance, etc.), trace their origin to the classic mime, which, in turn, originates from religious drama, the holy game.[9] Thus all forms of the profane dance can be linked back to their religious origins. The medieval Marian legend (1200) of the Juggler of Notre Dame, who, unable either to read or to sing, danced before the image of the Holy Virgin until he collapsed, retraces this art to its consecrated heart.

PROCESSION   A pure and universally preserved relic of the cultic dance is the procession. In all cultures a parade is a kind of social mobilization in which all the people involved appear in a fixed order, to show themselves to the spectators. Especially in processions we find a latent awareness of the rhythmic background of life; when things are serious, we do not simply run to and fro in confusion, but group ourselves according to a definite, conventional order. In the procession, the movement of the group attains a fixed form. For this reason, even today, nobody can do without it: not the Church—not even the Reformed Church, which still has a procession to the pulpit, even if on occasion the celebrant may precede and the attendants follow; not students, who usually grasp every opportunity of documenting the rhythm of their lives; not politics, which drives the people into the streets and gives to their undefined desires the festivity of ordered steps and ordered relationships; not even science, which arranges its servants in procession, if not according to the rhythm of the intellect, then at least according to that of their length of service. Something of the compulsive power of rhythm is preserved in the indispensability which the procession still retains even for us. In Central Africa, the drummers drum "forward" and "backward," and the rhythm controls the movement.[52]

Whenever we feel the need for the consolidation of life, we subject ourselves once again to rhythm. A funeral, a wedding procession, even modern traffic, demand an ordered movement, which, if not always necessarily beautiful, is still an attempt at beauty. I have seen a traffic policeman in Hamburg who was practically dancing. If traffic attracts our attention more than it does at present, not as a means to an end but for its own sake, then we may hope for a general rhythmicization of our movements on the streets. We shall then progress or come to a stop only in fixed columns and groups, at definite signals defined by a fixed rhythm.

For this it is very important for everyone to be in the right place. We need only think of the quarrel of the queens which brought about the tragic events of the *Nibelungenlied*, or of the difficulties of protocol which have disturbed history. But besides providing order, the procession is also a useful tool, in fact almost a weapon. In China, processions with music and dancing are held against cholera. The Church does the same thing when it holds processions to ward off hail and all other kinds of dangers, for the sake of a successful harvest. Here the circular procession holds a special place. It forms a magic circle, a "witches' circle," which brings the circumscribed object within the power of whomever describes the circles, whether for the purpose of harming or protecting it. Jericho fell at the sound of the trumpets, by means of a procession around the city. The ancient Romans led the sacrificial animals of Mars, the pig, sheep, and steer (the suovetaurilia) in procession around the *ager Romanus,* thus purifying and protecting the commonwealth. The *Fratres Arvales*, an ancient society of priests, were responsible for carrying out this ritual. The Feast of the Procession (the Ambarvalia) in the month of May assures fertility for the coming season. At the so-called lustrum, the Roman *exercitus*, in its full company, stood armed and battle-ready on the Field of Mars, and was there purified (lustrated) by the process, once again, of having the holy sacrificial animals led in procession around the assembled multitude. The strength of the people was assured and preserved. In the plain, every village and every field was thus protected by a procession. M. Porcius Cato, in an old handbook, "On Agriculture," has transmitted this ancient rite to us. The field should be purified as follows: "Order [the peasants] to lead the suovetaurilia about"; then follows in archaic language the formula used on this occasion:

Mars, father, I pray and beseech thee, that thou mayest be favourably inclined and disposed towards our house and towards our servants; therefore have I ordered that the suovetaurilia be led about my field, about my meadow, about my land, that thou mayest keep, drive, and chase away from us all diseases, visible and invisible, infertility, and destruction; that thou mayest cause the fruit, the fields, the vines, and the garden to grow and to prosper, and give health and strength to me and to our house and to our servants.

The Church, too, has processions connected with the growth of the fruits of the field. In many Roman Catholic areas of Germany the blessing of the weather takes place on Ascension Day, when the Blessed Sacrament is carried ceremoniously through field and meadow, and at four places (or at the four corners of the field, so that once more a magic circle is formed) the Gospel is read. At the feast of Corpus Christi the holy Body of Christ, visible to the entire assembly, is carried through the congregation. The power of the concealed Saviour is, so to speak, brought out. We have here a new element, the carrying about of the holy object, which has a parallel in many heathen processions in which *sacra* (holy objects of various kinds) are carried. The power which proceeds from the movement of the congregation, the mobilized society, is here concentrated in a holy object, and is thus spread over field and meadow.

Of course we must not forget that, even in this case, aesthetic and recreational elements are involved; when a whole village is set in motion, life is still lived in unity. Thus the procession also plays the role which is filled in our modern, diversified culture by open-air plays, masquerades, etc. The pageant and the Italian *trionfo* are related phenomena. The latter is actually an imitation of the Roman triumph, the victory procession of the victorious emperor, in which, arrayed and worshipped as a god, he made his entrance into the city. But soon the Italian Renaissance, which loved display, transferred the *trionfo* from the entrance of a prince or conqueror to every ceremonial or festive occasion. The procession, now become completely worldly, assumes the character of a social mobilization, a means of ordering the events of daily life in a beautiful form.[53] The *trionfo* becomes so popular that Burckhardt expresses astonishment that even funeral processions are not thus organized.[54] In the twenty-ninth and thirtieth cantos of *Purgatorio*, Dante uses the form of the *trionfo* to represent the victory procession of the Holy Church, once more reuniting the secular and ecclesiastical forms. Upon the *carro trionfale*, in a cloud of flowers, Beatrice is enthroned—the beloved of Dante and at the same time the wisdom of God.

In the processional form we meet three kinds of movement: mobilization, the carrying out and about of a sacred object, and the mimetic representation of personalities, events, abstract characteristics, or virtues. The word "pageant" only gradually reached its present meaning of "parade"; originally, it meant only a movable stage. The idea of movement remains central. In the processional form, the power or the effect of this movement is coupled with a specific content, whether this be the grace of the Lord, concealed in the Sacrament, or the renown of a display-loving Renaissance prince. The power which proceeds from ordered movement extends over the whole congregation and averts evil influences. At solemn moments and in representative events, our culture still senses the same thing as the primitives do. The bridal procession which enters the church is still a kind of parade. The representative formation of the Prussian Guard, marching in goose step, has a parallel in the solemn parade of the participants in the *korrobori*, a holy feast of Australia, in which exactly the same movements are made. The word "representation," besides, indicates that the movements of life are perceived as an expression of a higher power which lies behind life. A man who gets out of his car to have a cup of tea walks with a different gait than the minister who, in the name of the queen, closes the sitting of the States-General. Even a boy who has been commissioned by his friends to ask the teacher something moves more ceremoniously, more purposefully, than when he simply comes on his own. "Something" is present which can be represented: a supra-individual power which constrains free movement. In our own day this is well known, and is much more primitive than we are wont to assume. The innumerable demonstrations, meetings, witnesses, to which our social and political differences give rise, are actually only primitive forms of the dance. Seen in the sober light of the modern point of view, there is nothing more laughable than a mass demonstration. The cause is not improved; not a single argument is advanced by a parade, not even when the parade carries banners and placards. But who will deny that power issues from these demonstrations? This power is directed both inwardly and outwardly. It strengthens the persuasive intensity and the spirit of the demonstrators, and concentrates an attack upon the offenders. All institutions which have understood mass psychology have known perfectly well the power of the parade, from the Roman Catholic Church to the

Salvation Army, from the great kings and emperors to socialism and National Socialism.* [55]

Of course, the procession is not a dance in the full sense of the word. We may view it best as a petrified dance, the movement monotonous, no expression of counterpoint. But rhythm is present. There is no chance of its being left out. And yet we must not view the dance as being somehow the predecessor of the procession; the procession is rather a special form of the dance. We ourselves recognize procession in a circle as a dance, the round dance. In ancient Greece, the women danced around a holy tree identified with Dionysus. The same is still done today with the tree (Maypole), the symbol of fertility. Humanity is sparing with its symbols; the revolution can find no better way to honor the power of freedom than with a dance about the (freedom) tree.

With this thought we return to dance, the great conqueror. "Girls and guns will last forever." War and love, related as they have always been, have best preserved the original significance of the dance. It is true that war dance has become parade step. Still, in every act of war, ordered movement is indispensable. That the dance can still awaken love we know only too well. In recent times we have even taken over the exhibitionistic dances of uncivilized peoples. It is a long way from the belly dance of the savage to the waltz of Johann Strauss: the road from barbarism to culture.

But the essence has not changed much. Through ordered movement the power of love is released. When life presses heavily upon us or weighs very lightly, when it seems to falter or drags us along on its mad journey, we not only feel the need for rhythm, ceremony and protocol; we also become aware that life does not need to be stylized. It has its own style, and does not need to be rhythmicized, because rhythm beats within it. We do not have to give it a beautiful background, because it has its own deep and mobile background. But the passion of the artist, the anguish of death, the dangers of war, or the delights of love are necessary if we are to be made aware of this background in the "diversity of life." We may watch a dance, perhaps even a religious dance; but for ourselves, we dance only for pleasure, when the occasion arises after the routine of our daily life is over.

* In National Socialism, demonstrations and parades constituted an indispensable part of the whole regime, which was a kind of secularized liturgy, having in the parade its cultus, in propaganda its sermons, and on the battlefields and in the concentration camps its hecatombs and autos-da-fé.

THE DANCE OF DEATH   The transition can be clearly traced in
the history of the dance of death. At one time these dances were actually
danced. The rhythmic background of life and death was felt strongly,
and so people incorporated their own movement into that of death and
life. In the fourteenth century this was done with a magical purpose, to
ward off the Black Death. The dance of death was performed at court.
But instead of a magical act, it became a representation of a powerful
and terrifying *memento mori*. The dead dancer, who takes the living,
became Death who spares no one, respecting neither age nor station.
Holbein's picture presupposes a corporality that does not mock the unity
of life.[28, 56]

The Greeks also had dances of death and games of death, whose
compelling rhythm supported tottering life and drew it past the critical
point. Many dances and games were of this sort. In the Middle Ages the
great movement of life and death was still viewed as a dance. The fantastic pictures on the bridge at Lucerne, together with many others, only
put in concrete form a general idea of the Middle Ages, that death and
life both dance. Originally it is not an abstract Death who grasps those
happily enjoying life, but rather one of those already dead. This is the
primeval concept of the dead man who returns, dangerous to those who
have remained behind. This dance of the living and dead was not only
pictured, but also danced.

In ancient Egypt, dances formed a part of the rites of burial and resurrection, performed by clownlike figures, the Muu. The crown which
they wore was the royal crown, and they were thought of as the souls
of dead kings. They were the protectors of the tomb, and by their dance
they prevented life from fleeing away. Whoever is buried with the aid
of the Muu shares the eternal life of the king.[28, 57] The dance of ecstasy
has become rare; one can find it on occasion among the acrobatic dancers. Although dance has disappeared as an immediate expression of life,
it still lives on as an indispensable element. There must be dancers at
every sad or happy event to continue the rhythm of life. So must we
understand the function of the burial dancers.

LABYRINTH DANCES   Today we have the most abrupt transition
where the dance ceases to be an expression of undivided life and becomes
a game for simple folk and children. That is not to say that children's
games, often of ancient origin and folkways, remnants of a culture which
is older than the pyramids, are not charming; but their charm is that of
a thing which is doomed to destruction.

Many ancient and modern games preserve the memory of the original meaning of dance as the cosmic movement of life and death. At Easter, in the province of Twente, in Ootmarsum, the children form a long chain, which proceeds in serpentine motion through the entire village, from house to house, first in at the front door and out at the back, then in at the back door and out at the front. Meanwhile they sing a very old Easter song:

> Hallelujah! The happy melody
> Is now sung loud and prettily.
> Hallelujah! Hallelujah!

and the possibly even older song, once so popular in the Netherlands, "Christ Is Arisen" (*Christus is opgestanden*). The snakelike movement of this dance, the *vlöggelen*, is very old. It belongs among the labyrinth dances which really (and this is still shown by the dances of Easter, the Feast of the Resurrection) represent the dark and inescapable path of the underworld and the way of escape from it. Other examples are the Dutch *sluip-door-kruip-door*, the German forest dance and Magdeburger, or golden bridge, the French farandole, and the *cramignon* of Limburg.[19, 58] Ancient England had the morris dance:

> The nine men's morris is fill'd up with mud,
> And the quaint mazes in the wanton green
> For lack of tread are undistinguishable. . . .

This dance reminds us of the mazes of our playgrounds, a form of amusement of venerable age. Another English dance, the furry or faddy dance, reminds us even more of Ootmarsum. In Helstonwake, the furry dancers, clad in oak leaves, dance through the entire town, in one house and out to the next.

In medieval Germany there were so-called "wonder circles." The father of German gymnastics, Ludwig Jahn, discovered a relic of one, which he then imitated on the Hasenheide near Berlin. Two people had to run through different openings, each aiming to be the first to the middle. At the time of the Renaissance, winding and sinuous paths were a form of decoration for royal gardens, like the later parks of Lenotre. Louise of Savoy writes in her diary for the year 1813: ". . . in my park, by Daedalus." Already in the Middle Ages this sort of object was named after the mythical architect of antiquity: *domus Daedali*.

They also have two other names, the one taken from Biblical antiquity, the other from classical: "Jericho" and "labyrinth." Jericho represents the city of death, which was captured by the forces of life. The labyrinth illustrates even more clearly the convolutions of the realm of darkness, where the way is known only by one who has overcome death. Thus Theseus, the mythical hero who slew the monstrous Minotaur in the labyrinth on Crete, becomes the prototype of Christ, who conquers the ancient monster, death. In medieval churches in France, and in a few even older ones in Italy, labyrinths are depicted on the floors in mosaics. The one at San Michele in Pavia has next to it: *"Theseus intravit monstrumque biforme necavit"* (Theseus entered and killed the two-natured monster).

Similar labyrinths, also called *"chemins de Jérusalem,"* are found at Orléansville in Algeria (fourth century), at Lucca and Piacenza (ninth century), and at Chartres, Saint-Quentin, Amiens, Poitiers, Sens, and Reims (thirteenth and fourteenth centuries).[60] A manuscript in Munich sees in the myth of Theseus a symbol of deliverance from Hell, for the Minotaur, like Hell, devours all.

Besides being a pious symbol, the maze is also a place of recreation, although with a meaning considerably deeper. Especially in the north of Europe, there are many so-called Trojan castles, bearing various names; among them we find the "Daedalus" again, as well as "Babylon," "Rose Garden"; in Iceland the "Völundar-hus"; "Trojan Castle" itself in Visby and other places; and "Dance Mountain" in Jüterbog.

The movement along the serpentine paths is older than the paths themselves: first came the dance itself, as we shall see. The many children's games which have such a movement retain the suggestion of a dance which represented victory over death. A graffito in Pompeii, scratched on a wall by a child, shows a labyrinth, with the caption: "LABYRINTHUS HIC HABITAT MINOTAURUS" (Here lives the Minotaur). It is not improbable that even at that time the labyrinth was the schematic representation of a children's dance, not unlike the figures which we still find on our sidewalks today, only, in this case, with reference to the mythical background. Many contemporary children's games also preserve the memory that there is more at stake in the simple game than the game itself. Hopscotch is called in German *Himmel-hinken* (hobbling to heaven). In many parts of Germany, the spaces which must be reached are designated "heaven" and "hell."[26, 62]

The whole story of Theseus, who saves the youth of Athens from the convolutions of the Cretan labyrinth and the claws of the Minotaur, is itself a dance which has become a myth, a dance with cosmic, death-conquering power. When Theseus lands on the island of Delos with the Attic boys and girls and Ariadne, the Cretan princess who had shown him the path through the labyrinth with her ball of yarn, they perform a dance which the Greeks called the *geranos*, crane dance. This dance, an ancient imitation of the movements of cranes (which we have seen depicted on the famous François vase), was a sort of *vlöggelen*, a snake dance. Plutarch speaks of imitating the detours and openings of the labyrinth. Theseus led the dance and led his people, so to speak, out of the path of death. The *geranos* itself, which, by another reading, was actually performed in Crete—in fact at the "Dancing Ground of Daedalus"—was thus a repetition of the procession through, and the escape from, the labyrinth: the dance existed before the myth, and the myth is a projection of the ritual.[63] This becomes even plainer when we look at the figure of Ariadne. We are told in the Iliad that in Knossos, Daedalus built a dancing ground for the beautiful Ariadne.[64] There youths and girls performed a dance which once again consisted of convolutions and chains. Ariadne and Theseus led this round dance of youth, as it was danced in Greece. It had religious significance.

Thus the labyrinth is not, as the Greeks thought, of Egyptian origin. The Egyptian building which the Greeks called a labyrinth has nothing Cretan about it, as it is known to us through coins. What mattered was not the building, but a conception, the conception of the snake dance. This explains the youths in the Theseus myth, the connection with the children's game at Pompeii, and also its use as a game and as a holy symbol in the Middle Ages. Even the medieval name Trojan Castle, although intending beyond doubt the ancient city of Troy (cf. Jericho, Babylon), has a predecessor in a Roman game described for us in detail by Virgil, which was called the Trojan game. This name was given it, not by Troy, but by an old Italic word *truia*. It was a kind of weapon dance, performed by youths on horseback. Its convolutions and complicated patterns of movement gave the poet material for a magnificent description.* And so it is not surprising to learn that the *vlöggelen* of Ootmarsum even today has a parallel in modern Greece, near Mycenae, where at Easter the boys and girls perform a dance which mimics the blind alleys of a labyrinth, just like the dance of Theseus and Ariadne. We are equally prepared to see that the transition from death to eternal life, the goal of the most holy of the Greek mysteries of Eleusis, was reached by a series of labyrinthine parades and processions along dark,

---

* Perhaps it was even the other way around, and "Troy was called Troy because it had many characteristics of a maze."

dead-end paths. The labyrinthine path through death to life is the path through the "bowels of the earth," whose human form is the womb.[65] Dance is rebirth.

We chose only one form of the dance (the snake dance) as an example of the religious significance of the dance in a time no longer primitive. In the labyrinth dance the relation to the overpowering trap of life is very clear. To disentangle the convolutions means to progress out of the kingdom of death. But other dances, too, no matter what their rhythm and movement, often preserve the memory of their origin in primitive universal religion. Lucian even says of the mysteries that their form of expression, their instruction, and their message are the dance.

And yet all this is a relic. Just as the snake dance became the country-dance and *contredanse*, the circle dance, which magically took hold of a blessing, gave way to the round dance, *ronde*, and finally the musical form, the rondo. Independent art forms split away from the unity of life.

LOVE DANCES   The transition to pure relic is radical in the case of love dances, whose prehistoric origin and whose structure, which remains eternally the same, we have already discussed. It is a long way from the miolithic man around whom nine women dance, to Apollo and the nine Muses, and to Krishna, who dances with the shepherd girls. But the way is still longer to the profane dance with the same structure, when we take part in the Dutch or East Frisian round dance whose old refrain is:

> I say of Jaapje, I say of Jaapje,
> I say of Jaapje, stand still!

To these words, in East Frisia, boys perform a dance around a girl who stands without moving, while the leaps of the dancers become wilder and wilder.*

The fandango and *Schuhplättler* are dances of the same kind. In West Australia, a dance is performed about a hole in the ground, representing the vulva, which is pierced with a spear, the phallus. Various obscene gestures are made at the same time, which go as far as exposure and masturbation, but not to sexual union.[9] For no matter how unambiguous these dances may be, they are rituals designed to aid fertility, and not, as

* To the refrain: *Ik segg der von Jabk: Stah still!*
        Warum soll ik dan stille stahn?
        Ik hebb di jo nix to Lede dahn![9]

among us, direct expressions of desire. The couple-dance is a modern invention which puts love-making in the place of ritual. With this development, dance becomes completely profane, no matter how many relics it has preserved in its structure and connected phenomena, such as exposure, approach, and separation.

3   ENMITY BETWEEN

DANCE AND RELIGION

HOSTILITY   The enmity between religion and the dance is ancient. Opposition arises to the dance in the early Christian Church, but at that time the dance presented no direct danger, limited as it was to the professional dance. But the Germanic folk dances were still based on the practice of life among Christians, and were thus still too "religious," in the primitive sense, for the Church to come to terms with. This opposition had its most relentless form in the late Middle Ages. A fifteenth-century manuscript from the Prussian State Library contains a detailed polemic against the dance. It does not differ essentially from the common argument of today: "For this reason St. John Baptist lost his holy head: that it was given to the daughter who could dance so well."[25] The circumstance that folk dances were performed joyously in or near the churches may share in the responsibility for the antipathy of the priesthood toward the dance, but the basic cause of the conflict lies deeper. We shall return to it presently.

There are conciliar decrees against the *chori secularium* and *cantica puellarum*. Nevertheless, the customs were retained with iron determination. We have already described the dances on the graves on the day of burial: the naked sword dance and the dance of the priests.

The feeling against such things is illustrated by a legend. At Kölbigk, in Anhalt, a procession of dancers refused to give obedience to the command of the priests to restrain their merrymaking before the Church of St. Magnus. As punishment, they were forced to dance without ceasing for the entire year. The pious authors of the legend take a certain pleasure in describing the suffering in detail: *Dat boec vander voirsienicheit Godes* (*The Book of God's Providence*) from the royal library in Brussels, which dates from the year 1478, gives three examples (on folia

234–237) as a warning of the dangers which await the souls of those who devote themselves to the pleasure of the dance or organize dance festivals. The devil seizes the body of a woman who was accidentally killed during the dancing. Robbyn the troubadour, "who often used to play the flute at the dances," falls sick and is represented at the dance by the devil himself; and whoever allows dancing in his house is treated, like the troubadour, by the devil as a slave of hell.[66]

Yet, as we have seen, the Roman Catholic Church has preserved the dance as an official holy act in a few rare instances. In Italy and Greece, the religious dance also occurs outside of the cultus proper. In the region of Salerno, the feast of the forty martyrs in August used to be the annual occasion for a wild dance at which the Bacchic drums were played. The streaming hair and heaving chest in the burning sunlight indicated that the concern was truly the development of "power." In Calabria, dance and procession are united to the extent that the standard-bearer of the parade performs dance steps; dancing with the heavy standard demands great skill and much practice. But, since even in non-Protestant churches, these and similar customs are merely relics, it is only natural that they have completely disappeared in other religious groups. Protestant churches in general are not favorably inclined toward the dance, and the idea of a religious dance is inconceivable to them.

As members of the Gerefromeerde Kerken, we know this attitude even better than other branches of the Christian Church. Our style of life is generally somewhat milder than that of the part of the Christian community which bears the stamp of Calvin. That is surely not mere Genevan rigorism or Dordrechtian narrowness. The church of Luther experienced and preached the ideal of renunciation of the world more strongly than the Reformed Church, which desires to proclaim the glory of God in all areas of life. For this reason, the Lutheran Church, when the challenge is made, must judge very harshly (in opposition to Luther and Melanchthon) both the dance and all other arts and worldly pleasures. It can do this and remain liberal in other areas of life. The Reformed Churches do not view this world as a vale of tears, but as the vineyard of the Lord, which is to be cultivated. They do not shun the world, but meet it, accepting the danger of becoming secularized in order to magnify God's name within it and by its means. Thus in the last analysis they subject nothing to a judgment of absolute condemnation. Everything must and can serve to the glorification of God, even art. We may recall the thought of the Neo-Calvinist Abraham Kuyper. Basically, the art of the dance should also be capable of being incorporated into the service of God. And there are tendencies in this direction: Calvin defended David's dance before the ark of the covenant; Marnix van St. Aldegonde wrote an "Apologia of the Dance," which is an especially significant work coming from such a deeply convinced Calvinist.[68]

But in this case the practice of life demands a fixed, easily recognizable rule. An asceticism within this world is the norm, but its application is difficult. The flesh is weak, and most men's powers of discrimination are small. Therefore, many areas of life are declared anathema, to be shunned with a passion and logic which the other churches, like the Lutheran and Roman Catholic, in principle much more ascetic, do not know. We find the strongest opposition in the Calvinistic world. But the well-known trinity of stage, cards, and dance is more an exception to, than the consequence of, the Reformation view of life.

A few examples may be introduced here. In a remarkable booklet, which can be found in the university library at Utrecht, we find the following polemic:

> The heathen are the inventors of the dance. Those who cultivate it are generally idolators, epicureans, good-for-nothings, despicable or dishonourable comedians or actors, as well as *souteneurs,* gigolos, and other dissolute, worthless, wanton persons. Its defenders and followers are Lucian, Caligula, Herod, and similar epicureans and atheists. With it belong gluttony, drunkenness, plays, feast-days, and heathen saints' days.[69]

Here, Voetius' puritanical spirit has already read the exception for the rule, and stifled primitive Calvinism.

We find a second example in a recent expression of antipathy toward the dance. In tone, and even in its examples, it evidences a remarkable congruence with earlier protests. In 1938, a member of a commission which was to study the social and moral significance of the dance received the following letter:

> In regard to the question of whether the dance is permitted, you should confront the questioner with the question of where it is written or can be found that the Lord Jesus Christ, our kinsman by blood, whose example we wish to follow, ever danced; in the second place, you should ask whether they know what the consequences were for Herod's daughter, who by her dancing caused

the death of a saint, John, which it were better had it happened to Herod's daughter; whether these two proofs are sufficient, you may judge yourself.

Here, clarity replaces what rationality leaves to be desired. The opposition to the dance is still by no means exclusively Puritanical or Calvinistic. Dr. Josephus Pollmann has recently shown in several articles that the dance was by no means always looked down upon in Calvinistic circles.*

DANCE AND THEATER   There are two reasons, as far as I can see, for the antipathy of the Church toward the dance. The first is the connection between the dance and the theater. The Church in its infancy became acquainted with the heathen theater, and this beyond doubt was more like vaudeville than like classic comedy or tragedy. Theater, dance, and salable love were inextricably bound up together.[70] The theater and the bordello were related concepts. The dance was considered one of the main constituents of the theater. The connection between the two still exists today, not only in the unity which the Reformation found so sinister of dance, theater, and game, but also in the need for ballet in the theater. The more the unity of life tends to vanish, the greater, remarkably, becomes the separation between theater and dance. Already the "ballet," as such, is a form of dance which has freed itself from its roots; a game, "no longer in the service of God and of nature, but of princes,"[9, 71] a play without religious foundation. I have already mentioned the court ballets of the sun king and his own dancing. If we compare this dance with that which the Egyptian kings performed as an important part of their accessions to the throne,[72] we can see an enormous gulf. If the ballet of the eighteenth and the first half of the nineteenth century still belonged essentially to the theater, so modern drama and modern opera have turned their backs on the dance and thus denied its origin. It is hard to imagine a play by Ibsen or Gerhart Hauptmann provided with a ballet.

On the basis of his universal concept of art, Richard Wagner arrived at a strict denial of the place of ballet in opera, insofar as it did not emerge directly from the drama. The members of the Parisian Jockey Club whistled their protests over the absence of the ballet in the second act of the opera *Tannhäuser*. They were accustomed to appear in the

* We have already referred to the masterful exposition of the dance and Calvin's moderate disapproval by Marnix van St. Aldegonde.

theater only at that time, and did not want to be deprived of their ballet. But the dramatic context made it necessary to have the ballet on the Venusberg take place in the first act, as a part of the action of the opera. As soon became clear, the inner connection between dance and theater was so great that the excuse for a ballet was gratefully seized, not only in *Tannhäuser*, but also in *Meistersinger* and *Parsifal*. Meanwhile, where the gentle muse reigns and where artistic development remains rudimentary, the dance has maintained its ancient claim on the theater without limitation. In England, "going to the theater" often means a chorus line, and the unspiritual intrusion of the chorus girl is the revenge of the dance upon a refined, autonomous artistic development. The time should not be too far off when the dance will celebrate its return to opera and drama. But even the increasing separation between dance and theater has been unable to arouse religion to any sympathy for the dance.

THE BODY CULT OR CULTURE?   The second, deeper reason, lies in the close connection between the dance and eroticism. Almost always the dance partially involves exhibitionism, be it the charming innocence of the child or young girl, or the enticing beauty of the fully developed, inviting body. In addition, couple-dances, such as we have had for ages in Western Europe, are at the same time an erotic approach, where the dance spans a scale of nuances from the most innocent embrace to the most obscene contact. The dance, even the simplest and most proper, brings out the glory of the body; and even in its most innocent form it serves for the mutual attraction of the sexes. In other forms—I am thinking of many primitive dances and of modern ones which we have borrowed from the primitives—it can, either as solo or couple-dance, provide very strong sexual stimuli.

But almost from the very beginning, Christianity has been the outspoken enemy of the body and all sensual pleasures, which it never considers innocent. It seeks the secret of all guilt in the lust of the flesh, *concupiscentia*, which transmits sin as an inheritance from generation to generation. Christianity knows no innocent sensuality, nor the glory of the body. It knows only the ideal of virginity and the mortification of the flesh. It must reach a compromise with sensual pleasure, because without it the world would not continue to exist. But even in the most proper liaisons it sees, if not sin, then at least weakness, which only the fullness of merits of the chaste can make good. "Chaste" does not mean "free of immoral desire," but "virginal." It is obvious that a view of life which shrinks from the body cannot stand for beautiful movement; that a religion which exalts virginity above all else must hate the enticements of the moving body; that the hope for release from the body of this death expects no benefit from any expression of feeling, and certainly not from any expression of the holy, through dance.

It is equally self-evident that this Christianity which can still be found in broad strata of society, Catholic as well as Evangelical, is not true Christianity. It is a Christianity which has gone to school at the feet of Orphism and Neoplatonism, and has there forgotten its Jewish heritage.[73] It is a Christianity which, in an unfortunate hour, took over from the Greeks, along with the idea of the divinity and immortality of the soul, the idea of the evil of the body. This is a Christianity which almost replaced "good" and "evil" with the concepts "material" and "immaterial," and for which virginity was of more value than holiness.

True Christianity knows that body and soul were both equally created by God, equally attacked by corruption, and equally saved by Christ. The resurrection which the Christian Church preaches, in opposition to Greek immortality, is the resurrection of the body. Genuine Christianity is in no sense dualistic. Therefore, the idea that the movement of the body could express the holy is equally as right or wrong from the Christian point of view as the idea that the holy may be expressed through speech. Equally wrong, because nothing in this world is able to express the holiness of God; equally right, because a duty has been given man to glorify God with all his powers. Equally wrong, because corruption resides in every human expression; equally right, because man is created in the image of God.

The cult of the body is characteristic of our century. Of course, in the training and glorification of the body we have come nowhere near the grace and spirituality of the Greeks, however paradoxical it may sound. It is obvious that we have not been able to translate joy in the beauty of the human body into the joyous art which the Renaissance produced. Our cult of the body is predominantly American, and up to the present has had more to do with world records and sensuality than with beauty. But in spite of everything, the fact remains that men of our age are no longer ashamed of their bodies and emphatically demand rights for everything connected with their bodies. Physical culture has begun to take over a larger proportion of our education. It is high time, otherwise the matter of most concern to adolescents would be completely shunted out of their education. In the matter of clothing, the Greek idea of nakedness, which reigned for a while under the Directoire, has won a clear victory. In entertainment the dance plays a major part.

These phenomena may be judged as you like. In no case should one be blind to their excesses and dark sides. But I do not hesitate to greet it as desirable that the body is no longer considered a negligible quantity. Not that we wish to rejoice with Heine over the emancipation of the body. This movement turned against the spirit. Possibly that will also happen, in the end, with the modern reaction. The glorification of stupid film stars and animalistic boxing champions at any rate betrays no trace of the spiritual. Yet we shall not go far astray if we see, in the continually growing demands which things of the body make upon our culture, an expression of the same spirit which, in psychology and philosophy, once more desires to view man as a unity; not as a soul in an accidental body, but as a single organism whose deepest essence expresses itself as much in the least movement of the body as in speech or thought. We have thereby gradually reconquered for ourselves the possibility of expression through bodily movement. As rudiments, we have always had the gestures of the speaker and the mime of the actor. Modern dance, since Isadora Duncan, has taught us that the whole body can be an expression, an expression of all that moves the person.

But if the dance is to become a religious expression, more is needed than its mere reappearance as an art; the dance must become for all of us an expression of life. It may no longer be thought of only as unattainable art or all too easily attainable pleasure, but rather it must become a natural and healthy expressive possibility once again. The folk-dance movement, taken over from England, has already achieved much in our own land. Young people again dance naturally. Here, those remarkable words "youth movement" have received new and good meaning. Much has already been achieved by various youth organizations.[74] May the folk dance become a natural movement of all young people!

Then the possibility may someday arise, even if in the distant future, of expressing once more the holy through beautiful movement. Perhaps we shall even advance to the point where we can once more learn the hymn, which, according to an old French fairy tale, poor souls learned from a good girl, and which must be danced: "All godly souls praise God, the Lord, who shall save the world, both good and bad."[75]

4   RELIGIOUS DANCE:

INFLUENCES

If we are now to discuss the unity of beauty and religion as manifested in many forms of the art of the dance, we should examine some points at which religion and the dance touch and interpenetrate, before drawing any general conclusions. We must trace the influences which contribute to their *rapprochement* and the manner in which this takes place. We shall do this first quite atomistically, taking up one influence at a time. There is one point, though, which we shall examine at the start, since it is present in other arts, too, and since its presence has occasionally been cited as an explanation of the connection which exists generally between religion and art.

THE ANCIENT   The experience of the "wholly other" in art is very often occasioned by ancient, archaic forms. C. Lalo, in a remarkable article, has even tried to explain the essence of religious art completely on the basis of this aspect: "Art never is religious; but it becomes religious."[76] The religious nature of a particular art would then exist only in the fact that this art makes use of ancient modes of expression. Religious art is the art of yesterday or the day before. A specific form, the chorale, or a specific instrument, the organ, seems religious to us because the ancient form, the ancient instrument, makes an impression upon us which is different from anything in our daily experience and which suggests another world to us.

Doubtless this idea contains a germ of truth. We recognize this phenomenon in other areas also. The language of the King James version has a devotional effect because of its archaisms, and no modern translation, however excellent, can replace it for religious and cultic use. The language of many sermons is only too greatly the language of yesterday, while the preacher's gown was in earlier times the usual costume of the learned. Quite apart from their content, the Gregorian chant, the chorale, and organ music can independently conjure up a religious mood. The ancient psalm tones, which are no longer "in our ears," precisely for that reason are able to give us the consciousness of distance. We have seen that the oldest Javanic dances, the *badaja semang* in Djokja and the *badaja ketawang* in Solo, were revered as a holy inheritance. Their melody, too, is considered holy, and may not be performed except on official occasions.[19] For this reason we must probably admit that the quality of age is one of the most important means which enables art to express the holy.

The chorale is only an ancient song form. Before it received its numinous overtones, the organ was a very secular instrument, somewhat like the saxophone in our modern jazz bands, ". . . the organ, in whose presence darkness listens and is still."[77]

Today it is ecclesiastical and religious to a degree that scarcely any other instrument is. It is often noticed that an ordinary secular concert at which the organ is played by a soloist accompanied by the orchestra has many more "Christians" in the audience than an "ordinary" concert. The organ attracts their religious spirit. And it will probably escape the attention of many of them when the soloist introduces, besides purely religious art, some which is beautiful but by no means religious. In other words, the ancient can effect a purely outward connection between holiness and beauty, which brings us no further.

It would be completely false to conclude with Lalo that the religious does not belong to the essence of art, that the holy does not permit of being organically united with the beautiful, and that an expression of the holy is attained only through association. If the religious nature of art could be completely explained by its old-fashioned form, it would be difficult to understand how the music of, say, Gustav Mahler, or in even more modern terms, an expressionistic picture, can evoke clearly the experience of the holy, while so-called religious music, in the standard canonical forms or ecclesiastical paintings based on well-known motifs, leaves us cold, religiously speaking. The modern piano or orchestra can move us religiously, while the ancient organ, when not played religiously, by no means speaks to us in the language of the holy. It would be irrational to say that the chorale is religious and that the equally ancient folk song, which is formally often identical with the chorale, is not. On the other hand, religious songs of modern form, such as hymns, or songs like Negro spirituals, whose form is similar to the "blues," make the experience of the holy possible. Besides, we must re-alize that in a certain sense everything is "ancient." The tambourine and flute have prior rights over the organ as holy instruments. Yet if one were to introduce these as accompaniment to our congregational sing-ing or use them in place of the common electronic organ, they would probably make an impression of "modernity" in every respect. The large drum, which is probably the most ancient cultic instrument, is used by the Salvation Army precisely for the purpose of sneaking in spiritual meaning through secular music, and its use shocks every re-ligious person who is conscious of tradition. It is necessary to admit the connection between music and religion if the great drum in the finale of Beethoven's Ninth is to be seen as a religious element. Hardly anyone would reach the idea that the holy is expressed by the honorable antiq-uity of this instrument and its associations.

And so it is impossible to ascribe the essence of religious art in general and that of religious dance in particular to the effect of age. Neverthe-less, the ancient, as that which is widely separated from us, is an im-portant means of marking the distance of the holy. Then, to use Otto's terminology, the ancient becomes a schema of the holy.

APOLLONIAN MOVEMENT   Rhythmic movement in itself—we touched upon these matters and discussed them earlier—can be an ex-pression of the holy, either by being understood as Apollonian, as order in the sense of Nietzsche, or as Dionysiac, as ecstatic intoxication. The opposition "Apollo-Dionysus," the restrained and ordered as opposed to the ecstatic and surrendered, is eternally human, but specifically Greek. Apollo's lyre and Dionysus' flute still battle for control over our movements.

The difference between Dionysiac and Apollonian music re-mained preserved, and this differentiation, which our modern com-posers have inherited and preserved, can be traced back to two different tendencies within ancient Hellenistic religion.[78, 81]

Plutarch says:

For the one [Dionysus], dithyrambic songs, full of passion and change, hesitation and confusion—; with moving sound the dithy-ramb is said to accompany Dionysus, going mad with him.

For Apollo, on the other hand, the paean is sounded, "well-ordered and cultured."[79] The Greeks heard the difference in sound between the lyre and the flute. We hear it when we place Gluck or Mozart beside Beethoven or Wagner. We see it when we compare Raphael with Michelangelo, Frans Hals with Rembrandt. Apollonian movement is, above all, order, which calms the soul and fills it with quiet: "He [Apollo] gives the zither and presents the Muse to whom he will, pouring peaceful calm into the mortal heart."[80] It feeds *sophrosyne*, the untranslatable Greek virtue which extends a happy heaven over the soul and protects it against everything which exceeds the mean, against everything unrestrained, wild, wanton. To this, Dionysiac movement stands in complete contrast. It arouses man, puts him beside himself; it lets the bacchantes forget their children, separates the mother from her son and brings all human relationships into disorder, and it nourishes *hybris*, the equally untranslatable Greek vice, which is a brilliant sin with heroic, rebellious features.[81] Both Apollo and Dionysus order life to the extent that its depths become visible and its undertones audible.

Here the dance even today asserts its ancient rights. It is not only ecstatic flight from life and stormy conquest of the higher realms of life that cause men to dance. Peaceful, serene ordering of life and the need to trace the complicated multiplicity of life back to a fixed foundation, summon man to dance. The girls in the Vosges, who perform a round dance in the middle of winter about a well decorated with a sort of Maypole, constitute a remarkable and peaceful contrast to the Greek women raving on the mountains in the winter nights. Not only the wild orgy, not only the intoxication of the mystic who forgets all, demand dance. An active thankfulness, too, expresses itself in the movement of the dance: "Then Miriam, the prophetess, the sister of Aaron, took a timbrel in her hand; and all the women went out after her with timbrels and dancing" (Exod. 15:20). In addition to ecstatic and erotic elements, and presumably in greater measure than these, it is the awareness that there is a peace for the soul to be attained which again and again compels young people to dance. Spranger, in his discussion of the dance and youth, penetrates deeply into the psychology of the dance:

The growing girl puts the entire grace of her soul and the entire fervour of its feelings into this form of expression, which in earlier times was rightly thought of as worship. The male youth is by nature less capable of pouring his entire soul into rhythmical movements of his body. But one can see on the faces even of quite simple couples that a deep seriousness and a holy unawareness of self is effected among both sexes by the dance. It is really God who leads the chorus. One would like, of course, once more to ban the faun and satyr from the dances of our children. In truth, it is not the children who have introduced them![82]

The movement of the rhythm awakens the awareness of a background to life, a cosmic order, which extends this life to its limits, where it has no purpose other than through and in that which is beyond, the holy.

The music of Mozart in all its sunny depth, its open clarity, is surely the most beautiful revelation of Apollonian movement in the modern world. Everything dark, everything ecstatic, everything intoxicated and disintegrating, everything infinite and unaccountable is excluded, and yet, whoever has heard the music of Mozart revealed, that miracle of God, knows that therein sounds not only the depth of life, but also the melody of the beyond. We must here also refer to a portion of the art of Bach, in which the transparent architecture creates a shining world of fine lines which cross and then diverge, drawing us inescapably and yet filling us with awe.

For Apollonian calm is capable of silencing neither terror nor enchantment. It can be shown that rhythm arose at the same time as Eros, the oldest of the gods, who ordered Chaos and began the round dance of the stars.* From this point comes the transition to complete peace. The Japanese and Chinese Buddhas may serve as examples. On the other side, we have the transition to ecstatic dance, with its powerfully active, stimulating rhythm. Thus there is within many Israelite war psalms a rhythm which is certainly not Apollonian, but which, on the other hand, is no confused, ecstatic intoxication. Whoever has heard the 144th Psalm sung in the arrangement of L. Algazi understands how a march can be filled with burning, divine activity. Actually, we should have known this all along from the biblical story of the march through the desert.

DIONYSIAC MOVEMENT   Dionysiac rhythm lives ecstatically in the raving dance of the dervishes and maenads. In mysticism it becomes the symbol of dissolution, of the complete loss of self to the god. The dance of the Mevlevi dervishes, which we have already mentioned,

* For what is that dance of the stars and that regular, hidden movement of the planets relative to the fixed stars, and the measured union and beautiful harmony of their movements, if not examples of a primordial dance? (Cf.[29])

takes place within a bounded circle. The leader takes up a position to the east. The whole dance illustrates the Sufic theory of emanation: the first semicircle representing the emanation from the godhead to the animal kingdom, ending in man; the second symbolizing the reverse ascent of man to the god. This explanation was already given by the founder of the Mevlevi order, the great poet Dshelal-ed-din-Rumi.[35] Thus he could also say, "Whoever knows the power of the dance resides in the god, for he knows how love kills."

Mania, madness, which according to Plato (whom we are still more ready to believe than Cicero) is the precondition for any contact with the Muse, inspires and overpowers, but also empties and discards what it has conquered with full hands. The highest goal of the Sufi mystic is *fana*, actually "being blown away," any condition of ecstasy and self-forgetfulness, indeed of unconsciousness, which can be attained with practice. Music and dance are said to put man into this state. The dervishes dance until they have forgotten everything. Earthly, bodily life is discarded, blown away. Dancing is not a secular pastime, but training for blessedness. In ecstasy, the body becomes light and the chains of the soul loosen. "When the heart pounds and ecstasy grows, when excitement is revealed and conventional forms disappear, then it is neither dance nor bodily pleasure, but release of the soul."[83]

The personality is lost in the whirlwind, while the narrow confines of the body and the environment are extended to infinity. It is a strange thing, which nevertheless plays an important role in the history of the human spirit, that poverty, insofar as it is intentional, often means wealth. The mystics know this when they seeek the highest riches and find them in the greatest renunciation, in stripping their thoughts and feelings to the extent of completely emptying their souls, in order to find the point of connection with God, indefinable and without content, there, on the ground of their soul. It is thus not astonishing that the dance belongs to the technical apparatus of many types of mysticism. We have spoken of the dervishes; we know that the Quakers received their name from the peculiar spasmodic shaking which seizes the pious at the moment of illumination. The Old Testament, too, knows the dance of prophetic ecstasy:

> After that you shall come to the hill of God, where there is a garrison of the Philistines; and there, as you come to the city, you will meet a band of prophets coming down from the high place with harp, tambourine, flute, and lyre before them, prophesying. Then the spirit of the Lord will come mightily upon you,

and you shall prophesy with them and be turned into another man [I Sam. 10:5–6].

In the parallel narrative (I Sam. 19) we read, in addition, that Saul stripped himself of his clothes and prophesied. Common to both stories is the contagious power of prophetic ecstasy, whereby it could now be said of Saul, who certainly had no intention of being drawn along, " 'Is Saul also among the prophets?' " William Oesterley, in his explication of this passage, comes to the justifiable conclusion that the infection must have been transmitted through the dance, even though the words speak only of music. Dancing, playing, and taking off one's clothing also go together in the story of David and Michal (II Sam. 6:12–23; I Chron. 16:28–29).[84] There, upon his return from the land of the enemy, the king dances in light clothing before the ark of the covenant, the throne of the presence of God, in the midst of the people. Ecstasy is not actually the involvement here, but rather a joyous outburst of energy which the sullen Michal cannot get used to. To her objections David answers with spirit, " 'It was before the Lord . . . who chose me . . .' " Joy over the reappearance of the presence of God is here naturally and obviously translated into dance. Michal, whom we must not view as a narrow, Calvinistic opponent of the dance, has reservations precisely about this lack of restraint unsuited to a king. The controlled energy of a ceremonial procession would have been more to her taste. The disintegrating energy of the free dance is too overpowering for her. Dance and music —and the latter in its primitive stages is even more exclusively rhythmic than in its later melodic and harmonic development—bring out this overpowering energy, but they also pour strength into a man. Elisha the prophet asks for a minstrel. "And when the minstrel played, the power of the Lord came upon him" (II Kings 3:15). The maniacal character of the dance remained preserved, for example, among the Portuguese *folias*, dancers clothed as women.[9]

Even more strongly than in the Old Testament, which as a rule is very cautious about ecstasy or the domination of holy powers, we find the transformation into another man, the loss of individual personality, the possession by a strange power, and finally unconsciousness under the influence of rhythm (Saul lay thus for a day and a night) in Hellenism, so much closer to nature. In *The Frogs*, Aristophanes has the chorus sing a dance hymn in honor of the Eleusinian god of fertility, Iacchus, in which this self-forgetfulness and ecstasy are clearly put into words:

Iacchus, thou who livest
In the revered shrine here, Iacchus, Iacchus!
Come to the meadow, to the chorus' dance,
To the festal madness of your holy people,
Let the sumptuous crown of myrtle,
Placed on your head,
Shake with the fragrance of berries!
Beat out the measure with brazen foot,
For the wild and drunken celebration!
Come to the dance, the blessed,
Delightful, thrice-holy mystic round!
Let the blinding torches flame up!
Yea, come, O Iacchus,
Swing them in our hands,
At the dark feast of the morning-star!
With lights the meadow is blazing,
Even the old raise their knees,
And shake off the load
Of their cares and their years from their heads,
Made young by the joy of the feast!
But you, O holy one, shine the way
With the guiding star of your torch,
To the field decked with flowers,
To the swirling round of the youths.[85]

This dance song is an epiclesis; that is, the chorus calls upon the god
and beseeches his presence. The dance compels the gods to come. This
was true even in the most ancient period, when the women at Elis sum-
moned Dionysus, the fertility daemon (whom they still half thought of
as an animal), with the song: "Come, Heros Dionysus, to the holy temple of Elis, with the Charites—raving, with your ox-foot." The throb-
bing life of nature takes on form in the figure of the dancing god who,
as savior, brings new life.[86] To look at the beautiful vases on which
Dionysus is represented with his maenads is to come under the spell
of the rapture which reigns in this religion.[87, 88] Most suggestive of all is
the picture of the god with his head raised in frenzy toward heaven. In
the cult of Dionysus, the joyful lack of restraint in the god of Spring has
led to ecstatic mysticism. The Thyiads, female disciples of the god who
were considered the prototype of the maenads, the frenzied disciples of
the myth cult, even in historical times went at night to the mountains to
dance there to the stimulating music and to "rave the god."[81, 88a] There
was nothing immoral or even questionable, in the usual sense, about this

frenzy. Its ultimate goal was for a woman to leave behind all that reminded her of her own narrow and encumbered life, to feel how broad
and powerful a flood of life flowed through the veins, allowing all restraint to be forgotten. For this the dance is once again indispensable;
indeed, it is the major component. The bacchantes and satyrs dance. The
dance has become their rhythm of life. "They have left their children at
home." Thus Euripides characterizes the Thyiads with a single, acutely
noted metaphor. The bacchantes dance until every human feeling is lost,
until, amid the ruddy glow of the torches, the divine animal appears in
the supernatural light, leading to the ancient, drastic act of communion,
in which the flesh of the divinity is devoured raw. Then the bacchi are
silent, for there is nothing more to be said. The rhythm, which was at
first loud and general, with the sound of the flutes repeated in the lines
of the dance, now becomes wholly interior.

We find a remarkable parallel to the Dionysiac intoxication in the
Perchta dances (and also the *Schönbartlaufen*) of parts of southern Germany. Perchta, or Bertha, the wild huntress who on stormy winter nights
rushes through the air with a swarm of the dead, infects her train with
her frenzy. Her followers race through the villages on her day (January
sixth), dancing and leaping. When the dance has reached the point of
frenzy, Perchta herself is said to be with the crowd. Another example
of an ecstatic dance which leads to union with the divinity is found in a
Russian sect. The moment of ecstasy is reached by a spinning dance
which becomes faster and faster. The excitement continues to grow
until someone cries out, "He comes, He is here, the Holy Spirit!"

According to Aristotle, the Phrygian flute makes the souls who
devote themselves to the service of Dionysus "enthusiastic," filled with
the god.

The rhythm of the Dionysiac dance creates in the soul an emptiness
in which the god can live, a freedom of the ego from itself which binds
it to the god. The movement releases power, dissipates it, so to speak,
and empties the soul so that it may be filled with the god. But at the
same time life is grasped and ruled. The dervish who has attained the
highest level of ecstasy is a saint, armed with supernatural powers.

Thus there is a mutual interaction between the freedom of the spirit
and its power. Rhythm which has become independent leads to the
rhythm of life itself. For this reason all the gods of the Central American peoples dance. Even the corn mother dances, the goddess of fertility
from whom springs all life. That is, the parental, basic movement of all
life is the dance. We do not need to go to the Indians. Eos, the goddess

of dawn, dances; she has her "residences and dancing-places" (Odyssey
XII, 4). It is just at this point, where we are concerned with the powers
of life, that the dance shows its nature as a universal and all-inclusive expression. When one wishes to describe the course of the world, one
cannot avoid reaching back to the image of ordered movement. It is for
this reason that the Muses and the Graces dance, Apollo and Dionysus,
Shiva and Krishna. For this reason Plato describes the eternal ascent of
the souls of gods and men to true being as a gigantic procession. For
this reason, at all times and in many lands, the gods are taken out of their
quiet temples and carried in parade through the streets of the city.

We can understand the metaphysics of this dance when we listen to
the highest forms of dance music. Beethoven's Seventh, justifiably called
the apotheosis of the dance, is inspired with a truly Dionysiac passion
which seems not to rest until the entire world dances with it. A similar
impression is made by the powerful march (*allegro assai vivace*) in the
finale of the Ninth Symphony. There is a small fugue by Bach[89] which
seems to contain the dance of the world in delicate miniature.

In the Middle Ages and later, innumerable dances were made into
music. The sung dance, *cantilena*, with its alternation of *responsorium*
(*represe, volta*, refrain) and *versus*, still has a liturgical form. Soon there-
after it becomes a song, either in its simplest form as rondo, or as *ballata*
(*cantio, chanson*, with the form a-b-b-a).[9] Finally the dance song becomes a basic form in modern instrumental music.

THE HUMAN   Any expression of the divine through the human is,
naturally, in a very special sense the prior right of the dance. The movement of the body often expresses more of the totality and the background of life than words or sounds are able to do. It is all very human.

Through the shaping power of art we experience that humanity
genuine and unfalsified, as we experience the beauty of a dancer in
her dance. As long as we are concerned with this type, she dances
her beauty. Not just to put it vainly on display; no, because only
through this process does she express her essence, and always more
purely, more fully, the better the shaping succeeds. Here, within art,
the human discovers the most difficult test of its capacity to bear
weight; for it does not appear before us "in" various roles, nor only
in work "on" a work of art. No; it must assert itself through itself.[90]

5 RELIGIOUS DANCE:

HARMONY

It is possible for beauty and holiness to interpenetrate so that one must speak of a harmony. We shall find the most beautiful examples in music and painting, but they are not lacking in the other arts, even the dance.

I am thinking above all of the Indian dances on Java, on Bali, and in Indo-China. The movement of the body is here so spiritualized, every nuance of spreading the fingers and moving the arms becomes so much an expression of the movement of the soul, and every movement of the soul is so much a step in the great progress of man to, from, and in God, that we must speak of a complete harmony. I cannot pursue this topic further. Here, only the specialist has a right to speak. Therefore, I can only refer the reader to the book of Th. B. van Lelyveld.[19] ("The West dances with its legs, the East with its hands." (Cf. 91.) But anyone who has ever watched Indian dancing senses that here the inner movement of the mystic ascent of the soul to God has become visible. The body has completely become an instrument. Often almost motionless, but always in the highest degree expressive, the body is as far separated as is possible from what we in the West call "sensuality."

Thus we in the West do not find this harmony, except in heaven, or in what the mind has reached in literature, in music, and in painting.

THE HEAVENLY DANCE   Amidst all the multiplicity of its purposes, we found in the rhythm of the dance a twofold mode of development: grasping life on the one hand, and discarding it on the other. Obviously this would by no means suffice to prove the religious significance of the dance, if life itself were not discovered to be "holy"— it does not matter whether we mean life itself in the primitive sense, or a life which extends far beyond the everyday world. As we have seen again and again, this is precisely the case. No matter whether we come to the dance as a natural and universal expression of a spirit to which the unity of life is still obvious, or as a relic in the midst of a culture in which there are various modes of expressing life, within the dance will always be found the awareness of a broader, wider, deeper background than everyday movement offers. The life of the dance has an independent existence. It awakes the serene knowledge of spiritual release, and the blessed consciousness of being transported by a sovereign power. The surrender of oneself to a stronger power, the unification of one's own movements with the movement of the whole, is what makes dance religious and lets it become a service of God. Whoever dances after the manner of the primitives or of religious ecstatics, indeed whoever in our modern culture subjects himself to a predetermined rhythm in a parade or a procession, understands, whether clearly or vaguely, that his movement is a reflection of primeval movement; that the rhythm of his dance is like the distant sound of breakers which emanates from the beat of waves in the heart of the universe. Just as at the high point of the Christian liturgy the earthly voices unite with the chorus of angels and "with angels and archangels and with all the company of heaven laud and magnify his glorious name," so man tries in the dance to follow the rhythm of the angels and the movement of their heavenly round. St. Basil spoke of a *tripidium angelorum,* a dance of the angels, and of the blessedness of imitating this dance upon earth. There is dancing in heaven. To die on earth as a martyr brings heavenly joy. According to an old prayer from Bremen, the eleven thousand virgins dance in the heavenly feast chamber before Mary.[66, 92] In Fra Angelico's *The Last Judgment,* the virgins and martyrs dance the heavenly dance.

The singing of psalms and their antiphonal reading, which the popular imagination of even our strict Calvinists cannot do without, is a loose, boring drama, which lacks the invigorating rhythm of the dance. Luther describes the garden of heaven for his small son. He saw ". . . a beautiful meadow, which was arrayed for a dance. There hung lutes, pipes, trumpets, and beautiful silver cymbals." There is a moving little song which girls in Bailleul used to sing at the burial of their dead playmates, which speaks of a heavenly dance:

> In heaven high there is a dance,
> Hallelujah,
> And there girls dance, one and all,

> *Benedicamus Domino,*
> Hallelujah, hallelujah.
> It is for Amelia
> That all we girls are dancing now,
> *Benedicamus Domino,*
> Hallelujah, hallelujah.

Thus the ancient idea of a dance which leads to heaven reappears in the imagination of children. Naturally, adults and adult Christianity have scrupulously closed heaven to the dance. Even in the hymns of the churches, with their love of resplendent imagery of heavenly joy, the dance is almost always lacking. A powerful, almost ecstatic hymn, such as "Wake, Awake, For Night Is Flying," leads us to expect any minute that the Gloria "which men and angels sing" will be translated into a heavenly dance. But it remains only an invitation to the dance, which still sounds bacchantic:

Des sind wir froh,	(We joyous go,
Io! Io!	Io! Io!
Ewig in dulci jubilo!	Ever in *dulci jubilo!*)

But even that was still too much for a more sober world, and was replaced with a trivial:

Und leben so,	(. . . And will live so,
Ewig in Wonn und Seligkeit.	Ever in joy and blessedness.)

Even the beautiful Jerusalem hymn of Johann Mathäus Mayfart stops with heavenly music, although this is admittedly so powerful that, instead of its inhabitants, the city of God itself begins to move:

> With sound of joy and instruments of gold,
> In choirs without end,
> When that sweet sound through all the heavens rolled,
> The ramparts did attend:
> With tongues surpassing number,
> And voices even more,
> Forever without slumber
> The hosts of heaven adore.

Folk poetry is somewhat more courageous, but even where "the little bells ring" the dance is not expressly mentioned. Only the hymns of mysticism have no reservations at this point. A nuns' hymn, from about 1440, reads:

> Let us all together go
> On the road to heaven.
> There, where joyous music rings,
> We shall with angels dance along,
> To the sweet heavenly strings.

We have seen how there is dancing in Dante's heaven, and also in the heaven of Vondel: "We dance to the honor of God's name." In the latter case, the heavenly dance is like the ballet in many respects, not that of Louis XIV, but that of the Renaissance, such as Leonardo da Vinci put on, in which the entire cosmic order was danced.[9] In any case, Western culture had to see the harmony between dance and religion in heaven. On earth it did not exist.

Our torn-up age is characterized by a strong yearning for unity of life, for harmony. The separation between individual "areas of life" is perceived to be artificial. But we shall have a long time to wait until we achieve that unity again. We cannot become primitive once more. Archaisms and revivals do not mean progress. For this reason the attempts to bring ancient folk dances back into our life is welcome only when the reintroduction is equivalent to a rehabilitation of the dance in the consciousness of the people. Even if there must be moments, like that in Mozart's *Coronation Mass*, when ". . . the Saints may dance on the cornices of the reredos,"[93] it would still be senseless at the present time to propagate the dance once more as a religious expression in divine service. We already have enough trouble with the other arts.

One thing is very gratifying: besides this yearning for the lost unity, our time has a healthy and salutary antipathy toward any ornamentation which is useless. This has had the result in the art of dance that we have learned to realize how unworthy an art is which is offered only for entertainment, as a spiritless display. In this connection I shall again mention with honor the name of the person who for the first time revealed to us the majesty of the dance, and that is Isadora Duncan. She has already had many excellent successors, but she was the first. Only when the dance as an art has once again achieved respect, when the possibilities within it for universal expression have again been revealed by beautiful examples, only then will it all be able once more to become an expression of the holy. The metaphysics of music we can experience, those of the dance only, and not without effort, understand. But why should not mankind speak again in its most ancient language of the great mystery of movement and countermovement: the one movement which proceeds from this world to God, and the other movement which proceeds from God to this world?

I may close this section with a reference to two beautiful stories, both having a tone of gentle reconciliation. First the wonderful sketch of John Galsworthy: *Salta Pro Nobis*. A dancing girl, caught and condemned as a spy during the war, is spending her last hours at a cloister. To distract her from her dismal thoughts, the Mother Superior asks whether she would not like to dance for the nuns. She gladly agrees. And the power of dance is revealed so strongly in the girl who is condemned to death that the Mother Superior asks herself, Is what I did the work of the blessed Virgin or of the devil? Here all the scruples of the Church peep around the corner for a moment. Shortly afterward, as the shots of the firing squad ring out, the dance reconquers its rights in the soul of the Mother Superior: "The Mother Superior prayed for the soul, dancing before her God." In heaven there is dance; but the scruples, too, are justified. For on the next day the youngest and prettiest of the nuns has secretly returned to the world.

The other story is of earlier date, the fine dance legend of Gottfried Keller. Musa is a religious child. But when she does not pray, she dances. Even when she goes up to the altar, she dances more than walks. Once, alone in the church, she begins to dance, and David himself comes to meet her, and they perform a skillful dance. He offers to let her enjoy eternal bliss in endless, glorious dance. She accepts gladly. But the condition is that for the entire period of her earthly life she must renounce the dance. The girl then asks whether there really is dancing in heaven, for the condition seems hard to her. But David shows her "in many biblical passages as well as through his own example" that the dance is indeed a sacred occupation of the blessed. When Musa still hesitates, the king lets a few measures of heavenly music sound, and now she notices that her body is much too heavy and stiff for this music, and she accepts the condition. She lives three more years in quiet loneliness, her tender feet fastened together by a light chain. Then she dies as a saint. The chain breaks of itself into many pieces, the heavens open. . . . We let Keller tell the ending with his fine humor:

> There one could see many thousands of beautiful girls and young gentlemen, in bright illumination, dancing in an immeasur-

able ring. A majestic king came on a cloud, upon the edge of which stood a small supplementary orchestra of six little angels, a bit towards the earth, and received the form of the blessed Musa before the eyes of all present, who filled the garden. One could still see how she leaped into the opened heaven, and in the twinkling of an eye was lost to view, dancing in the resounding gleaming columns.

In heaven there is a dance, and that is more important than the dance upon earth. It may be that the example of little Musa is worth imitating; nevertheless, we cannot think of the little feet chained together without a great feeling of pain. It is like a strangled voice, a cracked note. Musa's feet move in our time once more, somewhat more freely within their chains. We can only hope that sometime they may be completely free, so that here on earth we can receive a foretaste of the rhythm of the heavenly round.

6 THE THEOLOGICAL

AESTHETICS OF THE DANCE

The problem is now to find, using the dance as a point of departure, an entrance to the problem of the relationship between beauty and holiness. Up to now we have been groping about the edge. We must now try to achieve greater clarity. We can succeed only to a certain degree with the dance. It is the oldest, and to a certain extent the most elementary religious art, but certainly not the most theological. In the case of each art we shall discuss the relationship with God.

The dance, as such, is nothing other than ordered movement. The man who invented the dance did not only discover himself, he discovered God. For he stepped into a new dimension of his existence. To dance means always to see oneself dancing, feel oneself dancing. The man who dances discovers that there is a power which enables him to give a new character to his own movement: by dancing to a fixed beat, to develop a new essence, so to speak; thus we read in Robert Marett.[10, 47]

This is what makes the dance as an art so broad and inclusive: the boundaries of the body and the soul open,[9] and whoever dances feels how boundary after boundary falls away. But this also limits it. It is the father of all other arts, but its children are richer than it is. "The dance is a special and very perfect form of the game as such,"[6] but the game immediately finds proper, special forms, and pantomime becomes drama. The pulsing rhythm demands accompaniment, ordered movement, a mistress. Or to put it another way, in the words of a fine musician, "The melody sounds until rhythm takes it and, dragging both down, creates form. From this arises music. Rhythm withdraws into the wings like a good director"; but in the dance it is an autocrat.[94] The original art is in both cases the dance, which lives only through movement. It is difficult to discover from this point an approach to theology. For van Lely-veld is not wrong in saying that in the West the feeling for rhythm has almost died out.[19] Yet that is a theological mistake; for in the Bible, movement is everything; God is movement. His spirit broods over the waters of chaos, his pillar of fire leads through the desert, his prophets bring disquiet to a people that loves quiet, his Son comes down to earth, his spirit drives. His creation is no clumsy piece of work, but a progression into the world, which Dante follows in the last canto of his *Paradiso*: "Love, which makes the sun circle like the stars."[30] It is the curse of theology always to forget that God is love, that is, movement. The dance reminds it.

The dance is the discovery of movement external to man, but which first gives him his true, actual movement. In the dance shines the recognition of God, himself moving and thereby moving the world.

This is elementary, but it is not slight. It leads into the prolegomena of dogmatics. How important that is, is proved by the fact that at this point, as everywhere, dogma has its ethical correlative.

The artistic dance in our age has experienced a grand rebirth, as Duncan, Pavlova, the Russian ballet, the Ballet Jooss, and many others let us become aware once more of the beauty and value of the dance. Now the folk dance is reappearing also and causing our dull feet to move. It is high time; it is a theological and ethical necessity. For the "modern dances" are mirrors of our completely empty culture. Nothing more can be seen except an empty seriousness or a stereotyped smile. We turn away in disgust.

But that is not enough. The dance is not something in which we can participate or not, as we like. Whoever does not dance runs, races, waddles, limps—that is, he dances badly. We must all learn once more to dance, so that once again a general consciousness of life can be created, and finally perhaps even a style of life.

At this moment the body has apparently triumphed. But it is a body without spirit, a corpse that celebrates its victory in the dance hall and in the "nature bath." "Drives" reign supreme, and receive their psychoanalytical justification. But only the spirit can bring man to dance.

If we do not view the dance as a most meaningful social, aesthetic, ethical, theological concern, we shall return to the animal dances, to the moor hens and the cranes.

God moved, and he set us upon this earth in motion. That is sublime and impressive. It is the beginning of his work in creation and salvation. It is also the beginning of the dance.

PART TWO

Movements and Countermovements

1 HOLY PLAY

DANCE AND DRAMA   Throughout the world, the drama arose from a holy play whose purpose was to assure the cycle of life. At decisive moments, such as seedtime and harvest, or midwinter and midsummer, the holy play is performed. One or more speakers step out of the chorus, mimetically representing spring, winter, death, life, or the animals, daemons, or gods from whom an advantage is expected. This play of hawthorn and May king, banishing winter and ushering in summer, this *certamen* of Hiems and Ver, which is still found in a play by Shakespeare,[95] is the origin of the drama. Whether the players are clothed in green suits and decked with flowers, whether they appear as bears or other holy animals, whether they represent gods or spirits, in any case, they dance. Originally they only danced. The actor is originally the dance leader and interprets all that moves the entire company, in the literal sense.* In Greece, this development can be traced very clearly. The orchestra or dance area is the stage, upon which the chorus moves in slow dance steps. The chorus, the true actor of the drama, always remains the center of the action, whether in tragedy or comedy. The dance gives rise to music, the music to verse, and verse finally gives rise to the manifold actions of myth and saga in place of the uniform, typical course of nature found in undivided life. Yet the rhythm of the dance still beats in the powerful movement of the figures of an Aeschylus. Drama, too, consists of movement and countermovement. This remains true even when dance leader and chorus have long been replaced by a series of actors and the chorus serves only to accom-

* "The most ancient drama is only choral poetry bound up with dance and action. . . . Surely the religious, or, to put it more accurately, the magical, plays a large role in primitive poetry" (cf. [96]).

pany the action. When Aristotle, developing a psychology of the drama, sought the essence of tragedy in peripeteia and recognition, in the style of the holy play whose basis and goal are both the great cycle of death to life, the reverses of destiny and the painful or happy awareness of the connections within life, doesn't it bring to mind the image of the Labyrinth? The turns and twists, the sudden recognition of an unsuspected exit, or the dismay at happening upon an insoluble maze of passages?

The origin of Greek tragedy is a much-disputed theme. Many think only of the ancient agricultural games, others of mimetic interpretations of animals, still others of funerary games and dances. The most sensible course is presumably to try to give weight to all of these elements in an explanation. In one point they are all united: the dance is older than the drama; the oldest form of drama is the dance.

In Japan, drama likewise arose from the dance.[17, 91] • There are traces which point to the fact that Greek comedy arose from animal dances, that is, pantomimic dances with animal masks. Such names of comedies as *The Frogs, The Birds, The Wasps,* and *The Goats* remind us of this.[70]

DRAMA   But drama belongs neither to dance nor to poetry, nor to music alone, but to all of these. Indeed, it is also basically related to the plastic and tectonic arts, movement and countermovement in lines and surfaces. Dramatic writing, more so than mere theater art and play-acting, is in itself a rich art form. In several national dramatic traditions, as for instance in the wajang wong of Java, we find that dance, poetry, and music combine organically to make an artistic whole.[19]

Still, dance is beyond doubt the art which plays the most important role in the structure of the drama. The drama can do without words and without music, but never without movement. Even the shadow of drama, the film, reproduces this, since live movement is lacking. Rhythmic dance in itself is not yet drama. The latter only arises when movement meets countermovement; when two groups approach each other, avoid each other, entice each other, fight each other. When a leader emerges from the chorus, not only stepping forward, but placing himself opposite the others; when rhythm not only asks, but also answers; when melody joins rhythm, song and antiphony are born, recitative and

• The Japanese drama rose from the dance, the *kami asobi* (play of the gods) retraced to the mythical original of Uzume's dance before the grotto of Amaterasu.

refrain.* If the accent lies on the word, dialogue arises. But all this is subsidiary. The pantomime is genuine drama, even when no attempt is made to imitate definite situations by means of masks and costumes.

Here belong various more or less primitive forms, from the *pompa*, the parade, through the *saltatio*, actual dance, to *ludus*, the game. A very widespread form is the process of young men or children bringing blessing to the houses. Our Twelfth Night and St. Martin's processions are remnants of this. The Greek peasants went past their houses, wearing antlers and singing, "Receive happiness, receive the bread of salvation, which we bring from the goddess." M. P. Nilsson observes that in these simple, naïve customs are rooted two of the highest forms of expression of Greek art, those of drama and pastoral poetry.[98]

Folk games have a more dramatic form; for example, the practice which is customary among many peoples, or was until recently, of driving out death. A person who represents death and everything harmful is driven from the village with scorn and contempt. In Tuscany, this is said to represent "*fare il Giorgio*," the deed of St. George who slew the dragon.[99] An example which leads to rhetoric is the dialogue game of boys and girls in Tibet, Tonkin, Annam, and China. Each group represents one of the great forces: *yang*, which increases in the spring, is at work in the girls, and *yin*, in the autumn, is at work in the boys. Antiphonal choruses are formed which shout improvised questions and answers at each other. Thus arises a kind of erotic liturgy. The very concrete purpose is demonstrated by the fact that in Tibet the dialogue is often followed by mating in the forest. The same thing was true in ancient China. Antiphonal songs between the two groups insure fertility and health.[6, 27, 100]

From time immemorial, mankind has tried to give its life this dramatic form. Not to some particular event of this life, but to life itself in the greatest possible abbreviation, the résumé. Life and death, as they occur in nature and in the life of mankind, the eternal cycle of life to death, death to life, the monotonous but heart-stirring rhythm which pulses everywhere, within us and around us, are represented dramatically as movement and countermovement. Even the prehistoric rock drawings, representing hunting scenes among other things, are nothing else than dramatic representations. Man stylizes the events of his life through a predetermined movement, and connects this with something which took

* The Anglo-Saxon race, in its musical taste still perhaps the most primitive of the cultured peoples, has retained this form, not only in folk songs, but also in music-hall numbers and spiritual revival hymns.

place in primeval times. Thus life is given consistency, and happiness guaranteed.[101] A work of art arises which we call dance, game, drama, but also liturgy, and for which I suggest the name *sacer ludus*.

SACER LUDUS   The dramatic scheme which follows is found in numberless instances among cultured peoples, and still has power today among the primitives and in folk customs. From the group of young people, either girls alone or together with young men, a single individual, the dance leader, separates himself, gradually assuming more and more the role which actually is appropriate to the entire youth of the village or tribe, that of the bearer of life, the bringer of new life, the savior. He or she is led about in triumph, but comes to an unhappy, a mock end, banished, drowned, or burned. That is new life which ages and dies. Just as frequently, however, the concern is with old life that dies but rises again. The bearer of life is dressed as an old man or an old woman, is ridiculed or maltreated, is finally killed, but rises again after a short while. This is naturally only a schema. In reality, the *sacer ludus* occurs in innumerable variations. Often there are two actors, the one representing life, the other death; or better, the one the life which dies, the other the life which awakens. Then the theme of resurrection is dropped, and the drama takes on the form of a battle, a battle between two gods, summer and winter, death and life. The climax of the drama still remains invariably the same, the transition from death to life, and vice versa. That is also the significance of the stereotyped ending of many Greek tragedies, that drama which developed from a dance with animal masks to the highest of arts, but which always finally returns to a unity from the multiplicity and confusion of human affairs. This unity is brought about by a *deus ex machina*, or remains limited to a formula:

> A manifold form has the will of the gods,
> Their counsel is done without man's expectation,
> And what you imagined comes never to pass.
> The impossible yields its path to a god.
> Thus this event has its finish.[102]

The protagonist was originally a god or a daemon whose suffering and death represented the tragic element, and whose resurrection represented the joyous element. Greek tragedy is rooted in the sacral representation of the sufferings of Dionysus. The comedy is the other, the bright side.[103]

In folk customs this protagonist is often the king, and in antique and primitive people still remains so on occasion. The king, as no other, is the bearer of life for his people.

Frazer has brought to our attention an impressive store of innumerable variants on this pattern in his rich collection, *The Golden Bough.* He placed at its beginning the epigraph, *"Le roi est mort, vive le roi."* One can say that this motto comprehends not only the most ancient drama, but also the basic type of all drama, the primeval peripeteia. The lament over dead life and jubilation over the spring of resurrection have sounded for ages, and an echo of them is found in every drama: from the lament in the *St. Matthew Passion* to the sentimental emotions of *The Two Orphans;* from the exultation of *Fidelio* to the final close-up in a spectacular, where the hero kisses the heroine.

But less important characteristics also arise from this primeval drama. The comic element can already be found in a magical environment, such as when banished winter is mocked, or when it seems necessary to set up a temporary substitute for the king, who reigns for one day and then is maltreated and banished, or perhaps murdered; when the May queen changes place with an old woman, life with death, so as to make a fool of the young hero. The eternal type of the tormented fool, the comic old woman, and the derided king fall into place here. Shakespeare's Christopher Sly and Holberg's Jeppe fra Bjerget represent a primeval type. For example, in Cambodia, the king abdicates every four years. A pseudo king replaces him. Originally he was probably put to death, and probably, much earlier, the real king was killed. Today a few elephants trample down a pile of rice called the "scaffold"; the rice is used to fertilize the soil. Life is renewed through death and through resurrection, or through the replacement of the bearer of life.

An ancient game from Babylon has been recorded for us, in which the god Bel is trapped within a mound that represents the underworld. Nebo and the other gods search for him at the gate of the tomb. In the city, he is mourned. After three days, Bel is resurrected again, and consummates the sacral marriage with Belit-Balili, which brings new life. A pseudo king plays the role of Bel.[104] A dialogue between the pseudo king, who is in reality a slave or prisoner, and his slave, who is the real king, evidences a bitter, almost tragic, *vis comica*, which has characterized the figure of the clown for ages. The master always wants to undertake something, but every time he thinks of something, the slave flatters him, but insinuates the approaching end of his single day of glory:

KING. Slave, obey me.

SLAVE. Yes, lord, yes!

KING. Fetch my chariot without delay, harness the horses. I want to go to the palace.

SLAVE. Go, lord, go; all that you desire will take place, all will honor you.

KING. No, slave. I will not go to the palace.

SLAVE. Do not go, lord, do not go. Whither you do not wish to go you shall be sent; lands which you do not know you shall be forced to conquer.

Thus the pseudo king expresses desire alternately to eat, to love a woman, make sacrifice, etc. This entire life of the king is for him a single day. If only he knew how to begin. The bitter finish follows:

KING. Slave, obey me.

SLAVE. Yes, lord, yes.

KING. Now, what is truly good?

SLAVE. To break your neck; yes, to break your neck and throw you into the river, that is good.

We must presume that he followed the word with the deed.

To the schema of the *sacer ludus* also belongs on occasion the sacral marriage, which unites the masculine and feminine bearers of life with one another. The king and queen of the May are the classic example, which occurs in many variations. In ancient Rome, instead of the desired beautiful woman, the victorious hero found an old woman, Anna Perenna, so that the spectators laughed. It soon developed, however, that Anna Perenna was also a bearer of life. She represented only last year's life. She is the comic old woman who, christianized as Befana (from Epiphania), is still burned in Italy amid barbaric music and unrestrained merriment.

This is all in jest, but it is also liturgy. It is at once liturgy and jest and drama, as befits the primitive context of ideas. Later the tendencies will separate, and in the solemn liturgy of the mysteries the marriage will be holy, while on the popular stage it will only be an exceedingly coarse joke. But at this point life is still an undivided unity. One laughs at holiness and kneels before the power of life, even when it is revealed grossly.

The fertility of man, animals, and plants is the only theme of primitive drama. One thing only takes place; life is reduced to the simplest circumstances. One single peripeteia brings both tears and laughter. In the wajang drama of Java, Kekajon, or Gunungan, is the only scenery. It is a kind of tree or mountain, which ends each scene and represents the holy area in which, for the most part, the represented actions take place.[105] In this manner the various happenings are reduced to a unity. In the *sacer ludus* only one hero appears, or at most two, as enemies or lovers. Even the interjected jokes refer only to the most elementary matters, those of victory, defeat, and the most important thing of all, the relationships of the sexes. We are amazed to hear folk customs and primitive drama speaking and making fun of sexual matters, and even more to see how they are made unequivocally the center of attention. The older dramaturges, even Aristophanes and Shakespeare, still retain traces of this. We forget that we have banished to the revue everything which is humorous or coarsely sexual, and that it should not be counted among the glories of our culture that we can combine sexuality and humor mostly in situations involving adultery, and seldom under normal circumstances. For the primitives, liturgy and aischrology, drama and sexual intercourse, lie on the same plane. It is not only the popular plays, whose only purpose is to amuse, which know no limits in this regard. At the Greek mysteries, aischrology was a ritual gone through by proper matrons, and had just as much liturgical character as the obscene songs of the young girls at the Roman feast of Anna Perenna. There is no more majestic movement and countermovement than between man and woman, and joke and jest furnish both relief and assurance.

The English play of the May king and May queen yielded much amusement through the comic subsidiary characters of Robin Hood and Maid Marian; but it also led to immorality, so that bishops in the thirteenth century forbade the *ludus de Rege et Regina*. A few centuries later, a Puritan wrote that he had heard "of tenne maidens which went to set May, and nine of them came home with childe."[26] Here lie the roots both of the quarrel between theater and morality, which must break out as soon as the primitive unity of life is destroyed, and of the moral mistrust of the theater, which in any case can be justified historically. This strongly developed sexual character of the *sacer ludus* in the primitive environment does not prevent the persons who represent powers or gods from being holy. On the contrary, fertility and holiness lie close together, and both touch upon the mystery of life where it goes over to a "wholly other" atmosphere, or, better, where it seems to come from thence. The person of the actor is holy to the Greeks. In precarious situations no more suitable person than an actor can be sent out as a negotiator, as the Athenians did when they had to ask peace of Philip of Macedon. The "holiness," of course, includes less desirable qualities, while the actor is in control of fatal powers. In the Middle Ages, he can conjure up rain or storm. Even in the year 1596, the actor Monferino, who had requested permission to perform in the city of Aosta, was banished from the town because no one would stand for black magic.[106]

THE MASK   The mask belongs to the *sacer ludus* as the great means of stylization. Through it, all events are reduced to a single event, which is, at the same time, divine. At the Athenian Choe festival, a mask of Dionysus hangs on a pole during the mixing of wine. To it the new wine is offered first,[107] and the rites are performed under its surveillance. The god is a mask; the mask, a god. Through the mask one is transformed into a person in the sense of an actual, essential happening. The Etruscan-Latin word *persona* (*phersu*) means both "mask" and "god of the dead," or "dead man" (cf. the name of the goddess of the dead, Phersephatta, or Persephone). The name of the dead man becomes the name of the mask. The actors in the Roman drama, the *atellanae*, are called *personati*. Originally they represented the spirits of the dead.[108]

The mask removes human differentiation from the realm of the accidental and raises it to the divine, eternal, and meaningful world of ritual. It transforms that which is into that which should be. In a certain form of the Javanese drama, the topeng dalang, the actors are masked. But they do not speak. This is done by the dalang, just as in the wajang drama. In this, actors are "only a symbol of a world outside the usual world."[19] Through the mask, human actions receive a new dimension. It "opens a world in which anarchy and possession lie in wait. Whoever puts on a mask is no longer absolutely certain of himself. It might happen that he asks himself which is his true countenance, the mask or his own face."[109, 110] • Therein lies the uncanniness of all acting, all personification. Whoever is equal to it is transformed into another man and approaches the divine.

But this actually belongs to one of the following chapters in another connection. The primitive drama, monotonous in its power, powerful in its monotony, rises again and again from lament to exultation. The concentration of all the powers of life into movement and countermovement lends the drama such an intensive force, makes the high point

---

• "The stiffness of death is mimetically more vital than life: therein lies the secret of the mask." The Japanese Nō plays have very ancient masks with long noses (phallic symbolism), which are still reverenced today . . . (cf. 91).

so compelling, that even we can still feel the power of this holy action, which naturally is meant to be magical, and, admittedly, out of a different perception of life, join the jubilation with the song of victory in the play of death's banishment:

> Death is now safely banished,
> We bring summer in with rejoicing;
> Life from our house is not vanished,
> Joy in song we are voicing.

"The union of joy and terrible seriousness in the apprehension and representation of the processes of nature, together with the imitation of individual cosmic processes which go together with it, constituted the immediate point of departure for the higher as well as purely mimetic drama," says Preuss, who has written about these matters with equal sensitivity and knowledge.[13] The mimetic dance stands at the beginning. It stands also as summary and crown, once more at the end. Was Goethe right when he suggested that its impermanence damaged it? If not, mimetic dance would probably reduce all the fine arts to oblivion.[8]

2 THE BREAKUP OF

UNITY

ART IS NOT IMITATION   Art is not an imitation of the movement of life. Art has its own movement. "Art does not reproduce the simple object, but only the object which has already been perceived aesthetically. One might say, paradoxically, that art is not an imitation of things, but an imitation (arbitrary production) of aesthetic experiences."[3]

The independent life of art shows itself nowhere more clearly than on the stage. We do not see there our own world, but the world of the author; and the events which are presented obey the laws of his spirit. He puts life into a particular schema. Of course, he may not do this individually or arbitrarily. Or, to be more accurate, he can do so—and modern dramatists do so almost exclusively—but in so doing he approaches closer and closer the reproduction of life. That is not interesting: it is boring. There is nothing sillier than the cry for "naturalism" on the stage, whether attempted in outward forms or in the faithful reproduction of passions and idiosyncrasies. Opera is attacked for its unreality; but musical drama is more original and more real than spoken drama, because, by nature, man sings when he speaks. Of all operas, those which are "true to life" are the most improbable.

As long as drama springs from the unity of life, remaining *sacer ludus*, it does not represent the movement of individuals, but of types, the ideal representatives of the movement of life. To this extent drama is always marionette theater. A man who can breathe the life of movement and countermovement into ideal types fascinates, indeed terrifies, his audience. It is not unusual to see yourself in a mirror; but to see your own spirit, your own representative, in a strange world, that is extraordinarily absorbing. This has immediate significance for our relationship with religion. The holy does not stand in a relationship with humans who speak

86

for themselves, but only with representatives. The holy demands priests, servants, and therefore can be expressed only by an art which demands the same.

> The genre painter may represent whatever tragic or comic figures and scenes he likes; if, in addition, he has the good fortune to discover a diverting background, all demands are satisfied. But if I were to take even the most handsome beggar in Munich and place him in a tunic, I would still be a long way from having created a Brutus; and, if I paint a beautiful girl with butterfly wings on her shoulders, that is a disguised Psyche. But if I succeed in bringing myself beyond the model to a typical form, then I have created as an historical painter.[111]

What Anselm von Feuerbach says here about the art of painting is valid generally. For this reason the Punch and Judy show is a more religious and human drama than the modern problem play. Thus, besides the wajang wong, in which actors appear, the culture of Java also preserves with religious conscientiousness the wajang puppet play; in fact, as we have seen, the masked actors of the former were put to silence. For this reason, Heinrich von Kleist could say that marionettes, moved by a foreign will, best imitate the movements of men, and that movement is most purely expressed "in that form of the human body which has either no consciousness or infinite consciousness, that is, in the puppet or in the god."[112]

In addition it can be said, luckily, that dramatic art is probably the least subject to psychological individualism. The epic and lyric arts have gone much further in the search for an absolutely unique character development, for (to use Willem Kloos's famous definition of art) "the most individual expression of the most individual feeling."

The reason for this is that a novel or a poem either is read or remains unread. But a drama must be performed; and to perform means to represent, to serve.

Among the types which populate the oldest period of the drama are the comic doctor who assists in the fight between the hero and the dragon, and the stupid man who is beaten by his wife, only to turn around and beat her ("*Jan, die sloeg Lijsje*"). They all grow out of the ancient *sacer ludus*. The primal theme of all drama has been battle: battle between death and life, summer and winter; a battle ending with a mortal blow, though it is not final, since sorrow is turned to rejoicing. In the old English entertainment, Jan and Old Bet quarrel about a chicken which the one would like to eat baked, the other, roasted. Jan kills Bet, but the doctor restores her to life. In farce and comedy the old drama of life lives on, with the obligation of humor. It becomes secularized, but remains typical for a long period, and thereby in contact with the magical whole.

TIPI FISSI (FIXED TYPES)   Between classic drama, tragedy or comedy, and the *sacer ludus*, many typical transitional forms occur, the most peculiar (and simultaneously the most important for the modern drama) of which is the Italian comedy, *commedia dell'arte*.

Commedia dell'arte is a relatively recent name • for a very ancient phenomenon.[70, 106] *Arte* is to be taken in the sense of métier, the entire phrase thus meaning "vocational comedy." What unites it simultaneously with primitive forms is its collective nature. The actors compose the text together; there is not just one author. All the roles are conventional types, many borrowed from literature, such as the *inamorati* (whose characteristic role as *jeunes amoureux*, young lovers, or the like, we have preserved in our culture). Others are folk types which spring directly from the ancient mime. They are *tipi fissi*, and the actor breathes life into them, literally creating the role as he improvises. The actors limit themselves generally to one fixed type: a certain Zanotto was an *inamorato* into his seventies.

Behind this typification of life is a hidden wisdom.

In the nineteenth century our fathers were convinced that life had become so complicated that it was impossible to make do with a small number of basic characters. Francisque Sarcey wrote, "Balzac needed more than two hundred persons to represent his *Comédie Humaine*, and he did not include all the differences of character which appear in present-day society." Ph. Monnier was also of the opinion that to the Italian *commedia* "the whole multiplicity, the whole variety, and the whole transience of life remained a closed book." Today life has become still more complicated. Is it not possible that these opinions appear a bit naïve to us? The "multiplicity of characters could not be exhausted with two hundred thousand types; but the number of primary colors in nature, as on our palettes, remains no less limited than before."[106]

The *commedia dell'arte* has *parti gravi* and *parti ridicoli*, and in itself this would be a brilliant synopsis of humanity. But there are also *màschere*, and, as in real life, these masks assume the most important place.

• The name first appears in the eighteenth century; previously it was called *commedia a soggestto*, or *di zanni*.

To the *parti gravi* belong both pairs of *inamorati* (two pair have been retained well into the period of modern drama, as though a single love were no love at all and could only become interesting through the possibility of comparison); to the *parti ridicoli* belong the talkative Capitano, Plautus' *miles gloriosus*; the soubrette Fantesca; and Servetta, the clever servant girl, who still has her small role of intrigue in Molière, and, indeed, continues beyond him. The *màschere* are first of all the *zani*, known by the most various names in the world: Arlechino, Truffaldino, Pasquino, Scapino, Pulcinella; and internationally: Pierrot, Punch, Hanswurst, Jan Klaasen. No matter what names these may bear, the type remains the same, with two variants: alert and clever (Figaro), or stupid and clumsy. Then we have Pantalone, raging or grumbling, and the *Dottore di Bologna*, the scholastic scholar, cleverly ridiculous. The action snakes along with a little love, a little intrigue, a little mock pedantry, and above all, a lot of fighting. Not such a bad synopsis of human life. The simple man with the common name is amusing, but receives the beatings. * Often it seems as though the world contains nothing but administering a beating or being beaten. In this small world, at any rate, everything is constant. Capitano is always chattering. Characteristics and idiosyncracies belong to people, so to speak, by virtue of their office: the fool, the glutton, the miser, the *souteneur*, the whore, the nurse, the betrayed husband, the young lover, the comic old woman—each is all that his name implies, and only that. The servants have no existence of their own, but are there only to help the romantic couples. Characteristics and idiosyncracies, deeds, thoughts, and feelings hang like clothing upon their shoulders. The actor does not play the role of a man, but the role of a role. Art is not imitation, but reduction of everything to a single principle. Dramatic art is ritual.

Therefore the performance is always a burlesque. There are humorous and serious materials, but even the serious ones are never represented without humor. Harlequin, Pickelhering, Kasperl, Karagöz (in the Turkish puppet theater), satyrs, clowns, and imps always peep around the corner. The childbed stands on the stage, even in the Roman atellanae (farces), and even Goethe noticed it on the street at the Roman Mardi gras.[113, 262] Life is in no way romanticized. It is transferred to the middle of the street. There man can recognize himself in his full, essential absurdity, which simultaneously contains the nucleus of tragedy. In the

* *Zani* seems to be dialect for Giovanni; the hero has the most ordinary name of all: Pierrot, Jan Klaasen, Hanswurst, Petrushka, or Ivanushka (cf. 106).

drunken peasants of Shakespeare, Langendijk, and Holberg, the fallen king lies hidden.[114]

SECULARIZATION   The stage begins in the street. The English stage begins in the inns, half roofed over, after the example of bear rings in which bears were fought, or, better, baited to death. There was standing room in the pit, and there were seats in the galleries.[115] One might say that the drama emerged from the church to the church square, from the temple into the market place. The history of the drama is a history of secularization.

We can trace two different lines of development, one leading further and further away from religion, the other seeking the religious exclusively:

SACER LUDUS

Greek tragedy and comedy	Greek and Hellenistic mysteries
↓	↓
Atellan and mime	Liturgy of the Church
↓	↓
Italian comedy	Medieval mystery plays
↓	↓
Opera	Passion plays
↓	↓
Oratorio	Musical passion
↓	
Classic drama	
↓	
Bourgeois drama	
↓	
Music drama	

We shall first trace the path of secularization. Ritual becomes literature. Or it is relegated to the fair, whence it came. "As far as the fools and jesters of the earlier comedy were concerned, they could not stand the atmosphere of the century of reason, and were forced once more to climb up onto the portable stages of the fairs, which they had left two hundred years before, in order to fulfill their important artistic mission."[106]

Much is taken over into literary drama from the *tipi fissi*. The rest ends up on the stage of the revue and operetta, and above all, and certainly most honorably, in that venerable form which is more esteemed in Turkey and India than among us: the marionette theater. Goethe loved marionettes. The Munich artists demonstrated the indestructible freshness of the puppet theater to an age which thought that men were not marionettes. In the animated cartoon, we have a return to the marionette. The creator of the film is closely related to the man who moves the dolls, only he does it by a new means. We are not yet in a position to survey the problems which arise with this new art form.

In the course of history we have twice had a secularization of drama. The first time was when the Greek sacral play became specialized and began to represent the colorfulness of all human life. In content it remained bound to superhuman gods and heroic figures; in form it still was constructed about a change of fortune. But in its essence it had been freed from its ancient content and its ancient form. Heroes and gods have become men, all too human men. The single god who sang and danced in alternation with his attendants is replaced by a whole swarm of characters of all sorts. Where the hero is still truly a god, he appears as a *deus ex machina*, to cut through the tangled knots of human events. That is a relic of the ancient drama. There are many of these relics, even in the form. In Euripides' *Bacchae*, the original frame is still clearly visible: the death of the god, the lament for vanished life, and the resurrection amid songs of jubilation.[116] As we have seen, the chorus remained the central character, even when it was superfluous to the action or downright destructive.[81]

But the pathos of Greek tragedy, and to a lesser degree also of Greek comedy, has put a great distance between itself and the *sacer ludus*. The primal peripeteia becomes the bearer of the deepest Greek ideas of god and man, world and life, sharpest satire and most merciless reason. Greek tragedy is without doubt a religious art, but no longer in the magical sense. It has already gone through its secularization, and has achieved a new unity of holiness and beauty; it is indebted for this to its fierce, painful struggle for life, divine and human.

After Greek tragedy, the transition evidences an enormous gap (another proof of the fact that we are not dealing with a chronologically measurable event in the development of the primitive form, through outward context to secularization), a vacuum which stretches from the end of classic drama in Menander and Seneca to Shakespeare and Molière. In between, we have only the mime,[70] vaudeville-like farce, which brought the ancient fertility daemons and vegetation rituals to India and Turkey in the form of clowns and farces.

Modern drama begins as a comedy of types. Not only Scapin, but also *l'avare, le bourgeois gentilhomme, le malade imaginaire*, are types, not characters, in the modern sense of the word. Sir John Falstaff, Mistress Quickly, Aguecheek and the innumerable fools and clowns are *tipi fissi*. But just because they are types, they are also men, often on a grand scale. The ancient form is at once accepted and overcome. In Shakespeare we often find the old *sacer ludus,* even in the dramatic form: the joke of Christopher Sly in *The Taming of the Shrew*, the duel between Armado and Costard in *Love's Labour's Lost*. The action, except in the histories, is almost always typical: jealousy, childish ingratitude, self-doubt, misanthropy. Yet greater men never walked the stage than an Othello, a Lear, a Hamlet, or a Timon of Athens, precisely because their humanity is more than simple humanity; precisely because they are firmly anchored in an inclusive background. No one is Lear and everyone is Lear; no one is Timon or *le misanthrope*, but everyone recognizes himself in them. If drama completely renounces types, one individual remains indeed the hero, but he represents only a single person, who, we may hope, is not to be found somewhere in the audience.

In the golden age of the modern theater, material and form thus remain bound in many respects to the ancient material and the ancient form. Following the example of Greek tragedy, the persons remain mythological, or at least aristocratic. Gods, demigods, and kings stride over the stage. The others, if not clowns for entertainment, are messengers and servants, types. The author still does not trust himself to leave the principals to their individuality, but selects them by virtue of their office or birth: this, too, is a primitive conception.

When the "bourgeois" drama appears, secularization goes a step further. But the pressure toward the typical, the suprapersonal, remains strong. As soon as the type is abolished the symbol is introduced.•

LITURGY   Another path, besides the one to secular drama, leads out of the primitive unity. This path was taken by the liturgy of the Church. The *sacer ludus* can become secular or ecclesiastical. We can trace this twofold development in antiquity. At Eleusis, the holy play remained a liturgical action, a *dromenon;* but in nearby Athens it also became an action to which a background and scenery were given, until tragedy arose out of it.[117] Ancient Egypt, too, has a dramatic liturgy, in which the gods exchange questions and answers, and the holy action of the faithful or of priests is represented. We have a remarkable scenario preserved from a time more than two thousand years before Christ. Its subject is the quarrel of the gods Horus and Seth, and of the division

• Later we shall deal with oratorio and opera, in our treatment of music.

of the world between them by Keb, the king of the gods. It is a liturgical drama:

> Keb says to Seth—"Go to the place where you were born!" [Seth, Upper Egypt.]
>
> Keb says to Horus—"Go to the place where your father drowned!" [Pun on the name Lower Egypt, which is like the word drowned. Horus, Lower Egypt.]
>
> Keb says to Horus and Seth—"I have separated you, Horus and Seth." [Upper Egypt and Lower Egypt.][118]

The last words of each sentence are stage directions and mean something like: "Keb points to Seth and then to Upper Egypt," etc.

In another very ancient text we can see how liturgical drama arises from sacrificial ritual. In regard to a dead king, the goddess is asked:

> What have you to give, my lady?
> *Answer.* What the king likes, what gives the king joy.
> What have you to give, my lady?
> *Answer.* What gives the king joy, what pleases the king![19]

A very ancient example is the liturgical drama which was discovered not long ago at Ras Shamra. Here, too, we have a kind of scenario, or libretto, for a mystery play, which was produced at the autumn festival, at once representing and effecting the birth of the Year god. A funeral dirge for the old god alternates with a kind of "search" in the desert for the goddess. The piece begins with a chorus and ends with a sacrifice. This has been viewed, not without justification, as the primal form of the Mediterranean mystery play, from which Greek tragedy developed.[120]

In addition, the mysteries of Hellenistic times were holy games, and yet did not despise theatrical effects such as the sudden appearance of a bright light.

The liturgy of the Christian Church is without doubt the holy drama which comes closest to perfection. Out of it grew a liturgical drama typical of the transitional stage: the Passion play, Easter play of the Middle Ages, the "mystery play," such as lives on at Oberammergau.

In a manuscript from the ninth century we have a so-called Easter trope,[97] an extension of the melody and words of a liturgical verse, which contains the nucleus of dramatic representation:

> The angels keeping watch at the grave ask the women:
> *"Quem quaeritis in sepulchro, o Christicolae?"*

[Whom do you seek in the tomb, O worshipers of Christ?] They answer:

"Jesum Nazarenum crucifixum, o Coelicolae."

[The crucified Jesus of Nazareth, O inhabitants of heaven.] And the angels:

"Non est hic, surrexit sicut dixerat. Ite, nuntiate, quia surrexit de sepulchro."

[He is not here, he has risen as he had said. Go and proclaim this, for he has risen from the tomb.]26, 122, 123, 124

After this, the usual liturgy continues with the introit: *Resurrexi et adhuc tecum sum* (I have risen and am still with thee).

Here we can witness the development of dramatic liturgy into more or less independent drama. Thus numerous dramatic actions have their origin in the Church, where, in a few cases, they remained. We no longer have the Easter tomb, but we still have the Christmas *crèche*. When, in the thirteenth century, the stage was no longer erected in the church but in the cemetery outside it, when the actors were no longer priests but laymen,* and when the language, originally Latin, was replaced first by a half-Latin mixture, finally by the native language, it was clear that the drama had become independent.

This drama which grew out of liturgy is religious in form and content. In the thirteenth century the *clerici vagantes* still wear masks in the Passion plays. Many Easter plays include the entire history of salvation, beginning with the fall of Lucifer. In this craving for a single, all-inclusive peripeteia (which can still be witnessed at Oberammergau), we see the close ties with the *sacer ludus*. The manner in which one watches, or, rather, participates, also points in that direction. One does not sit as in a theater, but takes part in a cult. It is popularly believed that whoever sees on Easter the re-erection of the cross which was buried before the altar on Good Friday will not die during the coming year. The re-erection of the cross is a typical transitional form between liturgy and drama.122

Two ancient components are also present: first of all, the dance. In a Tyrolean Easter play a dance is performed around the tomb of Christ, and the *"currebant duo simul"* of the Gospel (John 20:14) becomes a race in the Easter plays. In addition, the comic character is present throughout the Passion play. As *mercator*, the seller of oils, he is just as indispensable as is Iambe in the holy drama of Eleusis, in Greece, the

---

* In the fourteenth century the market place becomes the locus for the stage, the guilds furnish the actors, and the *officia* become *spectacula*.

indecently funny servant girl who cheers the sorrowing mother, Demeter.* The keeper of the house where the Last Supper is held and, above all, the devils provide an occasion for laughter and revive the exuberance of fertility in their foolishness, irreverent and yet almost sacred. But we recognize that these humorous components, especially when they acquire more independent importance, must lead to secularization. Joy constrained by ritual yields to joy for its own sake. On the other hand, we are surely wrong in not giving more scope to familiarity with the holy than our Methodistic orthodoxy will allow. The Mystery play deals with holy persons in the same way that the fairy tale deals with St. Peter and even with God. Joseph becomes a deceived husband; Mary Magdalene is welcomed even before her conversion; Noah's wife becomes a shrew who hesitates before coming along in the ark.[126] Even Christ is not spared. It seems to me that the need for a contrast between the exalted and the comic, the compulsion to make the most terrible and painful things bearable through utter foolishness and impropriety, outweighs any lack of reverence. Actually, we sense this lack only because of a religiosity which is neither very noble nor very Christian. This compulsion is fully literary. It brought forth in Shakespeare the great contrasts in Hamlet and in Lear; it created Lear's fool, the maddest and at the same time the most touching figure in dramatic literature. The comic intermezzi of the Mystery plays are not exactly masterpieces. They come right in the middle between the ritually determined roles of the Attic matrons in the Eleusinian mysteries and the search of the artist for a counterpoise.** [91] The atmosphere was not always very devotional. The second Wakefield Nativity play begins with a complaint of the shepherds about the cold, their hard lot, and the behavior of the gentry, which is reminiscent of Leporello's complaint in *Don Giovanni*. The coarse joke about the mix-up of the child and the sheep takes up more time than the whole Nativity. The drama has become secularized, and it is not surprising that it did not immediately become an autonomous work of art. Thus in the Easter play we have the episode of the *mercator*, or *unguentarius*; in the Christmas plays, the episodes of the star, Herod, and the prophets; in the Procession on the evening of Easter, the loud knocking on the gate of Hell, the so-called "harrowing of Hell."

* Iambe's sarcasm is a mythological explanation for the sarcasm which characterizes the Eleusinia—that is, ritual aischrology (cf. 125).
** In one day at a Japanese theater five or six pieces are presented, before each of which come *kyoges*, that is, farces and jokes. This is the same pattern as in Greece: three tragedies with a satyr play following; and, in the Middle Ages, the *sotte clute* after the Mystery play.

In England the guilds take over the disposition of the roles. The sailors take part in the story of the flood, the goldsmiths in that of the Three Kings, and the carpenters in the building of the ark. "Expositors" or "doctors" explain the incidents. It is characteristic that the Mystery plays came to an end in England during the sixteenth century, on the one hand because of the growth of Puritanism, on the other, through the development of the secular theater.[115] In the Easter plays much space is taken up by the showing of the evidence for the Resurrection: *sudaria et vestes*, the sweat cloths and clothing, which formed part of the story as early as the famous sequence *Victimae Paschali.*• [127]

If we differentiate on a purely mechanical basis between comedy and tragedy, and obstinately insist on being serious in representing the holy, we block the path which leads us back, not only to our own dramatic past, but also to the times of Shakespeare and Faust, perhaps even blocking the path to true seriousness, which is not the same thing as impassive melancholy or sentimental emotionalism. What Beethoven demanded of music is true of religious drama in its ancient context, and possibly in a new one—that it strike fire on the souls of men.

• The Mystery plays were originally sung, but "The stage triumphed over music."

3 THE ENMITY BETWEEN

RELIGION AND THEATER

THE ENMITY   The conflict between Church and theater began a long time ago and still continues today. Everyone acquainted with our literature knows the bitter battle of the Amsterdam pastors against the academy for theater and poetry, which Samuel Coster founded in 1617. This battle was the occasion for some of Vondel's most biting satire. Here in Holland the interest in theater, which is just now awakening in Christian circles, is discovering violent resistance from those same circles. "A Calvinist does not go to the theater, even in a foreign country," a Calvinist once said. Little headway can be made against this kind of aversion by the more "moderate Christian." He is liberal in his views of drama, but, because he is a pastor, he is seldom or never seen in his local theater. And the complaint of Liselotte von der Pfalz unfortunately still holds true: "Is it possible that the ministers in Frankfurt are so stuffy that they attach more importance to comedy than to sin? Their ambition to rule over men is a much greater sin than watching an innocent spectacle which for a moment can make a person laugh; I cannot forgive any parson this farce!"[128] It is good, in the midst of picayune quarrels and narrow-minded liberality, to remember that the background of the conflict between Church and stage is that of history and the complex movement and countermovement of the human spirit.

The opposition of the Christian Church to the theater has grounds which are basically historical. In the historical conflict, there is a good measure of irony. We do not see theater and religion, but two different religions, one against another: the ancient fertility religion of the *sacer ludus*, with its candor and sexual symbols, and the new ascetic religion of Christendom. The theater must pay for its fidelity to the ancient primitive religious forms with the hostility of the new religions.

97

When Christianity conquered the ancient world, it did not find there tragedy or comedy, but only the least elevated dramatic forms, indeed the oldest, but certainly not the most venerable: mime and pantomime.[70] Today we would call it vaudeville. Not only the ancient forms of the fertility play, but also unavoidable objections to the lighthearted way of life of the actors, and, above all, of the actresses, were bound to bring down upon the theater of disintegrating antiquity the implacable hatred of Christianity.[70]

St. Augustine, for example, points out that the actors in Greece performed a religious function: since they propitiated the gods, they were honored by men. Examples are Aeschines, the statesman, and Aristodemos, the ambassador of Philip of Macedon. The function of the actors can be compared with sacrifice: they are priests. In Rome all this was changed.[129] There actors were engaged as a protection against the plague.[130] Tragedy and comedy no longer had the same importance they had held in Greece, and these forms were finally supplanted completely by the Atellan and mime. Even heathen writers did not have a particularly favorable opinion of the mime. The fear arose early that the populus would become degenerate and that honesty would suffer. A century and a half before the birth of Christ, Scipio Nasica opposed the building of a stone theater.[131] In the fourth century of our era the great enemy of the Church, the Emperor Julian, was just as strenuous an opponent of the theater as were his opponents, the Galileans. At that time people lived for the theater the way they live today for the movies. Theater and circus claimed complete devotion. The Emperor, who wanted not only to restore pagan worship but also to deepen it mystically, made himself unpopular by the infrequency of his attendance at the games, and became just as disliked as his opponents, the Christians. His path passed the theater and went directly to the temple, "because the theater is the most noxious activity, the most reprehensible manner of spending time." A Christian could not put it more strongly. The pagan priests, whose office and way of life Julian wished to elevate, were not allowed to visit the games. The theaters were to be purified and given back to Dionysus. Of course this proved to be impossible.[132, 133, 134]

The irony of history in this conflict is found above all in the fact that the mime was charged with putting gods on the stage. What sort of believers, asks Lactantius, are those who put on a front of honoring the gods, but at the same time let them be represented and laughed at in mimes? What sort of majesty is it which is honored in the temple and mocked at in the theater?[70] We may remember that the *sacer ludus* owes its sanctity precisely to the fact that the actors were gods, and that in the context of primitive magic, the powers to whom honor was given were represented dramatically everywhere in the world. The mime preserved the form. But what was once a note of sanctity is now considered a sign of irreverence: the nature of religion has changed. A striking proof of this irony is the story of the great actor who no longer wanted to hear the audience, and so every day presented his mime on the capitol for the benefit of the gods. He understood where the play really belonged!

In addition, the mime had its revenge upon the Christians. Just as it in no wise shrank from making the pagan gods seem comic on stage (for that was a tradition in the holy play!), so now the Christians, their customs and even their martyrdom are made the objects of coarse jokes with great gusto. Besides the other *tipi fissi*, the "Christian" comes on stage, and a whole category of Christological plays is born. Above all, the Christian "mysteries," especially baptism, are made to pay. Bishops, priests, and deacons come on stage to baptize the hero of the piece, he who sits in the baptismal font, in the name of the Father and the Son and the Holy Ghost. This is a most realistic parody, which was taken by faithful Christians as an attack upon everything they held most sacred.[70] Yet the Church had its own revenge in readiness. There are many stories of actors, who, at the very moment in which they scoffed at Christian belief in their roles, were converted. The most famous and striking example is the case of St. Gesenius, who in his play, when he was brought before the Imperial Court and accused of being a Christian, dropped his role and informed the people that he truly was a Christian: "Believe me, illustrious Emperor, and all of you who have just laughed at these mysteries [the quasi-Christians had previously been baptized on stage] . . . believe me, that Christ is the true Lord, that He is the light, He is the truth, He is piety, and that you can obtain remission of your sins through Him."[70] Among the actresses, we find not only Theodora, an empress who is anything but holy; but also a real saint, the beautiful Pelagia of Antioch, who was converted by Bishop Nonnos.• [70, 81, 91, 135]

• Hermann Usener sees in Pelagia one of the many forms of the goddess of love, which further intensifies the opposition between Christian piety and stage beauty. In Japan there are two kinds of theater, the Nō and the Kabuki. The actors of the former are held in quite high esteem; the Nō plays still belong to the type of the *commedia dell'arte*, with nine fixed roles. The Kabuki actors are of such ill repute that in the census they are counted with numbers which are otherwise used only for cattle—which, of course, does not prevent the Kabuki from being very popular and idolized. The Kabuki play has more of a bourgeois character.

The Christian Middle Ages had exactly the same kind of drama, exactly the same kind of actors, as late antiquity. The *joculatores* are the successors to the mime actors.[70] This explains the contempt which to this day is poured upon the actor, the *cabotin*, who is placed on a level with the mob at a fair; for this reason, also, servants of drama were refused a Christian burial. We must understand this, of course, in the light of the previously described ascetic nature of ancient and medieval Christendom. It is incomprehensible that an ascetic religion could find anything objectionable in a tragedy of Sophocles. But it is quite plain that it is bound to oppose a play in which the *mimus calvus*, with fat belly and enormous phallus, plays the leading role; or where bedroom, bordello, and fight scenes constitute a major part of the content, in which intrigue is always concerned with adultery and fornication. The Church could take no other position. That we can understand. For even if the ancient form had remained the same, there is an enormous difference between ritual aischrology, the jests and coarse jokes of the primitive context, and the comedy of alcoves and adultery of a culture which has long ceased to be primitive. Nevertheless, the toughness of the life of the *sacer ludus* is shown by the fact that the stage obviously can hardly get along without indecency.

The mime makes fun of the Church, and the Church converts the actor. But the mime retains the last word. Not only did the notoriety of the actors and actresses go hand in hand with popularity and boundless adoration, such as is given to their present-day successors, the celebrated film stars (unfortunately without the mimes' notoriety!), but the forms of the mime even penetrated the Church. The Salvation Army sings hymns to the tunes of hit songs; masses and chorales acquired secular tunes (as we shall see in another connection); and ever since the time of Gregory of Nazianzus, the author of the famous evening hymn, various ancient Church hymns have borrowed their meter from the strophes of the mime.

THE NATURE OF THE ENMITY   In the historical conflict, the irony of history lies in the fact that the drama was condemned by one religion because it evidenced connections, indeed a relationship, with another religion. But there is another, deeper conflict, which springs as the logical conclusion from the different natures of religion and the theater. As we have seen, dramatic art originally had only one object, one peripeteia: the alternation between death and life; between eternal dying and birth. The religious cult, too, knows only this one event, and can, therefore, scarcely be distinguished from the *sacer ludus*. But drama developed into a multiplicity, while religion remained with unity. The drama developed thereby in a direction which was directly opposed to that of religion. It included more and more of the whole motley richness of the world, while religion remained fixed on the single necessary object, which it calls salvation.[136]

In this regard it makes no difference whether the theater has a low or a high level, whether religion is ascetic or not. At this point the tendencies of drama and religion come to blows.

Ernst Theodor Hoffmann has said much of importance about this in a little-known article. Young cultures, he asserts, bind man directly to the absolute. In more ancient cultures, on the other hand, man seeks the absolute, the background to his life, in the theater. Thus is explained the mutual interaction of Church and theater, their natural affinity and their enmity. "In the Church, from the very beginning, there lives much of the theater." In the theater, on the other hand, there still reside many relics of the Church. Even in the worst trash there is still a "faltering breath which reminds one of the absolute." In great dramatic art this absolute comes clearly to light.

Even the drama which corresponds to the service of God—worship, liturgy—does not escape this conflict completely. It can happen that the forms of the liturgy seem to religion to be too rich, the movement too unrestrained. Then arises the demand for a more spiritual worship with extreme simplicity of form, together with the strictest concentration on the drama between the soul and God. The primitive Church expressed the striving of the entire communion of saints, living and dead, angels and archangels, toward God in the most venerable portion of its worship, which has been preserved in almost all churches: *Sursum corda!* (Lift up your hearts!) *Habemus ad dominum.* (We lift them up unto the Lord.) Calvin retained the idea, but stripped it of its dramatic form and transformed it into an exhortation to spiritual depth: "That in the days to come we may be fed with the true heavenly bread of Christ, let us not set our hearts on the outward bread and the outward wine, but let us lift them up to heaven, where Jesus Christ is."[137]

We can understand this conflict; we can even find beautiful its predilection for outward simplicity. But we cannot hide the fact that it is impossible to exclude drama without thereby damaging the dramatic character of the idea of the advent of salvation. The Calvinistic churches indeed succeeded in reducing the liturgy to a rudiment, but not in protecting the simple inwardness of the meeting between God and man from the nonsimple and undramatic surfeit of homily and sermon.

We must cite an often-heard objection on the part of religion toward the drama, even if only to reject it as unimportant. We are concerned with the statement that stage action is not "genuine." Many conclude from this that the stage is absolutely reprehensible, that men fall in love with mere appearance, and that the character of the actor becomes fundamentally degenerate. Others, on the basis of the supposed unreality of the stage, want to prevent the representation of anything really serious. For them, holy persons on the stage, again an irony of history, are an abomination; and holy actions, such as prayers, they find offensive in this context.

Of course no one can defend mockery of what is holy (but not what is hypocritical, O Tartuffe). We are not religious enough to laugh at the holy with impunity. But it is equally impossible to exclude one area of life, and that the most important one, from dramatic art. That would impoverish both religion and the drama, because when the sanctity of religion is not equal to the violent movement of the drama it has too much resemblance to an old, broken vase to be taken seriously.

The dramatic treatment of religious materials is very healthy for testing the "genuineness" of our religious life. Goethe formulated the "dangers" of dramatic art so well that they are refuted without refutation:

> Man sagt: es könne den Charakter verderben,
> Wenn man Verstellung als Handwerk treibt,
> In fremde Seelen spricht und schreibt;
> Und wenn man das sehr oft getan,
> Nehme man auch fremde Gemütsart an.

> 'Tis said, it could be very harmful
> To make profession of disguise
> And see and act through others' eyes;
> If this is very often done,
> A man becomes the other one.[138]

Dramatic art is thus characterized as the basis of all art and, we may safely add, of all humanity. For it is one of the most noble forms of the great human art of comprehension, of placing one's self "inside another." To find all men in yourself, that is the secret. And that is not only the secret of drama, but also the secret of forgiveness and of love. We shall return to this point. But this has already invalidated the argument of artificiality; for this argument proceeds upon the naïve assumption that art is only an "as if," an imitation, perhaps not totally for fun, yet still without essential meaning. But it is precisely within the basic experiencing of all feelings, even those of others, that therein lies an extremely important connection between religious and dramatic expression.

And so what originally seemed to be an element in the conflict turns out to be a part of the connection between religion and drama. The boundary vanishes. But this already leads us into the midst of the considerations of our fourth chapter.

4   INFLUENCES: HARMONY

We shall here illuminate two more single influences which clarify the contact between religion and dramatic art.

THE BROADENING AND DEEPENING OF LIFE   This is brought about through play and, through it, play occasionally becomes capable of giving expression to the holy. By being caught up in a dramatic movement, life is reduced to its simplest form, to its particular content, to its eternal nucleus. While in the context of magic this nucleus was visible to all, so that dramatic representation of life could be truly simple as soon as dramaturgy ceased to be primitive, it had to express the unity of life in terms of the multiplicity of accidents which a life of movement entails. Here we can find a religious aspect. A man who reaches the background of life, its ultimate basis, comes upon a boundary. Broadening and deepening, the sudden experiences of life as a unity bring with them the suspicion of holiness. Further, this unity and immensity of life are not generalities, which can be attained in thought but not in experience, but are, rather, extremely personal. The secret of all dramatic art is *"tua res agitur."* New tales of joy and sadness, mourning and rejoicing, appear out of the complex multiplicity of life. But amidst the great variety of occasions the same thing is felt. It concerns you or, rather, it concerns the power that resides in you, in God, in everyone. Aristotle's dictum that drama means a purification of the passions is the half-modern expression of the releasing, overcoming, life-giving force of the drama. Primitive man thought of it as magical. We try to understand it psychologically. In modern drama, too, the accidental circumstances of an individual life and of the persons represented vanish. They do not give way to a colorless generality, but to the consciousness of a greater, deeper life, of the one single life in a variety of manifestations.

Small boys were watching the Passion story in a puppet theater. "Yet when Jesus was bound and flogged, the boys felt shame themselves. They, too, had hated and persecuted. They were like the Pharisees, like the Romans."[139] Beethoven's *Fidelio*, which only through music becomes a drama, does not tell the story of a prisoner, but of the imprisonment of every man; and in the chorus of the prisoners we hear the oppression of our own subjection; in the trumpet fanfare, our emancipation from unbearable slavery. Shakespeare's *King Lear* is not an interesting story of thankless children, but the story of us all and of our relationship with our parents. The Gretchen tragedy is not a touching anecdote, but the story of the human heart. Great dramatic art is greater the more typical it is and the less it represents a unique psychological case.

Naturally the consequence of this development would mean the end of dramatic art. Drama would return to liturgy, whence it arose. Calderón is a borderline case: in his *Mysteries of the Mass*, he returns completely to a single peripeteia. From Adam to doomsday there is only a single event, a single peripeteia of salvation. Everything is liturgy: Adam prays the Confiteor, Moses the Introit and the Kyrie, the Patriarchs the Kyrie, Christ recites the Gloria, Paul the Epistle, John the Gospel, the Apostles the Creed.[140]

More clearly than in the drama, this broadening and deepening are expressed in the art and person (which are inseparable) of the actor. "The art of the actor, his entering into another character and speaking and acting from within him, ultimately is related to its original root, that transformation of the individual life which the truly enthusiastic participant in the nocturnal dance festivals of Dionysus felt happen to him in ecstasy."[141] Prophet, ecstatic, priest, and actor, in their service and official capacity, have a common origin. The actor loses his individuality. He puts on a mask which from time immemorial has been fraught with holy significance. He can "see himself transformed in his own presence, acting now as though he had really entered into another body, into another character."[142, 143] The only genuine actor is the one who does not play a role. As long as the mask is consciously worn, the role played, the action of the actor means little as art, and nothing at all in the religious sense. Only when the artist is his role, laughing and crying from joy, from pain of the character which he represents, suffering unbearably, joyously unrestrained—only then can one speak of high art and of a broadening and deepening which lead to the boundary of earthly existence. An actress in the full religious sense of the word was Eleonora Duse.[144] Lucian tells of a man who was amazed that the pantomime artist can play so many roles. But then he thinks to himself: You may have only one body, but several souls.[29] Since Hamlet, we know that we can learn from the actor about reality and depth of feeling:

> Is it not monstrous that this player here,
> But in a fiction, in a dream of passion,
> Could force his soul so to his own conceit
> That from her working all his visage wann'd,
> Tears in his eyes, distraction in 's aspect,
> A broken voice, and his whole function suiting
> With forms to his conceit? and all for nothing!
> For Hecuba!
> What's Hecuba to him, or he to Hecuba
> That he should weep for her?[145]

The answer is that Hecuba is everything to the actor, because he is able to give over his entire soul, because he reaches that boundary of life which is called love. Chesterton has his priest-detective Father Brown discourse about his apparently superhuman gift for following the trail of a murder. He possesses this gift, the priest says, because he committed that murder himself. When those who hear him are shocked, he explains that he puts himself totally into the soul of the murderer, experiencing the murder with him. For in each man all murderers reside. This putting himself inside he calls a "religious exercise."[146] It is his secret. The ability to get inside all men, murderers and saints, heroes and bunglers, Oedipus and Thersites, the Cid and Scapin, Henry V and Falstaff, Faust and Mephistopheles—that is the secret of the actor. On occasion, it is certainly also a religious exercise, because he cannot achieve it without love, which overcomes the boundaries of the ego.

I would call this secret the dramatic secret of us all, or the religious secret of the actor. Hugo von Hofmannsthal has expressed it beautifully in his poem, "In Memory of the Actor Mitterwurzer":

> Er fiel: da fielen alle Puppen hin,
> In deren Adern er sein Lebensblut
> Gegossen hatte, lautlos starben sie,
> Und wo er lag, da lag ein Haufen Leichen
> Wüst hingestreckt; das Knie von einem Säufer

In eines Königs Aug gedrückt, Don Philipp
Mit Caliban als Alp um seinen Hals,
Und jeder tot.

He fell: then all the dolls collapsed
Into whose veins his life-blood
He had poured; they died without a sound,
And where he lay, there lay a heap of corpses
Thrown down in disarray; a drunkard's knee
Pressed tight against a kingly eye, Don Philipp
With Caliban, a nightmare 'round his neck,
And each one dead.[142]

Indeed, without this secret of love the whole world is a confused heap of corpses. The one who breathes life into us at the same time takes our life into himself and bears our guilt:

Er war ein wilder König. Um die Hüften
Trug er wie bunte Muscheln aufgereiht
Die Wahrheit und die Lüge von uns allen.
In seinen Augen flogen unsre Träume
Vorüber, wie von Scharen wilder Vögel
*Das Spiegelbild in einem tiefen Wasser.**

He was a savage king. About his hips
He wore, like motley sea-shells on a string,
The human truth and lie of all of us.
Within his eyes our many dreams flew quickly
Past, like multitudes of wild birds
Reflected deeply on a standing water.[147]

A deep insight into the psychology of the actor and the meaning of his art is provided also by the novel *Broome Stages*, by Clemence Dane, in which she describes the experience of a dynasty of comedians, their sufferings and their joys, their temptations and their victories. Filled with great pain, Harry Broome looks into a mirror and starts to work out his facial expression, with twitching lower lip, as an expression of pain for stage use. The temptation lies in plundering life for the sake of the theater. But there is also a theater where life becomes broader and deeper.

* A fine apologia for the theater and an accurate comparison of the dangers which meet the actor and the pastor can be found in Björnstjerne Björnson's story *Fisker-jenten*.[148]

It is the same actor who tells how, after a bad performance in the role of King Lear, he gives an after-dinner speech to the company, which is almost like a creed:

> You are the priests of a temple: and likewise—for this is a unique, ancient office—the prostitutes of a temple, and you serve God both with your body and with your soul. Your duty is undivided service; and I warn you now that if you turn aside from this service, either out of ambition or for the sake of money or in a love affair, God will punish you . . . we, the priests of the most ancient temple, do we not have our God and our divine, holy book? I say holy . . . we of the theater are a peculiar people. The world comes to us to see itself, but we do not go out into the world to see ourselves. We have no selves, we are only the mouth of God. . . . For me there shall be no other God!

In the second place, there is an influence which is also very important in the other arts. I mean the human.

THE HUMAN   It is always somewhat difficult to rediscover pure humanity behind the profession of the theater. To express the holy by means of the human is certainly the most difficult and the most amazing problem which religious art has to master. For, as we have seen, it strives after the typical, the general. Dramatic art gave us a striking example; we shall see how this is even more true in music. But let us stay with drama for a moment longer.

As the *tipi fissi* gradually take on more and more human character, art becomes profane. The Greek tragedians, like Shakespeare, Holberg, and Molière (who still preserve a remnant of the *sacer ludus*, the mime, or the *commedia dell'arte*—of course in the primitive, magical form), stand closer to religion than does the completely free art of the modern drama. The latter, therefore, seeks out a new means of reuniting the severed threads. It finds this in the symbol. The human life is bearer of a more comprehensive, suprapersonal reality, no longer as type but as symbol. Henrik Ibsen is the classic example. His characters are people, not types. But at the same time they are bearers of a suprapersonal, eternal content, symbols of another world: Solness, the master builder; John Gabriel Borkman; Johannes Rosmer; and Rebecca West. Eternal values are expressed through their speech, their actions. When Rosmer and Rebecca West go at night to the millpond, a part of humanity goes with

them. Solness, who speaks to God from his tower, embodies the humanity of many centuries.[149] Borkman, who hears the metal sing, awaiting
the ambassadors who will offer him a kingdom; Borkman, against whom
there blows, out of that kingdom he desired so long and so passionately,
the icy cold of death, is the official bearer of a whole dream of humanity,
which calls and entices, inspires, disappoints, and kills all of us, from the
first to the last, from the bank president to the prophet, from the poor
writer to the disappointed woman. Today's generation maintains that
Ibsen's age is past. But he can wait; he does not belong to a particular
period. His genius was able to express general and symbolic truth, not
only typologically, but through the finest psychological analyses of
character. He anticipated Freud and Adler, but he did not remain stuck
in psychology; he understood how to create from it and with its help a
series of eternal symbols. Since he could serve, he belongs among the
greatest geniuses of all. The religious meaning of Ibsen's work does not
reside in religious or philosophical generalities, certainly not in the
so-called "Christian" element of the oldest portions of his work. It is in
the overwhelming power, in the disconcerting pathos of his plots, which
make us realize that here there is something quite ordinary happening,
something which could also take place in our own lives; but here it is
simultaneously the bearer of world-wide significance, eternal powers.
And to us it seems as though, with the help of Ibsen's dramas, we might
cast an eye upon the drama of God.

5   THE THEOLOGICAL

AESTHETICS OF THE DRAMA

LITURGY   From the point of view of theology, the place of dramatic art is in the liturgy. For whether it is rich or impoverished, developed or truncated, the liturgy of the Church is in any case drama, and it is in any case art. "Look at the liturgy: among the forms of Christian art, it is the transcendent and dominant one; the Spirit of God itself formed it, in order to have pleasure in it." It is not as though the liturgy represented primarily a work of art: "Therein the Church seeks neither beauty nor decorative motifs, nor does she seek to move the heart. She desires nothing more than worship, and to unite herself with her Saviour; and from this loving worship there streams of its own accord a boundless beauty."[137, 150] The Church is by no means a dramatic institution. The beauty of the liturgy belongs among the glorious gifts of God which are granted us when we seek the kingdom of God. In any other instance, the liturgy becomes a spectacle and a sin.

But that does not change the fact that in any case liturgy is drama and so also art. A sermon in every instance is a form of rhetoric, even if the preacher does not deliberately strive for beauty. We have seen that drama grew out of the primitive liturgy, and that in the course of its history it has split into spiritual and profane drama, liturgy, and theater. If we now wish to trace back the drama, not to its historical but to its theological origin, to its origin in the creation of God, then the two paths must meet once more; then we must once more return to liturgy. We do not now mean the liturgy which is found everywhere at the dawn of history, but the liturgy of the Church of Christ, the service of God, which begins with the "Song of the Angels" from the Apostle Luke, and which ends with the hymns of the blessed before the throne of the lamb, as we read in Revelation.[137] From the Christian point of view, the movements and countermovements from which drama grows have their origin in the movement and countermovement of man to God, in the holy encounter.

Just as in the other arts, liturgy must hold to the ancient. To be modern is the greatest mistake into which a liturgy can fall, says Friedrich Schleiermacher.[151] The forms of the liturgy* are always the forms of yesterday.[152] That is no romanticism or love of the archaic, but a means of attaining objectivity. In the sermon, the language of our day is spoken, or at least should be. But in the liturgy one speaks either another, special cult, language (originally Greek, then Latin), or at least a language which is far removed from today's. "In the Church, the difference between today and yesterday must be done away with; nothing must look as though it has its origin in the present day."[152] The ancient forms, the ancient language, are more suitable for the word of God than the daily forms, the daily language. For this reason, when the Church goes out into the world to teach and to preach, she speaks the language of the world. But when she returns to worship and fellowship with God, she speaks the language of the liturgy, in which so many generations already have carried on their conversations with God.

In times of secularization and rationalization this is not understood. The liturgy is deserted or modernized to correspond to the spirit of the age. Thus, for example, the Renaissance exerted a fatal influence on the liturgy through the "relativization of the holy through what is humanly beautiful." Much vanished, including the sequence from the music of the Church. The texts of the hymns were thoroughly rationalized. But the worst was that a separation had been made between liturgy and popular devotion, between liturgical and daily life—a separation, under the unhappy consequences of which the Roman Catholic Church primarily has to suffer today.[153] That is all the result of a fatal, morbid pride, which tempts man to take himself so seriously that he forgets that human life has the nature of a game. And at the same time he forgets God. For the meeting of God with man, of man with God, is holy play, *sacer ludus*. The theological nature of the dance, as we discovered, lies in movement; that of the drama, in movement and countermovement. God moved; he came down to earth. Then the puppets on earth moved also; or, if one prefers, the bones in the dry valley of Ezekiel. God began; we followed. For we are only "God's masques and costume balls," as Luther says, or "God's toys," as Plato puts it.[6] The most ancient drama, the drama that rules the world, is the drama of the meeting of God and man. God is the protagonist. We are only his antagonists. And we play a dangerous game,

* Including liturgical vestments; even the gown which Luther wore in 1524, having a revolutionary beginning as an academic gown, became a sort of Protestant chasuble.

for we share this honor with the devil. When the liturgy does not bring us to adoration and sacrifice, we even begin to imagine that we had given the impetus to the drama. The dramatic vanishes from our lives, and we are suddenly once more dead marionettes, to whose countermovement movement is lacking.

Among primitive men, every game, even a game of chance, is a religious activity, a contact with invisible powers.* [154] On the one hand, the game is bounded: it needs a closed order, a limited freedom of movement. On the other hand, the concept of game ranks above that of seriousness. For seriousness tries to exclude the game, while the game can easily include seriousness. For this reason, cultus and custom are a game: "for one does what is solemn."* * [6] For this reason, the game points beyond itself: downward, to the simple, ordinary rhythm of life; upward, to the highest forms of existence. The game of love, says Buytendijk, becomes love, spectacle becomes drama, melody becomes art.[156] Play is the prerequisite for those forms of existence which strive toward a communion with the other, and finally for a meeting with God.

In that sense the drama between God and men is also a play: it is played in a limited space; the infinity of philosophy is strange to it; it is concerned with a small land, a small people, a single man, a particular period of time. A deeper seriousness is concealed here than we usually understand by the word "seriousness": it is the meeting of man with God, God's meeting with man.* * * No speculation, no meditation, no theory knows that the relationships of God to us are essentially dramatic: question and answer, movement and countermovement. In the interplay of creation and re-creation, the means by which God himself acts, the drama has its place. It is to be conceived just as broad and just as narrow as the *Val de Grace* is described:

> The world has only rest upon the narrow space where God
>   in peace dwells with his creature
> In inward unity, and no one knows the beginning of his
>   grace, and end of nature.[157]

So it is not only the boards which represent the world: it is also the narrow space, defined by boards and wings, which pertains to more than itself.

* For this reason the primitives do not stop playing until they have nothing more to wager.
** I know of no other way than the game of dealing with great problems: that is an important prerequisite, as an indication of the size of the problem (cf. 155).
*** Buytendijk points out that not only do I play with something, but also that something (a ball, for example) plays with me (cf. 156).

PART THREE

Beautiful Words

1 HOLY WORDS

THE WORK SONG We know of songs which, in an earlier age, were sung during work, and which even today occasionally accompany some activity. The work song is, or was, known during tamping down of soil, grinding, rowing, sowing—during all work which demands regular movement. Even those jobs which are not typically rhythmic make use of accompanying words. "If there's no song while it's brewing, the beer won't be good," says an old German proverb. Travelers in the Indonesian archipelago have observed that the song which accompanies rowing exerts a visible influence on tempo and power. We have received reports from American factories that experiments have been made toward increasing production with the help of recorded music.

We are still aware that, under rhythmic constraint, words exert a force. Even when no longer reinforced by a rocking cradle, this force is exhibited by the cradle song. Where does the source of this force lie? Surely not in the content of the words. At the magical, primitive stage, the beauty of words does not reside in their meaning, but in their rhythm, in their meter. The words generate a certain power which is fixed, controlled, and concentrated by the rhythm. Therein lies the religious significance of the work song. The man who discovered that was Bücher. He thought he must remain unpersuaded of any religious significance, since the content was fully profane, being related either to the work itself or to completely foreign matters. But we are dealing here with art; and art, by its very origin, is connected with power. Thus the work song is a religious and magic instrument. The mere recounting of the various movements of the job has magical effect. In his milling song, the Greek sings of the "great Pittakos," who was himself a miller.* In the process

---

* ἄλει μύλα ἄλει. Χαὶ γὰρ πίτταχος τας μεγάλας Μιτυλάνας βασιλεύων.

In the temple service at Jerusalem, frankincense was crushed fine to the song *hadek heteb hadek* (crush good and fine). The spices benefited from the noise. This information from Dr. J. Premsela.

of tamping down earth, Haman* is brought in:

> Haman had a scaffold built
> To hang both Jews and Christians,
> Alas, he had to climb it himself,
> With his shoes and stockings.

American Negro field hands bewail the great danger that awaits the sinner:

> Oh, poor sinner, now your time has come,
> What will you do when your lamp's burned low?

What is sung is not important, since we are not concerned with Pittakos or Haman or the burning low of the lamp of life, but with the power necessary for work which is magically strengthened. In the view of the primitive mentality, as we have seen, the religious or magical cannot be separated from the profane. Every power which attracts attention, which calls attention to itself, is power.

Words possess this kind of strong, insistent power. About the origin of language we know nothing. But we can picture to ourselves what effect organized language, beautiful words, must have. Of course, we cannot picture the transition from the call of the animal to the articulated, sensible word.** But we can understand the surprise at the discovery of the formula. A formula has a liberating effect and possesses power. Even we modern men live by formulas, though we may not generally like to admit it. A thing only comes alive for us, becomes a part of our own life, when we have found a formula for it. For ancient formulas we have a certain disdain; or, rather, the organized and powerful words of earlier generations make us feel ill at ease. For this reason people state that they don't "like" the liturgy. They mean that they are afraid of the concentrated power of the formula. But while we reject the formulas of earlier periods, we are all the more in need of the formulas of the day, "of the day" in the literal sense that the newspaper creates them for us. In political and ecclesiastical life we find a plethora of examples. War is justified as "intervention on behalf of the rights of small nations," or as "preserving our culture," or as the "fight against communism." One

---

* Haman, as seen here, is a figure out of Dutch folklore, although he is widely known from the Book of Esther.

** Richard Thurnwald holds that expressions of emotion and desire stand at the beginning of the development of language; still, work songs—such expressions joined together into a work of art—do not occur among the most primitive peoples (cf.[158]).

party needs "the little man"; the Social Democrats need the "proletarians"; the National Socialists needed the "demo-liberal Jews"; others need a "Protestant nation." Ecclesiastical politicians speak of the "Church Universal" or of the "rights of minorities." These formulas are not pure cant, but represent a very real power, even if they are by no means identical with the actual objects of concern. A formula concentrates power. It fixes it and extends it.

RHYTHM   For this reason, it is almost premature to try to speak of verbal art at the primitive, magical stage of life. There is only a rhythmic art, and a boundary can hardly be drawn between word, music, and dance. Even when the words have content, the rhythm exerts a compelling force. Through the Middle Ages a solemnly formulated prayer retained just as much effective power as fairy tales, which are the echo of primitive mentality.[160, 161] We know the power of cursing and blessing; we are dealing with phrases that "work." Every word, even when expressed accidentally, has an effect. But metrically organized words develop a concentrated power which is feared. Rhythm compels the movement of the soul, even the soul of the gods, says Nietzsche. This is a purely primitive perception.

Rhythm is strengthened by stricter control through repetition, parallelism, refrain, rhyme, or alliterative verse. We call all these means "artifices" for achieving an aesthetic purpose. But they are equally, indeed primarily, magico-religious means of retaining power and controlling it. At this point religion and art cannot be separated—indeed, they can hardly be told apart. Ancient Egyptian sacrificial texts and ritual formulas exhibit parallelism and obligatory repetition of the spoken word; the Psalms, which to a great extent owe their beauty to their parallelism, almost allow us to forget that such control of expression is more than just artifice. Ancient Germanic sacrificial texts are ordered by alliterative verse. Popular wisdom is formulated in meter and rhyme. In a certain sense, every primitive poem is a work song: it develops power through its conventions, either as work song in the strict sense, or as a song of war, love, or play, or as a dance song. Energy is concentrated and released. Primitive art is never without purpose. It always has a very definite goal which can almost be expressed in economic terms. On the other hand, song is a release of surplus energy. The Botokude has only one song: "The chief has no fear," *da capo*, without end, and in a fixed rhythm. For an Australian, song is the same thing chewing tobacco is for a sailor, says an ethnologist. When he is angry, he sings; when he is hungry, he sings; when he is happy, he sings; when he is drunk—as long as he is not too drunk—he sings more happily than ever. M. Julius Grosse, in his reports on these observations, compares this justifiably to the improvisational singing of our children: the same soberly objective or nonsensical refrain is repeated endlessly. The child is giving vent to his stored-up energy. Power is released. Thus primitive song is never what we call "musical." It is used to transfer energy either to a job or to another man, or occasionally after the manner of an adjuration of gods or spirits. Or purely negatively, it serves for the release of surplus energy. The first function we call—depending on its goal—religious, magical, or economic; the second, aesthetic. But both intersect. And the power which is put in motion is always holy power. In this mentality the beautiful word is always the powerful, creative word, such as we have in its most sublime manifestation in the prologue to St. John's Gospel.

THE IMAGE   Even though meaning is secondary to primitive man, a word still has meaning. In addition to its sound, a word also creates an image. An image conjured up by a word should call forth an idea of the object mentioned. But it is quite wrong to expect to find a really exact transcription for the object in question. The image is rather an "image" in the sense of a metaphor. On the other hand, it is not a poetic simile in our present sense. It is far distant from the detailed Homeric metaphor: just as when . . . so also. . . . It is concerned alternately with avoiding and seeking power. Beyond doubt there was a connection between the oldest images and the so-called language of taboo. "Poets did not make use of images because it was fun to change the words, or because they stood under the constraint of a poetic form; they found them ready-to-hand in the language of taboo."[162, 163] Not only among the primitives, but even in our modern culture, we have all sorts of special languages which particular groups have created and which are often secret. Even today we know the language of hunting, the "view" in fox hunting. Malayan warriors have a special name for the ear, which they call "hearer"; for the wind, which they call "blower"; and for the pig, which they call "short legs." The argot of criminals still lives among us.

Many professions use a more or less private terminology, just as children often have their private expressions. Among many primitives it is forbidden to mention by name certain powerful animals, such as the lion or tiger. The names of persons are not mentioned when they are engaged in hunting or in battle. It is equally impermissible to mention the name of the king. All these words and names are taboo; one avoids releasing the force which might be addressed by means of the creative word. Thus the use of metaphor does not come about through exuberance, but through necessity. The power of the dead is feared; this power resides in the name. If the name is mentioned, the power is released. For this reason, it is the custom among many primitives not to mention the name of the deceased. The name of God is also avoided. To pronounce that name releases the power of God, which could be destructive. Thus it is not reverence which keeps the Israelite from mentioning the name of his God, making him refer to Him as "Lord." It is the avoidance of an overwhelming power, the taboo.

Heinz Werner speaks in this regard about the ambiguous sense of an image: the open mystery and mysterious openness;[163] intimation and avoidance; setting force in motion and damming it up. In West Africa, the report of a death is given with the words that such and such a one has "moved." The ancient Egyptians called a casket the "Lord of Life"; death, "entering into life." These are not euphemisms, but attempts to neutralize the power of death by overcompensation. In the jargon of modern psychiatry, which is itself a kind of language of taboo, this is called an "abreaction." Traces of this can be found in our linguistic habits, when we say of the dead that they have "passed away" or have "gone to sleep" or have "departed this life."

Everything which possesses power must be approached with care. The Dakotas had a hunting song which went as follows:

> Out to the hunt,
> Cinch up the saddle;
> Precious children
> In half a day
> I will surely kill!

The "precious children" are buffaloes, whose latent power must not be awakened by public mention of their name. Especially dangerous is the area of sexuality. What makes primitive man and antiquity prefer to hint at sexual matters rather than naming them freely (though for our taste they still do so freely enough) is not shame or timidity, but the awareness that they are dealing with "powerful" things. For this reason, in this domain more than in all others, the symbol reigns, and one can say without exaggerating that the symbols of love hold true in all periods, and in all literatures, and are rooted for the most part in the double tendency to avoid and to preserve power. We, too, have a whole series of terms for sexuality which fulfill simultaneously the primitive purposes of concealing and revealing. Too often among us they have a questionable nuance. Modern psychoanalysis brings to light from our present-day intellectual life exactly the same primeval symbols which have always obtained. After the birth of a child, our children still say that their mother was bitten in the leg. All periods and almost the entire world know that the phallus is a snake. Wonderfully beautiful, spontaneous, and naïvely pure, this phallic symbolism returns in Mörike's "First Love Song of a Young Girl":

> *Was im Netze? Schau einmal!*
> *Aber ich bin bange;*
> *Greif' ich einen süssen Aal?*
> *Greif' ich eine Schlange?*
> *Lieb' ist blinde*
> *Fischerin;*
> *Sagt dem Kinde,*
> *Wo greift's hin?*
> *Schon schnellt mir's in Händen,*
> *Ach Jammer! O Lust!*
> *Mit Schmiegen und Wenden*
> *Mir schlüpft's an die Brust.*
> *Es beisst sich, o Wunder!*
> *Mir keck durch die Haut,*
> *Schiesst's Herze hinunter.*
> *O Liebe, mir graut!*
> *Was tun, was beginnen?*
> *Das schaurige Ding,*
> *Es schnalzet dadrinnen,*
> *Es legt sich im Ring.*
> *Gift muss ich haben—*
> *Hier schleicht es herum,*
> *Tut wonniglich graben*
> *Und bringt mich noch um.*

> In the net—what's this I feel?
> Fear my heart is binding!
> Do I grasp a tender eel,
> Or a snake unwinding?
> Love is played in
> Hide and seek;
> Tell the maiden
> **Not to peek.**

It slips through my fingers—
The worst and the best!—
And suddenly lingers
Uncoiled on my breast.
Oh, wonder, it bites me!
And pricks through my skin.
Oh, Love, it affrights me,
That strange javelin.
Oh, why do I shiver?
That terrible thing,
Its tongue all a-quiver
It coils in a ring.
Poison it, kill it,
The slithering threat.
I fear its deep thrill, it
Will murder me yet.

The image which is here formed completely unconsciously does not affect us as something out of place, but as being just as much the product of necessity as the symbolism of the folk songs with their rose gardens, their clear fountains, their apples which are ripe for plucking, etc. In an incantation of the Kubu from Sumatra one can see how the poetic image arises from the language of taboo:

Oh, oh, from what in days gone by the bird [man] arose,
Whose shadow [sperm] fell on the sea [vulva],
The shadow of Malim [a demon], who was
As beautiful as the moon,
He was the first to make the bird arise.

Alberta Portengen has shown us how the so-called *kenningar* of ancient Scandinavian poetry form a transitional stage between circumlocution and avoidance on the one hand, and the language of poetry on the other. The king is called "distributor of gold," a "reconciler of men"; the queen, "mother of heroes"; the son, "tree of the race"; sleep, "gathering of dreams"; being born, "awakening."[162] Among the Israelites we find similar circumlocutions: Jacob is called the "peeler of rods," the "flatterer," the "tent-dweller"; the temple is called "Lebanon"; and prayer is called "singing." We call the mode of expression used by Oriental peoples, especially the Japanese and Chinese, "flowery." But the flowers are rooted in very real earth.

THE POET   The poet is the man who controls the power of the word. For this reason he stands in close relation to the prophet. The word which he speaks is not the product of himself, but is a power which surpasses him, which he sets in motion. If, in this magical environment where every religious perception still concentrates on "powers," we could speak of God, we might say: he speaks God's word. But that is not the case. Still, he is the bearer of holy power. The later idea that the poet is inspired has its origin here. *Es deus in nobis.* . . .

The poet is, in the strict sense, a mythologist, a creator of words. The word which he creates is an image, a living image. He does not use the jargon which we commonly call "everyday language." He does not speak in "concepts" or "abstractions." All of those are ways of stunting the language of poets, the living language. It is not romanticism which made Hamann and Herder speak of poetry as "The mother tongue of the human race";[164] and Matthew Arnold said: "Poetry is nothing less than the most perfect speech of man, in which he comes nearest to being able to utter the truth."[165] Poetry is not an artificially exaggerated language, but the peculiarly human language. What we write and speak as language in our daily lives is a language estranged from its basic nature and robbed of magic. The poet speaks; teachers and professors, on the contrary, use means of communicating ideas. The poet serves the word; "writers" and "speakers," like ourselves, make use of verbal fragments and abstractions.

Two poets in recent times have been strongly conscious of this: Victor Hugo and Stefan George. Hugo is a mythologist through and through. What he touches with his word lives; everything speaks to him. Thus he can say: "The roaring of the abyss—that is the exertion the world makes in order to speak."[166, 167] The gift of bringing everything to life through a word, of letting everything speak, says Charles Renouvier, "consecrated him a poet in a way which long had been lost to view."[167] The great poets are always primitives. They return to the primeval force of life and language. Viewed psychologically, this "primitive" mentality is actually not so strange to us if we will only disregard for a moment the useful effect which words can have. In all periods the poet says more than he intends. His background goes deeper than he himself realizes. His word carries further than he is aware. Democritus wrote: "What the poet writes, filled with the Holy Spirit and with God, is very good."[168]

At the primitive stage of life the poet is not a specialist. He is everything at once: physician, exorcist, chronicler, and much more. But he always makes use of the word, the word of power. The oldest names for rhythmically organized words point to a magical or religious origin. The Latin *carmen* was a formula of exorcism, a legal phrase, a cultic formula, and had to be recited with painful exactness in a specific intonation. Brahman in India is a song, a formula, and further points to the power that resides within it. In Greece, the paean, before it became a hymn, was a prescription, a formula for recovery, an incantation, and it later became—so great was the power which resided within it—itself a god.

It is by no means always true that we can determine the author of a primitive song. Although today we no longer assume that the "people" itself makes songs, as an older school thought, at least it cannot be denied that primitive rhetoric, by nature and origin, is in a great degree collective, and that no unusual importance was assigned to the poet who did the work of redaction. Lyric and epic, in the primitive environment, almost always arise as choral works. "The singing chorus is primeval."[169] Primitive culture expresses itself collectively, just as primitive art does. The more that culture becomes modern, the more the social systems disappear. Then art becomes either "the most individual expression of the most individual feeling," or groups are formed for the exclusive purpose of "practicing art," and for this purpose societies and clubs are formed. The primitive choral lyric, which formed the basis of Greek drama and epic, presupposes a tightly knit, unified culture. In the folk song, a form of song with choral refrain, a bit of this has been preserved. As soon as everyone in a modern culture becomes aware of his own feelings and thoughts, a collective rhetoric becomes impossible or, at least, problematic. The fixity of the religious, liturgical formula becomes thus a problem for a humanity which assumes that everyone must pray in his completely personal way to a completely individual God, in order to achieve a private kingdom in heaven. Primitive man expresses his feelings collectively and narrates collectively. The choruses which we have in classic tragedies still tell of feelings and events. Unintentionally, the power of rhythm once more makes itself felt. No matter what the individual may do, the chorus, the crowd, is bound to movement in society. This is guided by a leader of the dancing and singing (the *exarchos* in Greece), but he is only *primus inter pares*. The development from *exarchos* to individual poet and singer is not only important for the development of Greek literature, but it provides us with a picture of the transition from the primitive to the modern mentality. A history of literature can be conceived—and it would certainly not be the least interesting one—which measured the importance of a poet according to the degree of his relationship to the primitive chorus leader. Does he speak only for himself or is he one among many? Is his meaning exhausted in his own meaningful perceptions or does the moving chorus stand behind him?

WORD AND GESTURE   In art and religion great importance is ascribed to the word. It is a living image, which moves in a set rhythm. But even at this point it should be stated that there is no basis for doing what theology might perhaps wish to do, and give words an exclusive or even a preferred position in the relationship of man to the "other," in the religious sense. Later we shall also have to deny such a claim to the special position which is put forward by philosophy in regard to music. We believe in the incarnation of God. But we do not have to believe that God must make use of a single, definite human mode of expression in order to reach us. Words fulfill a very important function in the revelation of God to man. But that does not mean that all other forms of expression are excluded. Later, in our treatment of the theology of the word (in our sense), we shall return to this point.

Words do not even represent the original form of human expression. For the first word was a gesture.

> Man thinks with his whole body, with his feet, his hands, his ears, as well as with his brain. . . . Psychological activity is an activity of the total organism, not a local activity. There is only the *commutateur* (controller), not the *détermineur* (originator) of thought. A man dancing and gesticulating mimetically in the light of the sun or the hearth-fire must have seen how his body was projected on the rock walls surrounding him, and this drama may have given him the idea of fixing statically the most typical moment of the processes of nature. . . . Thus those men fixed objects and scenes in their characteristic moments; they described the mime of their bodies and not their ideas. Thus the word "mimogram" should replace the false expression "ideogram." And these mimograms might be the most ancient graphic representations, with whose aid man tried, in the darkness of those centuries, "to make eternal the gesture of the moment."[170]

In this way man first "spoke," first "made poetry." The moving shadows on the rock walls of his dwelling were the pattern of his dance, were his holy drama. Gesture is not only an important part, an elucidation of the word, but is its predecessor. Word and shout reinforce gesture, clarify it, not vice versa. The words are secondary. This by no means lessens the enormous importance of the word for culture, for art, for religion. But it keeps us from making the word into a unique mode of expressing the holy. First we must view words less pretentiously; even so, they are still important enough.

"... A GOD GAVE WORDS TO TELL MY SUFFERING" We have seen how the holy power which resides within men is loosed by the spoken word. It can be directed toward a specific goal: toward the hunt, or toward war. That is the magical transfer of power, which is of prime importance for the practice of primitive religion. We might call this the economic purpose of rhetoric. But it can also simply be set free. Then we speak of rhetoric as an art, of its aesthetic meaning. In this respect the psychology of the poet, which Goethe summed up in a few words, holds true for the magical mentality:

> *Und wenn der Mensch in seiner Qual verstummt,*
> *gab mir ein Gott zu sagen, was ich leide.*

> And when the man fell silent in his pain,
> A god gave words to tell my suffering.

He says the same thing more directly in a letter he is writing to his "falcon": "My Giovanna probably has much of Lili Schönemann in her nature, together with something of Frau von Stein; perhaps it will do me good for a brief while to convert my faded sorrows once more into a drama."[171] Schopenhauer once made the following malicious remark about this connection between poetry and life: "If Petrarch's passion had been satisfied, from that moment on his song would have fallen silent, like that of a bird which has just laid its eggs."[172] But that turns the story of man unjustly into the story of nature. The man who is a true poet sings because he is never satisfied, even when the eggs have been laid. His song is more powerful than he himself. This is beautifully clear in a prototype of Goethe's poem which is found among the Ewe of West Africa. There, when something happens to a person that is too terrible to remain hidden within the heart, he says: "Sing me my suffering." He then goes to people "to whom song speaks," who can express what we vainly try to clothe with words. Upon them "song has fallen." And they sing:

> Not of myself did I become a singer,
> What is too heavy to be borne—
> That is the singer.[173]

In the structure of the primitive mind, the ends of practical religion, economics, and aesthetics are always bound to one another. They are bound by religion in the widest sense of the word, through the holiness of power. It is always a god that opens a man's mouth. And thus Hugo is right: "The point of departure of religion is always also the point of departure of poetry."[174]

2 THE BREAKUP

OF UNITY

FROM CARMEN TO LITERATURE   An ancient Egyptian pyramid text, which, like all others of its kind, is a formula of incantation, in its introductory words separates itself so far from the realm of magic that there must have been room here for a completely independent joy in the dark beauty of what is pictured:

> The jackal awakes, the moon arises,
> The sleepers awake, the men of Nubia awake,
> For the great bittern which came from the Nile,
> For Anubis, who came from the tamarisk grove;
> Pure is the mouth of the king. . . .[119]

The purpose of this text is to protect the departed king from dangers in the next world and to assure him of eternal life. With "jackal" and "great bittern," which are mentioned in the introduction, in all probability the king himself in his irresistible power is represented. But literature conquers religion. We feel how the incantation is becoming a work of literary art. But such an introduction cannot exist for long independently of the religious text. We call it then a lyric poem. Poetry awakes.

RAIN MAGIC BECOMES POETRY   Poetry also awakes to life in a song of the shamans of the Tarahumare, reported by Preuss:

> The wild tomatoes stand in bloom,
> They stand in bloom and ripen.
> There upon the ridge hangs the fog,
> Water is near.

127

> The fog rests on mountain and mesa.
> The bluebird sings and hums in the trees. . . .
> The turkey plays, the eagle screams,
> Therefore the time of rain will soon set in.[175]

This is a true song of spring; now everything, everything must turn! Among us, the cuckoo would call instead of the bluebird. This song is sung by the shamans, to the accompaniment of a rattle, while the participants in the feast perform and dance to bring fertility and growth.

We can see poetry becoming independent in the same way in the harvest songs of the Toradia, which have the form of an incantation, but actually are already moving poems. Thus we have a song to ward off rain:

> It's not the rain that roars there:
> It's the brook, which gaily runs.
> It's not rain approaching:
> It's the brook, which happily splashes.

During the time of harvest, rain is gladly dispensed with, but wind is wished for. In order to summon it, the song runs:

> Wind, where can you be today!
> All the leaves are hanging limp.
> Wind, begin and strongly blow,
> That the leaves wave to and fro.
> Wind, arise and strongly roar,
> Then I'll suffer thirst no more.
> Wind, cool off the burning day,
> Since I'm not yet allowed to bathe.[176]

Drinking and bathing are prohibited during the harvest.

POETRY BECOMES PROSE   Every spoken or written word is under a certain constraint. Even "free style" is determined by convention. In every kind of rhetoric, therefore, "style" is the discovery of the holy word. Dependence on rhythm, phrase, image, antithesis, etc. is a continual symptom of the transition from original religious unity to the separation between worship and "literature." Without such constraint, no style and, therefore, no art is possible.[177]

But the more the unity dissolves, the weaker the constraint becomes. Thus arises the peculiar form which we call prose: not the prose of an artist like Lodewijk van Deyssel, but that of M. Jourdain, who did not know that he was speaking it. We have seen that poetry, song, and dance once formed a unity in the *molpe*. First, dance vanishes, then song becomes melody, while the meter is retained. Finally this latter, too, is lost; and in prose, the characteristic Greek and modern form of human expression, that reserve and individualism come to light which are introduced by contrasting man to the world. Originally the spoken word was called *epos* or *mythos*; later it was named *logos*: that is, something arranged and calculated. Then *epos* and *mythos* retire; *epos* can only signify verse, *mythos* only myths, while *logos* indicates at the same time both "prose" and "reason."[33] In this respect, too, poetry is a transitional phenomenon. Originally, poetry was sung. Speech is a stage in the decay of song.[97]

Now, speech is certainly not a phenomenon of degeneration. In speech is manifested the spirit of the man who places himself outside the world, who wants to perceive sharply and clearly, and wants to take account of the world in clear outlines. This even begins with musical poetry and continues with prose. The poet sings in the world and with the world; the writer wants to give himself an account of the world. The poet finds image and rhythm in the world; the writer wants to balance the books of what he has found.

But, thank God, prose is always interrupted again and again by poetry, and even in the driest argumentation the original power of the holy word is never completely absent. In general we discover that the *molpe* is replaced by verse, verse by prose, and agitated, poetic prose by the lecture and report. The greatness of man lies in the fact that he always fights against joining in this transition and, stepping back, asserts himself. The ancient *epos* was still sung words. A modern *epos* scarcely exists any more. We have lost our breath and are no longer able to sing so long; surely Milton was the last great epic poet.• Only in his land could the great prose epic of the English novel develop, beginning with Fielding and Jane Austen, continuing to provide pleasure into the most modern period with its great art, at once controlled and uncontrolled, through storytelling.

THE FAIRY TALE BECOMES THE SHORT STORY The fairy tale, which surely was not told originally without purpose or useful magical effect upon the hunt or at work, loses its typical characteristics in its transitional stage. In the true fairy tale the hero has no name, or such

• A single exception: Stephen Vincent Benét: *John Brown's Body*. Garden City, New York, 1928; a verse epic about the American Civil War.[178]

a common name that it scarcely defines him; he is a type, with at most the name Joe. Further, he is very stupid or very noble, very strong or very small and insignificant. What he experiences, even if it is miraculous, is basically nothing more than that which every man experiences or would like to experience: birth, eating and drinking, marriage, and death. Death is presented in the form of an adventure in distant lands or of service to a cruel master; marriage is glorified as the rescue of a beautiful princess or the finding of a husband believed lost after a long, faithful search. Even birth is elevated to the stature of a "miraculous birth," so that from the beginning the hero is differentiated from other men. Apart from the immediate magical purposes which inhere in the fairy tale (the Pawnee Indians tell such stories of a hunt in order to capture buffalo), it retains the nature of magic when it is set in a context which has long been nonmagical, which it turns from wish into reality. It has been observed that many German fairy tales took on their present form during the period of the Thirty Years' War, and for this reason deal largely with eating and drinking well; the poor, who told these tales to each other, were hungry. And we are all hungry, for a beautiful woman, for fame, for riches, for the wonderland in which everything is good, whether we banally call it dreamland or romantically name it Bimini or Christianize it as heaven.

Then, in the period of transition, the heroes received names, and the events became temporally and locally fixed. Thus a historical saga can grow, such as the Nibelungen Saga or the romance of Arthur and the Round Table. In the process many mythical elements are preserved. But fairy tale can also become short story or fable. It can be set into an artistic frame with many other stories. Then it becomes literature. André Jolles counts the fairy tale among simple forms, in contrast to the short story, which is an art form.[179]

Boccaccio and Straparola made old fairy tales into amusing or pertinent, but always entertaining, stories; Chaucer into a sensitive poem; Charles Perrault into something of an impudent narrative with a final moral; Musäus into long-winded, ironic stories for popular taste; and Hans Christian Andersen into true works of art full of bitter sarcasm, gentle sadness, and romantic idealism. But in all these cases the fairy tale is no longer a fairy tale, but a literary form. In the context of magic, rhetoric is symbolic—forms and figures always are significant. The words are actors; they represent something. Things live and mean something; men are types of their species, representatives. Literature, on the other hand, tells stories with words which mean precisely what can be found in a dictionary; their objects are objects and are so treated; their men are just men. The finer the psychology and character of an individual is drawn, the truer the depiction of circumstances and objects, the further are we removed from the religious context. Of course, the tie can never quite be broken. In every literature there is symbolism, and even the dictionary meaning of a word can have a deeper meaning than the schoolboy suspects as he looks it up. Absolute literature, autonomous rhetoric, would mean the end of all literature. But a certain kind of naturalism and the modern, ultrarefined psychological novel are already approaching that limit. In the golden age of French naturalism there is said to have been a book which described the life of a man during a single day, including the tiniest peculiarities of his toilet, his nourishment, etc. Such is no longer art, because it is nothing but art. And the books of Marcel Proust, however admirable they may be as psychological analyses, do not always have very much to do with art.

The result of all this is that there exists an inner connection between verbal art and religion which can never quite be broken, even when the structure of the transition tends in that direction. Type and symbol maintain a distance. And without distance, life is neither beautiful nor holy.

3 THE REJECTION OF
THE WORD BY RELIGION

THE FORBIDDEN IMAGE   Whoever speaks, participates in time and space. He sings and represents. The graphic power of words, once a holy and mighty power, becomes—when the structures of transition no longer hold together—in its antithetical structure, the rebuke of the beautiful by the holy.

The image no longer represents something bound by the holy, but rather something typically human. Man is able to construct images only in the forms which he sees, and the highest and best form is the man himself. As long as—within the structure of magic—God could be represented as an animal or a fetish, no danger threatened. But as soon as the human form of God becomes something obvious, religious man fears the withdrawal of magic from religion. That he cannot imagine God otherwise than in the form of a man—that cannot be changed. But art must not make a virtue of this necessary poverty.

God is not the only thing humanized by verbal art; it humanizes everything that is holy. It must hope that the great Lord will speak humanly with it, too, as Goethe has Mephistopheles say of God. But this congruence between the spoken word and Mephistopheles has the effect of putting religion on its guard. If God speaks humanly, then either a miracle has occurred, or sacrilege has been committed.

Thus Xenophanes and Plato make the poet responsible for much evil. They simply were compelled to work evil; they had to represent divinity, and found only human forms. They may occasionally have had love, but they did not possess the tongues of angels. They were not forgiven. Poets, says Xenophanes, have ascribed all human failings to the gods. The tragedians speak the same language. And Plato prohibited them in his ideal state. Of course, this indignation had a particular reason in Greece.

Poets saw themselves confronted with the task of creating order out of a chaos of local and other powers. This could only be achieved with the help of a theogony, which brought the gods together in family relationship, but at the same time brought human frailty and evil into their circle. But behind this particular reason there lies hidden a deeper and more general cause: the poets had to create forms. Homer is the great creator of living, half-divine, half-human beings. This necessity remains in force even when quite different conditions obtain than in Greece.[81] Even the Old Testament, the more it banished the image of man from the idea of God, had to correct all-too-human characteristics: God repents—no, he is not a man, so he could repent of nothing; he tempts David into an evil deed—no, Satan was the tempter.

The problem of the relationship between religion and art touches here upon another, greater, problem—that of form in religion. How much space can and may imagination occupy in our thoughts of God? Something like the idea, "You heard the sound of words, but saw no form; there was only a voice"? (Deut. 4:12) • Here, then, is the parting of the ways of religion and art, of religion and literature. For word is voice, but also image.

In the popular faith of early Greece, Helen of Troy was a goddess and a very primitive one: a holy tree. Homer gave her human form— and how superbly! As the most beautiful of women, she was to bring delight even to modern peoples. And as the object of love, for whose exalted beauty the battle between men and gods burst into flame, she will always be rediscovered by other poets. She will enchant anew even wise old age, as she enchanted the old Trojan at the Scaean gate; and she will always call to life the smoldering hate of injured right. She lives and will live always, "Admired much and muchly blamed, Helen." But she will live as a woman, not as a goddess. Legend relates that the poet Stesichorus, who took over the beautiful story from his predecessors, was punished with blindness for his unholy conception. In contrast to Homer, Stesichorus recognized his guilt and composed a famous palinode in which he used an ancient motif from a fairy tale to represent matters as though Paris had only brought a phantom of his beautiful beloved to Troy, while she herself went to Egypt, waiting there under the protection of Proteus until Menelaus took her home again. Immediately upon this penance, Stesichorus regained his sight.[180]

It is remarkable that it is often the artists themselves who avoid the

• The problem of form in religion will be treated in detail later on, in the consideration of the fine arts.

frivolity of form. As Nietzsche said, Plato, who drove the poets from his Republic, invented the artistic form of the dialogue, and could not do without forms, even for representation of the divine essence.[81] Over a period of time the image cannot be excluded; so what can be the grounds for the rejection of the word by religion?

We cannot here deal with the arguments, so often tossed out and so rarely treated properly or even honorably, as to the moral or immoral implications of a work of art. We are not concerned here with the relationship between art and morality, but with the connections between art and religion. It is true that there is a close connection between morality and religion, but they are by no means identical. On the contrary: just as the relationship between religion and art is problematical, so there is also an unsolved difficulty, indeed a conflict, between religion and morality. We can hardly solve the one problem by means of the other, and had best leave the amoral nature of art out of our examination.

But there is something else which brings verbal art, together with the others, under the judgment of religion. "I the Lord thy God am a jealous God." Clearly it is impossible to serve another God besides him. But art also demands that she be worshiped as a goddess. And thus we return to the artist, who sells himself to his art, both life and death, and to beauty, which is a stern mistress—at least as jealous as the God of religion. Henrik Ibsen, in his dramatic epilogue, represented the tyranny of beauty over the artist in the form of the sculptor Rubek.[181] Beauty leaves no more room for heavenly love than it does for earthly faithfulness. This conflict exists not only in literature, but in every art. Ibsen expressed that very well, and in a form which is generally valid, in his poem "Paa Viddeme." It is the confession of a man who has withdrawn to the plateau of beauty, and from there looks down upon the madding crowd. For him, nature remains only a means of attaining beauty: "He knew how effectively the glow of the fire and the flood of moonlight worked together to form a composed illumination of the evening."

Stefan George makes a strong accusation against this aestheticism in the rebuke which the king gives to his harpist:

> *Mein schwert mein schild, von fürchterlichem saft*
> *Noch klebrig, klopfst du an dass es dir klirre.*
> *Ins wasser wirfst du dass es tanzt und ringelt*
> *Geschoss wie ich es zum verhängnis wähle.*
> *Die früchte meiner felder—siedend mühsal*
> *Der langen sommer—gehst du achtlos schütteln*
> *Und kühlst mit einer du den satten mund*

Dir dienen fieberqualen meiner nächte
Um sie in ton und lispeln zu verwehn.
Mein heilig sinnen drob ich mich verzehre
Zerschellst du in der luft zu bunten blasen
Und schmilzest mein erhabnes königsleid
In eitlen klang durch dein verworfen spiel.

My sword, my shield, which are still ghastly moist
And sticky, you clang together for your music.
To see the water dance you toss in it
A bullet, such as I would choose for doom.
The fruits of all my fields—the seething toil
Of a long summer—shake so carelessly
And cool your pampered mouth with one of them.
The fevers of my nights lie at your service,
To waft away with sound and whispered song.
My holy thoughts with which I am consumed
You shatter in the air like brilliant bubbles,
And all exalted royal suffering melt
To silly noise with your accursed playing.[182]

This is the charge made against a service of beauty which plunders life, against the poet who falls in love so that he can write a sonnet, who murders so that he can confess, and who fiddles while Rome burns. This danger confronts every artist; the less of an *artiste* and the more of an artist he is, the more aware of it he becomes.

It is a danger to which one may not yield, but which also cannot be avoided. For it is a result of the necessary gulf between life and art. Actually every "art" is already art—where there is no artistic life, there are also no "arts." Art tears life loose from its moorings and gives back to it a radiant beauty, admittedly without responsibility toward God.

For this reason, religion must mistrust art, even verbal art, and especially lyric poetry, since it is the most closely related to life. "A lyric poem makes possible, in the sequence of its verses, the experience of a unified event; not of the actual event which inspired the poet, but of that which the poet puts into the mouth of an ideal person."[183, 184, 343] Actually it is only modern poetry which presents this problem. In it, immediate experience (event) has replaced tradition (the petrified experience of peoples), like the so-called *Erlebnis Lyrik* (poetry of an experience) which arose from our pietism. Then there exists the great danger of desiring experience in order to write poetry, which finally leads to experiencing nothing. It is the tragedy of art that its conflict with life only becomes acute when it is closest to life, more acute than in its less personal stages in which it is content with beautiful illusion. This is by no means to say that battle with life must always mean battle with the holy. Thus it develops that there exist poets of various kinds, pious and atheistic, Christian and heathen, St. Francis and Baudelaire, Dante and Goethe, Homer and Aeschylus, Guido Gezelle and Willem Kloos; but it is precisely the most serious and deeply religious among them who have felt so strongly the conflict between the art of words and the service of the holy. Spranger mentions Plato, Rousseau, Goethe, and Tolstoi:

> Plato, who was surely an artist, rejected artists because they could only reflect and imitate, and were not capable of attaining truth, the archetype. Rousseau saw the danger of writing novels, at which he was a genius, in the fact that it arouses passions without bringing them under control. Goethe experiences something of the destiny of Tasso in himself. Tolstoi does battle with himself, or at least with a dimension, a side of himself, when he persecutes the immorality of art purely as art. And yet all these men had to use language to speak. They wanted only to surpass it by declaring war on the aesthetic form of life. . . . Thus in the battle against aestheticism on the part of many we see only their pain in realizing that it is denied them to express that which is highest, and represent it in themselves.[3]

These sentences open to us broad and fertile perspectives, which we shall consider as we come to them in the peculiar conflict of each art with the holy. Only the great artist experiences this deepest conflict. He despises art as an illusion, because he observes after its manner. He abhors Romeo, who is in love with love, because he wants to serve love simultaneously with and in beauty. He curses art in the name of the jealous God who demands truth and perfection. But the jealous God is master of his art. He opposes the service of beauty, because he wants to serve the holy, which is differentiated by its complete otherness from everything illusory, and which, in its absoluteness and perfection, turns its back on all that is partial and divided. But this holiness is not a foreign power. It is the holiness of his art, even when it is only visible in a distant perspective. Every true and high art points beyond itself.

THE FORBIDDEN WORD   Nevertheless, it does not point to a "Christian" art. It points to an art which is no longer an art, because it has completely fulfilled the task of art. It points to a heavenly art. The human word, which breaks down in trying to express beauty, points to the word of God.

Formerly, words possessed a power which forced men to use them with care. Words could bring blessing or curse, good or ill. *Favete linguis* (beware of the word). Now, in the antithetical structure, words are forbidden, not because of their power, but because of their essential powerlessness. Contempt for words, which is deeply implanted in the souls of modern men, is on the one hand a negative reaction to the primitive or scholastic word of power ("just where concepts are lacking, at just the right moment a word appears"), and on the other a positive reaction to the insufficiency of all images and sounds. Where it would be necessary to say something important, there remains only silence. Thus outward means do not help in the conflict between literature and religion. A "Christian" literature is sought, no matter what it turns out to be. Non-Christian books would be thought excellent if there was not so terribly much cursing in them; there is no actual objection to novels, so long as they are not terribly "naturalistic." And so on. It is not even noticed that this attitude not only contributes nothing to the solution of the conflict, but that the real conflict has not even been broached. It is precisely the same on the other side: glorification of the music of words at the expense of "meaning"; the construction of a definition of literature which is completely independent of all spiritual life, of religion, of philosophy, or of science; artistic impoverishment of life until all that is left are a few feelings. We in Holland have become all too well acquainted with this, even if we have come to know, after the lyric poetry of the eighties, both the verses of a Guido Gezelle and of a Roland Holst, of a van Eyck and of a Gossaert, after the beautiful, pitiful novels of poverty, those of an Alie Smeding and a Hendrik de Man. We know also that this attitude does not lead us to the conflict. Whoever reaches the conflict may not achieve a solution, but he attains unity. It is the religion of art that opposes art for art's sake, not the religion of those "devout souls" who do not always look upon art as an innocent accessory. In their eyes this problem does not even exist. It exists just as little for the devotees of "culture," who see religion as something of a cowardly sport. They have not even begun to come to grips with these matters.[185]

The word of God, which desired to be word of man, is a guarantee that unity exists. Most of the writings of the Old and New Covenant belong to the highest level of art. And even if Genesis and the Psalms, Job and Isaiah, John and Paul, were not the great works of art that they are, they would still prove that verbal art can be an expression of the holy. Certainly they, too, are inadequate; they, too, point beyond themselves to a word which is neither sound nor image, but form. And where God reveals himself to the world in the form of a man, there we do not need to look upon the forms of our intellect merely as schemata.

4 INFLUENCES

TOWARD HARMONY

THE SUBLIME   The motif of the sublime is related to that of the monumental; this we shall find above all in architecture, in the solemn calm of its noble line. In addition, however, the sublime is conveyed by an inwardness which reaches into the depths of our soul. We find it in all the arts, but literature has perhaps the best examples of it:

> In the year that King Uzziah died I saw the Lord sitting upon a throne, high and lifted up; and his train filled the temple. Above him stood the seraphim; each had six wings: with two he covered his face, with two he covered his feet, and with two he flew. And one called to another, and said:
>
>> "Holy, holy, holy is the Lord of hosts;
>> The whole earth is full of his glory."
>
> And the foundations of the thresholds shook at the voice of him who called, and the house was filled with smoke. And I said: "Woe is me! For I am lost; for I am a man of unclean lips, and I dwell in the midst of a people of unclean lips; for my eyes have seen the King, the Lord of hosts!" [Isaiah 6:1–5]

This simple immensity, this reverential terror, these basically quite simple words are a perfect example of the sublime in art, because behind the strict rhythm of the account we feel the strongly restrained inner movement, for which there is finally no other expression than "Woe is me!"

"We call that sublime which is simply great," says Kant. Besides Isaiah 6, we could cite a whole series of other passages from the Bible

139

which are filled with the same greatness. We think also of Vondel and Goethe, who, no matter how different, agree in this regard. Further, the famous series from Vondel's tragedy *Lucifer* is a paraphrase of Isaiah 6. In the "Prologue in Heaven," of Goethe's *Faust*, adoration is addressed more to nature than to God, but at least to a nature which is boundless in its majesty and delicacy:

> *Da flammt ein blitzendes Verheeren*
> *Dem Pfade vor des Donnerschlags;*
> *Doch Deine Boten, Herr, verehren*
> *Das sanfte Wandeln Deines Tags.*
> *Der Anblick gibt den Engeln Stärke,*
> *Da keiner Dich ergründen mag,*
> *Und alle Deine hohen Werke*
> *Sind herrlich wie am ersten Tag.*

> There flames a shining devastation
> Before Thy thunderbolt's display;
> Yet angels praise with glad ovation
> The gentle progress of Thy day.
> Thy sight makes strong the heavenly city,
> Since none may seek to probe Thy ways,
> And all Thy works, both high and mighty,
> Are glorious as creation's days.

LIGHT   Light is as present in literature as it is in painting or music. This is what we mean when we say of a landscape that "it is transfused with a supernatural light"; it is something graceful, almost gay, which reminds us of "God's friendly countenance," possessing "joy and light" for all who approach it in childish simplicity. As examples, we mention the incomparable hymn of St. Francis, and, in Dutch, a fragment from Herman Gorter's *Mei*:

> Thus I feel, too, the while I play, quite
> Quite far, over the fields comes early evening light
> Of words, and dreams when sleep my mind makes numb—
> Therefore, my young, sweet sister, come.

> Come, my young, sweet sister, come,
> Too long you've listened to the sickle's steady hum,
> Come, sister blond, out from our sunny corn!
> For hark! Oh, hark! The people distant-born

With eyes like sun are dancing, there are some
With music and with incense, come, sister, come!

SILENCE AND NEAR SILENCE   Silence and near silence are primarily constituents of music. But we find them also in verbal art, even if
it is more difficult for literature to deal with the "paradox of expression"
than for music: the art of saying something by saying nothing or, at most,
very little. It is concerned with what is written between the lines and
discloses unsuspected depths. The little "Evening Song" of Tersteegen
not only speaks of quiet; for the most part it is quiet:

> Now sleep is here.
> If sleep does not appear,
> Then come with me, draw near,
> Praise Him who made us,
> Who day and night
> Receives upon the height
> All praise and glory bright.
> O Jesu, aid us!
>
> Away with fear!
> My Lord and God is here,
> I am his starlet, here
> And there to glisten.
> Now I must cease,
> Lord, may Thy word increase
> And come in deepest peace,
> And let me listen.

Let us also hear Goethe, from quite another world, as he speaks with
a voice which becomes ever quieter, almost completely silent:

> *Selig, wer sich vor der Welt*
> *Ohne Hass verschliesst,*
> *Einen Freund am Busen hält*
> *Und mit dem geniesst,*
> *Was, von Menschen nicht gewusst*
> *Oder nicht bedacht,*
> *Durch das Labyrinth der Brust*
> *Wandelt in der Nacht.*
>
> Happy the man without hate
> Who remains unknown

With one friend to share his fate,
  Shares with him alone
What remains unknown to the rest
  Or hidden from the light,
Through the labyrinth of the breast
  Wandering in the night.

THE HUMAN   The human as an expression of the divine is also a
"paradox of expression," though of course a paradox which is hallowed
by divine example. God reveals himself as man. Then we must not view
man as the highest development of a power given in nature, even less as
something that thereby is divine; but we must see in him an unworthy,
base, fragile vessel, into which God desires to pour his grace.

In verbal art it is lyric poetry which brings us closest to the human.
It is not as though the poem were the experience of the poet himself.
Only the poet who speaks on the mandate of society is really a poet.
Since religion demands something "official," we shall find religious poetry
only where individual experience becomes the occasion for expressing
suprapersonal feelings that are true for all humanity. Here lies a boundary, both for religion and poetry, and, *a fortiori*, for poetry which expresses the holy. It would be worth while to make up an anthology of
religious poetry with no regard to the religious object, using as its single
criterion that which is common to all men.

In this context I should like to cite a characteristic remark of Goethe
about the so-called continuous song. This form is customarily viewed as
an advance in respect to the strophic form. In a continuous song the
various moods indicated in the strophes which follow one another can
better be brought to musical expression. But let us hear Goethe; he tells
how reprehensible all such continuous composition of songs is, "wherein
the general lyric character is completely removed and a false participation of the individual is demanded and aroused."[186] Here, then, we see
again the fear of anything overly individual, overly psychological. Naturally I am not intending to claim that a "continuous" song cannot have
great value, even great religious value. Schubert's compositions to
Goethe's texts are the best counterexample. But that which is universally
human still is best exhibited by the strophic song; and it is certainly no
accident that Mahler, goaded by the structure of his beloved folk song,
returns in many compositions to the form of varied strophes.

HARMONY   Harmony between beauty and holiness we find most
often in words which are spoken to God and before his face, in hymns.

For ages the hymn has been a song, not about God, but to him, sung in his presence, an apostrophe, and an epiclesis. Religions have in their liturgies many such songs of summons. Even where they have become literary, they still preserve for a long time their hymnic character. Since catchwords mean nothing before God, and since before His face a lyric outpouring in which the singer simply lets himself go cannot exist, the hymn is differentiated from other poems by its strict tone. There is not one word too many, no surfeit of images, no unintegrated exclamations. There is only reverence for the word, which is not only symbol or inference, but forms the body for the soul of things. The hymn has always preserved a bit of the character of an exorcism, which, according to ancient Roman prescription, "may not be ambiguous." Thus Latin is also the language best suited to the hymn, being short, clear, and powerful. The best examples are found in the Latin hymns of the Church. We think of the *Veni, Creator Spiritus*, by which the Spirit of God is almost conjured down to earth, yet in which all speech is in humble style and every word is a holy word.[97]

But even in so-called literature, much that is hymnic has been preserved. I have in mind the two great figures of antiquity, Pindar and Homer. In the latter, above all, it is evident how the holy word carries the reader and drags him along. Horace was basically a rather frivolous man, whose ideas are not especially meaningful. But the form of song to the divinity makes him into a *vates*, a priest speaker, whose word accompanies the holy action:

> Songs, not previously
> Heard, I sing as priest of the Muses
> To girls and boys.[187]

In later ages, it was Friedrich Klopstock and, above all, Hölderlin, who discovered the sacral tone once more. In our own time, Stefan George was the first to consider words once more as holy. In his language, which is sacral in the fullest sense of the word, every word has the weight of a magical formula addressed to God:

> *Wer schauen durfte bis hinab zum grund*
> *Trägt ein gefeiter heim zu aller wohl*
> *Den zauber als begehung und als bild.*

> Whoever looks as far as to the depths
> Bears a charmed home for everyone's salvation
> Magic as image and as celebration.

Gertrud von Le Fort, too, in her hymns to the Church, recovers this tone of epiclesis.

Wherever the word turns directly to God or the gods, there rules a harmony between beauty and holiness. Of course, this does not have to occur exclusively in the form of the hymn; nor does it always have to be a ponderous, liturgical tone which conveys the word. We find this harmony between beauty and holiness in Dante, above all in his glorious final cantos of *Paradiso*, but also in the childishly simple Guido Gezelle, whose poems, precisely because of their childishness, reflect the harmony most clearly: each word that he speaks, whether it has to do with horses or with flowers, is spoken before the face of God.

5 THE THEOLOGICAL

AESTHETICS OF THE WORD

POET AND PROPHET In a small book which Albert Verwey dedicated to his friendship with Stefan George, there comes clearly to light
the conflict which arises as soon as poetry tries to return to its source, the
holy word. Verwey, who was more than just a rhetorician, opposed
the prophetic tone, the almost hieratic mode of expression, which is
found in George's poetry after *The Seventh Ring*. George speaks of the
transformation of the world, which he introduces with these words:
"When he said that, he was all passion, his whole body was movement.
What fascinated me in everything he said was the power of his faith.
That the world would be transformed, of that he was sure. Yes, I said, but
we must be only poets. There were times in the conversation when the
landscape, the mountain with the towers of Bingen on the opposite side,
seemed to have changed, as though on that height I were not walking beside a man, but beside an angel."[189] This prophetic office does not suit
Verwey. For him the poet is only one man among others, who expresses
what lives in all of them. His word is a human word, not a divine word.
When, in the First World War, Verwey views the political events as a
superficial movement, which does not touch the poet in spite of his clear
and sharp judgment, this leads to a break with George, who still feels
that he is both poet and leader of his people, as the one who speaks the
word, holds authority, the one who sings the *carmen*, the song of
magic.

This is not to maintain that on this account George is a greater poet
that Verwey. This he is, without a doubt, but not because he rediscovers
the word of the *vates*, which Verwey does not succeed in doing. In both
categories of poet we find the very greatest, both among those who

speak the human word and are satisfied with that, and also among those in whose words the divine word breaks through. In the second category belong Dante, Milton, Novalis, and Hölderlin; in the first, no lesser men than Shakespeare and Goethe. In the conversations with Eckermann, Goethe talks about the poems of Fleming, a superb poet, whose poetry was also taken over into the hymnal. Goethe says, half naïvely, half ironically, "I've done so many kinds of things, and yet there is not one of my poems which could stand in the Lutheran hymnal." To which Eckermann, fully naïve, and, in his innocence, getting to the heart of the matter, replied: "I laughed and agreed with him when he said to me that there was more to this strange statement than appeared on the surface."[190] Indeed, the hymnal is here very revealing, for Novalis was taken over. The "more" which Eckermann guessed is found in the fragments of Novalis in which he sketched the theory of a sort of cosmic hymnal. Novalis' songs are still sung regularly by congregations, even though they leave much out in the process.[191]

The hymnal, the "Christian road block" as Nietzsche called it, is here truly a landmark. Nietzsche was furious that the world had to wait a bit longer for his new Zarathustra gospel because of the five hundred thousand copies of the hymnal which Teubner had to print. Goethe was amused because he was no longer able to find true humanity in the pious, schematized emotions of the Church hymn. But no matter how much Novalis romanticized the hymn, he is aware that it is precisely this hymn which is the true word of the poet, the word which ascends to God because it has come from God, and which the poet can speak only because it was given to him. For this reason the hymnal remains the first among books of poetry, and it is no credit to "literature" that it must always be content with a small edition. For the genuine word of the poet is the poem of society, the song of the congregation. Here begins the theological aesthetics of the word.

For is it not thus: the word takes its own course? It has its own laws and its own demonic power. It finds its destiny and its fulfillment when it returns to the hymnal from which it had its beginning. That may be a heathen book, as it was in the case of Nietzsche and Stefan George. It can be a book in which everything unusual, including everything Christian, is caught up in romantic ecstasy, as in the case of Novalis. It can also be the Christian hymnal, in which we find the poets Vondel, Gezelle, Revius, Jacqueline van der Waals, Newman, and Tersteegen. The word then finds its proper place once more, from which it departed, in ritual, in society, in the hymnal, in the word of God. The theological place of the word is inspiration.

INSPIRATION   It is primeval. Garodman, the Iranian heaven, is the "house of song" into which the hymns of men ascend. Ecstasy gives rise to singing. And song builds the temple of the gods.[35] In Israel, *Yahweh* is enthroned on the praises of his people (Ps. 22:3). God's spirit always seizes a man and compels him to speak, to sing. Man meets his God in the word which proceeds from him, but which derives from God. The religious man who expresses himself, who speaks, we call a prophet; the servant of beauty who does the same thing, we call inspired. The impersonal nature of prophesy (it is not the prophet who speaks, but God who speaks through his mouth) we find in another manner in the inspiration of the poet, who surely says more than he intends. "Creativity has its impersonality; creativity is not a child of the will, but a child of this unconscious drive which is called inspiration; it seems to the creator as though someone else were acting in him, through him, subduing his personality and making of him a mere mouthpiece."[192] When we were young, we thought the inspiration of the poet came as a flash of lightning; we thought that he, who was born and not created, wrote down a poem in the frenzy of his senses, without consideration, his hand guided by a divine power. Whoever has seen the rough draft of a great poet, Shelley, for example, knows that this childish image is wrong. Much practice, much reflection, much conscious consideration, much technical ability, are necessary to bring a good poem into existence. But yet in the childish idea of inspiration there resides an eternal truth, for no more than the prophet does the poet speak in his own name or for his own purpose. He says more than he can be responsible for. He is a "*porte-voix*," a mouthpiece. Through him societies speak, powers of the most varied sort. His word is suprapersonal. It is given to him; it is entrusted to him. Albert Verwey once wrote to a young poet who had sent him his poems to be criticized: "Do not pursue the Muse, but let yourself be claimed by her when she needs you." This does not mean that the Muse will suddenly call upon someone who has not mastered the technique of poetry, to glorify the word of beauty. But it does mean that neither wisdom nor ability is of any use to the man whom the Muse does not call. Joachim Konrad names five characteristics of inspiration: (1) Passivity and constraint; (2) Immediacy of thought; (3) Necessity of form ("thus and not otherwise"); (4) "Emotional rapture"; (5) Need for relaxation through "broad rhythms."[193] He cites the superb picture which Nietzsche drew of his inspiration for *Zarathustra*, which we shall also reproduce here:[155]

> Has anyone at the end of the nineteenth century a clear idea of what the poets of strong ages called inspiration? If not, I'll describe it. With the tiny bit of superstition left in him, man would indeed hardly know how to avoid the idea of being simply an incarnation, a mouthpiece, a medium for overwhelming powers. The concept of revelation in the sense that suddenly, with ineffable assurance and sharpness, something becomes visible, audible, something which terrifies and overthrows a man in the very depths of his soul, simply describes the facts. One hears, one does not seek; one receives, one does not ask who is giving. Like a flash of lightning, an idea shines forth, with necessary form, without hesitation—I never had a choice. A rapture, whose enormous tension at times breaks loose in a stream of tears, in which my pace is sometimes impetuous, sometimes slow; a complete sense of being beside myself with the most distinct awareness of numberless fine tremors and shudders to the tips of my toes; a depth of happiness in which everything most painful and melancholy does not have the effect of an opposite, but as something conditional, something demanded, as a necessary color within such a superabundance of light; an instinct of rhythmical relationships which bridges broad reaches of forms. Length, the need for a large-scale rhythm is almost the measure of the intensity of inspiration, a sort of compensation for its pressure and tension. Everything is involuntary in the highest degree, as though in a storm of feeling of freedom, of being absolute, of power, of divinity . . . the necessity of the image, the metaphor, is the most remarkable thing; no conception remains of what image or metaphor is. Everything appears as the most immediate, the most correct, the most simple expression. It really seems, to recall a phrase of Zarathustra, as though ". . . objects themselves drew near and offered themselves to the metaphor."

It is by no means accidental that Nietzsche's language has a religious sound. Art is here represented as service, as duty. "I never had a choice." Things come to the artist with an absolute imperative. He does not seek for them in order to rule them, to put them into the chains of his form. They offer themselves to him so that he may serve them. Thus the concept of the "artist" receives still another content, other than that which we recognized at the beginning of our third chapter as typical for the phenomenon of transition. All artistic genius, no matter in what structure it appears, holds itself at a distance which we call inspiration, and thus becomes the same thing that playing a role is for the dramatic artist. Inasmuch as all artists are servants and must lose themselves, they are all equal to each other.•

The same thing holds for every artistic person. There exists, it is true, a great gulf between the so-called creative artist and the one who is only imitative, and further, just as great a gulf between the latter and the receptively artistic individual; but there also exists a unity among the three. In every creation there is something of imitation; in every imita-tion, something, no matter how little it may be, of creation. And "artistic" means nothing at all when the creative-imitative component is lacking. Whoever is receptive to art, letting art penetrate within him, whoever (as is said, using a very bad form of expression) "enjoys" art must under-stand the secret of imitation. The beauty which the artist created must be experienced and re-created anew in his soul, thereby revealing to the humble "lover of art" something of the mystery of creation.

"All artists are religious," said Friedrich Schlegel. Only the giving up of one's own life, only complete devotion to the "other world," enables a man to create and to imitate beauty. Here religion and art speak closely related languages.

THE DIVINE WORD   A word is sound, rhythm, and image. It drags everything along, but also sets boundaries; it constrains and it frees. By fencing off a portion of the world, giving form to a little bit of reality, it creates; by being rhythm and sound, it arouses. The poet calls into being things which do not exist. Therein lies his divine mission. And when he becomes aware that God stands behind him and breathes into him his creative spirit, he turns and sings his most beautiful song in God's presence, and in praise of him who put it into his mouth.

Without doubt there is a boundary between the poem and the hymn, or the song of praise (laudes); we have seen it in the case of Verwey and in Goethe. But there is also a path from the poem to the hymn. In this way we must understand the words of St. Augustine, which are all too well known, but not always cited in the proper context: "And yet man

• We find the reverse side in Thomas Mann: "You see, the man of letters basically does not understand that life still wants to live on, that it is not ashamed of living on even after it has been pronounced 'over and done with.' But see—in spite of any salvation through literature it steadfastly continues to sin; for every action is sin in the eyes of the spirit" (cf. [194]). Nothing more of "service" can be felt here. The artist is here also a "man of letters."

desires to praise Thee, a miserable sketch of Thy creation. Thou Thyself encouragest us, that praising Thee is joy; for Thou hast created us for Thyself, and restless is our heart until it has its rest in Thee."[195]

Whoever finds words can find God; whoever can write poetry finds the praise of God. For by its very nature all poetry consists of *laudes*. The theology of the word is expressed most beautifully and purely in a poem by van Eyck:

> Oft, tired of labour never bearing fruit
> (A poet's will is never absolute),
>
> I think how, with an unsuspected flight,
> Allowed by grace which rarely breaks the night,
>
> The soul at once extends its mighty wings,
> Inerrantly creating beauteous things,
>
> And then the breath is stopped before the face!—
> God speaks in human tongue with open grace;
>
> Many another, only because he
> (His will performing what God wills to be)
>
> Admits his work unexpiated sin
> And separates himself from what has been
>
> And sets his life upon a strict command
> So that a perfect poem at last may stand,
>
> Until to him who suffered through the flame
> The hour comes, and poet is his name.
>
> And labour, too, which conjures with the word
> (Behind which to the heart a song is heard),
>
> When sudden light goes through our souls at last
> And—since that light and song by God were cast—
>
> Brings us with love to that position high
> Where joy makes suffering vanish to the eye,
>
> Is—making good unexpiated sin—
> Fulfilling joy, the crown of discipline.
>
> If then my thoughts can make this song their own
> (For every beauty comes from God alone)
>
> In which all pain and pleasure of the earth
> Have lost themselves, denying all their worth,

So that the heartbeat coursing through the world
Softly remains within its song enfurled—

That which thus has deigned my soul to bless
Should I not worship, rapt in thankfulness?

Taught by fulfillment and denial mute,
Aware no poet's will is absolute,

And all is given to the man who stills
His own desire, as the Master wills,

And labours with his word, avoiding wrong,
Until he hears a brilliant, heavenly song,

I know my place and honor his command:
For every beauty flows from out God's hand. • [195]

• There is also a "theology of the word" which is not aesthetics, but is either the doctrine of the divine Word (i.e., Christ), the revelation of God (i.e., theology itself), or the doctrine of a specific position of human words in the revelation of God. This latter doctrine, disastrous when made into the only valid theology, is in itself indispensable. In any case, it can learn much from the theology of the word in the sense of the aesthetics which has just been summarized.

PART FOUR

The Pictorial Arts

1 THE FIXATION OF

AN IDEA AS A HOLY IMAGE

THE ART OF MOVEMENT AND PICTORIAL ART "Pictorial art" is a convenient expression, though hardly a happy one. It is wrong to limit the power of representation to painting and sculpture, in the face of the fact that it belongs, beyond doubt, as a major component of the other arts, such as dance and, above all, literature, and is actually lacking only in music. The ability to make images is primeval, and it is no accident that the earliest records of human activity show men making pictures. The prehistoric drawings and paintings on the walls of caves are not only evidence of the creative ability of man, but also evidence at the same time of his mastery.

If we wish to give an account of the importance of images for man, we shall still make a survey primarily of "pictures," that is, products of sculpture, painting, or drawing. And if we wish to know exactly what an image really means to a man, we shall do well to inquire as to the connection between the image of man and the image of God.

In the very ability to make images there is a religious component. Every art is movement. In art the objects of life obey a peculiar rhythm. But in the pictorial arts (and in architecture) this rhythm is fixed, movement is checked. Powerful life can speak from a painting or statue, but it is as though the life were caught fast at a particular moment, as though motion were frozen. Words, too, call forth images, but their movement is continuous. The image forms before our eyes and, scarcely completed, is replaced by another. Dance, too, has plastic character; but the image does not remain still, it forms incessantly, only to disintegrate again, equally incessantly. In a painting, in a statue, in a building, on the contrary, movement has passed from a fluid to a solid state. This results in very peculiar problems, which Gotthold Lessing discussed in his

155

Laokoön, and which have caused our time, less given to observation than to technicalization, to invent the film, or as it was called in our youth, "the moving pictures."

The film art is imperialistic. It claims both drama and dance for itself, and now, through a new technical *tour de force,* has also incorporated words and music.

Kierkegaard saw the perfection of art in its growing free of space in order to turn to time; in other words, art is the more perfect the more purely it is movement. Progressing from space to time, sculpture becomes painting. Music alone has time as an element, but it is lost, since it has no ground on which to stand. It pays for its existence with ceaseless movement, it "sounds in time, but fades away at once and has no duration." Thus poetry is perfect art because, unlike painting, it does not have to limit itself to the moment; but neither does it vanish with time, as does music.[197] One does not have to agree with Kierkegaard's evaluation to admit that he has presented the problem with unusual clarity. In addition, there is the fact that sculpture and painting (I omit architecture here, because in it everything is different) are bound by space; that they fix spatially, that they must interrupt the movement of life, also, perhaps even primarily, have religious significance.

I understand this religious significance in a double sense: positively and negatively. Representation as the freezing of the stream of life is a religious act which can be transformed at any moment into the opposite.

IMAGE IS NOT LIKENESS   "Pictorialization" is not the same thing as making a likeness. The man to whom it first occurred to fix permanently that which surrounded him did not intend to create a faithful reproduction. The pictures of men and animals which we have come to know from ancient cultures are neither likenesses nor portraits. At times, it is true, they may be amazingly true to life (think of the prehistoric representations of animals, their behavior and their movements, of the Egyptian geese, of the horses and asses, and much more), but no less frequently we find renderings which agree with "reality" only in a few points. Especially where human beings are concerned, representation is by no means true to nature (we think of Negro sculpture, of the statues which seem to us almost hieratic from the Old Kingdom of Egypt, of the most ancient Greek sagas). Representation is not reproduction, but a second thing is placed before and beside the first: it is the expression of a remarkable double experience, peculiar to man, regarding the forms which surround him. "Art is the signature of man," says

Chesterton. Man has the ability and the inclination to invent other forms besides himself and the forms which he comes upon. He creates symbols and, through them, represents the surrounding, living reality. He creates representatives of that reality, "images" in which the form he perceives and the form he creates fall together. An image is a representation, created by man, of a visionary form which in essentials is identical with that form.

ORNAMENT   Thus we are dealing with representation, not reproduction. In primitive art and the art of classical antiquity, this receives clear expression. One of the oldest forms of pictorial art is surely tattooing. We might think at first that the practice is purely decorative, but that is not correct. A pure will to ornament would not agree with primitive thought. Ornament as ornament does not fit into the unity of life and thought which we know from the primitive structure. We decorate our houses and furniture with ornaments. Primitive man does so, too, but for him the ornament has not only symbolic, but actual meaning. The legs of your chair are decorated with lion claws; the joiner did not give the matter any particular thought, but took the motif from the history of art. In ancient Egypt, the same claw at the foot of a couch is replete with meaning: one rests upon the lion, the sun god, who overcomes death. Thus rest becomes, instead of a likeness of death, a prelude to eternal life. Primitive and prehistoric man loved to draw the animals which he hunted, becoming master over them by depicting them.•[198] This agrees with the fact that primitive art often hints at more than it represents. What we call ornament has a very specific meaning on the Australian Tjurungas. We see nothing but lines and circles, but they represent women, houses, and animals. Something similar is true for the oldest, so-called geometric period of Greek vase painting, where every figure has its own meaning. In the oldest Egyptian drawings it still is not clear whether ships or villages are represented. Thus the question arose whether this ancient art had religious significance. We want to repeat here what we have said in another context, that the religious character of art is not conditioned by its subject, but by its purpose, by its character.

REPRESENTATION   The question then arises: What is its purpose? Why does man go to this trouble? We have seen that we may not picture

• Cf. also the placing of the head of an animal (Germany) or of an eye (Egypt, Greece) at the bow of a ship. The "ornament" is protection against evil influences.

the primitive man or the man of classical antiquity as a modern aesthete, something like an artist who creates art for art's sake, for his own pleasure, or, at most, for the enjoyment of the "happy few"; primitive and classic art has a clearly recognizable, practical purpose. One cannot always do as he likes with men, animals, plants, or other creatures, whether for one's own benefit or to protect one's self from them. For this reason the movement in which the creature is engaged is fixed in an image. This image represents a second form of that creature. It is believed that everything which happens to the image will also happen to the creature represented. (We, too, still speak today of a painting "representing" something; but we must take this word in its etymological meaning to understand what the actual function of the image is.) In our discussion of the dance we pointed out how primitive man dances to acquire everything. We discussed how primitive the control of power is in drama and the holy word, how it strives to exert an influence in one sense or another; on that basis, we called it by nature magico-religious (cf. page 17). We find the same thing here. Whoever influences a creature—be it a god, a man, an animal, or anything else—by means of an image, is likewise exercising a religious function. We have a clear instance in the so-called *defixiones* of Rome: the image of an untrue lover is cursed (it by no means has to be similar; it is a doll which is said to represent the beloved). The person is convinced that the curse will also strike the one represented. For the image is its being, even though it may be its second being.

Another example. We all know the name of Tutankhamen, the Egyptian Pharaoh, ephemeral successor to the great heretic Akhenaten. It is less well known that his name means "the living image of [the god] Amon," and still less that this title does not hint at an exceptional status, but a fixed relationship between the god and the king. The king is the "living image" of a god. "Tut" actually means "statue." When the king is said to be the living statue of a god, nothing can be meant except that he "represents" the god as the image does, but through his living form. Whoever sees the king, sees god. What the king does is the deed of god. Indeed, even the stone and wooden statues in Egypt are living. In the tombs are found, for example, the ka statues, that is, the images of the dead. At the same time is seen the ka, his soul, which is so like him that the two could be confused, born at the same time he is and bearer of his being. This image is treated in a manner befitting the dead man: food is set before it; it is spoken to; and various actions are performed before it which are to effect resurrection from death. The same is true, more or less, of all statues of dead kings and gods. "It is the convinced belief of the Egyptian that all incomprehensible phenomena, such as god, a dead man, love, the state, thought, need an anchor in the world of intelligibility; that they are present and effective only when living men force this hold on reality—rather like an antenna that emits radio waves only when electrical energy is influencing it. Thus the ka, the soul of the dead man, is in reality fixed to the statue, and comes to life in it through the force of a living man." Thus wrote H. G. Evers in a profound psychological study of the art of Egyptian sculpture.[199]

Greek geometrical ornaments, like the realistic prehistoric drawings of animals, are attempts to come nearer to creatures, to control them. From this point, two ways, which have proved viable in all ages, lie open to us. The first is comparable to the monotonous utterance of holy formulas, avoiding any expressiveness; the second is analogous to acribia, scrupulous exactness in the recitation of prayers or spells. But from the point of view of the word, both are, by origin and nature, holy action. The first way has as its goal abstraction—*nomos*—which is never attained. The image takes flight to space or time, in lyric poetry finally becoming music, space becoming time. The second way strives for reality and tries to achieve it by imitation, which it never succeeds in doing. Here the word becomes epic, finally losing its sound and becoming concentrated into pure sculpture.[200] The pictorial arts also choose both directions for themselves, in prehistory and early history as well as in the present where impressionism, expressionism, and cubism alternate with a new objectivity and a new classicism. The first way brings motion more strongly to a halt. This way is thus the one which comes closest to the unity between the fine arts and holy action.

This explains why primitive art is often indifferent to the image as it is seen, and why it pays attention to the image only as it is known, as it lives in the imagination. Perspective will hardly be found. In regard to ancient Egyptian art, Heinrich Schäfer has shown that this lack of perspective is no failing, not a case of "not yet having attained" that high level which characterizes the art of the Greeks, but is rather to be judged as an essential difference in the conception of the job of representation.[201] Similarly, Evers states that drawing in perspective means a change in the way man is situated in the world, to which he no longer belongs as one component among others but, rather, stands in contrast to, as an ego, freed from it. "This view of the world only became possible with Greek philosophy."[199] Primitive man no longer views the world from his own point of view, but from "another world" which provides the norm for this one. That is not a kind of supernatural world, but is the world as it ought to be and therefore also is, the world as symbol. He does not deal with the image as he sees it, but with the object as he knows it. He does not determine the relationship of the objects which he wants to illustrate according to the angle of vision, but according to the meaning they have for him. From this attitude he can then attain to a thorough-going realism, such as we are acquainted with from prehistory and from many primitive drawings of the hunt; or, on the other hand, to a thoroughgoing stylization and symbolization, as among the Egyptians, who draw the figure of the king twice as large as that of ordinary mortals.[202]

The function of imagination is even more pronounced in the case of masks. After our thorough discussion of masks in connection with dance and drama (pp. 84 and 85), we can content ourselves here with a few remarks.

W. Joseph de Gruyter explains the mask on the basis of the "ability of man to multiply himself or a part of himself, to project his humanity visibly into the nature which surrounds him." It may be assumed that mask plays belong to the most ancient ritual possessions of all humanity. Now, whoever puts on a mask does not do so for fun: "Putting on a mask does not mean a simple disguise, as for us, in which the individual remains what he is. It is the experience of a real transformation. The mask is for the head what the skin is for the rest of the body."[23] Those who wear masks "represent" what they resemble, in the most concrete sense of "causing that to reappear which has vanished, making it present again." In the mask, man creates a second countenance, a second form, and thereby doubles the power which he exercises. This can go so far that the mask becomes the most important thing—the second form becomes the first.

This is true not only for the mask, but for every image. For with every representation an attempt is made to approach what is represented, to hold it fast.

IMAGINATION AND REPRESENTATION   In other words, an image is a cult image, the word "cult" being used here in the broadest sense of holy action, "force," as Evers expressed it. A man makes for himself images of gods, men, animals, or other creatures, in order that they may be made to "function" as needed, just as in the masked plays the gods or spirits do what is necessary for man, and as animals subject themselves according to human needs of hunt and domestication.

As we said, the holy action consists in a man's overpowering a creature by constructing, re-presenting, a second, masked form. Still, the representation by no means has to resemble the "original." In Chinese sacrifices, ancient bronze vessels are used. They date to before the advent of Buddhism, and they were also used by the ancestors. "The power-principle of the family is embodied in them," where important events are maintained by inscriptions. By representing ancestors, these vessels guarantee their presence at the sacrifice. When the last member of the Chu dynasty had his sacrificial vessel stolen, he lost contact with his ancestors and thereby also the royal power.[203]

Through pictorial representation, an event is confined in a second form, thereby assuring its renewed presence and the effectiveness of its power.[204]

FREEZING MOTION   The holy action of re-presentation on the one hand brings forces into operation which on the other hand it freezes again. Further, the more an image differs from a reproduction of reality, the more it is a religious action. In other words, the more frozen the motion is, the better re-presentation succeeds. No apparent "lifelikeness" can help in the process. On the contrary, pictorial representation is a holy action precisely because there stands before the eyes of the first reality a second, which, in spite of its connection with the first, is a different one. It is just this peculiarity of being "other" that makes representation a religious action. We are touching here on one of the most elementary and at the same time most deeply rooted of human experiences. Whoever sees himself in a mirror sees himself and yet sees another; sees another and yet sees himself. The first confrontation with one's self is an enormous revelation for every man. Richard Wagner has pictured this for us with fine psychological perception in the first act of *Siegfried*, with words and sounds. One discovers one's self in the other, the other in one's self.

If at the same time a man has discovered his ability to make such images, the representation is no longer dependent upon accidental reflection in a brook or lake; but he will emphasize the "other" in the image more than that which is his own. For he is concerned with influencing what is represented. He presupposes thereby that what is represented is powerful. It pays to get this into one's own service, or to make it innocuous. Primitive and classic man thus represent primarily, in fact almost exclusively, those beings with whose power they are impressed:

gods, spirits, kings, animals. In them man recognizes a power which he does not possess at all, or only partially.

If he represents himself, he will emphasize those organs which he looks upon with religious awe because of their wonderful power. This is proved by the female figures such as the famous so-called Venus of Willendorf,[205] many statuettes and drawings of primitive peoples, and the innumerable images of women in the most varied cultures. In these representations the sexual organs are excessively emphasized. The complementary pieces are the ithyphallic male figures of Indian and Greek art, as well as many primitive works of art. They do not deal with what we call reality, but with the aspect of reality that they may represent, because it is powerful.

A clear example are the Hermes figures, which were erected in Greece at squares and along streets. They represent the god Hermes (frequently also another god). They have the head of Hermes, but the rest of the figure is nothing more than a pillar which has been provided with a gigantic phallus. The mutilation of a Hermes, of which Alcibiades and his friends were accused, thus did not consist, as we were tacitly led to believe in school, in the knocking off of noses and ears, but in knocking off the holiest, most important, most representative part of the figure, the phallus. Much evidence even points to the oldest Hermes having had no head at all, but consisting only of a phallus on a pillar.

Pictorial representation is re-presentation, and thus reproduction of power, fixation, and thus concentration of power. That is the reason why the puppet theater is once more winning acclaim and why modern actors, following in the footsteps of the Greeks and Japanese, are once more experimenting with masks. Rigidity better expresses the deepest nature of things than does movement. Aesthetically and humanly, the puppet theater ranks higher than the cinema. "The stiffness of death is more alive than life: therein lies the secret of the mask."[206]

THE IMAGE OF GOD   The image of God, which most unequivocally attempts to approach the other and the mighty, is the clearest example of formation of images in general. As we have seen, the primitive artist is intensely interested in what he represents, and this interest is neither purely sentimental (romantic), nor purely visual (aesthetic); his interest is, rather, conveyed by his entire personality, directing itself toward the entire being of what is represented.

From this point of view we can understand that fear of images which we meet with so often in the domain of primitive magic. Prohibition was directed against original images in general, preventing Judaism and Islam from giving birth to any of the pictorial arts (we owe to them the play of lines in arabesque). Through the image, the object appears; it is thus exceedingly dangerous to represent pictorially demonic or divine beings. They are conjured up by drawing them or erecting images of them. Without doubt, the prohibition of images originated in considerations of primitive magic, even if later it received new impetus from awe before the majesty of God.

The other side of the same affair is the worship of images. Divine power can be brought into the realm and possession of man by means of illustration. "Thou shalt make unto thyself no graven images"—for illustration brings one into all too dangerous proximity with stirring life. But, on the other hand, we hear that one should "make for thyself a god who shall go before thy face"; for it is very valuable to bring the powers of life under one's command.

We do not need to illustrate here the great importance which has been ascribed to the image of God in the religious worship of all periods. Puritanism thought it could get along without images, but, instead, wrote books. In order to fulfill their cultic function, "images" by no means have to be likenesses. A portrait cannot be made of God, but surely a symbol of his presence can. The lamb is just as much an image of Christ as is the Good Shepherd.•[207]

The law is valid almost everywhere, that the least appealing and the least human and the least "beautiful" images of the gods are wont to be the most holy. Primitive images of the gods seldom have completely human features. A good part of them are fetishes. It is by no means self-evident to primitive man that the god is to be pictured as a man. He finds, on the contrary, the distance which separates him from the wholly other to be better expressed by the non-human or semihuman. From the religious point of view, the Greeks ranked the xoanon, an ancient image of the god made of wood, rough and scarcely human, above the works of a Phidias or a Praxiteles. At the Panathenaea, the xoanon of the goddess was carried about in procession, and not the glorious work of Phidias. The Roman Catholic knows that the most holy images of Christ, the Blessed

• "Genuine symbols do not become boring, but always stimulate afresh, and are never completely exhausted. Precisely because of their depth, they are rich in complex meaning, and cannot be defined with a single, limited sense. They say one thing today, another tomorrow, one thing to one man, another to another, and still remain radically unified. Thus they are a true social art, because they offer to each his own and to society the whole, as St. Ambrose says of Christ, that he is at once *summa universitatis* and *portio singulorum*."[207]

Virgin, or other saints, blackened with age, are only rarely the most important works of art. In Italy, it is the "black Madonnas" which work miracles. Not infrequently, popular art is better suited to worship than something that is truly beautiful. In the chapel of a Jesuit monastery I once saw an ugly, conventional *Pietà*. The Father who was guiding me said to me that at first a genuine work of art had been placed there, but was later removed. "One must have something before which one can pray." Thus it is possible for faith to prefer the ugly to the beautiful, because a conventional form better preserves the distance which separates the holy than does the individual vision of the artist. The most ancient image—paradoxical as it may sound—is the fetish, the piece of wood or stone filled with power. From there the way leads via the semi-image to the pictorial arts in the modern sense of the word. From the point of view of primitive religion, a coarse piece of wood, *rude lignum* (Tertullian), a geometrical drawing, are images, for they partake of the nature of what they point to.

Humanization of form means atheism to the fetishist, for it is just the "monstrous, the sinister," which is holy, says Nietzsche with his penetrating insight.[208] The religions of the oldest periods of Rome, Israel, and Islam share this aversion to the human. Yahweh is not represented, not even in the unorthodox forms of worship. The bull of Jeroboam is no image of Yahweh, but rather an empty throne which stands ready for the god. The ark of the covenant is viewed very concretely as the present reality of Yahweh. It is his "image," yet not his likeness, but rather his symbol, his empty throne (Num. 10:35ff.).[209]

In this connection the history of the so-called Mathura Buddha is typical. Originally, Buddhism had no images of Buddha, but only the wheel, symbol of its doctrine, the bodhi tree under which the teacher received illumination, and the footsteps of Buddha. In pictorial representations from history, the form of Buddha himself is purposely omitted. Thus Prince Siddhartha, as he leaves his ancestral dwelling, is represented with a horse and empty saddle. In the pictures the central figure is always absent. When, under Hellenistic influence, people began to represent the Buddha, two completely different schools emerged: the one, the school of Gandhara, puts its emphasis on human beauty; the other, the school of Mathura, is completely Indian in character, and here the Buddha is often even repulsively ugly. What is important in the latter is not beautiful appearance, but rather making in the image an instrument (*yantra*) for purification of the soul and the practice of asceticism.[210]

COMPLETE STASIS In Japanese and Chinese art it is very apparent that freezing of motion must be thoroughly carried out if it desires to reach its goal, the influencing of the power which resides in the objects surrounding us. The pictorial representation of Western cultures is primarily representation of the self. Since the Greeks, it has rested on a self-awareness which results from the idea that man has of himself. In the foreground of our European art stands the human form; even the art of landscape painting could develop only by excusing its representation of nature, so to speak, through the figures of a few hunters, shepherds, or soldiers. The landscape, as such, is at any rate a modern invention. Japanese art is completely different. Behind this art there stands the religious experience of the world as a totality, as an uninterrupted continuity. Man also fits into this continuity, but he may not dominate there; he may not rule his environment. In addition, nothing there must stand independent; everything exists only through and in connection with the whole. Upon this feeling of life rests the so-called framelessness of Japaneses painting. There is no boundary. The landscape is not a closed composition, but continues infinitely.[17, 91] For this reason the Japanese paints on the *emakimono*, a roll of what is actually very impractical material with an inconvenient format. "But herein we see the unconscious effort of the ancient artist to point in a very primitive way, yet unmistakably, to the uninterrupted continuity of the true form of the world."[17] And Tsudzumi declares emphatically that this consciousness of "framelessness" is of religious nature.[17] Fixed boundaries with their frozen self-awareness are lacking. Man does not place himself outside the world, but within it. That is clearly expressed in the human figure itself. It is never represented without clothing; the artist can never conceive of the man outside his environment.[17] This is no sovereign man, who takes account of the world. In fact, it is not man at all. There is only a play of divine powers in which we, too, fulfill a function, albeit a subordinate one, and are never in control.

At the beginning of Greek art, too, the human form is represented clothed. This was true, even and especially, of the forms of the gods. "To walk the streets in Grecian nakedness" is by no means universally Greek, but a discovery of classicism. Only with time does man discover himself, his body, in its sovereign beauty and strength, and at the same time his spirit, the measure of all things. The great accomplishment of the Greeks is that they discovered man. Phidias played just as great a part in this as did Socrates. Clothing is laid aside as belonging to the world; the human form arises in its full, independent power. Immediately, Philo will continue the tradition and condemn the body as belonging to the earth; the naked soul then appears in place of the naked body. But in both cases man asserts himself emphatically in contrast to the world and God.

In the Far East, this self-assertion was unknown. The Oriental represents himself and the world with nonpartisan humility. In view of the charming attention to nature which characterizes Japanese and Chinese art, the human figure gets short shrift. In his book about China, Lin Yutang says:

> In the representation of man, of course, the Chinese remained far behind. Perhaps there existed among them, too, a valuation of the female form as such, but nothing can be seen of this in their painting. The female figures which occur in Ku K'aichih and Ch'iu Shihchon are not meant to express the beauty of the human body, but the pattern of curves which the artists had observed in wind and waves. The cult of the human and especially the female body is, in my opinion, a quite infallible note of Western art.[211]

The same author pictures Chinese intellectual life as humanistic through and through. It is the more remarkable that "strangely enough, no one in China ever thought of calling the human body beautiful."[211] Chinese art is concerned with "mountains and seas" whose movement must be frozen, perhaps in the original, drastic, primitive sense, in order that they may be usefully employed or warded off, later with the promotion of mystic contemplation.

Thus sculpture is far less respected in China than painting, for with its three dimensions it comes closer to represented reality than does two-dimensional painting; it is more imitation and less representation.[203] This Chinese point of view is in remarkable agreement with that of the icon painting of Eastern Christendom.

Thus thinks the cosmically oriented East. But the West, too, taking man as the point of departure and depending upon him, knows that law of pictorial representation according to which movement is fixed and a reverent distance from the object is preserved. This is shown most clearly in the form in which the Christian West brings to expression humanly the power of God, in the figure of Christ, the God-man. A glance at collections like *Das Bild Christi im Wandel der Zeiten,* by Hans Preuss, or *Le Visage du Christ,* for which Pierre Mornand wrote a very significant introduction, is very instructive.[212]

The figure of Christ adapts itself to all ages and to all cultures. It forms itself by the most varied nuances of religious conceptions and reveals the lack of the same. In Raphael and Veronese, there is only a completely external connection between the figure of Christ and the divine-human power which it is to express. In Rubens the figure which is taken down from the cross is "a good-looking Flemish worker who has fallen from the fifth floor." The more the artist departs from "reality," the more real and impressive is the expression of the holy.* We have ascertained this a number of times. Those early representations of the crucified, which do not intend to convey the idea of real, human suffering, but put the Lord on the cross as a king in the Byzantine regalia, the purple, scepter, and crown, give the greatest impression of holiness.[213] If one would compare to such a royal crucifix the famous *Dead Christ* of Holbein, one would feel the difference between an image which approaches the realm of divine omnipotence and a very skillful realistic likeness.[214]

Instructive also are the *Scenes from the Life of Jesus,* a collection of Chinese works of art which appeared shortly before the Second World War.[215] They are the well-known motifs which came to the Chinese through mission sermons. But the effect is completely different. There is almost no scene to which the landscape does not contribute. Occasionally it even plays the major role. There is no "background"; the holy is here expressed in a very unusual way. Thereby the human retreats. Very fine, for example, is the representation of the storm on the sea, where the calm figure of Christ and the anxious figures of the disciples clutching one another are completely embedded in the powerful movement of the water. It is a representation of Christ; but we find the real image of Christ in the rebellious water, which leaps up on all sides with high, foaming waves, and yet is completely controlled.

We do not have to turn to China for confirmation of what we have asserted here; the European East has understood all of this better than the West. Even a *Maiestas Domini* from Siena expresses the holy much better than does the usual image of Christ as it developed in the West. Still closer to it comes the Byzantine "stasis." In the art of icons we shall find our statements confirmed.

THE LIVING IMAGE   The image of the god long remains the bearer of the divine life which it represents. It works miracles, it is worshiped, it

* At the Council of Constantinople (692), even the representation of Christ as a lamb was forbidden.

fell from heaven (the image of Athena Polias under Kekrops), or it came to its worshipers in a quite extraordinary way (the xoanon of Hercules at Eritrea, which came on board a ship; the sacred stone of the Magna Mater, which was taken into Rome in miraculous fashion); it descends from its pedestal and helps man (Beatrijs), or it falls from its pedestal because a powerful god will not stand for it (Dagon); it is bound, so that its power may not become too dangerous. In short, it is replete with powerful life.

Sometimes divine life is breathed into the image through a kind of consecration. "We reverence images which are hallowed by consecration," the Christian apologist Arnobius has a heathen say in defense of idolatry.[216] Or the image lives because a spirit resides within it: the Korwars of New Guinea shelter gods from which oracles are asked.[217] It is still a very long way to the aesthetic in our sense, but the ancient Egyptian ka statues were already the first good portraits.

But they are not that by their own nature. Up to this point we have ascertained an obvious unity between the holy and the beautiful image. From these latter observations there arises now a differentiation. If we examine the outward points of contact between the fine arts and religion, we shall be amazed to see that here a greater gulf opens between art and religion than where both come into open conflict. Iconomachy is a religious phenomenon.

2   UNHINDERED

PICTORIAL REPRESENTATION

REAL AND DECORATIVE NAKEDNESS   Religious reverence paid
to human likeness (idolatry) is by no means primitive. We have seen, instead, that primitive man worshiped fetishes, animals, forms, mixed forms
of men and animals, monsters, but seldom or never realistic likenesses of
gods or demons in human form. Primitive man can certainly not be said
to have made his god in his own image. The bond between the representation and what is represented is not realistic, but magical. In the image, in
the representation, the creature is contained, no matter how little outward similarity it evidences with the thing represented. The fact that
objects and animals, but not men, are often represented extremely realistically, agrees with our observations. When art frees itself from its sacred
ties, it breaks through the identity of image and object.[218] From this
grows the need to proceed "realistically," by illustrating that which is
seen. When the existential connection with reality is lost, a visual connection replaces it.

In the naked form we see man in his full beauty. Homer, and after
him, the Greek sculptors discovered the glory of the human body and
gave this, the most beautiful thing they knew, to the gods. The
Renaissance, which in this sense was indeed a rebirth, repeated this discovery by opposing the glowing nakedness of their worldly spirit to
medieval timidity. Before the Middle Ages, nakedness was still ritual,
specifically "heathen" (and thus called *ritus paganus*): witches are naked,
and the devil; anyone who wishes to engage in magic in the dead of
night must usually unclothe himself for the purpose.

In primitive Greek art we do not usually find the gods naked, but
represented clothed. The naked Knidian Aphrodite was not accepted
by the inhabitants of Kos for their temple.[78] In the primitive context

of life, as in the Middle Ages, nakedness is viewed as ritual. Through it, a distance is removed with magical power. Religion, on the other hand, strives to maintain this distance. Through pure joy in a beautiful body, recognition of separation is lost. The representation of the divine, both in Greece and Egypt, long remains immobile, antirealistic. And clothing contributes to this.

"To the art of the Renaissance, the divine is not mysterious, but human."[219] Now even the completely human can contain a hint of the holy. In Demeter of Knidos, in the Sistine Madonna, or in the Assunta of Titian, it is not difficult for us to experience the revelation of the holy. Occasionally that is also true for unclothed figures, like the Hermes of Praxiteles or the Christ of Michelangelo. But here one searches always for what is purely human, humanity in its perfection, which is far separated and hence can be the conveyor of the wholly other. The purely human beauty of Aphrodite Anadyomene is overpowering, awaking awe rather than a feeling of "humanity" in the sense to which we are accustomed. The religion which speaks to us here may be a kind of religious humanism, but it is religion in any case, and we become effortlessly aware of the harmony between holiness and beauty.

But that changes as soon as harmony yields to external continuity; as soon as what is humanly beautiful is still perceived as beautiful, but no longer as divine, no longer as holy. The Apollo Sauroktonos, Apollo Belvedere, the Zeus of Otricoli, the penitent Magdalene of Correggio,* the Madonnas of Rubens or Vandyke, all those beautiful men and women which classical antiquity, the Renaissance, and the baroque created for the Holy Story are neither gods nor saints. Greek piety wrestled with the beautiful, as did medieval artistic sensibility with that of the Renaissance. Now man creates God in his own image, and at the same time he creates only himself. The divine man and the perfect woman become athletes, hetaerae. The Mother of God becomes a touching human mother.[220]

This secularization brought many advantages to art, incredibly extending its domain. This was shown most clearly when the Dutch school renounced religious subjects and took up genre painting, so that liberated art could now feed on the beauty of country inns and interiors. We experience the same thing in the birth of landscape painting. The landscape no longer serves only as a background or ornament, but is painted for its own sake, first, still, with a small human figure as an excuse, then

* Baton (1780) was the first to represent the Sacred Heart of Jesus. A typical example of an all-too-real symbol.

only as beautiful nature. Nature, which for religion took on the form of nymph and satyr, received meaning for art only when it did away with its beautiful inhabitants.

EXPRESSION OF THE HOLY BECOMES EXPRESSION OF HOLY FEELINGS   We have seen how the feeling for distance vanishes more and more in the pictorial arts. Greek art does not depict according to the imagination, as it lives within the artist, but holds itself to what it sees. Thus it does not ascribe to the object its own value, but imports its own psychic preparation of the object into the work of art. This reduces the separation between subject and object. The magical mental structure was able to express the holy through art; the spirit of the transitional structure always expresses primarily itself. As Schäfer justifiably noted, impressionism up to now represents the last stage of this development which began with the Greeks.[201] Expressionism goes still further and seeks to import the content of the impression into the object. Perhaps a "new objectivity" will again come somewhat closer to primitive art. The latter at least left the thing itself its own value, with the exception of the cases where it is extremely realistic (prehistoric, primitive, and Egyptian animal and plant drawings), or where it proceeds ornamentally or geometrically (primitively, the geometric period of Greek vase painting). It conquered reality by remaining at a reverent distance from it. The art of transition, which tries to express religious feelings, is thereby less religious.

"It would not say too much if one were to ascribe to a still life by Cézanne or a tree by van Gogh more of the quality of holiness than to a picture of Jesus by von Uhde," says Paul Tillich.[221] But the paving stones executed by A. C. Willink, demonic beings rushing upon us, once more come nearer to the "quality of holiness," precisely because they are unmistakably stones.

In New Caledonia, a man was seen whose legs were tattooed with sacral figures in the traditional fashion. Young students of the mission school, whose parents were already Christian, made fun of him: "He wanted to make himself look pretty." But a wise old man said, "It's because of the lizard." The lizard represented the Great Power, and the figures were supposed to control it.[15] The young people were aesthetes, the old man magical, existential. Perhaps the happy wearer of the tattoos found himself where we find ourselves, at the point of transition between both types of thought.

TRANSFERENCES   By "transferences" we understand, in the phenomenology of religion, uses of the same motif for different contents. A
bell is rung to ward off evil spirits. It is also rung to summon the faithful
to the house of God. We find the same phenomenon in the phenomenology of religious art, particularly under the influence of the transition to "wordly" art. The heretical king Akhenaten, who in many
respects gives a "modern," humanistic impression, takes over a primeval
artistic and religious motif. It was the custom to decorate the four
corners of a sarcophagus with the figures of four goddesses; according
to the primitive idea that the being is present in the image, the goddesses
of death are to protect the dead man. Akhenaten leaves the four
figures unchanged at the four corners of the sarcophagus in which the
body of his young daughter is laid to rest. But he gives to them the
face of the queen, the mother, who in this way protects her daughter
even in death. The thought, no matter how beautiful and impressive it
may be, is not an expression of the holy, but of tender human feelings,
and, incidentally, gives evidence of human sensitivity to the holy. In a
similar way, the king proceeds with the canopic vases, which held the
entrails. Since ancient times the heads of four gods had formed the
cover: the head of a jackal, of an ape, of a hawk, and of a man. That is
barbaric, but truly religious, because these four gods are the gods of
the dead, who lead the dead man safely along the paths of the other
world. Again Akhenaten preserves the form, but he covers the vases of
his daughter with wonderful portrait busts of her mother.[222, 223]

The regency of this great king means a golden age for Egyptian art,
which shakes off the archaic stiffness for a short while, searches for
freedom and truth, and breaks through the old forms. Formally, too, this
period means a temporary retreat of the primitive imaginary images
which are not determined by what is seen. The great artists of that time
did not preserve the distance from the objects which at other periods
of Egyptian art was especially great, but placed the object into their
own lives and filled it with them. The stiff mask and the realistic portrait, which ruled the older art alternately, were replaced by a kind of
dogmatic realism, which forces its own vision upon reality. A royal
statue of the older period withdraws from our perception behind the
mask of its immobile office. The famous *Village Magistrate* is a simple
man, in whom the vision of the artist hardly appears. But the portraits
of King Akhenaten and his wife are neither masks nor realistic forms.
They overflow with life and movement, but it is the life and movement
of the soul of the artist.[222]

In the art of the transitional structure, which is at the point of liberating itself, the primitive method of expressing the holy is avoided, or given another meaning: for example, the gesture of the Astarte figures from the Near East, pointing at the sexual organs. The figure represents the worship of the holy power of fertility. We find the same gesture again in the most perfect thing that Greek art produced: the gesture with which Aphrodite Anadyomene covers herself; here the expression of purely human, purely feminine, modesty is the point of the work of art. To the degree that it frees itself, art loses the possibility of expressing the holy, that distant thing which needs the mask, the stereotyped gesture, in order to make room for the living expression of the human. Thus, the art of Amarna, as well as that of the Golden Age of Greece, no matter how high it is judged from the artistic standpoint, must be viewed as a retreat of religious art. Beauty kills holiness. All the prerequisites for a conflict are present.

OPPOSITION BETWEEN IMAGE AND LIKENESS   It is not as though realism were particularly unreligious. Impressionism is no less so. But there is another kind of realism which brings us very near to the holy. We have already spoken of Willink's stones. The powerful realism of Grünewald's Isenheim Altar is religious art in the highest sense. The pictures which this master created are something completely different, much more than a mere likeness of gruesome reality. The holy is not afraid of reality, but of naturalness.

Here we must refer to the icons of the Eastern Church, where image stands in genuine opposition to likeness. The iconostasis—the screen of images which we find in every Orthodox church, which has no sculptures but only paintings on which Christ, his Mother, and the saints are represented, grouped in a fixed order—is actually nothing more than a particular form of the cancelli. In the West, too, this separated the place in which the holy actions are performed from the place in the church where the people are located. Possibly Byzantine theater motifs have influenced the development of the cancelli into the iconostasis.[224] More important is the fact that this screen of images completely hides the altar space behind it, thereby setting it apart as a genuine *adyton*, an unapproachable shrine where, in secret, the action of the mystery is performed. For the iconostasis cannot be pushed aside. It is interrupted by only three doors, through which the priests enter the church in procession at the high points of the liturgy.[225] Thus the screen is not a barrier in the sense of a wall. It is, rather, a living creature, and indicates the presence within the church of a divine world. This image screen is not a "symbol" in the modern sense, not even an object of devotion, such as the images of saints or altar pieces in Western churches. It is an "image of the cult and stands in the order of the liturgy. . . . The unification of images into a unity is the gate through which this world is bound to the other."[137] The people, who have the world of the saints represented to them in the church, participate in it and know that they are transferred into the divine world.

This function of the image in the Eastern Church rests on a theology which developed during and after the great iconoclastic controversies of the eighth and ninth centuries. Every icon presupposes the possibility that God can be represented in man in the immediate and concrete sense previously described. "God cannot be represented in his eternal nature, but in his revelation to man he has a face and it can be described. Otherwise the divine revelation could not have taken place," says Boulgakoff, who in his summary of the doctrine and nature of the Orthodox Church devotes a very thorough and complete study to the icons.[225] In other words, the painting and cultic use of icons rest on the doctrine of the image of God, which at creation was put into men, darkened by the fall, but never destroyed. The most important place in the iconostasis is therefore occupied by the so-called *deësis,* the representation of Christ with his mother Mary and his forerunner John at either side. Both of them, as humans, stand nearer to Christ than do the angels. The angels, it is true, bear the image of God, though not in the fullness it has been granted to men, who through their bodies participate in the earthly world. Angels live without body, without world, in God. Men, on the other hand, bear his image in their bodies.[225] The earthly, material world is therefore capable of being bearer of the divine. That this is so derives from the fact of the revelation itself, for in Christ, God took on human form.[226]

Even better than from theoretical considerations, the nature of icons proceeds from a way of life, as it is pictured for us by Nikolai Leskov, above all in the wonderful story, *The Sealed Angel,*[227] in which the ideas of the so-called Old Believers are reproduced. They protect their icons like relics. The icon controls all of life. When a petty official took an angel, the holiest icon of the congregation, and "sealed" it with lacquer and desecrated it, all the members were stricken with an eye disease. Since the angel was blind, they all became blind.

A people lives with its icons. The simple peasant can distinguish all the schools of icon painting. The painting itself is a holy action. It is

done exclusively by monks, in a continuous fast, and with paints that
have been mixed with holy water and relics. The purpose is certainly not
to make a "work of art," or even a likeness. "The icon is not so much a
likeness as the archetype or original of a pneumatic creature, saved by
belief in the incarnation of Christ. . . . For the Greek Christians, the
image was and is basically a mystery; they think of it as a sacrament, as a
vehicle of divine power and grace. . . . The incarnation of the Logos so
ennobled human nature that it provides a worthy form for the representation of Christ."[228] The icons are pure fixation; the freezing of representation in their making is a purely holy action. The West sees in images
only instruction, education, edification; the East, on the other hand, sees
mysteries which effect salvation. Therefore, their painting (sculpture is
forbidden) is a piece of genuine tradition, not the invention of "artists."
"Human artists are only able to paint the image of Christ when they
receive it from the hand of the Church, and when they are illuminated
by the Holy Pneuma."—"Whoever looks at the icon of Christ, sees
Christ in it. . . . The image is no mere symbol of the archetype, but Christ
becomes present in and through his icon."[229, 230] The icon is thus a
sacrament, and the Council of Nicea in the year 787 indicated its desire
that at the adoration of the Christ icon the following be said: "This is
Christ, the Son of God." It is therefore no wonder that many miraculous
effects are ascribed to an icon: it protects against hail, drought, and
sickness. One is found in every house, even in the poorest, in the *Krasnyi
ugol,* the "beautiful corner." Even the origin of the icon is viewed as
supernatural, the beginning of painted pictures that "were not made by
hands": *acheiropoietoi.* When we know all this, we understand the
overpowering impression which the ambassadors of the Russian Vladimir
received at their visit in the churches of Byzantium, an impression which
was decisive for the conversion of the Russians to Greek Christianity:
God walked there in beauty among men.[231]

But whoever expects a luxuriance of beautiful forms in the art of the
icons will be disappointed. The divine has a form, but it is the broken
form of Christ; it is an image which is bearable only when a person renounces all outward beauty, all luxury of form. The icons are removed
as far as possible from "reality," so that divine reality is brought into the
realm of men. Everyone who has ever seen an icon is aware of this
difficulty. The battle of St. George with the dragon, for example, is
not represented as a fight: "Upon a solemnly advancing horse, St.
George gives the dragon the death blow with a calculated gesture.
Actually, the dragon is already vanquished."[231] To the dismay of the

Old Believers, the modernistic tendency represented the archangel Michael as a second Prince Potëmkin, and gave to Christ, the Saviour, the features of a Jew. That is shameless, because "an empty drama destroys the clarity of the spirit." The degeneration is irremediable as soon as images of saints become portraits of saints.[227] With a decree of the modernist Peter the Great in 1709, separating the painting of icons from "secular" painting, the degeneration became final.[231] Thus the art of icons as painting was eliminated in favor of autonomous art, which made humans for humans. The aversion to the "real" also explains why sculpture was very early banned from the Eastern Church. The Council of Nicea in 787 forbade plastic representation of Christ and the saints. Later, when artists emigrating from the West brought statues of the saints to Pskov, the people were scandalized and refused to pray before these figures. Thus no "figure" will be found in a single Russian church. Painting is able to deal with unworldly forms far better than is sculpture.

TRANSITION   In the art of icons, the image opposes the likeness, and true holy art comes into being. In the Far East, we find the continuation of this effort to the point where every connection with reality is surrendered. Chinese calligraphy *(shuhua* means both calligraphy and painting) renounces content for the sake of pure form: "Whoever admires a masterpiece of Chinese calligraphy does not think for a moment of the content of what is written, but admires only the lines and forms for their own sake. A painting must transmit an objective impression; a beautifully written character, on the other hand, transmits solely the beauty of its outline and structure."[211, 231] We find the same aspiration in Arabian calligraphy in the form of the "arabesque." Pictorial art ceases with the complete denial of reality, just as the representation of the holy ceases where reality becomes all-powerful.

THE PROHIBITION OF IMAGES

AND THE ICONOCLASTIC

CONTROVERSY

THE PROHIBITION OF IMAGES   We have seen how the pictorial arts, outside their existential context, lose their distance from their subject and devote themselves more and more to representation of human feelings. For this reason, they maintain only an external connection with religion. Thus the mind which has become "modern" loses its ability to see anything in the pictorial arts other than the expression of the human. This brings about an important transfer: at first, the prohibition of images was explained by the danger of reproducing the holy, the divine, thus bringing it into an immediate, terrifying proximity; but now the prohibition is motivated by awe in the presence of the divine being. This awe is intended as a protection against humanizing the holy, thereby robbing it of its strength and impairing its immediate effectiveness. Man must not make any graven image, because the god confined in the image will harm him, says primitive man. He must make no likeness, because the god which he so represents is capable of nothing, says "modern" man. The prohibition of images underwent this transfer early in the history of Judaism and Islam. The prohibition in Exodus 20 is based in Deuteronomy on the intangibility of the form of God, who speaks but remains invisible (Deut. 4:15 ff.).

Classical antiquity is also aware of this intangibility of God. Heraclitus expresses his indignation at those who "pray to these images as though they wanted to talk to buildings; they do not know the true nature of the gods and heroes." Herodotus tells the story of Amasis, who had an image of god made out of a spittoon, a foot basin, and a

177

chamber pot. The Persians are praised because they did not use images. The Roman historian Varro sees much good in the absence of images at Rome under the monarchy, an absence which lasted more than a hundred and seventy years. Religion was purer then, and its decline was brought about only by the introduction of images. Just as the poets of Greece had to live with the accusation that they had turned the gods into men, so did their successors, the sculptors. A Phidias is unthinkable without Homer, who created the "forms" of the gods. We have spoken already, in an earlier chapter, of the evils of representational poetry; but Phidias was guilty of hybris, of presumption, when, forgetting the separation between the human and the holy, he represented on the shield of Athena Parthenos an archer who looked like Pericles. Similarly, Paolo Veronese was attacked by the Inquisition because of his representation of Levi's banquet: it is a real Renaissance dinner, with fools and drunken soldiers as auxiliary figures. Christ, too, is there. Replying to the expressed misgivings, the artist responded arrogantly that the painting was correct as it stood. The Inquisition declared itself satisfied, but religion cannot do so. When it uses images, it retains the old fetishistic ones.

Friedrich Theodor Vischer speaks in this connection of the right of "barbarity." In a work of art, religion fears the presence of an idol, and with good cause. Therefore, "the rough and ugly image is of more service to it than the beautiful one; it does not draw the spirit out into the fullness of the world, where it can enjoy itself in freedom, but throws it back upon itself with a violent shove." For this reason the Greeks preferred the xoanon to the works of art of one of their great masters. But it is also quite possible for religion to reject all images, the ugly as well as the beautiful.

We have already asserted that freezing of motion through representation is a holy act, which can change at any moment to the denial of motion. We have also seen how the art of icons had to protect itself from becoming too lifelike, and how even in the East, representation time and time again fell into danger of becoming mere copying. The fixation of motion of life in this case takes on an absolute character and does not allow room for any other possibilities. It binds the free imagination. It leaves no scope for thought above and beyond what is represented. It drags down instead of lifting up; it holds fast instead of goading on. Such representational art has, to use an expression borrowed from mysticism, no more *epekeina*. It exhausts itself in the actuality of its object, leaving no room behind or beside it. It is rhetoric which forgets the most important thing, the suggestion of the inexpressible. It is pictorial art which forgets the most important thing, the hint of the invisible. The art of representation carried through to its conclusion is a valley without a view, a house without windows. It is a failure as a holy act, unfruitful as art.

In the Ten Commandments it is striking that the concern is not with the representation of God or gods, but with all that Creation contains. Power resides in everything, and this power may not be overcome arbitrarily. Awe in the presence of this power, primitive as it may be, is an expression of this consciousness, that the holy can neither be represented nor described. The same Israelites who viewed man as created in the image of God said of the appearance of Yahweh on Mount Sinai: "You heard the sound of words, but saw no form; there was only a voice" (Deut. 4:12). The image of God has here become a voice; pictorial art dissolves into words and then into music. And music is preserved longer in worship than is graphic art.

For Calvin, the prohibition of images is absolute. He directs it not only against graven images, but, with what is plainly a reference to the Greek Church, also against painted images. The making of an image can be an act of self-assertion, of autocracy; and this it is when it succeeds in freezing motion completely. Then religion, whose essence is the ceaseless movement of God toward man and man toward God, can do nothing but turn against the images. Iconomachy is just as much a religious phenomenon as iconolatry, the prohibition of images grounded as deeply in religion as the shaping of images.

The difficulty in expressing the holy through the form of an image lies, then, not in materiality, which every art, and especially the pictorial arts, needs. The sculptor and painter belong to that class of men for whom, in the phrase of Théophile Gautier, *"le monde visible existe"* (the visible world exists). The believer, on the contrary, seeks the invisible world. The painter lives through the grace of form, line, and color; the believer lives through the grace of a Lord whose kingdom is not of this world.

Here there is a real conflict. But it is not a conflict between religion and art, still less between religion and pictorial art. Religion, it is true, seeks something other than this world; but as long as it does not surrender to asceticism, it does not seek the supersensual. Likewise, art could never attain the purely "spiritual" level, because it can never do without something which is visible, audible, or tangible to the senses. Music has been called the least material of the arts because it needs "only" the sense of hearing, and uses no images. For someone who knows how to listen, however, the sense of hearing is material enough. Everyone who knows the least bit about music is aware that it certainly does not lack concreteness (for this is what is actually meant). And that is fortunate.

Hegel's influence has strengthened this conception of materiality being the actual opposition. According to him, the beautiful is the appearance, in a material form, of an immaterial idea. In the last analysis this is a Greek idea, which cannot coexist with an organic view of man as a unity. "Spirituality" and belief are not coextensive. The Christian Church has always believed in the resurrection of the flesh, and thus left room for the possibility that God will glorify this world. What is wrong with this world is not its concreteness, its sensual perceptibility, but rather its sinfulness. And sin destroys both spirit and matter. The Greeks thought the flaw lay in dead matter, salvation in the living spirit; but the Christians, who believe in the Son of David, see the flaw in the spirit as well as in matter, and salvation only in God. Besides, it is not dead matter which is the object of pictorial art, but, rather, matter which has been awakened to life by the touch of the artist. Otherwise a still life would be only some fruit and a wine bottle. "The actual aesthetic object is not the stone or the metal, but the construction of the phantasy occasioned by it, a movement of the soul which has become visible and been transferred to the objective world. Beauty increases both sensual and spiritual perception. Harmony may inflame a worshiper, but it does not shrink from raising the tone of a banquet." We conclude that art, precisely because it does not derive abstractions from material postulates, is better able to convey the holy than is pure idea. Its point of departure is the whole man, body and soul, an indivisible unity. The holy, too, is concerned with the whole man, not with an abstract "spirit" which might be hindered by a material body. Besides, when religion desires to express itself, it can no more do without material means than can art. Without myth, without symbol, without "costuming" in words, movements, tones, religion cannot exist.

When we ask ourselves what men, from the primitive to the most "modern," have meant by "religion," we find it again and again brought into conjunction with the visible. What conveys the power that is sought for is a holy object, holy food, a holy action, a holy man. I can neither write poetry nor preach without addressing myself to the whole, bodily man. I can produce no drama, administer no sacrament, without depending on hearing and sight. In this respect, religion and art are fully alike.

Where, then, is the difficulty? We have already touched on it when we mentioned that lack of distance, that autocracy, which conquers the power residing in or behind objects, only to experience how quickly it volatilizes. Rilke says in this regard:

> *Wir dürfen dich nicht eigenmächtig malen,*
> *Du Dämmernde, aus der der Morgen stieg.*
> *Wir holten aus den alten Farbenschalen*
> *Die gleichen Striche und die gleichen Strahlen,*
> *Mit denen dich der Heilige verschwieg.*

> *Wir bauen Bilder vor dir auf wie Wände,*
> *So dass schon tausend Mauern um dich stehn.*
> *Denn dich verhüllen unsre frommen Hände,*
> *Sooft dich unsre Herzen offen sehn.*

> We cannot paint thee at our own desire,
> Thou twilight, out of which the morning rose.
> Our ancient palettes were our one supplier
> Of all the pattern and of all the fire
> With which God worked, thy beauty to enclose.

> We make our murals of thee, unforbidden,
> So that a thousand walls rise up to blind our sight;
> For thy pure beauty by our hands is hidden
> As often as our hearts see by thy light.

Of course, the autocracy involved in making an image can be strengthened by unbridled sensuality. In Rubens, the distance from the holy is much greater than in Giotto or Rembrandt. But the actual conflict still lies in the autocracy of pictorial representation itself. For this reason the pictorial arts (and verbal art, too, insofar as it is representational) prove to be the most recalcitrant toward the holy. Music, on the other hand, which is least representational, is the most pliant. All representation is subjugation, is violation and self-assertion. It is of the essence of painting and sculpture that motion stagnates: precisely therein subjugation attains permanence, and autocracy becomes fixed. The prohibition of images is therefore very deeply rooted in the nature of religion. Even when done as a holy act, the fixation of motion can evoke an opposite effect. The spoken word goes its own way; music, dance, and drama have their own movement; but in pictorial art, motion is fixed, representation is complete—and terminal. Therefore, the unification of art and religion, as one of the possibilities of expression for beauty and holiness, is an even greater miracle in the pictorial arts than in the others.

ICONOMACHY   For this reason, many do not believe in this miracle, and destroy the images. Iconoclasm is a phenomenon not only of the Reformation period. The Greek word carries us back to the Byzantine Empire. Even much earlier, in classical antiquity, there was a reaction against images.[216] We have seen the judgment of Heraclitus and Varro. Behind Paul's speech on the Areopagus: "Being then God's offspring, we ought not to think that the Deity is like gold, or silver, or stone, a representation by the art and imagination of man," stand not only the prophets of the Old Testament, but also the Stoa (Acts 17:29). As formerly it was made from the primitive consciousness of God, so now, protest is made from refined, cultural consciousness of God. Whoever defends images does so either for pedagogical reasons, or to help the untaught, or on philosophical grounds. The human body is beautiful and useful and contains the divine Logos, and can thus be used as an expression of the divine (so Cicero and Posidonius).[216] Behind this pedagogy hides a fundamental aversion, but behind the philosophy is a degree of anthropomorphism which flees from religion.

It is identical in Christianity. Here, too, exaltation of the concept of God has kept man from viewing images as essential vehicles of the holy. But the theory that the worship of an image is transferred directly to the prototype of that image has been invented as much for reasons of expediency as has the argument, which reappears here, that images help the ignorant who cannot read. The difference between worship, which is proper only to God, and veneration, which likewise is expressed by kneeling but is appropriate to Mary, the saints, and the images, gives the impression of being an excuse. The primitive influence was (and is) too strong. In broad strata of the Christian community this conflict is not perceived, and the holy is identified with its pictorial representation. The miraculous image is still one of the most powerful motifs of popular piety, but not without protest, even from the Roman Catholic side, as the titles on many crucifixes in the south of Holland prove:

> Christian, reverently draw near,
> Christ's image, but not Christ, is here.
> Worship neither wood nor stone,
> Worship Christ, your God, alone.

Here two possibilities lie open: either devotion to the human, or its complete denial. Nakedness, which is basically ritual, can, in the first way, become an expression of human perfection and self-sufficiency.

The early female figures of the Near East and Greece are naked because nakedness constrains the powers, because the naked body is valued as an independent power and not as something of which man is proud; it is something divine. Exposure constrains these powers. A naked female figure conjures up fertility. In classical Greek art—with the exception of vase painting where nakedness was avoided for a long time—nakedness is the peculiarly human element in which man moves freely and lightly.

Here are revealed the two ways open to art: naturalism or asceticism. Or perhaps we should say, with Jacques Maritain, that art has the choice between *moyens riches* and *moyens pauvres,* abundant means and scanty means.[240] The first way is by no means a discovery of the modern era, nor even of the Renaissance. Already the heretical Egyptian King Akhenaten opposed the free flow of the garment, the realistic reproduction of the body, to the religiously constrained sculpture of his time. His sculptors created not kings, but men.[222]

The second way, asceticism, leads ultimately to doing without images. This expresses itself, then, either in prohibition of images or in iconoclasm. This, too, is not limited to the sixteenth century. At that time, it is true, it became evident how easily destroyed are images which were not created out of a strong belief in the revelation of God in human form, but had to be defended by pedagogic arguments, as shown in a dialogue between a Roman priest and a Baptist:

> He [the priest] said, "The images you see
> Do no one evil by their presence;
> Wherever they are found to be
> They are the Bible of the peasants.
> Take what you think is better,
> The image or the letter:
> Is their difference in their teaching?
> Are they both not dumb and dead?
> Thus an image, as I said,
> Serves as well for God as preaching."
> Then I spoke and answered thus:
> "As the Bible's grace was given
> By the Holy Ghost to us
> That we might be led to heaven,
> To pay an idol awe
> Is set against God's law.
> Those who engage in idol-making
> Will taste eternally

Accursed by God's decree
Hell's flames and torments never slaking."

The arguments of the opposition, insofar as they did not consist simply of hammer and chisel, were themselves extremely humanistic and rationalistic. Thus, Erasmus says: "I am not such a fool that I need carved or painted images, which often hinder my worship, since among the rude and stupid masses these figures are honored as though they were the saints themselves." The disciples, too, worshiped, but only in spirit and in truth, and it never occurred to them that "it had been revealed to them at that time that a picture drawn on the wall with charcoal was to be worshiped in the same manner as Christ himself."[242] On the other hand, Constantijn Huygens' reason is genuinely religious, and typical of the Reformation. The sermon must be freed, the word lying in chains behind the stone must first be broken open:

> With such a thunderbolt God's word broke through from heaven;
> If any think it be not reason and not right
> To start the Church's holy work with breaking as a leaven,
> Tell him iconoclasm preceded sermon's light.[243]

How much more justified was iconolatry (and even iconoclasm) in that earlier controversy of the iconoclasts of the Greek Church in the eighth and ninth centuries. Then, as we have seen, the cultic use of images was interpreted as the immediate corollary of the incarnation of the Word, so that sacramental meaning was ascribed to the holy image. Under strong Mohammedan influence, Emperor Leo the Isaurian (c. 680–740) ordered the removal of all images. Thereupon he was accused of heresy. Whoever denies images to be vehicles of divine power opposes the revelation of God in the human form of Christ and puts himself on the side of Mohammed, who would stand for no mediators. Thus he is *Sarakenophron;* that is, he Saracenizes. Women, monks (the painters of the saints), and the Roman Popes (Gregory II and III) join together to defend the images against Emperor Constantine V Copronymus *(eikonomachos)*, the fighter of images. The monk and theologian John of Damascus, from Jerusalem (died c. 754), indicates the theological basis of iconolatry: "I shall never cease to revere the material, through which my salvation became reality." The dogmatic core of iconolatry is incarnation, which ennobles nature.[228] But the Synod of Constantinople, in 754, decides that the elements of the Eucharistic Sacrament are the only permissible likenesses of the Saviour, and condemns John. All subjects must swear an oath that they will not worship any images. The emperors were brought to this first by the desire to purify the cult of its Mohammedan influence, of all that they thought was idolatry, and by the effort to strike at the Church and, above all, the monks. Empress Irene, nevertheless, at the Council of Nicea in 787, has the decisions of Constantinople reversed: salutation *(aspasmos)* and reverent honor *(timetike proskunesis)* of images are permitted, in fact are obligatory; actual worship, however *(alethine latreia)*, is reserved for God alone. The genuinely orthodox reasoning is notable: if the images are discarded, damage is done to Christology, for the possibility of pictorial representation preaches the true human nature of the Lord. In addition, the East and West are of the same mind about images.

But at the beginning of the ninth century, two emperors again take the field against images: in 832, a new prohibition of images is promulgated. Again it is a woman, the Empress Theodora, who must save the images. In 843, a synod renews the decrees of Nicea. The Feast of Orthodoxy still reminds us today of the meaning which the Eastern Church ascribed to images, and still ascribes to them. But since that time the Western Church has turned aside. The Imperial Synod at Frankfurt (794) condemned the decrees of Nicea. • [244] In this conflict it is shown very clearly how, in this fight between religion and images, two different religions are battling each other: the rational, exalted, deistic religion of the emperors under Mohammedan influence, and the primitive, but strongly Christian, religion of the women and monks. Basically this conflict concerns an opposition within religion itself, which cannot avoid form, and yet ever again becomes aware of that within the forms which is autocratic.

We have seen the importance iconomachy had for the Reformation. The Humanistic Enlightenment, with its view that God is too exalted to be represented; its fidelity to the Bible, which values the respect paid to the letter of the Old Testament prohibitions; its ecstatic personalization, which endures neither constraint nor image nor sacrament; the protest of the poor against the riches of the Church—all of this together has the effect first of destroying the images and then shunning them more or less rigorously. Calvinistic worship, completely without images, beyond doubt gave a great impetus to profane Dutch painting. Even today, besides hate of Papists and bourgeois narrowness, there hides behind

• The French Church under Charlemagne opposed iconolatry, and the Papal consent read: *nec cum illis frangimus, nec cum istis adoramus* (we neither destroy with the ones, nor adore with the others).

the Reformed Church's fear of images a residue of aversion to anything autonomous, the fear that it is possible to approach too closely to the majesty of God.

The holy image again and again causes that primitive confusion between image and likeness, which could come too close to God's glory. "The barbarity of the iconoclasts is not to be judged from the aesthetic point of view; it was fanaticism directed against that confusion and, from the religious standpoint, quite well motivated."[218]

Thus, while on the one hand religion demands forms, it discards them on the other. It destroys representations, those bibles of the ignorant, in order to impress upon them more emphatically the images of the Bible itself. To express the holy, one declares one's self free from line and color and turns to the spirituality of the word. But this has by no means done away with the image. For no religion speaks in abstract concepts; religion speaks in myths, that is, in the language of images. And no religion can get along without symbols. For "whoever becomes an iconoclast out of protest against drawings and pictures, sets up pictures himself. The more consciously a Reformed Church is formed according to this lack of images, the more it becomes an image," says the theologian Hans Asmussen.[245] For even the bare walls and central position of the pulpit are "symbols." One can, nay must, not lose the image. At any rate, not in Christianity. One expression of the holy is the Son of God, Christ's form of the servant. This is no autocratic shaping, no human overpowering of the majesty of God; it is the deed of God himself, which took form—it is the Word that became flesh. Thus Christology was justifiably called to witness in the Byzantine controversy: if God was able to assume the features of a man, then the image of a man cannot be completely unworthy of expressing the holy. In Rilke's poem cited earlier, there is also something of the paradoxical, the impossible but imperatively necessary, of genuine religious art, of wonder at the mutual interpenetration of holiness and beauty.

Iconomachy does not have to assume tangible form. Mysticism, too, contemplative and little given to revolution, turns aside from images; not only from the concrete image, but also from those that fill the soul. In all the mysticism which has invaded the West since Neoplatonism, from the Mohammedan Sufis to the German mystics of the Middle Ages, and from St. Theresa to the Quietists of the eighteenth century of the likes of Madame Guyon, ideas and images are systematically banished from the soul. Even the facts and forms of the Gospel have only temporary pedagogical value. Where human life empties into divine life and unites with it, all images pale. "Do you want to know how I passed beyond the creation of images?" This question of a medieval mystic reproduces the mystic experience superbly.• [136]

Thus, representation always moves between two dangers: the perfection of the image (the autonomy of what is depicted) and the disappearance of the image (the prohibition of images, iconomachy, and finally the dissolution of contours into the nothing and all of mysticism). Religion calls the first danger idolatry; art opposes the second danger with the motto "art for art's sake." But the theology of the Christian Church circles about the problem of the image of God as about a midpoint. The concern is not peripheral questions nor liturgical problems, but the central facts of revelation of God and man. The relationship to "pictorial art" is determined by the relationship to the great doctrines of the creation of man in the image of God, and God's incarnation.[230]

Finally, the concern here is about the problem of creation of form as such, that is, an aesthetic problem, assuming that we are not taking the word "aesthetic" in the narrow sense that aesthetes commonly give to it. The painter and the sculptor are not imitators, but shapers. The action connected with pictorial representation leads them to a new, different reality. A work of art strives for independent life. The object does not matter. Whether the dove of the Holy Ghost is painted, or the dove of the gutter, whether one paints a still life of bread and a cup, or calls to mind the holy symbols of the Eucharist, the attempt to penetrate to the ultimate reality of what is represented will always lead to another reality, to a second form. This second form draws more and more into the background. The greatest painters know that best. No mastery, no trueness to life, can help when the vision of the spectator does not again and again see another image through color and canvas. The true painter is always at work on the one masterpiece that is never created. If it should be accomplished, it could not be seen, for in the perfect image there is nothing more to see.• • [246, 247] But there is no perfect painting; thank God,

---

• In the circular paths of the Boro Budur on Java, statues stop where the round terraces begin: the phenomenal world does not accompany one to the highest stages of mysticism.
•• The painter in Balzac's "The Unknown Work of Art," like the tailor in "The Emperor's New Clothes," but in good faith, points out to his pupils all kinds of details in a mass of colors and lines which are not present. "*La*," says one of the pupils, "*. . . finit notre art sur la terre.*"—"*Et de la, il va se prendre dans les cieux,*" answers the other. At the other pole of human imagination we find the Greek, alike to Homer in thought, who scratched onto an archaic statue of Apollo by Manticles: "Ugly guy." He did not need distance, only humanity.

there is none. And perhaps there is also no problem; or, better, perhaps it solves itself. The pictorial arts move between two dangers. It is a wonder that they survive. But they do survive, and bloom in our midst. And that is the miracle of representation that surprises us, so that we say again with van Eyck:

> And then the breath is stopped before the face!—
> God speaks in human tongue with open grace.

4   THE HOLY IMAGE:

INFLUENCES

PATHS AND BOUNDARIES   "Art is the signature of man."[248] The first thing we know of prehistoric man is the fact that he drew. It is hardly conceivable that such a typically human form of expression as art, or more comprehensively formulated, such an essentially human awareness as that of beauty, should find no entrance to that deepest depth into which religion leads us. It cannot be assumed that holiness and beauty are hermetically sealed off from one another. But we have seen how both tend to draw apart, how they attack one another. On the other hand, they always search for one another. Again and again religion searches for art, because it cannot live without form and figure. Art always comes to religion as to the broader and deeper stream into which its floods can pour. The religious work of art, an expression of the holy through beauty, is not a mere pipe dream, but reality; a reality that we find less rarely since modern man lost the approach to the magical, existential context. On the contrary, we can say of almost all great artists that they have religious meaning and try to express a particular aspect of the holy. That is true for Rembrandt and Goethe, for Beethoven and Ibsen, for Michelangelo and George.

The perceptive statement of Schleiermacher is still true: "Religion and art stand beside each other like two friendly souls whose inner relationship, if they suspect it, is still unknown to them."[249] And thus we shall patiently have to search out approaches and boundaries. In the process we shall put much emphasis on the absolutely incomprehensible in the holy, so that we shall have to seek the approach to the beautiful from the holy, rather than vice versa. In spite of this, we shall keep clearly before our eyes the fact that art is not a derived or secondary form of life, but validates its own right in the same measure as life itself:

"Art is neither the imitation of life nor empathy with life; it is a primary form of life, which thus receives its laws neither from religion nor from morality nor from science nor from the state, nor from other primary or secondary forms of life."[250]

FASCINATION   Fascination, the attraction exerted by the holy, can be expressed through color, through sunlight in contrast to darkness, of which we shall speak presently. One of Alfred Römer's students speaks of a "liberating patch of meadow" which contrasts with the dark forest. Another pictures a "golden veil" which lies over the landscape at sunrise.[251] We think of the white grace of the temples of the Greeks, which yet are strongly filled with the sense of the numinous, earthly likenesses of the *olympia domata*.

THE AWE-INSPIRING   The awe-inspiring, divine *òrge*, that about the holy which excites fear, is expressed above all by sculpture and painting. Otto has pointed out the deliberately ugly, even monstrous, character of many Indian deities. Less barbaric, but still repulsive enough, is the effect of the threatening majesty of Byzantine art. And even more, modern art knows the "fear of the Lord." I am thinking of that *Christ With the Crown of Thorns,* by Dürer or one of his pupils, which brings us involuntarily to a "Lord, depart from me, for I am a sinful man." I am thinking of Michelangelo's damned, the face reflecting absolute terror of the holy.

THE GHOSTLY   A nuance of the awe-inspiring is the ghostly, the ghastly, which Grünewald was able to express in the terrible glory of his colors and the demonic richness of his insanely impossible movements. Before his picture of the resurrected Christ we are first gripped by fear of the specter, just as are the soldiers we see in the foreground, their limbs distorted with fear. The phenomenon still does not lack the majesty of divine terror.

In the "Crucifixion of the Isenheim Altar," though, the awe-inspiring is free of the ghostly: gruesome reality suffices to terrify us and cause us to tremble. Horror seizes us. But the mighty finger of John the Baptist points away from the human to the divine.[252]

DARKNESS AND SEMIDARKNESS   We come still closer to the holy through the influence of darkness and semidarkness. We are dealing here with a technique analogous to the *via negationis* in the development of the concept of God: by denying everything human and earthly, one comes closest to the nature of God. In the temples of many peoples, the deity has dwelt in the dark for ages. This does not mark it as a "Spirit of Darkness"; rather the contrary—through the impenetrable darkness is indicated the fact that the deity "dwells in unapproachable light." All earthly contours, all perceptible forms take flight and dissolve where the holy appears. Herein we recognize once more the "paradox of expression"[253] which mysticism, above all, knows well. He speaks most clearly about God who keeps silent. He draws the image of God most sharply who keeps it veiled in darkness. This darkness, of course, can never be total; if it wants to express something, then it must be perceptible, and if it is to be perceptible, then light, too, must be there. Therefore, we would do better to speak of semidarkness. We know it from the Romanesque churches, with their narrow windows admitting little light. The art of chiaroscuro makes a strongly numinous impression. Rembrandt understands not only how to veil the descent from the cross or a birth in eloquent darkness, he also knows how to unite the element of darkness with that of transition, and give a numinous effect to the most brilliant light in contrast to the dark background *(Simeon in the Temple, The Hundred-Gulden Note)*. In the Far East, emptiness corresponds to darkness. Chinese painters purposely leave empty spaces in their work. In this manner the Tao best flows through the work, for the divine can only be brought to expression negatively. Where nothing is, is the divine. For the value of a bucket does not reside in its wall, but in the space enclosed, in the emptiness.[203]

THE HUMAN Plainest in the pictorial arts is the influence of the human. The human form in fixed movement, the human face in set expression, can here become expressions of the superhuman and supernatural. If stiffness, the nonhuman, is to be avoided, this designates an enormous task, one which can be accomplished only by the very greatest. It is no wonder that they succeeded best when they tried to reproduce the form and features of the One who in his humanity expressed the entire fullness of the holy. I shall return to the meaning of Christ for the bond between holiness and beauty. It is enough to affirm here that the Christ experience of the Church, and the master who works in and through its strength, made this influence one of the most exalted of revelations of holiness through beauty. Thereby everyone creates his own man.

Thus the great painters offer us ever anew the drama of superhuman

miracle through the most varied human characteristics: *Ecce homo.*
Leonardo expresses in Christ an infinite; Johannine, mildness; Rembrandt,
the humility of the despised Jew; Michelangelo—in *The Last Judgment*
of the Sistine Chapel—paints the hero and judge, the terrifying gesture
of whose hand condemns the sinner to Hell. But he does not leave it at
that; that is not miraculous enough for him. The miracle lies primarily
in the unity of hero and Saviour, of judge and God of mercy; and
therefore next to the Son stands the Mother, a delicate, merciful figure
who pleads for grace. The Christ of the Cathedral at Perpignan (1529) is
conceived realistically, indeed more than realistically, and is able,
through superabundance of the all too human, to suggest the divine.

Everything in one and the divine in the human; the human without
softness, the divine without hardness . . . to give expression to all this
is not within the reach of even the most gifted artist. Nearest to
it comes that miraculous work of expression which, in my opinion, is the
highest religious work of art in the realm of the pictorial arts, combining
hardness and love, majesty and mercy, the awe-inspiring and fascination
in glorious manner: the picture of Christ in Albrecht Dürer's *Sudarium
of St. Veronica.*

HARMONY   The paradoxical function of the image in the relationship
of the beautiful to the holy results from the fact that there so seldom
occurs a harmony between the two in the pictorial arts. One or the
other almost always dominates. Almost always there is "something
forced," "something contrived"; precisely those artists who were most
deeply penetrated by beauty and holiness struggled with both: Rembrandt, Michelangelo, Dürer. Only very rarely does the sun break
through, only when both, faith and beauty, are childlike, youthful, with
pure, happy colors. The Italian *quattrocento*, Fra Angelico above all,
occasionally also the Flemish Renaissance, van Eyck and Memling, attain
that harmony.

THE THEOLOGICAL AESTHETICS OF THE IMAGE   In accord
with the structure of the previous chapters, in which we treated the
other arts, we could here add the theological aesthetics of the image. In
another place in this book we shall treat the image, which we have already
discovered in literature, in the dance, and in the drama—and which we
shall find in architecture—in a general theological aesthetics related to all
the arts, conceiving it more thoroughly as the principle of art in its
totality (see page 304).

PART FIVE

The House of God and the House of Man

1   THE BUILDING OF
THE HOUSE OF GOD

THE HOUSE OF GOD   In the context of our lives, "building" means constructing a house of God. It has this meaning even when we are not speaking of a temple or a church. House or city, in the same way as temple, is the bearer of a divine power, which is fixed in a particular place through the act of building. The boundary which separates the building site from the rest of the world is thus one of the most important constituents of primitive architecture. Whatever lies outside offers no security, is surrendered to all powers. The power which is known, and for which a house is built, resides within. The ancient Roman *pomoerium* is the holy boundary of the city, indicating the limit of the sovereignty of the gods. The ancient Germanic enclosure (*Einfriedung*) is a guarantee of peace (*Frieden*), with its boundary a boundary of power. Even today, the British Queen must beg entrance from the authorities of the City of London at the Temple Bar.

It is thus of greatest importance that house and city have the proper location, that is, a location which corresponds to the conditions of power. Upon this axiom rests the science of "orientation," which occupied so much space in ancient culture and was also determinative for the building of a Christian church. A specific point is chosen to provide direction, forming the focus of holy power. This can lie in the heavens and be the point of ascension of a star; or it can be a sign of the zodiac and stand in connection with the rising or setting of the sun; it can also be a holy place on earth, Jerusalem or Mecca. This principle developed most strongly in the world of ancient Asia: there a building reflects the construction of the world. The Sumerian King Gudea found the plan of his buildings in dreams, which his protecting goddess revealed to him.[254] Moses was to build Yahweh a house after the image which was shown him upon the mountain (Ex. 25 and 26).

Power actually resides in the house.

> The creation of architecture, as it actually proceeded on earth, has as little to do with our idea of "dwelling" as the creation of sculpture has with our joy in seeing. Quite different needs and abilities caused the first heaps of stones to arise. In them dwell hidden powers of the earth; indeed, there that which lives has itself been bound and become stone. The more stone, the more powerfully life can work upon the body of the dead.[199]

A house is an enclosure of power. The oldest houses are the dance houses in which the power of motion is fixed. Older still are the enclosed dancing grounds, such as the Maga in ancient Iran, where ecstatic singers and dancers assembled, developing their powers in the "closed circle." After dancing ground and dance house follows the temple. In undifferentiated life, a house is a temple in which the holy power of the family or clan resides. Churches were originally dwellings; temples likewise. The Japanese Shinto temples developed out of the primitive dwelling hut,[17] the Roman temples from round peasant huts made of straw. They became houses which belonged only to God, later to fall to the status of places for prayer or instruction, such as the synagogue or Japanese Zen temple, which are really schools.[17] In ancient Egypt, temple hymns were sung in which the opening of the temple doors was represented as an opening of heaven and earth. The temple as house of God has existed since the beginning. In Babylon, hymns of creation were sung at the consecration of the temple; and yet today, in Roman Catholic worship, Psalm twenty-four, which begins with the praise of God in creation, is the psalm for the consecration of a church.

BUILDING   Building is thus a holy action which is connected with manifold rites and sacrifices. Architecture is nevertheless the youngest of the arts. Primitive man finds shrines already present in nature: the holy glade (*lucus*) and the holy mountain are places hallowed without human action. And the shrine of nature long remains beside the building as the most holy thing, just like the fetish beside the image. Yahweh finds the simple tent more fundamental than the artistic temple: "I have not dwelt in a house since the day I brought up the people of Israel from Egypt to this day, but I have been moving about in a tent for my dwelling" (II Sam. 7:6). Thus he who builds must take precautions, perform building sacrifices, recite formulas, and, above all, take care that his work is in agreement with the power. Building is dangerous. The same thing is true, in this regard, that was earlier pointed out in a different context: "Unless the Lord builds the house, those who build it labor in vain" (Ps. 127:1).

Those who build are genuine "men of deeds"; "artisans" in the medieval sense. In architecture, workmen come into their own much more than in the other arts, for the latter are always exposed to the danger of becoming a luxury. By reason of its unavoidable utility, architecture retains its original social character. The religious does not exist in art in inverse proportion to utility, but in direct proportion. The artist must adjust himself to the demands of the work, says Maritain, according to rules and values which were not created by him, but are external to him. That is even more true for the architect:

> He needs a certain heroism if he wants to assert himself in the direct line of his work, and not sacrifice his immortal substance to the devouring idol which he carries within his soul; in truth, the artist can free himself from conflicts of that sort only when a deep humility makes him, so to speak, unconscious of his art, or when the all-powerful unction of wisdom lends to all that is within him the calm and peace of love. It is not accidental that Christ wanted to be an artisan.[150, 255]

Thereby he was at once an artist and an ordinary man. For an artist is not an extraordinary man, a "genius," but an ordinary man who has so much humility that he understands his task. This role of the artist is represented most purely by the master builder. Thus his art is also the most noble. The greatest humility achieves the most mighty result.

Thus in the twelfth century the French cathedrals were built, one after the other, through decades. Unknown builders, that is, the French people, filled with life and enthusiasm, brought material from far and near. Thus arose those miracles of skill and worship, that great art, out of the deepest need for worship; thus arose those houses of God which wanted to comprehend the entire world, *"miroirs du monde"* (mirrors of the world), in which everything was symbol,[256] beginning with Adam and Eve at the portal, and going to the Last Judgment at the far end. Therefore, architecture, which freezes motion as no other art is able to do, can hold fast the lines and forms of many cultures: "The art which was once called a symphony in stone gave to innumerable centuries a clearly comprehended form."• [172, 190, 257] Therefore, architecture, in that century which knows no fixed forms, no pure lines, in that century in which we were born, was doomed to break down completely.

• Goethe called architecture "frozen music."

2 THE HOUSE OF GOD

BECOMES A HUMAN HOUSE:

ALIENATION AND CONFLICT

THE HOUSE CAN NO LONGER BE A TEMPLE In this realm alienation proceeds from two sides: first from religion, which no longer wishes to store its goods in the house of art; and from art, which wishes to build its own house where it may dwell all alone. The house can no longer be a temple; in fact, temples can no longer exist. God is too great to be able to reside in a house that was made by hands, so says religion. It speaks classically and beautifully in Solomon's prayer of consecration before the new temple. This is called the dwelling place of God, a "place for him to dwell in forever"; it is still said that God's "name," that is, his being, shall be within it; yet it is clearly recognized that no human edifice can shelter the holy: "But will God indeed dwell on the earth? Behold, heaven and the highest heaven cannot contain thee; how much less this house which I have built!" (I Kings 8:27) And "the place of God's dwelling" is heaven, from which he hears and forgives when someone prays in the temple. God does not hear in his house, but in heaven: thus the king prays "that thy eyes may be open night and day toward this house," which was made by men (I Kings 8:29).

In the place of the house of God comes now the house of prayer. Man no longer builds a holy place, but rather builds himself a place in which he can pray to God in peace. If the synagogue and basilica had simply been places of assembly for quite some time, now the Christian church once more becomes the house of God, in which his immediate,

199

miraculous presence resides upon the altar. Even today the Catholic goes to the house of the Lord in the literal sense of the primitive structure. Even the Calvinistic Protestant, who has probably made the prayer of Solomon most thoroughly his own, perceives no contradiction between his sober house of prayer and his beloved hymn in which he sings of an ascent to the altar of God. Along with the name "house of God," the churches of the Reformation, even though they often became almost completely houses of prayer and even places of religious assembly, preserved much of the original power of the house of holiness.

Among us in the Netherlands, succeeding generations have done everything in their power to make of the church a meaningless space. Our knowledge of God's presence had to feed on the heritage of the past. In the place where the altar once stood, vestries are enthroned today in their full glory. People are generally quite contented with good acoustics and comfortable pews, wanting at most a bit more atmosphere. Every symbol is still feared; and Hyazinth, from Heine's *Travel Sketches*, is still right in saying that the hymn board is the only thing to which a person can hold fast in a Protestant church. Our native Church even gave it its due in a way that was not intended, when it wanted to wager on the numbers in a lottery. . . .

There is actually no such thing as Protestant church architecture. What is meant by the term—and there are glorious buildings among them—are imitations of Italian churches of the type of Santa Maria della Salute in Venice. There is nothing Protestant about it, and as far as the interior is concerned, "Protestant" usually means secularization. In the so-called "baptismal gate" we recognize once more the form of separation between choir and nave, now emptied of meaning. In the pews of the vestry we see the secularized pews of the choir. The symbolism in the carvings and statues of the pews, the pulpit, and the organ screen is overwhelmingly heathen, with hourglass and scythe, and *putti* with or without trumpets. The beautiful New Church of Haarlem, dating from the seventeenth century, and St. Mary's Church of Leyden, along with others, are products of the spirit of the Renaissance, not the Reformation.[258, 259] The feeling for style is retained, but little or no religious feeling. Naturally, even the former ultimately vanished, and the monstrosities of the nineteenth century arose.

But we must not complain. Church architecture is a problem, and will remain so. Nowhere do we live in a structure more transitional than here. We are aware that we no longer want the ancient Christian form, which has God's presence as its focal point and the form of the cross as its plan. But we do not have the slightest idea what we would like in its place; indeed, the uncomfortable feeling is abroad that if we limit ourselves to building a church for sermons, we are no longer even dealing with a church, that, in fact, a theater shows more characteristic forms than those places of edification which nothing differentiates from conference rooms. Transition succeeds transition until one day we shall return to the form which strives to be an expression of the holy.

Luckily, a strong reaction has made itself felt. In advance of and more consciously than the theologians (who clearly are afraid to refer their doctrine to life), architects have reached the point of demanding a peculiar character for the building of a church. Houses of God are to be built again; enclosures are to be created in which the meeting of the holy and the human can take place. The Church follows only with hesitation. But when she becomes conscious of her nature once more, that nature must necessarily be expressed in her architecture.[260]

THE TEMPLE BECOMES A HOUSE Primitive man could build houses of God because every house he built was, in a certain sense, a house of God, and every hearth an altar. But in periods of transition, the house in which men are to dwell creates its own demands, possesses its own character. There is a laboratory in Groningen that looks like a church, and a statue on it might be thought a Madonna, until one discovers that it represents one or another of the sciences. We feel that this is false. A laboratory is, and remains, a laboratory and should not give the appearance of something else; a factory is, and remains, a factory and should not give the impression of being a church. But just in this "desire to be something different" lies the recognition of transition. We have completely separated the human from the divine. We have built houses for our own power and temples for the power of God. We have lost the true relationship between the two. Since the Renaissance we know how good private and public buildings should be built, and only the nineteenth century—that century dark as scarcely another—temporarily forgot; but since the Renaissance we *have* forgotten how to build houses of God. The Renaissance had forgotten that God dwells in darkness, that he "breaks out of the dim halls of the Gothic cathedrals"[261] into the bright light of the human world. Faust is the modern man, freeing himself from his dependence on power, leaving his dark cell "where even the

blessed light of heaven breaks cheerlessly through painted windows,"
who, on the joyous morn of Easter leaves behind the narrow alleys of
the medieval city and rejoices in man:

> *Denn sie sind selber auferstanden . . .*
> *Aus der Kirchen ehrwürdiger Nacht*
> *Sind sie alle ans Licht gebracht.*

> For they themselves have now arisen
> From the Church's venerable night
> They have been brought into the light.

GOD NEEDS A HOUSE   Primitive man thinks that God needs a
house, and so he builds him one, as Solomon did. But in the king's prayer
we have already found criticism: no house can contain God. At first the
criticism gains strength only gradually. We have seen that even we, no
matter how Calvinistically we may think, have not been able to free
ourselves completely from the idea of a house of God. We shall probably never succeed. On the contrary, everything points to the fact that
the primitive form of thought of God's dwelling in a house built for him
has been given up, but that the essential content of that idea is once more
receiving new life. A previous generation rejoiced that God was everywhere, upon the mountains as well as in the valleys; today's generation
is beginning to realize that God is no longer a universal concept, but
allows himself to be recognized only in personal meeting.

However that may be, when God needs a house he lays claim to
everything. There beauty may serve, but not rule. We are not thinking
of the ugliness of carelessness, of that horrible negligence which often
characterizes our Protestant churches. We are not thinking of a negation, but of a positive demand. In God's house God must reign; his
thoughts must find expression in the building, and if men are not otherwise able to understand them, they must be expressed at the expense of
beauty. Here lie the preconditions for a conflict.

We find an excellent example of this contention in ancient Egypt.
The so-called Sun Temple of King Ne-wsr-re (c. 2700 B.C.) at Abu
Gorab consists of a very large open courtyard, which is connected with
a gatehouse by a long passage. In the courtyard stands a gigantic obelisk,
imageless image of the sun, upon an enormous pedestal. The passage
circles the courtyard and continues into the pedestal. The light

of day is completely absent there, so that torches must be used. After many turnings, the passage emerges at the foot of the obelisk. There the visitor has the rising sun directly before him. "It cannot be denied that the ancient architect let a magnificent effect escape him here, perhaps had to let it escape him on ritual grounds: by means of high side walls, he greatly blocked off for the slowly ascending visitor the view of the shrine lying before him, and its obelisk which towers far above everything else," was the first thought of Ludwig Borchardt, the excavator of the temple. At a later stage of the excavation it became clear that the passage was closed on all sides, and the "visitor" therefore received not a glimpse of the impressive building.[262, 263] We do not have to go far to find the reason: the artist was not concerned with "visitors," but with believers; not with men who came there to look at something beautiful, but with the reverent who wanted to behold the face of God.• Therefore, he expended everything on expressing the contrast between the cheerless darkness of the ascent (the kingdom of death) and the gleaming light of the sunrise at the end, where one leaves the passage and emerges at the foot of the obelisk. The "visitor" thus experiences the transition from death to resurrected life, which rules Egyptian sun worship to such a great extent. Expression of the holy and expression of the beautiful could not go together here. A similar conflict was observed in the architecture of the pyramid of King Sahure, which comes from the same period. There the ascent was covered, and the ceiling painted like the starry sky. Daylight could penetrate into the passage only through narrow windows. According to our way of thinking, says Ludwig Borchardt, this long, closed ascent has something hideous about it. "A hoselike covered viaduct almost 400 meters long, in which one ascends in semidarkness without any view of the pyramid plateau which lies outside, is unbelievable to us."• • [264, 265] Here the demands of religious

---

• An analogous architectural example is the Boro Budur on Java. The amazing wealth of motifs and ornaments which characterizes the square base ceases suddenly when one, arriving at the top, discovers oneself in the midst of round stupas, crowned by the central stupa. Here, at the goal of the pilgrimage of the faithful, there is no ornament, no relief, no image to be found. It is clear that (although the effect of this sudden transition from wealth to poverty is by no means unaesthetic in the judgment of connoisseurs) religious, not aesthetic motifs, dominate here; the path of the development of man is to be represented, he who withdraws from the world of phenomena in order to enter complete poverty and the highest spiritual riches. "The stupa became the material representation of the doctrine of salvation itself."[263]
• • Another example of building which is hostile to architecture on religious grounds is found in the Iranian temples, where the original open cultic space was essentially retained.[265]

experience carry more weight than aesthetic experience. We may think of the statement of the ancient topographer Pausanias concerning the buildings ascribed to the mythical architect Daedalus: "What Daedalus made is somewhat clumsy to the eye, but there is something divine about it."[266]

MAN NEEDS A HOUSE   God must reign in his house, just as man claims his house completely for himself. Master Builder Solness stands on his tower and speaks to God: "Now hear me, you mighty one! From now on I will be a free master builder, I too. In my own field, as you in yours. I shall never again build churches for you. Only homes for human beings!" And the modern house arises, the house without holiness, without a hearth, without penates. It took man a long time to remove his gods from his house completely. In the peasant house the hearth long remains much more than a source of warmth; the door is still a holy boundary and not merely an entrance. With the ancient, originally sacral forms, vanishes now also the last remnant of the primitive continuity of life, the awareness that our house is actually God's house. Inventions such as apartment houses and central heating are not inconsequential for our inner life, and also not accidental. In our time man has conquered his own house for the first time. It does not give him much pleasure. Master Builder Solness built a tower on his house, only to be able to speak with God. And he does not hold to his decision in regard to building homes for human beings. "I will say to him, 'Hear me, almighty Lord . . . You may decide about me according to your own judgment. But from this day on I shall build only what is most beautiful on earth. . . .' "[267] That is a castle in the air.

NO ONE NEEDS A HOUSE   There is a way out of the difficulty. It is that of mysticism. The God of mysticism needs no house, no more than do his servants. Each finds himself and the other in the holy of holies, in the *cor cordium.*•[172] The relationship between God and man no longer has extension. It needs neither space nor a roof. It has become a unity in the inmost part, where fixed contours can no longer be distinguished. The true *qa'aba*, says the Mohammedan mystic, will be built in the hearts of the faithful.

To the nonmystic believer, all of this appears differently. The heart of man is not the true temple of God; rather, God builds it as he thinks

• Thus Schopenhauer can evaluate architecture only as the "lowest stage of the objectivity of the will: hardness, heaviness, stiffness."

good, without human help. The superfluity of human building is not perceived as a demand, a norm, but eschatologically, as a boundary. The City of God, the New Jerusalem, needs no temple, "for its temple is the Lord God the Almighty and the Lamb" (Rev. 21:22). But in the old Jerusalem, building must go on; God's house as well as ours.

3 INFLUENCES

TOWARD HARMONY

THE MASSIVE AND MONUMENTAL   The first influence which forces its attention upon us here is the massive, the monumental. Architecture provides the most eloquent examples. It works by nature with large masses. But it can work in two directions: either overcoming mass as well as it can, removing its weight, thwarting its lines, or by letting mass itself speak.[268] As soon as it does the latter, it possesses a means of expressing the holy in a particular side of its nature. Again we think of the gigantic "Daedalus" buildings of ancient Greece, which gave Pausanias an impression of the divine. We think of the megaliths and the gigantic constructions of prehistory, their simplified mass, powerful gesture, which appears to us as divine movement. Above all, we think of the architecture of ancient Egypt, of the oppressive weight of the monstrous pillars of Karnak, placed all too near to each other, a divine oppression which compels us to flee; and we think of the superhuman gesture of the pyramids and obelisks. A learned Egyptologist once called the building of the pyramids—so much effort and expense for the grave of a king—"an infinite waste of material." A man with deeper understanding feels the titanic resistance to death of the divine life given to the king; the pyramids lie there like a mighty memorial to the battle between god and god. Let us look once at the famous rock temple at Deir el-Bahri. Simple rows of pillars form the entrance to the dark interior of the temple in the rock. But they find their end, their crown, and their absolute destruction in the enormous rock wall which towers vertically above them. It is as though the architect wanted to express his human vision in divinely threatening masses of rock, make his own work worthless, as though he wanted to say that the divine is invariably greater and of higher rank than what humans build. Here we also find the aspect of negation, to which we shall return presently.

Still, we cannot claim this influence for architecture alone. Egyptian sculpture, too, occasionally expresses the holy through its massiveness. The Sphinx, which in Egypt is by no means the feminine riddle it is in Greece, but rather a symbol of the masculine and divine might of the king, lies in the sand of Giza like a gigantic fragment of divine might. The enormous royal statues which watch over the lonely rock temple of Abu Simbel make us aware, solely through the majestic calm of their gigantic stature, that we are entering another world.

Not only architecture and sculpture, but music, too, can express the holy through the massive and monumental. There is music, even if it is only rarely found, which piles up stone blocks and awakens the experience of the divine solely through its massiveness. We think at once of the symphonic works of Anton Bruckner. Mahler's *Eighth Symphony* is likewise such a breaking through of power. The method of building sounds—in itself no guarantee of aesthetic effect, and not even above suspicion—is here used to interpret the experience of the wholly other. It is as though the entire world were dissolved in sound; we collapse under the weight, and feel ourselves enchained and repelled simultaneously. In many of Bach's organ works, the master, even if the architectonic line of his work is as fine and clear as everywhere in his music, seems to be playing with blocks of stone, like a prehistoric giant (*Toccata and Fugue in D minor, Fantasia and Fugue in G minor*).

It is no wonder that the massive and monumental possesses numinous power. Even primitive man heard in thunder the voice of God. A good criterion of the religious value of massive music is whether or not it is possible to perceive God's thunder behind it.

PROFUSION   Profusion is a nuance of the massive and monumental. I do not mean multiplicity, motley richness, but the fascinating inclusion which we find primarily in Indian art. The endless rows of identical stupas in the Boro Budur attempt, through repetition, to express the holy. We find in literature an analogy to this extension of structure in the piling up of epithets in the *Mahabharata*, which seeks likewise to awake the experience of the infinite through the endlessness of inclusion;[269] a typically Buddhistic infinity, image of the series of infinitely many Buddhas which in the endless change of birth still incarnate the same formless divinity.

EMPTINESS   The influence of emptiness, too, is found in architecture, especially in Islam. Rudolf Otto has drawn attention to this.[270] In the empty mosque the eye is irresistibly drawn to the empty niche which shows the direction of Mecca for prayer. The denial of all content receives positive significance. Therefore, emptiness comes after darkness as a means of expressing the holy. Among the most difficult problems of rejuvenated Catholic and Reformed architecture is the space to be filled with seats and pews—in contrast to a church which is empty, to which one brings one's own kneeling cushion. Stuffing a church full of furniture is indefensible, not only aesthetically, since it destroys every architectonic line and makes illusory the effect of space, but also theologically, since the house of God is not an auditorium. Rationalism has given a fixed place in our churches to everything, with the exception of the one thing that should be fixed: the communion table. To arrive at movable church furniture is one of the most pressing problems to be answered by architects and technicians.

4 THE THEOLOGICAL

AESTHETICS OF BUILDING

In architecture, the principle of creation, which is so important in theological aesthetics, is manifested most clearly. Naturally it is indispensable in every art, but it is the law of life for the architect. A poet can be said to "construct" a poem, and even the composer speaks of the "construction" of a piece. The terminology is nevertheless derivative, or rather it points to the architectonic element which is contained in all arts. Therefore, architecture receives such a prominent place, both in the totality of the arts and in theological aesthetics. Whoever builds, creates. Naturally he does not create *ex nihilo*, and if one chooses, one can therefore say that he does not create at all. Only God creates in the absolute, actual sense of the word. But the architect makes new forms. He changes the reality that is given into another, and does so in the literal sense. From a pile of earth he makes a house, from land a dwelling. He gives form to the settlement, that most elementary act of man upon earth. With awe-struck reverence, he recognizes in the lines and circles of his blueprint simultaneously the outline of God's plan. He creates only in the literal sense, but his building partakes of true creation.* [271] The artist is like a partner of God; he creates from a level below.

This creation comes about only when it is experienced as service. In the medieval division of the arts, the principle of servility was opposed to the principle of liberality, freedom.

The *artes liberales*, "liberal arts," were music, arithmetic, and logic. The *artes serviles*, "servile arts," were the pictorial arts and architecture. Modern thought tends to see in freedom the mark of the divine. Thus

---

* Creative art is "to bring forth a capability, doubtless not *ex nihilo*, but from an already present material, a new creation, something original, which is itself capable of moving the soul of man" (cf. [150]).

Schopenhauer called music a true religious art, and found architecture the heaviest, the most limited, the least divine. A renewed and converted thought will discover the divine in servility, and discover, with the indescribable melancholy which all music leaves in the soul at the hearing of holy sounds, that God has already gone past.

For creation and service belong together. God himself served the world when he created it. His creation is not the arbitrary act of a great Lord, but the humble service of Christ. The eternal truth is that all things are created by the Word, through the doctrine of the Mediator of Creation. When God created the world, he did exactly the same as he did when he sent Christ and in him redeemed the world. The same immeasurable love moved him the one time as the other. Therefore, the true master builder is also God's humblest pupil: "It does not suffice him to be a pupil of the masters; he must be God's pupil, for God knows the law for the creation of beautiful works. . . . The artist, whether he knows it or not, draws on God for advice, by his observation of things." Thus did the great masters of the cathedrals build: "They believed; and as they were, so they did. Their work disclosed the truth of God, but without doing so purposely, and precisely because it did not do so purposely."[150] The true master builder does not make a "Christian art," but discovers to his amazement that God builds by his hand:

> So it is true that I bore God in me, since he proceeds from me.
> It has sufficed, so he reflects himself within this wall and in this gold.
> It was enough for him that I should end my work, so that he might begin.
> And since it is so, it stands there now, ready to receive you, the cathedral I created, unaware, like a rose in its innocence.
> So it is true that something in me never lost the capacity for this ineffable childhood.[273]

But to be able to build thus, the master builder must, in fact, have ceased and God begun; the blueprint must have proceeded unconsciously from that well-built city whose artist and architect is God.

PART SIX

Music and Religion

1   HOLY SOUND

POWERFUL SOUND   In the world of the primitives, music is never an end in itself, but has its effect only in combination with other actions such as dancing or work or the recital of poetry. The situation remains thus for a long period, as the history of music teaches us.[274] Music for the sake of music is a "modern" invention.

Music is rhythm, melody, and harmony. Of these, rhythm is the most primitive. In primitive culture, melody plays a much less important role, and harmony is usually completely absent. Since rhythm is a constituent of music, but actually belongs to the dance, this means that dance is more primitive than music, and that we have already said what is most important about music in our discussion of the dance and of verbal art. Everything that was true of the work song is also true of music. Rhythm constrains the gods;[275] it can only be strengthened by the effect of melody.

Therefore, the drum is the original, the basic instrument, and among the primitives, especially in Africa, by far the most popular. It is the repository of the divine power which is poured out over life in war and in love, with dance and sacrifice. It would be impossible to imagine a bushman from Surinam without his drum. He speaks with great reverence of his *kobuwa-bensi-ankama*, his wood-hide-and-lacing.* Making music is an action just as useful as dancing, constraining power, and forcing it in a particular direction. Orpheus' song subdues animals and moves stones. At the trumpet blast of the children of Israel the walls of Jericho fall. The servants of Saul say to him: "Let our lord now command your servants, who are before you, to seek out a man who is skillful in playing the lyre; and when the evil spirit from God is upon you,

* Information from W. F. van Lier, 1938.

213

he will play it, and you will be well" (I Sam. 16:16). Thales of Crete, according to Plutarch, drove the plague from Sparta by means of music. The medicine men of uncivilized peoples proceed against the most varied evils with the aid of music. Here and there lives on the memory of a quack named Sequah, one of whose statements is preserved in a folk song: "You'll get well with music." Since ancient times the sound of bells has served as a protection against being struck by lightning and other evils. Therefore, bells are baptized. As late as 1700, Liselotte von der Pfalz saw how the people of Paris streamed together to attend such a bell baptism and began to ring the bells: "They think it will protect them from thunder."[128] Even today the bell towers still sound their *fulgura frango* over town and country.* This formula is perhaps recalled from the epigraph to Schiller's "Song of the Bell." When, in the fourth century, St. Ambrose introduced hymn-singing into the worship at Milan, making a great impression, the Arians accused him of working with magical formulas. The consciousness of the unity of sound and power was still so alive in the bishop that he did not reject the charge out of hand, but explained that the hymn really exerted power: "For what can be more powerful than the confession of the Trinity, which is daily witnessed by the mouth of the entire people?"[79, 277] St. Ambrose used the word *carmen*; it still means incantation, prayer, and song simultaneously.

Music wins goods of every description. The old Malayan of whom we spoke earlier not only danced before his mat in the house of the spirits, but also sang. The "good" which music evokes is quite various. In the West Indies, a flute is used together with a charm to entice a woman or calm a child.[278] In Indonesia the flute is the favorite instrument; full of the power of life, it conjures up renewed vitality. The flute is blown while one circles about the sacred post in the middle of the dwelling. It brings forth the spirits, and the production of sound by the player is a miracle. Women are not allowed to see the flute, whose power is strongly sexual. An angry man says to his wife, "If you don't shut your mouth, I'll pronounce the name of the karawari flute, and you will die on the spot!" The flutes have feminine names, and in them women are present as the bearers of new life. (It is typically masculine to keep a woman's own secret from her.) Playing the flute is an aid to fertility • •[279] We have seen that not only words, but also pitch and in-

* In regard to the magical significance of musical instruments, cf. W. Heinitz.[276]
•• To the primitive Papuan mind, flute and vagina are one and the same, just as flute and penis still are in the vernacular of Holland.

terval are determined by a formula. The formula must be pronounced in a specific way, but it is not a melody, at least not in our sense; it is more like recitative. In ancient Egypt, possession of the "right voice" was the path to righteousness among men and gods. Whoever possesses the "right voice," that is, whoever knows how to pronounce the holy formulas with the proper intonation, controls even his own eternal destiny. The same is true for song. It conjures up power, salvation, the Saviour. It leads, with inescapable force, to his Epiphany.[86] A powerful formula demands rhythm and also melody.

Primitive man knows that beautiful sound conveys all his feelings and thoughts more powerfully, more fully, and more exactly than does the individual word.[23] He even ascribes magical power to sung incantations.• [280] As late as 1316, the Council of Cologne forbade the singing of the famous hymn of mourning *Media in vita in morte sumus* for anyone, unless special permission were given. The song of death brings about death, and not even the Council wants completely to forgo practical application of this possibility.[280] Even we cannot tear ourselves completely loose from the power of song, no matter how secularized we are. The simple man, who does not know the nuances of the speaking voice—that educated form of conveying information which accents words according to their logical connection—repeatedly falls back into a psalmlike cadence of magical origin.

Anyone who has ever heard a representative of the old school read from the Bible knows that even a Calvinist is not content with the bare word, but seeks to constrain holiness through cadence and pitch. Whoever listens to the melody of many sermons can hear the same thing in less pleasant form; let us call it "atonal."

Sermon intonation is only differentiated from Gregorian chant by the imperfection of its structure. It does not differ at all from the magical formulas of primitive tribes.

Not only the Roman Catholic and Greek Orthodox Churches are wise enough to prescribe song at least for the liturgy: the Swedish, Anglican, and partially also the Lutheran Churches do the same thing. Whoever praises God, sings. If he does not sing, he is not deeply affected. "My heart is steadfast, O God, my heart is steadfast! I will sing and make melody!" (Ps. 57:7.) Gregorian chant is the perfect form of expression for the steadfast heart.

• "If a word has a certain real effect simply by being pronounced, a fortiori, it is either dangerous or beneficent when it is sung in the form of a modulated formula."

The solemn tones of the Gregorian hymns, to our present-day musical perception, are sounds from another, higher world, from the world of the divine. Its avoidance of polyphony and its monotony give it a stability, calm, and dignity which are never present in agitated, polyphonic music. On the other hand, this music evidences an astounding diversity; it knows how to set to music the finest nuances of mood of the liturgical feasts.[281]

Just as music binds power, so it also assists in its release. Here not only rhythm but, above all, melody and timbre, have an important function. Drums put the shamans into ecstasy, the flute the bacchantes. Many primitive peoples think the flute speaks with the voice of a spirit; others believe the drum is filled with spirits. The more the instrument is filled with power, the more violently the player or listener becomes "beside himself." Wild, stimulating music grips the spirits of men everywhere in the world.

2 THE TRANSITIONAL

STRUCTURE

LITURGICAL MUSIC BECOMES "CHURCH MUSIC"   Beautiful
sound reinforces the power of beautiful words. Singing is more effective than speaking. We saw this in our discussion of poetry (p. 129),
and shall return to it. Our modern times have almost forgotten this fact.
There are people who complain about the "unnaturalness" of opera, perhaps because the hero sings while he breathes his last, or, in naturalistic
works, sings when he asks for a glass of beer. There are also people—
and basically it is the same complaint—who complain about the "unnaturalness" of non-Calvinistic worship, in which the priest sings the Creed,
the prayers, and the Gospel. This comes about because singing has become a specialized field which has certain "artistic value," but may not
be brought into direct continuity with life. One does not sing at home
when one wishes to have a cup of tea, or when one dies, marries, or
otherwise does something that is "a part of life."

Everything is classified, and whatever does not fit in the frame is
unnatural. It is left to specialists, and they are generally all too happy
when others do not meddle in their business. For their own part, they
have something against "dilettantes."

Even in the churches which have liturgical music, the outward continuity of the transitional structure is often preferred. A powerful
movement within the Roman Catholic Church, led by the Pope, opposes
the secularization of music. But it is coming up against strong resistance:
"A profane art has not only withdrawn from the influence of the
Church, but has forced its way into the Church's holy of holies and
forced its authority upon the Church: the splendor of the Renaissance,
the expressive architecture of the seventeenth century, the debilitated

painting of the Jesuit school, the operatic music which has penetrated into High Mass."[152]

In the Roman Catholic Church, there is a movement which seeks to restore the choir to the position it originally occupied, where it belongs by nature, in the choir of the church, where the Holy Sacrament is celebrated. The dominant idea is that music in worship should be neither a decoration nor a spiritual concert, but that it is, rather, an essential component of the worship and belongs with the priestly bestowal of grace. In ancient times, therefore, the singers were placed directly before the altar and, like the acolytes, took part in the liturgical drama. The displacement of the choir to an organ gallery located at the other end of the church not only destroys the liturgical unity, but makes of the music an hors d'oeuvre, an attraction, removes it from the cult and places it in the world.[282, 283] In the movement, slowly gaining ground in Holland, in favor of a Reformed Catholic church music, the same problem immediately appears: does not the choir belong at the place of the cult, and are not the singers themselves ministers? All this is an attempt to become free of the transitional structure.

PASSION AND ORATORIO   The form of the Passion offers an extraordinarily instructive example of a work of religious art in the transitional structure. Half worship, half concert, it wanders homelessly to and fro between church and concert hall, and is nowhere quite at home. Here music has broken through the ancient form of the ecclesiastical liturgy, the *sacer ludus*. It has grown separate from it. In spite of this, we can understand the Passion better from the point of view of the liturgy than from that of autonomous music, or music only externally connected with the Church. This is true, above all, for Bach's Passions, especially for the *St. Matthew Passion*. It has been said to have strongly dramatic character, and that is true. The dominant role played by the text has been pointed out, and that is true, too. It has been suggested that here—as in many other places—Bach, the epic poet and painter, is speaking, and that the primary aim is to visualize the words musically. That, too, is true. But these three points of view are only true if we reserve a final judgment by liturgical norms. Only within this framework can they be given their relative due.[284, 285]

The *St. Matthew Passion*, in outward form, is a typical work of the transitional structure, a liturgical monstrosity and an aesthetic impossibility; but in inner form it is an incomparable liturgical masterpiece.

By its objectivity, the Passion is a sacral drama (cf. page 238) to which the chorales make a special contribution. The *St. Matthew Passion* has justly been spoken of as a mighty organ chorale. The chorales are more than mere pauses; they provide the actual structure of the work. Therefore, it is a fatal misunderstanding to have them performed too dramatically and emotionally, without accompaniment. In the chorales the congregation speaks, the whole speaks; they achieve the result that, in spite of the hybrid form which grafts Italian aria to popular hymn, in spite of the breaking up of controlled recitative by free declamation, in spite of the heavy drama of the mob choruses, the Passion has remained a work of primitive social art.[286]

But in external form the Passion belongs to the transitional structure which has outgrown liturgical form. Quite apart from the form of the Passion, the wonderful blossoming of German church music in the eighteenth century means a disadvantage for the liturgy. The classic form of worship could no longer comprehend the new musical wealth. The chorale was almost suppressed by the rank growth of polyphonic figuration. A Passion, and also a church cantata, as components of worship, are just as senselessly baroque as the altar shrines which in the same period almost became churches within churches.[284]

At the opposite pole of the transitional structure, close to the boundary of autonomous art, lies the oratorio. Of equally sacred origin as the Passion, developed from the medieval mysteries and moralities, its development does not differ from that of opera. Handel, the great perfecter of this form, writes heroic baroque music (to use a phrase of Paul Bekker's), at the base of which often lies a spiritual subject. This of course is not to say that Handel never wrote religious music: *The Messiah* proves the contrary. But there was no longer an inner continuity between the structure of his music and the expression of the holy. *Israel in Egypt* is a glorious choral opera, which could have some other subject as its theme. Generally speaking, music, like the pictorial arts, is stamped as spiritual only by its subject. The culture is not well enough saturated with religious elements that this often happens.

Already the appearance of polyphony was a blow against the objectivity which liturgical music demands. Homophony is the ideal and the norm of the oldest Christian music. The *una voce dicentes* of the Eucharistic preface very early gave evidence of that unity of belief which alone enabled man to sing the Trisagion.

In Paradise, of course, the fullness of polyphonic music is necessary:

> The various voices sing sweet tunes to hear,
>   The various stages also of our lives
> Bring forth a hamony from every sphere.[30, 133, 287]

WORDS AND MUSIC   The illusion of Christian vocal groups, that a sacred text makes a piece of music "religious," dominates the transitional structure no more than does autonomous music. Music is a servant, now of the Church, now of the world; it serves the dance and the theater, meanwhile quietly developing its own life, which lies hidden behind all kinds of forms.[274] Our entire modern music grew out of dance music and church music. Not only Handel, but also Bach, used the same music impartially for "spiritual" and "secular" texts. To us a chorale tune seems particularly religious. And indeed it does derive from the unity of life. It is therefore a piece of social art, just like the folk song, and so is religious to that extent. But it is not "spiritual." The well-known, common chorale form originated with the French troubadours, and was used by the German Meistersinger for all possible purposes, but above all for the service of love. "Two *Stollen* and an *Abgesang*," as David, in *Die Meistersinger*, instructs the knight Walter, who loves to sing; that is the form which long characterizes the secular folk song. It is at first a brutal shock to us to discover that the wonderful Passion melody, which has become dear to our hearts through Bach's *St. Matthew Passion*, and which we can only think of in connection with the words of Paul Gerhardt—"O sacred head, sore wounded"—that this glorious melody was not only first used by Hans Leo Hassler for another hymn (that is not too bad, for "How deeply I am yearning" is, if not a Passion hymn, at least a mourning hymn), but originally belonged to a *Minnelied*: "My heart is all confusion, this did a maiden sweet."• [288, 289] And it gives us pause when we discover that the melody fits the delicate folk song perfectly. At first it is not pleasant to discover that the scarcely less famous Passion chorale, "*Ich bin's, ich sollte büssen*," a verse from Paul Gerhardt's hymn, "*O Welt, sieh hier dein Leben*," was first an evening hymn, "*Nun ruhen alle Wälder*," and before that, a soldiers' song of leave-taking, "*Innsprück, ich muss dich lassen*." We must accustom ourselves to the fact that our psalm tune number sixty-five was actually a very secular love song: "*Petite camusette, à la morte m'avez mis*"; that the tune for Psalm one hundred originally had the words "*Quand Bourbon vit Marseille*"; and that many of our most beautful psalm tunes were originally dance tunes: for example, one twenty-two and one twenty-six, which are actually comprehensible only when the dance rhythm is restored. It is no different with other forms of hymns. Luther composed his famous Christmas hymn, "From Heaven High I Come to You," to

• The reverse is also true: the melodies of the sequences were widely used in the early Middle Ages for secular texts.

an old riddle in verse, "From foreign lands I come to you." The same development holds true for the hymn tunes which derived from Gregorian chant. Josquin Deprès, Obrecht, and Palestrina wrote Masses on secular themes: for example, on the theme of "*L'homme armé*"; others used the song which is still sung today, "*Sur le pont d'Avignon.*" • 97, 291

We must accustom ourselves to the fact that Handel's chorus, "For unto us a child is born," was first written with a secular text: "*Modi voi non vo fidamit*"; the splendid spiritual cradle song from Bach's *Christmas Oratorio,* "*Schlafe, mein Liebster,*" was originally a song by which lust tried to tempt the young Hercules.

But all this only serves to prove that the transitional structure still retains many elements of the structure of unified life. In addition, it proves how fruitless are all attempts to make music religious by external means. "My heart is all confusion" is not only a beautiful melody, but also one which, through the devotion and reverence it expresses, awakens the consciousness of the wholly other; of what is perfect. The inner communion of this melody with the words of Paul Gerhardt created a new work of art, but these words did not make the melody religious: it already was. Bach's cradle song is a masterpiece of gentle love. Out of the enticing swell of the song of lust, Bach made a glorious cradle song by darkening the tone. But it did not become religious music by being related to Jesus; it was not religious and it still is not.

REFRAIN   This second structure contains still other remnants of the first, remnants which belong to the unity of life, which bear witness to the magical nature of that unity. No small portion of musical forms has its origin in a distant, magical past. The refrain, which we know so well, is a primeval means of evoking the deity. The Greeks had the paean and the *euoi* of the Dionysus cult. The repetition of a particular exclamation gives force to an incantation. The Psalms provide many examples, and the force of repeated "Hallelujah" continues to live today in Methodist circles. The refrain may have a nonsense text (who knows exactly what "Hallelujah" means?), if only the chorus can join in strongly and "confirm" the words of the leader. "*Falderalderiere,*" "*juchheisassa,*" "*lon la lire,*" and many others fulfill this function. Jules Combarieu quotes a little song from the *langue d'oc* with a completely senseless refrain: "*La rousse à une fille, le pot, l'écuelle, la coquille—la rousse*

• The melodies of the synagogue, too, are mostly parodies of profane tunes, while already the musical directions for the Psalms point to similar appropriation.

à une fille, belle comme le jour."[291] We all know this sort of refrain, and know how suggestive its effect can be when it is used by a great artist.

I think of Shakespeare's songs in the dramas:

> Then hey-ho, the holly,
> This life is most jolly.

Or Rossetti's *Sister Helen*:

> O Mother, Mary Mother,
> Three days to-day, between Hell and Heaven!

The English especially have used the refrain again and again in their vocal music, from the hymn to the music-hall comedy. The refrain binds, arrests, holds fast in one single, magical, monotonous grasp all the particularities of life, which seem almost to disintegrate.

DA CAPO   Repetition, as a musical form, is a remnant of the magical structure. Combarieu has said what is most important about it. In all musical forms such as canon, fugue, dance, folk song and chorale, sonata, symphony, and liturgy, repetition plays a role.

> The ancients had an especial predilection for it; our contemporaries free themselves from it, but no one escapes it. Music which contains, like a lawyer's summation or the lecture of an academician, only a series of new formulas would be perfectly possible, but it would so go against what we are accustomed to that it would seem unintelligible to us."

Since ancient times man repeats his incantations. The Egyptian pronounces his formulas four times, each time facing a different point of the compass. Combarieu reminds us of the *ter dico, ter incanto* (thrice spoken, thrice sung). He points out liturgical repetition, the form of the Kyrie: *Kyrie eleison—Christe eleison—Kyrie eleison* which is then itself thrice repeated; and he demonstrates how this ABA schema remains usual in the most varied forms of vocal and instrumental music. The *da capo* form belongs to the basic forms of all music.[76]

Repetition is just as natural as song itself. We modern, intellectual men have become accustomed to repeating ourselves as little as possible. But a child stanchly repeats the same senseless verses he has composed himself, and the uneducated man keeps saying the same thing over and over in conversation. In this respect, too, we lead an artificial life, viewing our utterances as academic arguments, which must contain what we have to say as logically and simply as possible. Liturgy, music, and poetry in our lives are like the forms of expression of an old Adam who has been theorized almost out of existence; but like the old Adam, they still possess a really powerful life. For as soon as our spirit is strongly moved, we, too, repeat to the point of triviality. A man who has been beaten is capable only of repetition, through which he proclaims his defeat: "Dead! Lost!" And we feel, when we really shout "Hurrah!" with all our heart, that we have to repeat it at least three times.

IMITATION   It is possible that imitation, too, reaches back with its roots into a magical past, that its locus is found in the magical continuity of meaning. Onomatopoeia is surely primeval; and Siegfried, who imitates the bird, belongs to the type of the imitative musical man. Combarieu furnishes examples from Mexico, where imitation has magical significance: to imitate rain means to conjure up rain. In the transitional structure, the subjugation of life by imitative sound becomes artistic beauty of sound, such as we find, above all, in Bach.[280]

THE DECLINE OF CHURCH MUSIC   As we have already seen, the concept of church music itself belongs to the transitional structure. By intention it binds holiness and beauty to one another only externally, and receives signficance only through a process of becoming internal. The more sacral music becomes "church music," the more it loses its aesthetic and religious significance. Therefore, in our day, when life has been broken up, church music as a peculiar style and structure has almost died out. The good church music which is heard at worship or on other occasions is ancient. What is composed today has, sad to say, little significance.

Bach and Beethoven wrote Masses which were useless for worship, and just because at the same time they created truly religious music, the hybrid nature of that form is all the more clear to us: outwardly sacred; inwardly, already fully autonomous.[292]

MUSIC AND RELIGION   In the future, music will bring the holy to expression only as an autonomous, sovereign art. Servility is of no use either to it or to its masters; self-evident unity is gone forever. Corresponding to the external unity of the transitional structure, we shall again find religious music, in respect to its magical constitution, in the most varied sorts of music: in "church music" and in the dance; in opera and in the sonata. But we shall no longer find it automatically. We must search for it. Luckily, we have lately begun to do so once again. The result is, first of all, a rejuvenation of church music, even in Holland and the local Reformed churches. But if it is to achieve a new flowering, our ecclesiastical consciousness must become more inward and stronger, and national consciousness must be renewed within the Roman Catholic Church.[293] For, in the history of church music, new life always unfolds when a strong awareness of being called by God and being bound to him is combined with the determination to go out into the world and praise God. For then the folk song entered the Church, then the world seemingly conquered the altar; in reality the altar conquered the world. Then songs resounded, those "new songs" which ascended to God's throne when he had given them to us in his grace.[97]

Perhaps we stand on the eve of a general reaction against the idea that music must be treated as though it were meant only for connoisseurs in the concert hall and, according to which, paintings are dealt with as though they had to be preserved in a museum. It is possible that we shall once more achieve a healthy harmony of the arts. We have experienced the process of degeneration, in the course of which the song, which in ancient times was simultaneously poem, music, and dance, became printed verse and "absolute" music.[33] Possibly we are now witnesses to the first beginnings of a new turning, not in the romantic and pompous sense of an "art of the future," but in the simple manner of the folk dance, folk song, and hymn.

3   DISCORD

NO CONFLICT?   In regard to music, one might wonder whether even to speak of a conflict. With the possible exception of architecture, music, of all the arts, stands the closest to religion. Music continually places itself at the service of religion: it seems as though the old forms of Mass and Requiem allow themselves to be filled infinitely with new musical content. On the other hand, there is in religion no serious opposition to, and no open conflict with, music. Almost all worship uses music. Of course, there are often arguments as to the nature of the music. In the Roman Church, for example, it is the quarrel of strict liturgical music against a popular musical taste which loves kettledrums and brass in the church and sings the *Tantum Ergo* to the tune of an Austrian folk song. On the Reformed side, doubts exist whether music other than the Psalms is suitable for the "proclamation of the word." The tendency dominates to relegate all other music to the plainly less sacred "second feasts," those days on which one may ride the streetcar in even the most orthodox parts of Holland. Still, this does not touch the core of the problem. With few exceptions, Christian and general worship is not easily possible without music.

It develops, then, that religion can no more do without the singing than it can without the word. But this has not covered the entire matter. Music outside of worship might be more dangerous to religion than that within worship. There it is connected with the theater; there it shows itself publicly as what it actually has always been: dance music. Meanwhile, religion seems to have no objection to beautiful sounds per se. Music is praised as the least sensual of the Muses. All things lead to the question whether there is not a particularly strong affinity between music and religion. Before we discuss this question in more detail, we

225

must first discover that a conflict does exist, admittedly not in public where it could express itself in particular cultural forms, but nevertheless a conflict which goes so deep that it usually remains hidden.

MUSIC, NOT TONAL ART   The opposition here comes not from religion outside of music, but from religion within. Having arrived at the greatest height, music finds the air too rarefied and itself superfluous. No art points beyond itself more decidedly than does music. The statement made by the painter Runge, "We must go beyond art; it will be unknown in eternity," is true above all of music. That is not to say that music does not possess eternal value, but rather that, in contrast with eternity, it sees itself as art and is thereby aware of its insufficiency. This results from the fact that in the structure of music, expression of the holy is understood as an essential demand; this cannot be said, for example, of painting.

Ferruccio Busoni has perceived this and expressed it well. Music never reaches its goal, it only arrives at the gate. For it is tonal art, not music. "To the portal, to the gate that separates men from eternity or opens to admit what is already temporally past. On the other side of the gate, music sounds, not tonal art. Perhaps we shall ourselves have to leave the earth before we can perceive it. Only to the wanderer who has learned how to free himself from his earthly shackles does the gate open."[294]

Whoever desires music and not tonal art must keep silent. The means of tonal art, however infinitely rich they may be, desert him. The compass, the tonal value of the instruments, the expressive capacity of the human voice, the forms of musical composition—in short, the entire musical structure—seems to him insufficient. He has heard the harmony of the spheres and cannot find it again. Bach finally arrived in his *Art of the Fugue* at the "dogmatic" fugues; Beethoven at his *Last Quartets* and occasionally at the "boundary of what can be represented by sound."[295] It is a tragedy which adheres especially to tonal art that, at the height of his creation, the composer must confess that he can never say what is essential, that is, the other. In the impatient violence with which Beethoven, at the end of many of his compositions, throws in new final chords, almost unable to find a conclusion, we see not only the exuberant nature of the greatest of musical heroes, but also the gesture of a man who knows that silence is the highest expression, yet who cannot keep silent; as the Greek bacchantes, raving about Dionysus, fall silent at the moment of utmost ecstasy. Music, not tonal art. A whole history of music could be written about this phrase. Music represents the great struggle of reaching the wholly other, which it can never express. The conflict between religion and art, between audible beauty and the holiness which forever withdraws, is here most violent and most painful, precisely because it does not become open, does not assume a socially demonstrable form. Here art becomes aware that it is only art, yet simultaneously yearns for something higher. Later we shall see that the other, the higher, is not only the goal of music, but its precondition.

SILENCE, NEITHER SPEAKING NOR SINGING   Since music thinks thus about itself, it would be surprising if similar thoughts did not occur to religion. Nor, indeed, are they absent, although they have not taken the outward form of musical iconomachy. There is thus an opposition external to music, as well. As Calvinism condemns theater and dance, so Buddhism rejects theater and music. Wherever the will to live must be suppressed, where salvation is sought in destruction, where God represents the great "No," the only appropriate musical expression is the rest. "Over man's entire life the great *fermata* must extend, to bring to silent termination everything which affirms life."[296] In the nullification of the entire world is contained that of music. Where every expression is insufficient, music can hardly find the proper tone to sound the holy.

Thus the conflict between religion and music, although it scarcely shows on the surface, leads to the deepest depths of our problem: both religion and music can demand silence. When the holy girds itself to put beautiful sound to silence, it can be that the latter has already fallen dumb.

ALTERCATIONS   Meanwhile, there have also been many altercations which have not led into the depth. Just as in the case of theater, this is explained partially by the position of music in heathen culture. The flute player, the *tibicen*, anciently performed a sacred function; his playing at the sacrifice supported the epiclesis of God. Thus whoever plays the flute summons the gods, or, in the Christian view, the demons.[133] Chrysostom can declaim: "Where flute players are, there Christ can never be."[133] Because instrumental music has its home in the cultic-ludic complex of ancient culture, music is forbidden to Christians. Whoever plays the *kithara* or a wind instrument must give it up, says the nomocanon of Michael of Damiate, and in the *Canons of Hippolytus* it says: "Whoever performs in the theater, or is a wrestler or foot racer, or a music teacher, or a comedian, or a gladiator, or a priest of idols, none of these may be granted entrance to a holy address until they have been purified of these unclean works. After forty days they may hear the sermon. If they prove themselves worthy, then they are baptized."[133] This explains why instruments were scorned even when music blossomed in the young Christian Church: the Church accepted the heritage of the synagogue, but not of the temple. "In place of the playing of tympani, let the singing of hymns resound," says Gregory of Nazianzus; the *Sibylline Books* (Oracles) of the second century contrast the rejoicing of holy voices, the sweet Psalms, and the dignified hymns of God, to the glittering pomp of the heathen cult.[133] Actually, this avoidance followed a heathen argument, because, in his *Laws*, Plato found pure instrumental music opposed to *logike latreia*, the inner worship of God.[133, 297]

Thus, instruments were excluded from worship for centuries, and even today they are really a foreign element. Both the Gregorian and the Reformed hymns are meant to be sung without any accompaniment. Nor can it be denied that the objectivity, the purity of expression of unaccompanied singing, seems better guaranteed than when the voices are carried along by the flight of instruments. In Reformed worship it was a long time before the decision was taken to admit the organ for the accompaniment of congregational singing. Only thanks to the warm defense of the poet Constantijn Huygens was the organ introduced in the course of the seventeenth century as an accompanying instrument,[298] and even he defends it because he was himself opposed to instruments in general: an organ postlude lessens the effect of the sermon and sets ten madrigals against one Psalm.* Therefore, the organ can better be used to accompany the singing of Psalms.

Still, one could not remain blind to the fact that the always latent conflict between music and religion is not identical with the conflict between voice and instrument. Already the canons of Basel prescribed that the singing at the altar should be not with pleasure but with wisdom, and even then, Psalms exclusively. This anticipated Calvin, who also objected to instrumental accompaniment and restricted the singing to Psalms. Calvin did much for congregational singing and set up superb guidelines for it.[299] But his aversion to all polyphonic music hindered the development of Church music among us just as much as did his restriction to Psalm texts. In this conflict the relationship between word

* That Calvinism was a promoter of the organ is a remarkable argument of the nice little book by A. Bouman, *Orgels in Nederland*.

and sound again plays a part: in polyphony the text becomes incomprehensible. But there is also a danger which will remain as long as there is music, even if it is of the most extreme simplicity. That is the danger of pride and *lascivia animi* during singing, which was also warned against by Augustine, to whom the strict method of chanting prescribed by Athanasius—more like solemn reading than singing—seemed less suspicious than an overly beautiful rendition; and who allowed music in church, much as he himself enjoyed it, only out of consideration for those weaker in spirit. It has seldom been recognized how powerful this danger is, and that it holds true for all human forms of expression, for words as well as music, for the *pronuntians* (to use Augustine's phrase) as well as for the *canens*. Among us this conflict has led not only to the dying out of church music, but also to the shrinking of that music which was left, which *collegia musica* and organ works were able to keep alive only with difficulty.• [300, 301]

• In opposition to music, Zwingli went further. His damning judgment of Gregorian chant, which appears in the Confessio helv. post., witnesses to his ignorance, and is a blot on the Reformation (cf. [245]).

4   INFLUENCES

THE LAST DEFENSE OF EXTERNAL CONTINUITY   In our search for the essential continuity, we must once more protect ourselves against the external continuity which forces itself upon us. Nine-tenths of the "religious works of art" which we know evidence no inner, essential continuity between holiness and beauty, having only a purely external connection, which admittedly can be very refined, violating neither art nor religion, but not proclaiming their unity.

I purposely choose my examples from great art. Bach's *St. Matthew Passion* and Wagner's *Parsifal* are both, in their own way, religious art of the first rank. But it would be false to believe that the organic connection between religion and art, the flowing together of the holy and the beautiful, can be found on every page of the score. On the contrary, we find complete interpenetration of both elements in these works only on a very few pages. The lament of Jesus and the lament of Amfortas for the Grail have religious themes, but these laments are not, thereby, religious in themselves. Instead of being expressions of holiness, they can be expressions of purely human grief. The glorious duet from the Passion, "*So ist mein Jesus nun gefangen,*" is surely one of the most compelling pieces of music ever written. But it could still refer to a theme which is not numinous. The only religious effect lies in the text. On the other hand, the small chorus, "*Wahrlich, dieser ist Gottes Sohn gewesen,*" brings the holy very near to us by the wonderful exaltation of its majestic line. The grieving accents of Amfortas could just as well express grief other than that of lost holiness, perhaps an exalted pang of love or the suffering of a father for his son. But the mighty exclamation of Gurnemanz, "*O Wunden-wundervoller, heiliger Speer,*" and his blessing, "*Gesegnet sei, du Reiner, durch das Reine!*" are clearly numinous. Here horror, shrinking away, is connected with fascination, with painful attraction; here is the ultimate word.

And so we would do well in the future to free ourselves completely from the religious occasion of a work of art. We must dig deep, and Busoni has well recognized that "depth of emotion has its roots in the complete comprehension of every mood, even the most trivial."[294] Even when we know that depth of emotion by no means needs to be religious, the holy begins to appear in the striving for the absolute. Busoni's remark that "In the so-called 'Champagne Song' from *Don Giovanni*, there is more 'depth' than in many a funeral march or nocturne," we can so interpret that in many a seemingly nonreligious work such as Mozart's "Champagne Song," there is more depth, more awareness of the holy, than in many an oratorio or hymn. When we come down to fundamentals, the "last word" about champagne is nearer to the word of God than is an empty word about God. The somewhat crude deistic frenzy in the choral finale of Beethoven's Ninth is religious music, while the glorious adagio which immediately precedes it, which can be played with great effect in any church after the sermon, admits of doubt. •[302]

THE SUBLIME   Music attains sublimity by slowness of tempo. But this is not the only means, nor does it offer a guarantee for true sublimity, as many "religious" composers seem to think. To slow tempo belongs majestic reserve, chaste restraint. And even this remains nothing unless everything points to an emotion which admits no more violent expression. Here Palestrina is probably the greatest example. We have already mentioned examples from Wagner's *Parsifal* and Bach's *St. Matthew Passion*.

If we ask whence it comes that the massive, the sublime, often moves us religiously, indeed seems to be an expression of the holy, we find that this lies in its overpowering character. We cannot escape it; we find ourselves in the presence of the wholly other. It cannot be better expressed than in the words of a student who was the subject of a psychological experiment conducted by Alfred Römer. The student reproduced the impression which listening to music awoke in him: "We are on a ship. The waves are smashing violently against the sides of the ship. We feel different."[251]

•Baensch represents the finale as a victory over the despair of the first, the gaiety of the second, and the delicacy of the third movements, a victory which is expressed by the appearance and disappearance of the principal themes of the first three movements in the introduction to the fourth.

This overpowering can be fascinating or awe-inspiring. It can enchant, captivate, illuminate, remove a burden from the heart. It can also oppress, bring fear, cause horror and terror. Wherever the accent may lie, according to our working principle, no work of art can be an expression of the holy unless it contains both elements. It may be that terror dominates, but fascination must not be absent. It may also be that we are so enchanted that we revel in bliss; but if every tremor is lacking, it is a false bliss, even if we may be confronted with real beauty.

LIGHT　　Music, too, knows the divine light. Romanticism played with sounds which were visible and colorful. It thereby posed a psychological problem which remains acute.

> Horch, es klagt die Flöte wieder
> Und die kühlen Brunnen rauschen.
> Golden wehn die Töne nieder—
> Stille, stille, lass uns lauschen.
>
> Holdes Bitten, mild Verlangen,
> Wie es süss zum Herzen spricht!
> Durch die Nacht, die mich umfangen,
> Blickt zu mir der Töne Licht.
>
> Hark, the mournful flute is sounding,
> Cool fountains softly sifting,
> Golden sounds come downward drifting—
> Quiet, hear the song abounding.
>
> Blessed asking, gentle yearning,
> To the heart it sweetly calls;
> Through the night about me turning
> The light of sound my sight enthralls.[303]

Here we are involved with more than a psychological game or even a psychological problem. The light of golden tones comes into the darkness; all seems gentle enchantment; only night brings a brief tremor of fear.

Bruckner's Third Symphony is a glorious example of the breaking through of sounds in divine light. Hermann Hesse speaks in a novel[304] of another musical light, which is not romantic and emotional, and therefore perhaps expresses the holy even better: "I reflected, and there came to me pieces from Mozart's *Cassations,* from Bach's *Well-Tempered*

Clavier; and everywhere in this music that cool, starry brilliance seemed to shine, that ethereal clarity to whirl. Yes, that was it, this music was like time which had become frozen to space; above it there hovered endlessly a superhuman gaiety, an eternal divine laughter." In the music of Mozart's operas, above all in the ensembles, is contained something of this divine levity, this unearthly gaiety which is like the whispered laughter of stars, sublime in spite of its exuberance. Here, of course, we are far removed from all "religious" objects and every standard religious style. But Don Giovanni's Champagne aria, the great ensemble with the minuet from the same opera, Cherubino's "*Voi che sapete*," and the finale in the fourth act from *Figaro*, the trio of three boys and the overture to *The Magic Flute*, are religious music in the noblest sense. Here we find what is absolute, what is perfect, through which the young love of Cherubino, the drunkenness of Don Giovanni, in themselves become absolute, something which does not exist here on earth. Here we have reached an immense separation from everything that is earthly. Ever and again this divine gaiety is interrupted briefly, very briefly, by a sound of a different sort (the chords of the adagio in the overture to *The Magic Flute*), which briefly causes us to shudder, but only briefly, just enough to let us feel not only enchantment, but also fear. It is actually not necessary. For pure, complete enchantment is seldom heard and is no longer fascinating. "The stars, they are not longed for, they are enjoyed in their glory."

SUSPENSION   Just as in the dance, ecstasy is one of the means of expressing the other, reaching a new reality. Dionysus was not only the originator of the dance, but also of music. "Music, dance, prophecy, these three perfections, appeared as the glories of the original world renewed, as blessed miracles, out of the Dionysiac madness."[88] From the walls of the Villa Item in Pompeii, the ecstatic face of a singing silenus looks upon us, incarnation of ecstatic music.[305]

Music, freeing itself from the world, rises up to heaven in silent or occasionally loud ecstasy. When we are considering the expression of heavenly immateriality, we think first of Gothic architecture. But music, too, contributes its part: for example, the aria from Bach's *St. Matthew Passion*, "*Aus Liebe will mein Heiland sterben*," in which two oboes without the usual foundation of basso continuo accompany the flute and soprano voice. Here heavenly love emerges freely. [284]

The most beautiful example from the present day is the Negro spiritual. In these songs of an oppressed and faithful people there is perceptible something of that ectasy which inspired the Hebrew Psalms and the early Christian pneumatic hymns.[97] This is clear to anyone who has heard them sung by Robeson or by Marian Anderson. Still, that is a cultured form of singing. It is even clearer to whoever can listen to the song in its original form, which reminds us of the ancient examples of the primitives, Jews and Greeks. There is a leader, accompanied by a chorus, which then sings the refrain each time and improvises in part. Everything sounds less finished than in the production of the great Negro singers. But there is a strong movement of the soul contained there, which flees the earth. The spirituals actually developed from the sermon. Gilbert gives examples of Negro sermons which are sung in a rigid recitative, while the audience occasionally breaks out with melodious, ecstatic cries. Song breaks forth from the sermon. We can only long for a sermon which will so move us that the listeners can no longer control themselves but must shout, cry, and sing.[306]

THE HEAVENLY   The influence of the heavenly, expressed in many works of Richard Wagner, is formed differently. The pilgrim motif in *Tannhäuser*, the Grail motif in *Lohengrin* and in *Parsifal*, the Valhalla motif in *The Ring*, all bring up the image of another world in solemn, unearthly chords, filled with longing. In contrast, Bach, who knows the influence of the heavenly well, but stresses the distance much more greatly, frees the expression from all human longing. The symphony in the *Christmas Oratorio*, for example, has the sparkling melody of the violins with the effect of a glittering, starry sky, in contrast to the pastoral shawms of the shepherds.

A modern example is the Apostles' Creed in *Les Prières* of André Caplet, in which a mighty climax of faith is borne higher and higher, to the countenance of God, and, so to speak, achieves heaven from below. Bach, heavenly to begin with, does without an ascent. Nevertheless, Caplet's piece is very beautiful and devout.

THE TRANSITION   The same is true for sudden, unexpected transition, which we see in music as a surprising modulation, but which we have also seen in architecture in the form of contrast (for example, in the Egyptian Sun Temple). • [307] It is not necessary to take the famous modu-

• It must be stated emphatically that these "influences" by themselves do not express the holy. In certain cases they can provide the means. The same means can also be used on occasion for other purposes. Thus C. Höwler points out that contrast in tempo, pitch, rhythm, and general rest in music can be means of expressing the comic (cf. [307]).

lation to C major in Haydn's *The Creation* at the words "and there was light" numinously; it can be understood artistically, although here the expression is of something of the wonder of creation as a work of God, and not of man. But in Beethoven's Ninth there can be no doubt. I am thinking of the transition in the finale at the words "*Und der Cherub steht vor Gott.*" "*Vor Gott*" is repeated twice, but the second time the key changes, and only then does the word "God" seem to receive its full significance; it is as though the doors of heaven were opened, as though we were truly standing before God, and the music of the angels could reach our ears.

Filled by a completely different consciousness of God, but just as strongly numinous, is the transition in "Siegfried's Rhine Journey" from Wagner's *Götterdämmerung*. The sudden, almost brutal, modulation into another key corresponds to the change of the motif: the nature-earth motif, which expresses life as it slowly grows and unfolds, is transformed without preparation to the *Götterdämmerung* motif, whose falling line proclaims the end of all growth. Here one experiences the divine proximity of the fate of the world, the impersonal power which ranks above gods and men.

A very fine example of the expression of the holy through a change of key is offered by the soprano recitative from the first chorus of the *St. Matthew Passion*, "*Er hat uns allen wohlgetan.*" At the final words, "*Sonst hat mein Jesus nichts getan,*" the key changes to C major, so that the spotlessness of the divine radiates in glorious light. If the soprano has a high, brilliant tone, it seems at this point as though, after the gentle description of Jesus' work of love in the restrained song of the oboes' *da caccia*, we suddenly perceived the dawning day in the midst of death and woe.

Transition can also be occasioned by a sudden, complete change in the character of the music, the tempo, the rhythm, or the expression; for example, in the final aria in Bach's beautiful cantata "*Wachet, betet, seid bereit*" (No. 7). A powerful, majestically moving bass recitative has just pictured the terrors of the day of the Last Judgment. Slowly, hope breaks through and is finally transformed into joy. Then the aria begins, with an incredibly beautiful vocal melody: "*Seligster Erquickungstag.*" But it is suddenly interrupted by a violent presto in the accompaniment, one of the "knocking" themes so loved by Bach: "*Schall, schalle, letzter Schlag, Welt und Himmel geht zu Trümmern.*" The world is being annihilated. The voice, too, begins to rage rhythmically, fearfully sounding the cry for help; the orchestra races on without letup. Finally, the voice sighs, breathless, *"zu Trümmern."* The transition at this moment has a numinous effect. Without a break the vocal melody begins once more from the beginning with an indescribably lovely effect: *"Jesus führet mich zur Stille."* The presto becomes an adagio, the knocking motif a broad, singing harmony, and the fearful agitation is dispelled in the great, endless calm of heavenly bliss. • [292]

Finally, transition through the introduction of a new instrument can also become an expression of the holy. The most beautiful examples of this which I know are the two places in Saint-Saëns' Third Symphony where the organ enters: in the first movement, where an *adagio religioso* follows the agitated beginning, which is later taken up by the violins and transformed into a living prayer; then in the second movement, where the majestic fortissimo chord of the organ follows the Wagnerian ending of the winds, which seems to transport us to another world.

DARKNESS AND SEMIDARKNESS   In music, too, there is chiaroscuro. I point to the beginning of Beethoven's Violin Concerto, the four soft beats of the tympani and the chord which follows them, a mystic semidarkness from which the light of the melody at once arises.

SILENCE AND NEAR SILENCE   What darkness is to architecture and the pictorial arts, silence is to music and verbal art (cf. page 227). "The Lord is in his holy temple; let all the earth keep silence before him." Of course this silence, if it is to express anything, cannot be pure silence. It must begin and end, or, to use the musical term, it must be a rest. Or it must be a semisilence, corresponding to semidarkness. It is not the silence of a man who has never spoken, but the falling silent in the presence of the holy—holding one's breath. For before the wholly other, one stands in silent reverence. Music can indicate this numinous silence, which is like an echo of the "silence in heaven" (Rev. 8:1), by a pause or a rest, as happens in unrivaled fashion at the transition from the third to the fourth movement of Beethoven's Fifth Symphony. After the agitated, somewhat sinister and ghostly movement of the allegro, the motifs fall silent; finally, there remains only a mysteriously whispering drum roll (it is remarkable that just here the "most primitive" instrument is used), then follow broken chords succeeded by the powerful crescendo leading to the eruption of the *allegro maestoso*.

An example from a completely different realm is the recitative from

• Cf. also the mysterious transition at the *"Confiteor unum baptisma"* in Bach's *Mass in B Minor*, adagio: *"Et expecto resurrectionem mortuorium."*

the *St. Matthew Passion*, "*Mein Jesu schweigt zu falschen Lügen stille.*"
Silence is here already suggested by the text, but the music is much more
than a mere illustration of the text: the shrill staccato chords are an expression of unbearable tension before Jesus' death. "What in the music
of today approximate most closely its original nature are the rest and
the *fermata*. The tense silence between two phrases, itself music in this
environment, expresses more than the more definite, but therefore less
flexible, sound is able to do," says Feruccio Busoni.[294] The pause, the
"rest" as we call it by an extension of meaning, is by no means something
negative, but the negative expression of something most positive. It is, in
genuine mystic fashion, a rich poverty, a full emptiness. Camille Mauclair speaks of a sounding silence: "Silence can only be transcribed by
sounds. Certain pauses in Beethoven's symphonies have a radiant character."[308] Musical silence is thus by no means a "rest," but the greatest possible tension. In his sketch for the *alla marcia* of the finale of his Ninth
Symphony, Beethoven writes: "Turkish music—first pianissimo—a few
loud ppmo—a few pauses—then the complete power." About this,
Baensch says: "It remains unclear what 'a few loud ppmo' is supposed
to mean."[302] I venture to suggest that this lack of clarity has the following meaning: the pianissimi speak precisely because of their almost complete inaudibility. A "loud pianissimo" is a paradox, but not nonsense;
the expression indicates perfectly the character of numinous music,
which is to express what is inexpressible. • We find glorious examples of
"loud pianissimi" in the "*Incarnatus*" and "*Crucifixus*" of Bach's *Mass in
B Minor*; in the initial chorus of the *St. Matthew Passion*, at the words
"*auf unsere Schuld*," where the world seems to hold its breath; the choral
recitative in the *Christmas Oratorio*, "*Er ist auf Erden kommen arm*,"
where the soprano voice sings the drawn-out notes of the ancient chorale
to the delicate accompaniment of the oboe, giving rise to an impression
of loneliness, as though representing the kenosis, the self-emptying of
Christ. Here we stand in the immediate presence of utter abandonment,
which discloses itself in miraculous fashion as richest communion. In
many cults we find "holy silence," which is both the highest worship
and deepest communion with God, "sacramental silence."[152, 309] To be
silent is not to be inactive, but is the greatest receptivity and highest ac-

---

• It is also possible that we are going too far behind Beethoven's note, that the "first
pianissimo" refers to the chords for bassoon, contrabassoon, and bass drum, interrupted by long pauses, while "a few loud ppmo" could refer to the repetition of
those chords with the addition of the clarinet; the latter, in actual fact, gives the
music a completely different character.

tivity. We recognize this only when we deliberately keep a common silence in memory of a dead man, or when we turn within ourselves.

THE ENDLESS   In the realm of music, the influence of endlessness is best approached through seemingly endless repetition. Even monotonous repetition, which is like a moving *fermata*, through its apparent poverty attains the riches of suggestions of eternity. Thus the redemption motif at the end of Wagner's great *Nibelungen* trilogy, which seems to transform the wealth of lines and colors into an eternal, no longer audible, melody; • [274] the melodies of the "Liebestod" in *Tristan und Isolde*, which strive for nirvana and silence; the endlessly, monotonously repeated "*ewig, ewig*" at the end of Mahler's "*Lied von der Erde*"— these are examples of an approach to infinity which is probably more common in Asiatic music than in our own.

The "uncanny emptiness of long, drawn-out notes" in Bach, for example, at the words "*ewig, ewigkeit*," has the same effect.[310] There is a good example of the numinous effect of long notes at the word "*patris*" in the *Cum Spiritu Sancto* of Bach's *Mass in B Minor*.

OBJECTIVITY   The most beautiful example of the expression of the holy through objectivity is the way Bach, in the Passions and cantatas, continually sublimates the subjective sufferings and joys of the faithful into a suprapersonal expression of faith.

Every action, every word of Scripture, but also every emotion, every movement, and every burst of anger are immediately reduced by Bach, the great priest, to the "*Credo*" of the congregation. Upon the anguished, human "*Herr, bin ich's?*" follows at once the confiteor: "*Ich bin's, ich sollte büssen.*" We are immediately transported to another atmosphere, as though we were ascending from the rough sea to the firm land. The congregation knows of that guilt which is greater and lies deeper than the individual sin of a disciple; of that great guilt which comprehends the entire world.

Upon "*Gegrüsset seist du, Judenkönig!*" powerfully agitated, follows the salutation of the congregation: "*O Haupt voll Blut und Wunden.*" Upon the dramatic description of the watching of Jesus and the sleeping of his disciples follows the description of the watching of the faithful and the falling asleep of their sins. Thus we could continue our analysis

---

• Cf. Paul Bekker's discussion of the theme of redemption in Wagner and the striving for resolution in romantic-harmonic music generally: all romantic music is music of redemption.

through the whole Passion: everywhere human events, perceptions, and observations are reduced to objectivity; the wealth of images is again and again reduced to a single image of the history of God and man.

This liturgical character is also expressed by small features which are taken over from the *sacer ludus*. The comic chatter of the two witnesses whose words are parodied by the uninterrupted continuo, the crowing of the cock—all this has been reduced from a comic intermezzo to a mere hint, but is still reminiscent of the old spirit of the holy play, in which humor possessed as much ritual power as seriousness. But those are rudiments. As far as the actual structure is concerned, as in the "Choral Fantasia," think of the glorious small choral preludes of Bach, those variously rising and falling, appearing and disappearing, lines which wrap themselves about the one simple melody of the congregational hymn. The rich multiplicity, the dramatic agitation of the Passion narrative always returns again to objective resolution and the simplicity of the chorale. •

The evangelist relates the Passion narrative. A series of events and persons passes before us. The narrative possesses epic fullness and dramatic movement. Still, it is neither epic nor drama, but liturgy, the service of the congregation. We groan with Jesus in the Garden of Gethsemane; we are enraged at the priests; we shrink in terror at the cry of the wild mob which wants to see blood; we are torn back and forth continually between fear and hope, love and hate. Our pent-up emotions find release: the believing soul may watch with its Lord, weep when he is betrayed, plead for mercy when he is scourged. Yet the work does not thereby become a subjective expression of inner feelings; it is neither lyric poetry nor epic nor drama. For the many-sided, powerfully agitated narrative, the delicate language of the tortured soul, torn by grief and love, all rest in the great peace of the faith of the congregation. Everything particular, everything individual, everything human, all grief and all joy, all hate and all suffering, all pleading and all thanksgiving, all despair and all hope, finally end again in the simple, noble witness of the Church, in the objective, calm word of faith. In the mighty final chorus of the first portion, all emotions of the believing soul are expressed by the alto, tenor, and bass, through the glorious symphony of the orchestra, through the monumental choral melody, *"O Mensch, bewein dein Sünde gross"*— that is typical of the entire work.

• Of course, this objectivity could not move us as art if we had pure liturgy before us in the *St. Matthew Passion*. But since it is an autonomous work of art which bursts the external form of the liturgy and only retains its "inner form," within the liturgy it obviously becomes the highest means of expressing the holy through the beautiful.

The greatness of Bach lies in the fact that not only does this liturgical foundation permeate the literary form of the work, but also that the literary form completely coincides with the musical. Just as the multiplicity of events and persons, emotions and thoughts, is constantly simplified to the confession of faith, so also the agitated richness of the recitative (in which a greater "drama" unfolds than in many other dramas all taken together) becomes quieter, and the violent, passionate lyrics of the solo and chorus arias always find their way back to that simple line, that fixed inviolability of the chorale melody.• [284, 285, 292]

A few additional examples: In the *St. John Passion*, the evangelist tells how Pilate answers the protests of the Jews: "*Was ich geschrieben habe, das habe ich geschrieben.*" An answer of perplexity, a weary answer, a human, all-too-human answer. Bach the theologian directly opposes to it the word of faith in the chorale: "*In meines Herzens Grunde, dein Nam und Kreuz allein, funkelt all Zeit und Stunde, drauf kann ich fröhlich sein.*" Human perplexity becomes the courage of faith; what man has written becomes what God has written in the hearts of the faithful; the fate of man has become salvation given by God.

Jesus prays in Gethsemane. The tenor of the first chorus describes his sufferings in emotional accents, distorted by grief. He is accompanied by flutes and oboes, *da caccia*, shrill, almost unbearably sad, ever and again soaring upward as in a wail of grief. In the depths throbs the staccato bass of the continuo, like the feverish pulse of the sufferer, a musical description of grief such as was never created with more genius and unbearable intensity, so human, all too human. But then we hear, softly and gravely, played by the solo violins, supported by the second chorus:

> *Was ist die Ursach aller solcher Plagen?*
> *Ach, meine Sünden haben Dich geschlagen!*
> *Ich, ach Herr Jesu, habe dies verschuldet,*
> > *Was Du erduldet!*

> Who was the guilty? Who brought this upon thee?
> Alas, my treason, Jesus, hath undone thee.
> 'Twas I, Lord Jesus, I it was denied thee:
> > I crucified thee.

• This is analogous to the way Verdi uses ecclesiastical recitative in his *Requiem* (in the "*Libera*"). From the midst of all human anguish and sadness, this altar music sounds as the anguish of the Church, which conveys reconciliation. Therefore, Verdi can also close with it. Bach, too, knows how to use ecclesiastical intonation as well as the chorale, as in the Credo of his *Mass in B Minor*.

Both the objectivity of the confiteor of the congregation and the exalted calm of the chorale melody have the effect that we hear differently the lament which follows. Music has passed from an expression of utmost grief to expression of the holy.

For even over the sufferings and doubts of Christ himself in their earthliness is raised the witness of faith. The anguish of Gethsemane finds its sublimation in a mighty hymn: *"Was mein Gott will, das g'scheh allzeit"*; from the human point of view, Jesus, standing silent before Pilate, is addressed presumptuously: *"Befiehl du deine Wege und was dein Herze kränkt, der allertreusten Pflege des, der den Himmel lenkt."* When, after the violent action of the narrative, emotion overpowers us and the pain becomes unbearable, Bach the theologian thinks of the salvation which was granted us in so much suffering, and he has his congregation pray: *"Wen ich einmal soll scheiden, so scheide nicht von mir."*

The cantata *"Wachet auf, ruft uns die Stimme"* is an example of Jesus mysticism inspired by the Song of Solomon. The marriage of Christ and the soul is depicted for us in sumptuous colors, especially in the duets; the whole of the gentle inwardness of eighteenth-century mysticism is contained in a beautiful recitative. But the figured chorale with which the cantata begins surrounds all with the strong cry of faith, *"Wachet auf!"* and the whole awe of the congregation which kneels before God's face in holy darkness. The final chorale, not figured, is the Church's song of praise, in heaven as well as here on earth. And the greatest miracle of this superb composition, the chorale verse in the middle of the work, *"Zion hört den Wächter singen,"* makes the melody rise high and pure as *cantus firmus* above wedding music, which is amazingly reminiscent of a popular holiday tune. Thereby, the physical picture is given solemnity and depth, humanity is glorified, and the language of faith sounds the more nobly and purely.

Although Bach's work is the crown of the union between strict polyphony and expressive Italian monody, he knew how to retain objectivity in a very special way. This is shown by the dynamics of his choruses, which are not actual dynamics, but registration, reinforcement by the so-called *ripieno* (additional) voice.[311] It is shown by the way he succeeded, above all in the Passions, in always subordinating lyric and operatic elements to the reading of the Gospel. A Passion is not an oratorio with solo pieces, but a collection of biblical scenes, conveyed and unified by the contemplations of the believing soul and the chorale of the congregation. It is shown by the way he opposes the spirit of the times, retaining the unabbreviated and unparaphrased word of the Bible.[312, 313]

Thus Johann Sebastian Bach performed the awesome miracle of combining his service to the congregation with his service to art, the liturgical structure of his work with its aesthetic structure. The artist is priest, is himself a theologian. A miracle was developed by him. Here art has become in truth a holy action.

Thus another great composer and priest (Heinrich Schütz) could die with the words: "Thy statutes have been my songs in the house of my pilgrimage" (Ps. 119:54).

5   HARMONY

In the examples we have cited, the holy often breaks forth violently from the beautiful. Not infrequently, very impressive religious music is anything but harmonious, as in the instances of Beethoven's Ninth Symphony, and Bach's *Mass in B Minor*. Violence and struggle join in every chord.

There is also religious music in which the struggle can no longer be felt, in which only a gentle melancholy remains. Peace has been attained, a foretaste of the calm of paradise is received. There is music which reminds us of Michelangelo (Beethoven) and of Rembrandt (Bach); there is also music which reminds us of Fra Angelico.

I am thinking first of Gregorian plain song, the sung prayer which has ascended to God through all centuries and in all churches, and to which Pius X referred as "praying in beauty." The Gregorian melody breathes a peace and a clarity, a calm and a self-possession, which make it comprehensible that the Church (and also "secular" music), having progressed through the dizzying heights and chasms of polyphony and romanticism, always returns once more to the unison of Gregorian plain song. Nor will a revived Reformed Catholic Church music be able to do without it.

But there are also other examples of harmony in the history of music. The most noble and most beautiful is probably found in Mozart. To attain that harmony, one must either remain a child or become a child once more. This is fully and completely true of Mozart. We even discover that toward the end of his life he belonged more and more to the kingdom of children: *The Magic Flute* was his testament, and at the same time the most charming and childish of his works. Henri Ghéon, in his fine book about Mozart, has said such important things about this childlike harmony that I should not like to let the opportunity pass without quoting it: "We have stressed enough that Mozart thought only in music, no matter how clear his exalted destiny was to him; that he by no means imagined he possessed a divine secret different from what is taught to anyone. He did not view himself as a Messiah."[93] Here we find the guilelessness, the unself-consciousness, which Maritain demanded of a holy work of art. "Mozart's essence is not the man himself, but this gift within him, the charisma of sounds, the angel which dictates the music to him." He knows that he is only an instrument: "If one occupies oneself with Mozart and tries to fathom his soul, one finds at the point where one loved him and bowed before him quite another than him. . . . I believe in the angel in Mozart."

To attain such harmony demands complete dedication, a will only to serve. All artistic pride lies far distant.

He was unable to say, "This is unworthy of my art"; the duty of art is to make everything worthy. He would never have said, "It is unworthy of my art to adjust itself to the commission"; all his works arose in this way. He would never have said, "It is unworthy to let oneself be inspired by the art of others"; this he almost always did. He would not have said, "It is unworthy to follow the dictates of fashion"; it is important to learn how one gains approval. He could not have said that it was "unworthy to serve as entertainer"; he himself was entertained the most.

Thus there can shine forth from a minuet of four notes something of what lies behind all things. The humble service of what is least brings forth what is greatest.

Therefore, Mozart is one of the greatest religious composers, not primarily because of his church music, not even because of his *Requiem*, that glorious miracle, but because of the reverent joy with which he served his art: "A neophyte in the age of the apostles would have been able to sing like Wolfgang. . . . When a child prays, he is superior to us." •

Another composer can scarcely be named beside Mozart, except that other great child produced by Romanticism: Bruckner. With him, everything has more heaviness, but the guilelessness and humility remain the same.

• There is a noteworthy comparison between the famous sonnets from Dante's *La Vita Nuova* and the arias of Mozart, which presumably were written without knowledge of the forerunner: "*Donne ch'avete intelletto d'amore*" became "*Voi che sapetre che cosa amor*," from *Figaro*; "*Amor e'l cor gentil sono una cosa*" became "*Bei Männern, welche Liebe fühlen*," from *The Magic Flute*. Mozart's texts are clumsy, but the full content of Dante's sensitivity lives in the music.

6 THE THEOLOGICAL
AESTHETICS OF MUSIC

MUSIC, THE "TELEPHONE OF THE BEYOND"? Does music here occupy an exceptional position? Does it possess a direct relationship to God, unhindered by any resistance? We have briefly rejected this assertion, but it is too weighty and throws too much light on our problem for us to be able to proceed without treating it at greater length.

Nietzsche, once himself a zealous devotee of the ideas of Schopenhauer, in the footsteps of Wagner, later had only scorn for the musical theories of this philosopher. According to Schopenhauer, the musician is a "mouthpiece of the perseity of things," a "telephone of the beyond," in fact a "ventriloquist of God"; music is the language "from the abyss,"[275, 314] pure metaphysics.

Which of Schopenhauer's ideas earned him such scorn after his initial glory? We can summarize it in a single sentence: "Music is therefore by no means, like the other arts, the image of ideas, but is the image of the will itself."[172] Schopenhauer says the same in scholastic terminology: concepts are the *universalia post rem*, that is, universal abstractions which are formed on the basis of reality; music, on the other hand, conveys *universalia ante rem*, the essence of things, which precedes any giving of form.

Or, to express it idealistically, art is not governed by things in their particularity, nor by the abstract concept of the thing, but only by the idea, conceived platonically as the essence of the thing. Art is the image of the idea. Schopenhauer adds to this idealism his own doctrine of the will: the idea is the objectification of the will, which is the essence of the world. Every art attempts to express these ideas through the representation of specific things. Thus every art objectifies the will only mediately, via the idea. Every art does so, with the exception of music, which makes clear to us why Nietzsche spoke of a "telephone of the beyond," for music omits the ideas: "Since our world is nothing else than the appearance of ideas in their multiplicity, by means of entrance into the *principium individuationis*, so music, since it omits ideas, is completely independent of the phenomenal world, simply ignoring it, could still exist in a certain sense even if the world did not exist, which cannot be said of the other arts." Art needs the world of phenomena, it lives off it. The painter and the poet both need images. Music is a direct objectification of the will, as immediate as the world itself.

Schopenhauer evolved this idealistic view of art, which makes a realistic exception only for music, in very compelling fashion. The base is raw mass, which lies behind all life; above it are the baritones and other voices, which correspond to the world of animals; "finally in the melody, in the high, lyric, unconstrained free will which controls the whole, in uninterrupted, meaningful continuity of a thought which progresses from beginning to end, a principal voice representing the whole, I recognize the highest objectification of the will once more, the rational life and aspiration of man." The return to the keynote brings satisfaction, slowly and sadly, or quickly and gaily.

This parallelism between our world and the world of music has nothing to do with individual phenomena. Music can never express a specific joy or a specific grief, always just "joy, sorrow, grief, horror, jubilation, happiness, peace per se, to a certain extent *in abstracto*, their essence without any accidents." Music expresses only the quintessence of life, never its accidents. Therefore, program music, onomatopoeia, is evil, as Schopenhauer demonstrates to us with Haydn's *Seasons*. Of course, music can unite with words, with an action; yet even then it no longer expresses the action or the words themselves, but something which goes much deeper: "the most secret meaning of the same." Thus the world could be called materialized music just as well as materialized will. Music needs no content, because it is itself a world. The text of a song, the action of an opera, "are never bound to it by absolute necessity, nor do they correspond to it; they stand to it in the relationship of an arbitrary example to a general concept. They represent in the particularity of reality that which music expresses in the generality of pure form." Music expresses the inner essence, the perseity of the world. From it sounds the will, and this will is a suffering, partially terrible, partially miserable. As imagination, the world becomes bearable and consoling. In music we have a repetition of the world which is more than consoling: it is redemptive.

The work of art attempts to show the world as it essentially is; tries to drive away the fog of accidents. Only music, by way of contrast, for example, to architecture, succeeds completely.*

I am not able to escape easily the attraction of this metaphysics of music, especially not when I consider how what is constructive and arbitrary in Schopenhauer's thoughts took on living form in the passionate words of Nietzsche and the mighty music of Richard Wagner. Nietzsche did not always jest about "God's ventriloquist." The wonderful little book, *The Birth of Tragedy from the Spirit of Music*, stands completely under the sign of a metaphysics of music. Apollo and Dionysus there are symbols of the *principium individuationis*, and liberation in the essentiality of things:

> Apollo stands before me as the transfiguring genius of the *principium individuationis*, through whom alone redemption can really be achieved in the world of appearance; while in the mystic shout of joy of Dionysus, the spell of individuation is broken and the way lies open to the mothers of being, to the inmost core of things.

The "mothers of being" (*Die Mütter! Mütter, 's klingt so wunderlich,*"—The mothers! Mothers! How singular it sounds, says Faust) are the matrices, the archetypes of things; not abstractions, but yet universals, from which the individual forms of this world take shape. But they also are the ground swell of this world, the mighty movement of the will, which, painfully and nobly in this world of beautiful appearance, receives sound solely in music. "Madness, will, misery," those are the mothers of being.[142]

Even more powerfully, more compellingly, the metaphysics of music speaks to us through the work of Wagner. Song arises from the "morning dream," the state between the waking of day with its clear apprehension of contours, and the undivided, blessed, unconscious life of night. Song interprets the dream, it is a *Morgentraumdeutweise* (way of interpreting the morning dream) and, while it sounds in the appearance of things, the will sings nobly and sadly in the bass, which "renounces." If ever a theory of music was justified by its living form, it is that of Schopenhauer through the work of Wagner, above all through *Die*

---

* Within music, too, there are stages, from the bass to the descant. Schopenhauer's doctrine was given a beautiful form in Herman Gorter's *Mei* (see p. 140): Balder's song and Balder's words directed to Mei; see P. N. van Eyck's introduction to the edition of Mij. van Ned. Lett.

Meistersinger.[315] While the manifold forms of life pass in review before us, while Eva loves and Walter declaims, the apprentices beat each other and Beckmesser intrigues, again and again sounds from the deepest depth that wonderful phrase which is called the "renunciation motif," the will which destroys itself, which is the origin of all the superficial activity, which in its own right, in agreement with Schopenhauer, is nothing more than illumination, the example of its noble subterranean return to itself. On the stage of the world reigns madness. The great "thrashing scene" from *Meistersinger* is not only the last round and culmination of that endless series of fights and beatings which runs through drama from tragedy to the Punch and Judy show; it is also the eternally true expression of the madness which surrounds our life. And the love which follows the battle, as it also preceded it, is likewise madness, "madness everywhere." But where everything tells lies, music speaks the truth, that deeper truth which comes from another world. Music is a direct revelation of the secret of the world.[316]

MUSIC WHICH LEADS TO THE DEPTHS   Beyond doubt, the trinity of Schopenhauer-Nietzsche-Wagner laid hold of something important. Music dramatically raises us above the accidental and lets us differentiate between essence and appearance. We saw that *Fidelio* does not tell us of the imprisonment of Florestan, but of the imprisonment of every man; not of liberation from the power of Pizarro, but of that liberation in its broadest and deepest sense, which we call redemption. We found the religious character of music precisely in its dramatic movement, its conveying of the elementary, the "total"; and we experience it from a distance, which makes us perceive it as the wholly other. This is true first of all for dramatic music in the strict sense. While everyone on stage is deceiving everyone else, the orchestra speaks the truth. Grétry praises the instruments which delightfully betray a girl even as she denies her love.[317] Wagner made disclosure through the orchestra into a system. Alberich, in his hate, suspects Wotan of the worst despotism. But the orchestra knows better, and the departure motif hints at the melancholy thoughts of a man who goes through the world as a wanderer. Hans Sachs, with his unrestrained, bourgeois, happy shoemaker song, angers the town clerk Beckmesser. But right through it, oboes, clarinets, horns, and bassoons play "very expressively" the renunciation motif which discloses the noble soul of the poet-shoemaker. He, like Wotan, not only looks on and renounces, but also attempts, "as madness is well able to guide, to perform a noble work."

". . . the mighty orchestra . . . conveys all the motifs of the action battles and the world-will of Schopenhauer's philosophy, struggling for redemption," says Nietzsche. Ernst Theodor Hoffmann, uninfluenced by Schopenhauer and Wagner, has the same idea when he discovers, in his enthusiastic study of Mozart, that it is as though "all the characters could not speak otherwise than with the powerful accents of music, as though the realm of miracle were opening. . . ."[318]

But it is no less true for all other music which possesses dramatic movement. Paul Bekker shows us how Beethoven progresses from program music to purely instrumental music, seldom suggesting the experiences which gave rise to his creation. "What was important to him could not be forced into the traditional paths of external events. Only the souls of the events find sonorous expression."[295] Here is the path which leads in a direction completely opposite to true dramatic art; but both paths reach the same goal. We can also express it with the words of Jean Paul, who cites Schleiermacher's *Karoline*: "Music never weeps or laughs over individual events, but always only over life itself."[319]

By understanding the nature of music in this way, we turn aside both from a metaphysics, which would dissolve it in a universal idea that pretends to be true reality, and also from a purely formal aesthetics which desires no content. Since music, no more than the other arts, is likeness, imitation, and a description of reality, it may be said that, unlike science, the reality would be there even if the music did not exist. Neither music nor the other arts are like science, which loses its meaning as soon as it turns aside from its object. In science I could never speak about Napoleon if he had not existed. In art, on the contrary, I can very easily do so; in fact, in art I never speak "about" Napoleon. The poet who set out to dedicate an epic to the hero would no more speak "about" him than did Beethoven in his *Eroica*; both create a world, a form. Precisely speaking, the historic person of Napoleon is indifferent. Even the form of a "fictional" person is "fictional" in a sense other than that in which we commonly understand the term. For a fictional person is never that, because he could not be "real"; on the contrary, and rightly so, a work of art is judged according to the "trueness to life" of its figures. Figures must be created, not only in painting and poetry, but also in music, even if their forms are of a completely different sort than those of the pictorial arts. But the important point is that art never took those forms from "reality." Always and everywhere, in music as well as in the other arts, they constitute a new reality, a new creation. That is the truth behind the proud phrase of Schopenhauer that music (we would say *art*) would exist "even if the world did not exist at all." It is not that the world exists and art is an expression of it, but that art exists, "*fiat ars, pereat mundus.*"

It goes without saying that art is a world which has reality. Music, with its mathematical basis, might lead to the thought that it is not, for mathesis is the science of unreality, of bare validity. But ultimately, architecture and the pictorial arts also have a geometrical basis. That art is more than a relationship expressible in numbers can hardly be doubted. It is, rather, that we do not find the essence of art in this world, but the essence of art coinciding with the essence of this world at a point which is hidden from our view. "Art does not tell us of life, but it speaks to us of that higher life of which life, too, itself tells us something. This brings us again to religion."

This was already recognized in ancient China, where music was put in direct connection with the Tao, that hidden power behind all of life: "Therein was expressed a hidden will, something supernatural. It was of the greatest importance to understand this secret regularity and to observe it. The deep impression which music made upon the mind and heart, in spite of all simplicity, was connected with this hidden power. The sad, the gay, the melancholy, the unrestrained, the sensual character of many melodies was viewed as the expression of the most important powers which rule and guide human life. From thence there flowed a very important stream of life into the Tao of the state, filled with meaning, so that there was a close connection between the music that was performed in a state and the destiny of that state."[320]

Thus the Japanese music of the Tokugawa period was built up on five notes, because there are five planets and five elements.[91] It is universally known that similar observations were taken up in the school of Pythagoras. As Plutarch states, the ancient philosophers of the school of Pythagoras and Plato were of the opinion that "the tempo of what exists and the movement of the stars does not arise and continue without music, for everything is prepared by God in harmony, so they say." Conversely, music appears again and again as an expression of the movement of God and the world, for example in the beautiful "*Et incarnatus est*" from Bach's *Mass in B Minor:* "The violins develop successive themes in six-eight time, which rise over the words, roaring like the beating of the wings of the Holy Dove: *de spiritu sancto. . . .* These syncopated figures, which descend from the heights of heaven without cease, like falls of identical notes, are like a musical expression of the desire of centuries, which Isaiah put into words: 'Shower, O heavens, from above, and let the skies rain down righteousness' " (Is. 45:8).[152]

But it seems as though, confused by the many possibilities, we have more than ever lost the right way. Is music, is art, an expression of the holy? Or is it more than mere expression, is it the movement of the holy itself? Or is it less, only an amusing game of lines, colors, and sounds? We shall once more test all the possibilities conscientiously, first in regard to music. A suitable guide is offered by the introduction with which Felix Gatz precedes his collection of musical-aesthetic literature.[321]

First there is the possibility that music reproduces particular content and is simple imitation of reality. It can also reproduce sensations, such as joy, grief, and love. Or more subtly still, the mere essence of those emotions, the essence of joy or grief in general. Thus we found it in Schopenhauer. Apparently, but only apparently, the opposite is asserted by that interpretation which says music has only formal meaning and actually expresses nothing. We experience it only as though it expressed something; and we hear it as though it spoke to us of joy and sorrow (Ambrose). We need both aspects of music: it must tell us something, that is, speak of something nonmusical, something which has no sound. Up to now our entire treatment has been opposed to this conception, not only in regard to music, but in all the arts.

Then secondly, we have what Gatz calls "incarnational aesthetics." Here we are no longer concerned with an opposition between form and content, but with the opposition between appearance and essence.

Music is the appearance of the essence of the world, embodiment of the ground of being, the will, in Schopenhauer. This incarnational aesthetics is no longer idealistic, but sacramental. Music is a revelation of the nature of things.

Finally, there are the theories of autonomy. These exclude the possibility of music's having anything to do with something nonmusical, even if this were the grounds of being itself. As an example of this conception, Gatz justifiably chooses Edward Hanslick, the famous critic and enemy of Wagner. Hanslick, in turn, cites the beautiful poem of Emanuel Geibel:

> *Warum glückt es dir nie, Musik mit Worten zu schildern?*
> *Weil sie, ein rein Element, Bild und Gedanken verschmäht.*
> *Selbst das Gefühl ist nur wie ein sanft durchschimmernder*
>   *Flussgrund,*
> *Drauf ihr klingender Strom schwellend und sinkend entrollt.*

Why do you never succeed in picturing music with words?
Because, a pure element, it despises image and thought.
Feeling itself is but like a river bed, visible dimly,
Upon which its resonant stream, swelling and sinking,
    unrolls.[322]

The beauty of a piece of music is "specifically musical." The connection between the composition and the emotions which it arouses is
not causal: the same music has different effects upon different national-
ities, temperaments, age groups.[322] Music can only reproduce the
dynamics of emotions, their motion.[322] The different keys by no means
always have the same significance; minor is not always sad, nor does
"white" always mean innocence, nor A-flat major always mean fanciful.
What "emotions" are we to find in Bach's *Well-Tempered Clavier*, or in
the popular overture themes of Auber, Donizetti, Flotow?[322] "Connection with poetry extends the power of music, but not its boundaries";
Gluck's famous *"Che faro"* has brought tears to the eyes of innumerable
people, but to its melody, as well as:

> *J'ai perdu mon Eurydice,*
> *Rien n'égale mon malheur,*
> [I have lost my Eurydice,
> I can no longer be gay],

one can also sing:

> *J'ai trouvé mon Eurydice,*
> *Rien n'égale mon bonheur.*• [322]
> [I have found my Eurydice,
> I can no longer be sad.]

Of course, music cannot reproduce religious content when the
spiritual and secular texts have been proved interchangeable for the
same melody.[322] Not even nature can be reproduced musically. Any
material serves the composer only as an inspiration. If the title were not
known, no one would derive the figure of Egmont from the *Egmont
Overture.* "An inner singing, not an inner emotion, drives the musically
talented man to the invention of a composition."[322]
From all that we have said in the previous chapters, it is clear that

• Cf. also the characteristics of the plain-song modes of the so-called *octaechos*,
which Christianity took over from the Greeks, introducing, however, errors into
the assignments to the various modes, so that the characteristic is now referred to the
wrong mode, and this is not noticed.

we are in a large measure of agreement with the views of Hanslick. Nevertheless, it seems to us that they do not exclude the "incarnation theory." Music never expresses anything different, anything nonmusical, yet it can very easily be an expression of a reality which is by no means amusical, but more than musical. Music is neither the reproduction of the "world" nor of nature nor of the spirit. But in spite of this it can be the revelation of that of which the "world" is only an incomplete revelation. Heaven is revealed upon the earth both in the cup of cold water which is given to the poor man and in Michelangelo's *David*; in both the dance of a child and a melody of Mozart. In heaven there is music, but heaven is more than just music. If music were nothing more than "an inner song," it would have no form, it would be no creation, it would not be art. The theory of unlimited autonomy forgets that the particular form of music must still be measured by something else if it is to reveal itself as beautiful form, beautiful figure—as beauty.

Music is by no means purely formal in the sense that it has no shape. Otherwise it would be mathesis, and its essence, as well as its form, could be expressed in numbers. It has been pointed out that music does not use the sense of space, but only the sense of time, and that it is able therefore to unite the exterior and interior worlds. But even this reduction of visible form cannot rob music of its power. In fact, whoever hears music sees nothing; and if he imagines something, the images called forth in him by the music (a picture of nature, a funeral procession), or the notes as they stand in the score, have no immediate, essential connection with what is heard. Nevertheless, the world of music is complete. It is not like a world connected with time, but without space. Like Oskar Bie, we can seek for the analogy of time in the melodic element of music, while the analogy of space is to be found in the elements of harmony and counterpoint.[317] In any case, music is a world to itself, with its own space and its own time, in which not only spatial, but also temporal existence is subsumed. Movement, the essence of every art, demands both space and time. Therefore, in the pictorial arts we spoke of frozen movement. Now, in music, we speak of space which has become fluid. "You see, my son, here time becomes space," says Gurnemanz to Parsifal, as he points to the landscape. He could also point to the orchestra and say, "Here space becomes time." And whoever stands in quiet reverence before a perfect statue finds the perfect expression of his experience in Parsifal's words: "I am hardly moving, yet I feel myself already distant."

Music is a world in itself. But it is a particular world which we ex-

perience, and not, for example, a formal game of sounds or an equilibrium of relationships. Here, too, we arrive once more at an analogy:
religion has its own world which is not the one which surrounds us, not
the sublimation of its values and the projection of its content. The nature
of religion, too, can never be found elsewhere than in the religious. All
descriptions given of it, or which it gives of itself, are only analogies.
Nevertheless, its world is a world which is experienced. The Kingdom
of God is not of this world. But it is also no kingdom of ideas, no formal
construction. It is the most real reality which we experience.

The reason that we ultimately discard the attractive theory of Schopenhauer is that we are not concerned with a metaphysics, but with a
theology of music. Therefore, as was pointed out before, we may learn
much from Schopenhauer, but we are not able to follow him. True
reality lies for us, not in absence of images, but rather in the image itself,
indeed in the image of God. We cannot give music any prerogatives
before the other arts, because our point of departure is the category of
creation as such, not the eternal values of idealism. And, above all, the
path from art to theology, from God's creation to human creation, is to
be found in the image of God as a completely other reality—not then in
the beautiful sound, but in the image where art *represents*, does music
have its origin.(We shall return to this point more thoroughly in Chapter 7.)

It is good to hear Nietzsche once more on this point, in all his merciless realism: "How much unavowed and even uncomprehended satisfaction of all religious needs there remains in Wagner's music! How much
prayer, virtue, unction, virginity, redemption, still speaks there! Music
can do that without words, without concepts—Oh, how it turns this to
advantage, this crafty saint, who leads us back, tempts us back, to everything that was once believed."[323] That is completely true, and therefore
it must also be quite clear that music has no religious prerogatives. If it
takes the place of religion, it is just as much a surrogate as politics or any
other human creation.

PROGRAM MUSIC   From this point, we may return our view to the
apparently less important problems of music itself. It is precisely these
which are of great significance for our examination.

We have seen how Schopenhauer turned against program music.
Hanslick, taking his departure from the autonomy of sound, opposed,
consequently, any connection between word and sound. He emphasized
the problematic character of the opera, and called Beethoven's Ninth, in
spite of all the admiration he had for that powerful work, "one of those

spiritual watersheds which to a great extent lie visible and unconquerable between the streams of opposed convictions."[322] Both had, and have, many partisans, who consider instrumental music the only true music, but only when it does not attempt to depict, that is, when it does not try to be program music. Holland, especially, swarms with epigoni of this view, who see opera as a dubious triviality and feel themselvs duty bound by their "good name" to consider Beethoven's *Pastoral* as "less important" than his other symphonies. • [197, 324, 325]

Now we have, ourselves, emphasized the fact that music can express nothing. "Program music," whose primary aim is expression, depiction of an event, imitation of a natural phenomenon, and so forth, would already be condemned as music. But good program music is not so much concerned with the "program" (nor is the name, therefore, very good) as with the music. Those who rank instrumental music above all other music forget not only their "nonpartisanship," but also that instrumental music is of recent date, and that the entire development of modern music has its roots in the vocal music of the fifteenth and sixteenth centuries. In our view this makes no difference. For music which is real music does not illustrate the words, but exalts them, carries them along in order to annihilate them. Every text is destroyed by music in beautiful fashion. This also happens to the "program" which the composer made, and also to the subject of the opera which he composed. His music is never illustration, word, object, program; it is, rather, the occasion to create a new world. Beethoven himself felt this when he noted in regard to the *Pastorale*: "More an expression of mood than painting." As Bekker said, he is to a great degree an artist of ideas,[274] but the ideas are for him only dynamic impulses for pure musical creation: for example, the quartet movement, "The difficult decision"; or the *Eroica*, for which Napoleon was the occasion, not for a musical portrait of Napoleon, but for a new, purely musical, form; for a form, nevertheless, and not for a numerical system or a "pattern for a tapestry of sound." As Busoni remarked, there must be a third possibility which leads beyond the opposition between program music and absolute music.[294] All true music in this sense is absolute music, both vocal music, and opera, and so-called program music. There is absolutely no opposition between the Leonora Overture and the *Eroica*, between the Coriolanus Overture and the Fifth Sym-

• Kierkegaard already was aware of the most important point: "Music cannot express what is historical in a period." A. Schering says, "The sensible hermeneut does not attempt to translate music into concepts or words, nor to be a prophet of what the composer was thinking here or there . . . that would be presumption or charlatanry."

phony. For all true music is dramatic, and moves, like all art, in eternal movement and countermovement between form and formlessness.

We found in music an inclination to silence which connects it with mysticism. Similarly, we found in architecture and painting an inclination toward darkness. All music means a struggle for redemption, which would be the end of all music. But the struggle is a concrete drama, full of lines and colors, forms and nuances. Just as every religion is ultimately a struggle for redemption which finally does away with all religion, when God will be all in all. That struggle, too, is a concrete drama, in lines and colors, the flesh and blood of history. In music, color can predominate, in which case it will be primarily harmonic, with a strong emphasis on the middle voices; or the line predominates, and then music is melodic, the descant standing in the foreground. Or the architecture of the lines in their relationship to one another predominates, and then the strong foundation of the bass determines polyphonic music. Wagner—Mozart —Bach. These are oppositions which we can use better than such unimportant differences as that between so-called "absolute" (i.e., instrumental) and so-called "programmatic" music.[274] But in any case, music is never "absolute," unless it exists only in heaven.

IN PRAISE OF OPERA   I should like to sing the praise of opera. Not because it is the only, or the highest, form of music. That "impartiality" which is called love has the effect that any form is right: vocal, instrumental, song, or drama. In opera, music is truly music, a new world, not a harmonic reduction of the arts to an art work "of the future" (Wagner), nor the proved impossibility of that (Hanslick); it is a miracle which is granted us in spite of all human possibilities and impossibilities. The miracle of a new world, the blurring of contours, the fading away of colors, which are returned to us by the grace of God in a part of the great miracle through which God takes us all, only to return us renewed in even greater glory.

"The opera is an impossible art form." So begins Oskar Bie in his fine book, which is dedicated to this impossibility.[317] He exhibits eight impossibilities. It is precisely this impossibility which makes the opera such a wonderful proof of the breaking through of a new world into this one which surrounds us. "Invented through an error," amidst all the new theories, which were similarly new errors, it remained the pre-eminent miracle. Whoever is too disturbed by the impossibilities, the contradictions, the contrasts, the incommensurables, should take to heart the statement of Werfel: "The refusal of the 'nonsense of opera' is simultaneously the refusal of any sense which is not purely logically comprehensible."

Let us sing the praise of the opera. The impossibilities are laid forth thoroughly enough, beginning with the eternal conflict between words and music, to the bad temper of the prima donna. But the most tragic and glorious impossibility lies in the fact that the creation, which cannot be, is nevertheless present in the opera, that the form which vanishes blossoms again before our eyes. Every great opera dashes life to pieces, destroys it without mercy. Events are drowned in the current of music; characters disappear in a modulation; emotion becomes "feeling in general," that is, lack of feeling. But from the ruins of our life arises a new world.

Music leads into the depths of life, there where boundaries flee away. *The Marriage of Figaro*: ah, how beautiful is that life, the rococo life of the end of the eighteenth century! Our thoughts wander to the person of Beaumarchais, and we lose ourselves in cultural history. But the *"Cinque, dieci, venti"* makes us forget all literature and culture. We play like uninhibited children with Figaro and Susanna—until Cherubino appears and with his *"Non so pio cosa son, cosa faccio"* makes something of the eternally human, inextinguishable demand of youth for love, of "feeling per se," penetrate us. The trumpet sounds, Figaro leads the recalcitrant Cherubino to the war dance: *"Non piu andrai, farfallone amoroso."* We are children again, until our attention is drawn to the grief of the countess and the passions of the count. But at the *"Mi sento dal contento,"* the lament of Almaviva turns not only into joy, but into a duet so wonderfully beautiful that we listen only to the divine form and forget everything—the count, Susanna, their feelings, our feelings—to let ourselves be borne along on the flood of sounds. The wedding procession passes by us; we are children again until Susanna, in the clothing of the countess, makes us forget not only her own frivolous person, but also the elegiac figure of the countess, with her *"Deh vieni, non tardar."* And when at last the finale has united grief, joy, remorse, childish inhibition, cunning, calculation, courage, into a single, noble, yet so simple, poem, then we know that we have experienced all of that in that evening, that and more. But we recognize simultaneously that basically it was something else. We rub our eyes, we were dreaming—have we seen or heard another world? How remarkable and surely how "impossible" that this is never seen in an opera. We have dreamed it, and now that we are awake we carry within us the consciousness that on one single evening we have come nearer the secret of creation.

Remarkably, it is in opera that the religious nature of music is most clear to me. It is all so familiar: a little love, a little suffering, a little joy, and much intrigue (no opera without intrigue); and yet it is all so infinitely distant, as distant as the stars. It is near to us, and yet we cannot grasp it. In opera everything is very real; no one is afraid of trivial reality, what we humans in our blindness call comedy; no one is in any way embarrassed at those great realities, the presence of stage lighting and make-up, scenery, and all the trimmings. And yet all of this is very far removed, is another world, a new creation, in which God's hand reaches out to us just as incomprehensibly and really as in our "ordinary," miserable world; in that world of heroes and heroines, blunders and intrigues, we experience, if we will believe, God's creation. No—we do not experience it, we suspect it only, in trembling bliss. • [275]

MUSIC AS A GAME   In dance, in drama, in the mask, we spoke of art as a game. We compared it with the game of our life, the holy game which God plays with us (cf. p. 111). It is still common to call music-making "playing," and only in most recent times does play count as a waste of time, as something superfluous, as something lacking in seriousness, as something without value. In a famous passage, Sebastian Franck speaks of music: "A bird actually does not sing and fly, but is sung and transported through the air. It is God who in him sings, lives, builds a nest, flies." Man nevertheless has a free will, that is, in man God has become will. "We are all laughter, tale, and carnival before God."[183]

Music "to Bach and Mozart was supposed to be nothing more than the most noble of all diversions and the most skilled of all accomplishments, and it was heavenly guilelessness which raised it to unexampled perfection."[6]

It is not primarily the perfection of music which interests us in this regard, but its guilelessness, its innocence. For thereby it can grow from a beautiful diversion for men to a diversion for God, a work of that wisdom which in the beginning played before God's face.

• Nietzsche, too, sang the praise of the opera. "The persons of the opera are not to be believed 'upon their word,' but upon the music. That is the difference, that is the beautiful artificiality, which makes one go to the opera." Even the violent conflict with Wagner, which went deep into his soul, could not keep Nietzsche from admiring *Tristan* passionately: "Do not avoid *Tristan*: it is a capital work, and of a fascination which is without equal not only in music, but in all the arts" (to Carl Fuchs, December 27, 1888). His glorification of Bizet was only meant as an "ironic antithesis" to Wagner (see the same letter).

THE THEOLOGY OF MUSIC   Of what now does the essential connection between music and religion consist? Where does their unity lie? We have found two points of contact: first, the "other world," the new creation; and second, the inclination to the absolute, which is called silence. Or are they perhaps identical? Let us hear a few witnesses.

Romain Rolland's Jean Christophe says:

> Our music is a deception. Our scales, our sound sequences, are an invention. They correspond to not a single sound of reality; compared to real sounds they mean an intellectual compromise, the application of a metrical system to eternal movement . . . From time to time, a genius in transitory contact with the earth suddenly feels the torrent of reality which would like to break the frame of art. For a moment the dams burst. Nature gushes out through a crack. But immediately the break is stopped up. That is necessary for the protection of human reason. It would be destroyed if its eyes were to meet the eye of Jehovah.[326]

And Mauclair speaks of "metamusic": "Beyond music there is a highest language. . . . That is the rhythm which proceeds from the universe, and of which we are no more than a mere echo. And this rhythm alone is metamusic. In all other cases we can only use the adjective: the substantive itself is unattainable. Or better expressed: the metamusical state is silence, for rhythm makes no more sound than the movement through the ether."[308]

Metamusic is inaudible. We stand here at a barrier behind which images fade away. Actual music is inaudible. To our humanity, to our ear, to our feeling, it is only abstraction. Herman Rutters touched this background of music when he wrote about the first production of Bach's *Art of the Fugue* at Utrecht. Here is a work which no one knows how to begin. No hint, no dynamic markings. As far as instrumentation is concerned, it can be just as well (or badly) sung as played on the organ or the cembalo or by an orchestra. If you like, you can take it as an abstract amusement, like a difficult chess problem. A young artist ventured to score Bach's work, giving it sound. Rutters writes:[327]

> A case can hardly be thought of which would bring us nearer the mystery of the creating composer than this *Art of the Fugue*. In a certain sense, we stand in this work at the inmost point of his workshop. And yet we feel ourselves surrounded by all kinds of mysterious

riddles. Now, when we are so near the secrets, we first become truly aware of the inexplicable. We recognize through this music that Bach belongs to another world, to which we cannot find entrance. Here is music in its pure, abstract essence. Out of a seemingly insignificant theme develops a wonderful complex of melodic lines. The theme is like a magic formula. It is as though we were experiencing the whole story of creation. Chaos is ordered to a cosmos. But what else is happening in this work? What lives behind it? We, who were brought up to believe in the romantic expressive function of music, stand here in the presence of a strange discovery. Every association with a particular emotion is lacking. Ever attempt at paraphrase by images which, internally or externally, are borrowed from real life goes absolutely wrong. The *Art of the Fugue* exceeds everything material, even time and style. It belongs to that mysterious atmosphere where the physical becomes transformed into the metaphysical. It is a symbol.

But how can this symbol be explained? The *Art of the Fugue* is perhaps the purest manifestation of absolute music, of abstraction. But the sound is already something concrete, and even more so the timbre. Do we not speak of the warlike trumpet, the elegiac clarinet, the languishing oboe, the melancholy cello? But when we bring these timbres into connnection with the *Art of the Fugue*, do we not thereby drag it down from the height of its abstraction to the lower atmosphere of the concert? Do we not thereby overpower the actual nature of the work? Is there not a hint we should respect in the fact that Bach did not score his final work? It is a difficult problem, because instrumentation is the only means of bringing music to life for us, even in its abstraction.

I need not excuse myself for this lengthy quotation. It is a preeminent discussion of the problem of music, such as one rarely gets the chance to read, especially among us in Holland. Complete music is silent. Sound, for it, is a resistance conquered. But sound, and this also includes timbre, is "the only means of bringing music to life for us." Now silence reigns. Just as the perfect religion, which we call mysticism, is silent. Both dissolve into each other. Our problem is solved. Yet we can neither hear nor see the solution.

Temporarily, we are happy that music is not silent, that it resounds in all its timbres. But we must not forget that the precondition and background for its sounding is the great silence of God. Music comes to us as in a dream.

The point where religion and music touch can be found in every sort of music; but the point of meeting, intentional or unintentional, lies between art and service. Voices represent something; they do not sound for themselves, but for something else. The Orthodox liturgy has perceived this in its so-called cherubic hymn. The choir represents the cherubim, the voices sound in the place of angelic voices: "Let us now, representing the cherubim in mystic fashion, and raising the thrice-holy song of the life-giving Trinity, lay aside all earthly cares."[328] This representative music must not necessarily sound in the liturgy; not all religious music must be church music. But there is something priestly about it, whether it is Gregorian chant or opera, symphony or ballet. Like the cherub, it has stood before God, and speaks unconsciously in his name, at his behest.

It cannot do this without also speaking to him. Holy music is always a hymn, *laudes* in the ancient sense, the praise of God sung before his face. And behold, for here we have arrived imperceptibly in the midst of theology. For the original and only true meaning of the word "theology" is the same as hymnody, the praise of God.[329] Theology is not a kind of philosophical justification of belief. This occurs there; but it is essentially eschatological music.

ESCHATOLOGICAL MUSIC   The highest and best music is that which is more than music; not that which sounds with voice and instruments, but that which our voices and instruments remind us of:

Music is what wakes within you when you are reminded by the instruments,
It is not the violins and the horns, not the oboe nor the pounding drums,
Nor the melody of the baritone who sings his sweet song,
Nor that of the men's chorus, nor that of the women's chorus,
Music is nearer and further than these.[330]

In this sense, music is the last thing, that which remains. In the heavenly city which the Revelation of John describes, there is no more image and no temple: "The final thing is song."[331] The heavenly song cannot be heard on earth; it is that *canor* of which the mystics speak, the song which sounds first above, then within, the human being.[332] Earthly music can only remind us distantly of this song. The most beautiful music is only an echo of the eternal Gloria:

"To Father, as to Son and Holy Spirit,"
Began all paradise, "be honor given!"—
That song filled me with rapture just to hear it.
What I did hear seemed like the laugh in heaven
Of the whole universe. . . .[30]

    The doxology of paradise is like a laugh of the universe. Here we have fixed the position of music within theology. It is not as central as that of theological aesthetics, but it is very important. Music is a servant before the face of God; it has a priestly function. It speaks of the ineffable, it represents the *loci de sacerdotio et de finibus*.

PART SEVEN

Theological Aesthetics

1   PATHS

AND BOUNDARIES

At the end of each chapter we have attempted, in a preliminary "theological aesthetics," to indicate the theological significance and position of the art in question. The task now remains to seek the unity of art, as such, in a general treatment. What do all the arts have in common, from the theological point of view? What is the mid-point about which everything turns? And what have we discovered up to now?

The dance reflects the movement of God, which also moves us upon the earth. The drama presupposes the holy play between God and man. Verbal art is the hymn of praise in which the Eternal and his works are represented. Architecture reveals to us the lines of the well-built city of God's creation. Music is the echo of the eternal Gloria. In the pictorial arts, we found images:

> The best of artists never makes creation
> That is not hid already in the stone,
> In marble fixed; and yet the work is done
> By hand, which follows mind and meditation.[333]

So speaks Michelangelo, sculptor, painter, and poet. The artist makes visible the features of an image which is in the material. Out of raw marble he forms living images. What is the secret of the "hand" which effects the work of creation? And in what relationship does it stand to the creation of God? How is the "*intelletto*" of the artist related to God's holy, creative Spirit?

TO SEEK, NOT TO CONSTRUCT   We shall seek points of access, not construct them ourselves. If need be, we shall call a halt at boundaries, but we shall not string up any barbed wire. The question is not, How can we make art religious? Nor is it, When or how does art become religious? This would be too external, as though holiness and beauty were two ingredients which can be mixed together according to certain principles. We ask only, When and how is the unity revealed to us which was self-evident to primitive man, but which we can perceive only with effort? In other words, there is no particular art which can be designated religious. Still less is there a religion which one could call aesthetic. There is only a single art, and it is, first of all, art. There is only a single religion, and it is always and everywhere religion. But again and again we discern an essential unity between art and religion; again and again holiness and beauty appear to us in the same guise. With the assistance of our various "influences," we have examined the appearance of this costume. To return to our old image, we have again and again found points of access. It is now our task to see whether all these various points of access (and also boundaries) can be utilized, whether we shall succeed in finding a point from which we can survey the entire landscape.

I can imagine that a reader who has borne with me patiently may now become somewhat restive, and ask whether it would not be much simpler to come right out and state that all genuine art is religious, that the holy by its very nature comprehends the beautiful. Why was a whole book necessary to attain this simple conclusion? I reply that this objection is fully justified, that holiness always comprehends beauty, that their unity does not have to be discovered but can simply be observed. Yet there is nevertheless a need for a thorough discussion, which will have to be much more thorough and basic than our previous discussions have been if we are to pronounce this simple truth.

Let us first consider the fact that this truth is not reversible. Beauty is holiness. But holiness is not absolutely, not exclusively, beauty; it is more. "Holy" is the ultimate word; "beautiful," the penultimate. He who says "holy" says everything; he who says "beautiful" says much. In addition, there is the difficulty that although we can say that holiness is beauty, we only rarely experience this truth, and see it only in exceptional instances.

It is completely true that genuine, great art is, as a rule, also religious art; genuine, noble expression of the beautiful is simultaneously expression of the holy. We shall now attempt to penetrate to the heart of our problem. For this we shall omit all that is counterfeit, non-essential, or superficial, but hold fast to what we have discovered of the desired unity in work of art and in artist.

"RELIGIOUS ART" First we shall return briefly to the so-called transitional structure. "Transition" in the chronological sense is just as unknown to us as "beginning."• [334]

We are inquiring into the structure, not the process. Belonging half to the magical, half to the "modern" realm, art is still far removed from the solution of *"l'art pour l'art."* Culture is still a unity, all values are still catholic, and the awareness of life as a whole, which characterizes religion, still dominates the mind enough so that no artistic expression is possible outside of continuity with the religious. The breakup of the objective spirit into different, separate, autonomous provinces is still a long way from completion. But it has begun.

A typical example is the art of the Renaissance. At least in theory, the Church still rules all areas of life; all values are still judged by what is Christian. Nevertheless, the art of the Renaissance as a whole can hardly be called religious. The continuity has become external.

But we find a differentiation even much earlier. In Greece there was a Renaissance art, and even so-called "semicultures" (Egypt, Babylon, China, etc.) had "modern" tendencies. The structure of external continuity, as such, is always present, at least potentially, even in the most primitive culture. On the other hand, the magical view of art has never been completely lost, and it still lives on among us. The "primitive" conception is no longer possible for us, but we do not desire a rigorous separation analogous to that which Schleiermacher made between religion and ethics. We find ourselves, so to speak, always in transition from the primitive sphere of magical continuity to the differentiated sphere of the "modern" spirit, a transition which is eternal, because it is determined not temporally, but structurally.

In this transition the lines of communication between religion and art are almost unrecognizable. A self-evident, given continuity cannot be found. Nevertheless, the old connection is still sought, and so an external continuity, not organic but artificial, is striven for. This is done most simply by an appropriate choice of subject matter. The "religious subject," "spiritual material," come to mind. In Richard Wagner's *Meistersinger,* the good master Kothner asks the knight Walter von

---

• There seems to me no question that the results of ethnological studies in the field of art indicate that we may not speak of a "beginning" of the practice of art, as did the older school of "developmental theoreticians."[349]

Stolzing whether he would like to choose "sacred material" for his piece. The young knight answers by speaking of the holiness of love, in extremely poetic language. But the sober master says dryly, "We call that secular." The whole tragicomedy, the whole perplexity of the transitional structure contrasted with the real values of life and art, are contained in these words of Kothner. With an external division into "sacred" and "profane," one will never achieve an expression of the holy in art. "Holy" material is never the cause of art, least of all religious art.

Not only art frees itself from the organic continuity. It is not only the artistic sensibility of modern man which seeks its own paths. Religion, too, the religious consciousness, protests against a self-evident union with art. Holy power no more allows itself to be ruled by art than art allows itself to be constrained by holy power. There are, of course, certain forms of art which are accepted once and for all: holy words, many styles of building, a certain form of song, etc. But the religion of modern man is strongly inclined to let it go at that, and choose for religious expression a fixed artistic form, the sermon or edifying story, for example, and thus try to construct the necessary external continuity.

As far as music is concerned, for instance, our age has not only failed to overcome the external continuity, it is hardly aware of it. "Concert of religious music" is an announcement that always disturbs me. Of course it can refer to a beautiful and even edifying concert. But much misunderstanding lies in the term "religious." It is an expression preferred by those who think that art fulfills its function (and is unobjectionable to a Christian) only when it stands in the service of religion. It must be an "ancilla," a pleasant but nevertheless obliging "ancilla." And its servility, like the Amsterdam orphans of an earlier age, must be clearly recognizable by its costume.

This costume is of various design. Many think that part of the "religious" aspect consists of saying a prayer at the beginning or, occasionally, at the end. This, then, counts as an express emphasis on the desired continuity. Others do not find this necessary, but think that the holy must be expressed in the nature of the music, in the texts of the songs; or the choral numbers must be Biblical, or at least edifying. The spirit of the work itself is usually not considered. Not only is the spirit of the music forgotten, but also that of the words. Whether the Enlightenment (*The Seasons*) or Pietism (Bach) is confronted, it does not matter, unless one gets a whiff of the leaven of Rome. In such a case, accomplished artists know how to suppress Mary or the *Verum Corpus*, just as they can replace the profane object of a long-winded love poem with Jesus, in case that eases the mind of the church board. There are people, even musicians, who attend concerts not even knowing that Handel's "Largo," which is so extremely religious, actually does not sing of holy things, but of the beneficent coolness offered the tired hero of the opera by a shady tree. If the text is Italian, the content does not matter. If not, it suffices that in the text the name of God, or of Christ, or even of death or mortality (which are in themselves edifying), be mentioned a few times. The case is, of course, more difficult with instrumental music, which excludes an "appropriate" text. But in practice this impediment is scarcely perceived; it is quite easy to construct an external continuity. First of all, we have organ music. All organ music is "religious." Is not the organ an expressly "religious" instrument? In one of our large cities a few years ago a district judge determined that a piano is profane, but an organ edifying. It is, of course, suspicious that moving-picture theaters also acquire organs. There are people who assert that the organ did not always have such a serious aura, indeed that there was a time when the cymbal and tambourine were the true religious instruments; but this does not change the fact that many people still think that God created the organ deliberately for "holy" purposes. They would certainly be astonished if they did not find at least a small harmonium in heaven.

As far as the other instruments are concerned, a slow tempo usually suffices to suggest the holy. Thus the slow movements of violin-and-cello literature are plundered. Even a serious and perceptive man like Woldemar Voigt, who wrote a fine book about Bach's cantatas, does not escape this passion for slowness, but insists on a dragging tempo. The "eternal fire" of a chorus by Bach must not flame up too wildly, because the image is supposed to represent the Holy Spirit, as though the Holy Spirit were not wild. Voigt thinks that the essence "of every religious contemplation is quiet, reverent meditation," and as such is opposed to the essence of "dramatic progress," which is "movement, tension, surprise." He adds: "In my opinion, these are generally just the wrong elements to assure a religious effect."[310] What a confession of bankruptcy, not only for religious art, but also for religious life, which distortedly knows the "*ma non troppo*" so well. A religious life exists which understands no "surprise"; it is a relationship to God to which, as a rule, passion is alien, but it still must not be taken as an example. All of this is depressing. Music is never the servant of religion: it is the servant of God. And it does not fulfill its duty by singing psalms continually, but by being music, only music, and again music. "Religious" music in the true, deep sense is not only the music of Bach and Palestrina, but also a symphony of Beethoven, an opera of Mozart, a waltz of Strauss. All music that is absolute music, without additions, without anything counterfeit, is the servant of God; just as pure painting is, whether it treats religious subjects or not; and as true architecture is, apart from the churches it builds; and as true science is, even when it has little to do with theology, but busies itself with gases, stars, or languages.

Of course, the expression "spiritual art" can mean something more than the purely external continuity between religion and art. In this respect we are unconcerned with ecclesiastical art, liturgical music, the language of the altar, ecclesiastical ornament and architecture. To remain with music, for example, it is obvious that music used in worship must have its own style, its own character, which is determined by the form of worship and its historical development. Church music is not the same thing as religious music. Music can fulfill all the demands of ecclesiastical style and still not be religious. It can be filled with holiness, and yet not be church music. A symphony by Mahler can be very religious music, and yet not be suitable for worship. For here we are concerned, aesthetically, with a problem of style, and theologically, with a liturgical problem, not with the relationship between music and religion. But our superficial talk of "religious" music muddies a correct feeling for style. If a piece only has "mood" and is slow, it is thought suitable for worship. Thus, at worship are played Schubert's "Litany," the "Pilgrims' Chorus" from *Tannhäuser*, the "March of the Priests" from *The Magic Flute*, *Préludes* by Chopin, and much else of this sort. Liturgical consciousness of style lacks much, if not all. Of course, the boundaries of the various arts are differently drawn. The Roman Catholic Church could not accept an English hymn as church music; Lutheran and Reformed church music, based on the chorale, has a different character than that of the Roman and Anglican churches, which remained with psalmody. But there are very plain boundaries. The important thing is not "mood," but very sober stylistic sense.

For before one occupies oneself with the problem of ecclesiastical art, one must have something else in view, namely, true religious art. I do not object if by "spiritual" music one means religious music, yet that must be very clear. Spiritual music is music which is not only a revelation of the beautiful, but also of the holy, not through the subject matter of the text or the occasion for which it was composed, but through the fact that holiness and beauty have mutually interpenetrated. Such music can be church music or have profane character. It can have a text or not, can be opera or oratorio, symphony or dance. It does not pay to strive for it, for we do not attain it. It is granted us as a rare, disconcerting miracle.

THE ANTITHETICAL STRUCTURE   The structure of external continuity is replaced by that of opposition, of unity in enmity. The antithetical structure, too, is timeless, even if its contours are more clearly drawn in one era than in another. Only in the present day is the entire extent of the conflict visible.

The conflict can have many different causes. The limitation to time and space inherent in a work of art is felt as an impediment which opposes religion, the seeking of the infinite. Then again, art is accused of frivolity, no matter how exalted its forms are, as if it is ultimately not concerned with the final things, with truth.

On the other hand, art accuses religion of having neither eyes nor ears; the visible world does not exist for it, and it prefers the ugly to the beautiful whenever it thinks it has discovered a holy quality there.

Finally and ultimately, all the arguments are weapons in a struggle for power. Should the beautiful or the holy provide the measure and goal of life? When the structure of life splits up, art, science, ethics, and religion all rule, each for itself and each absolute. When they come together once more some day, it will develop that either one of them is sovereign and the others all mere vassals, or that all, no matter how different their paths may be, finally end at the "ultimate matters." Temporarily, they are at war with one another.

"ARTISTS"   Only autonomous, autocratic art has "artists." The quotation marks belong with the name. It is no wonder that the society which forms language has a stereotyped idea of the "artist": long hair, strange clothes, a lot of arrogance, and no money. The artist is actually a product of the division of our culture. He does not fit into our social order; there is nothing there for him. Skilled craftsmen and architects are better off, but poets, composers, and painters have no specific function. They despise "occasional poetry," and paint portraits only to earn their daily bread. There is no longer an inner necessity, an organic continuity, between culture and the life of the artist. Bach's works are, for the most part, occasional compositions; the pictures of the old masters were painted to order; Shakespeare wrote for production and nothing else. Franz Werfel, in his novel *Verdi*, puts the following well-stated words into the mouth of the artist: "This cursed and affected lying word, 'art!' Art, like everything holy, is only art when it does not know that it is. In my youth, the commission, the '*scrittura*' of an opera was an affair in which not much was said about art. But today the tightrope walkers no longer want to be tightrope walkers." In agitated, modern life the "artist" laboriously seeks his "opportunity"; he "delivers" only when he is inspired, and writes only for eternity. Every young artist in our divided culture appears with the pretension that he is creating masterpieces, and thinks himself justified in being angry or at least offended when no one listens to him. Usually society punishes him harshly enough for these pretensions.

The artist in divided culture is a bohemian, even if he has his hair cut and knows how to look after money. This is not a result of arrogance or eccentricity. His exceptional position rests on a base which goes much deeper. He is an "artist," and beauty rules him with a heavy hand. He may know no other laws, no other masters; he cannot be moral or scientific or even solely religious like other men. His beloved is a jealous woman, and only gives her favors to one who belongs to her, body and soul. No one knows this better than the dilettante. A good dilettante usually has much more insight into art than has an artist. But, confronted with an artist, he feels himself powerless in spite of everything, grotesquely incompetent. For to him it is not a matter of life or death. For him it is at most the beautiful drama of life or death of another artist, whom he sees dying in beauty before his eyes.

LA BEAUTÉ

Je suis belle, ô mortels! comme un rêve de pierre,
Et mon sein, où chacun s'est meurtri tour à tour,
Est fait pour inspirer au poète un amour
Éternel et muet ainsi que la matière.

Les poètes, devant mes grandes attitudes,
Que j'ai l'air d'emprunter aux plus fiers monuments,
Consumeront leurs jours en d'austères études. . . .

BEAUTY

You humans! I am beautiful, a dream of stone,
My breast, upon which, man for man, all wounded fell,

Attracts to me the poet through love's magic spell
Which, like the world, stays still, eternal and alone.

For poets, meditating on my carriage exalted,
Which I have borrowed from the proudest monument
There is no blame for killing hours which pass, unhalted.[335]

To be an artist is to be devoured by beauty. "All artists are religious, and to become an artist means nothing less than to dedicate oneself to the deities of the underworld. Only in the enthusiasm of destruction is revealed the sense of divine creation. Only in the midst of death does the flash of eternal life shine."[336] The reverse side of the coin is described by Thomas Mann very sharply and clearly in his *Tonio Kröger*: "To be clairvoyant even through the veil of emotional tears, to recognize, to note, to observe, and then smiling lay aside what has been observed in the very moment when hands clasp, lips meet, when human vision, blinded by perception, fails—it is infamous, Lisawetta, it is abject, disgraceful. . . . But in regard to the redemptive word, are we not dealing here less with a redemption than with a desensitization, putting the emotions on ice?"[194]

The fact that the artist represents a peculiar type has the result that more attention than usual is paid to his humanity. Of a devotee of beauty, one expects beauty in everything, or at least dignity. Therefore, artists are disappointing "as men," as the saying goes. That does not absolutely have to be the case in undivided culture, for there the artist is a normal human being who has his function beside others. As a rule, he does not even have a position, such as lends dignity and power to priests, kings, and others. The question of the artist as a human being appears only when he is no longer an ordinary human being. Then it often develops that his work claims his entire strength to such a degree that he has none left over to make his life a work of art. In spite of this, the very great, such as Goethe and Beethoven, partially succeeded.

"If the great artist is not always also a great man, it is only because he is not an artist in all the points of his being and all the moments of his life."[250]

STYLE   If the breaking out of art from the continuity of life leads to the position of "artist" and thereby to a consistently stronger predominance of the individual, complete transition from expression of the beautiful to that of "most individual feeling" is restrained by style, which not only asserts to a certain degree the collective nature of the expression, but also, as a result, keeps alive the consciousness of distance.

Style is a form of life. The style of a work of art is like the character of a man, taken in the broadest sense: the way he presents himself, his speech, his feelings, his thoughts, etc. To that degree style is also individual. An expert can recognize in a painting the style of a particular painter, in a piece of music the particular style of this or that composer.

But style is also what binds artists together, what makes an organic whole out of a group of men who belong to the same age, the same nationality, and the same school of thought. We speak of a romantic style, of *stilo novo*, of Italian style, of baroque, of expressionism, of the Amarna style. We are seeing then what is common to the work of a group of artists as a particuliarized structure, even if the boundaries of such a structure never remain fixed, and even if the essence of great artists is never subsumed in the style of their period or school. But in the fact that we recognize this common element as such, there lies a hint that form is more than individual genius, that there are certain forms of feeling and observing which are given to us as "objective spirit." We cannot free ourselves from these forms. We can indeed admire the Chinese style, love the baroque, but we cannot build like the Chinese or paint like the baroque artist, without imitation. Today a person can have his room decorated in the proper style by a furniture company. That is helplessness. The artist, no matter how great and independent he may be, creates within the forms of the structure which was given him. It may be that he breaks through those forms at important points, that he perfects the form and is its perfecter, like Beethoven for the symphony and Wagner for the opera, but even that proceeds from what is given.

Therein lies consciousness of distance and an approach to the holy. If our age is still seeking a style in almost every area of life, in music, for example, mixing apparently ancient forms with hypermodern ones, we recognize that the spirit of this age is not religious. The great changes in style, from Romanesque to Gothic, from the Greek of the fifth century to that of the fourth, all have a change in the religious consciousness of life as their precondition.

Every important change of style in the religious life indicates a turning point in the development of forms of style. The history of changing style up to the most recent period depends on the question whether an age was religiously or secularly minded, and how, in each case, the religious feeling or the joy in the world was directed.

An age is without style, groping unsurely amidst traditional forms, only when it is without fixed goals and ideals in either direction, in the forms of religious exaltation as well as those of enjoyment of the world.[261]

To which we should only note that conscious "enjoyment of the world" is also a form of religion.

It may always be a somewhat delicate matter to connect a style with a particular view of life, as Carl Gebhardt did with the baroque, Spinoza, and the Counter Reformation.[337] It is certain, however, that an age's feeling of life gives direction to art, that the capacity of a period to view life as a whole and to comprehend it, as well as its ability to produce life from itself, to objectify, are decisive for style. "Style" is another word for the expression of the holy, or at least for the possibility.

L'ART POUR L'ART   Together with the religious attitude, autonomous art also casts aside the religious subject. The continuity determined by subject matter can no longer suffice for it. Nor religion, either. The antithetical structure has in religion no need for expression of the holy through beauty, in art no place for anything but beauty: *l'art pour l'art*.[236]

Of course this isolation of art is artificial. Art cannot get along without life. If it turns away from life, a great degree of resignation is involved. Autonomy frees "the artist from external servility, but it at once falls into the danger of separating him from the ground of his life." The motto *l'art pour l'art* is valid whenever art must protect itself from subservience to any tyranny which forces its way in from outside. But one cannot say that art must have no "meaning," that a concrete goal in the context of life must remain denied it. On the contrary, art has always been greatest when it has placed itself at the service of a great idea, a great conviction, a great, suprapersonal emotion, assuming that this service is not a slavery but a community of life, an interpenetration of artistic form and the content of life. The poetry of pastors and priests is not worth much, yet Guido Gezelle was a great poet. "Patriotic" songs are, as a rule, not enjoyable, but Virgil was a genius, and Fitcht's *Addressses to the German Nation* is a masterpiece. It is not a healthy symptom for our age that religious, patriotic, even revolutionary art fail so miserably. It was one of the signs by which we recognized our new age, upon which we had set our hope, when out of the blood and tears, the enthusiasm and willingness to sacrifice, the hate and holy wrath of the years of occupation, a new song was heard. Many competitions for a patriotic song have failed wretchedly. But perhaps prison and concentration camp are better schools for a strong poetry, such as our time demands of us, than are literary salons. Lodewijk van Deyssel felt something of this alienation of art from its ground of life when he subdued the enthusiasm for art for art's sake and the hatred of versifying pastors which at that time ruled the magazine *de Nieuwe Gids,* by complaining about the lack of "thoughts." He was not serious, of course, but nevertheless had a perceptiveness which made the early barrenness of this individualistic art understandable.[338] "Feeling" was to take the place of "thought," and the end of the nineteenth century was no longer strong enough to understand that thought and feeling are one. The members of *de Nieuwe Gids* pointed again and again to the indissoluble unity of form and content, what is presently called the "inner form" of a work of art. In other words, in the antithetical structure, the breakdown of external continuity becomes visible, and each side now blames the other. Art blames life, and, above all religion, because it despises form or uses it without taste; life (and, above all, religion) blames art, because it allows itself to be led astray by form alone. Both are right: much in modern art is far removed from life and constructed according to the rules of a game; much in modern life—and now I am thinking, not of the particular forms of expression of religion, but of those of technology—withdraws temporarily, almost completely, from any artistic form. But the actual cause of the conflict lies deeper, in divided life isolating itself artificially into separated domains. We have set up a series of national parks and open-air museums, and they are our churches, universities, concert halls, and theaters. One must pay admission, prove oneself an "artist" or a "scientist" or a "Christian" in order to gain admittance.

SERVICE   When we were discussing the phenomena of the "artist" and "art for art's sake," we kept finding the double tendency to dominate and be subservient on the one hand, to free subjection and liberation from the alien yoke on the other. Signs of the divided unity. Where does the unity lie? The unity of life itself has divided; the unity of experience and art, of religion and art.

The servant of beauty who wants to serve God will be given no new instructor. Beauty will not let him go, and God never allows himself to be "added on." He who serves beauty serves God, at least if he serves faithfully. There is only one form of service.

Both the work and life participate in a supernatural vitality which binds them together and makes possible the growth of a work of art. We must view the much-discussed problem of the relationship between art and experience, between experience and poetry, in this light. Many think the basis of art is purely formal. We are only concerned with the structure of the work of art as it is offered us. The experience which inspires the artist to his work is almost indifferent to us; the work has its own life. There is much truth in that. Works of art do possess their own life; they perhaps mean something very different to him who receives them than to him who created them. Exegesis "*e mente auctoris*" here, too, does not bring us to our goal. It does not matter to me what Goethe experienced at the conception of one of his works. Ultimately I must understand it as it is given to me. But this does not detract from the fact that there must be an inner connection between the work of art and the experience, a congruence between the influences on the artist's life and the impulses of beauty which alone made the creation possible.

In this connection, the question arises whether one is to take the actual aesthetic quality of a work (following Kant and a whole school of aestheticians) as that which is "indifferent" in the nature of a beholder, that which sees and hears things but without actual participation, so that they do not have an effect in the context of life. "Taste," says Kant, "is the ability to judge an object or a mode of representation by like or dislike without any interest. The object of such liking is called beautiful."[339]

Most recently, Spoerri would even choose to see the major difference between religion and art in the fact that the former presupposes faith, the latter only perception.[340]

But this indifference of art is only a way of saying that it is not concerned with *this* life. Art does not desire to improve or to reform; it cannot believe. But its indifference is by no means lifelessness. The new world which it constructs is a creation whose origin can be found neither in the mental activity of man nor even that of the artist. The work of the artist is born neither out of his morality nor out of his science, neither from his passion nor from his wisdom. The work of art arises from the ground of all things. From the same ground of things is born the person of the artist. In that ground lies the close connection between experience and poetry.

Shakespeare's works did not grow out of his amazing knowledge of human beings. There have probably been other men who possessed this knowledge but could not create a dramatic world. The connection between experience and poetry is never direct. But on the other hand, the dramatic world of Shakespeare as a work of art is neither a formal whole nor a game, nor purely aesthetic in the narrow sense of the word; it is a world. In other words, the beautiful is not that which is beautiful apart from the good, the true. The beautiful is a new world which, in addition to the beautiful in the narrow sense, also includes the good and the true. If it were not so, only Raphael would be an artist, not Rembrandt; only Racine, not Shakespeare. Perhaps not even Raphael and Racine, but only Boucher and Stéphane Mallarmé. For the purely aesthetic does not penetrate even as far as the tragic or comic. Art is a world which is not simply "beautiful," but "a monstrous objectification of a peculiar sort," a second world in which all the components of the first live, but never as likeness, always on the basis of a new power inherent in them.[90]

The principle of form, the figure, is therefore that which in art rules everything, but not as pure form. Being beautiful is not art; intellectual, ethical, and religious values are not art. But the form of art gives to the values a "new mode of reality and thereby a basis of value."[90] Therefore, forming and experiencing are not separated, nor is forming a direct expression of experiencing, "but forming unseals experience, makes it possible, conveys it, exalts it."[90]

We have already spoken of inner form.

To separate form and experience is to destroy both. The work of art is never, even for a single moment, without an external, specifically aesthetic form. But equally it is at no moment without the entirety of life, without everything that penetrates and burrows into human life, thoughts, feelings, passions. The work of art is equally autonomous and of form.[236, 341]

The nature of the inner form is nevertheless a mystery. We cannot picture the essential connection between life and form, because we are not ourselves creators, but there is something creative in us. Among us, it always tends to pure form (game) or to pure life (no art). In life and in art, this new form comes from a world of the beyond.

It may be mentioned that there is also an art which has a certain nonreligious, perhaps even antireligious, nature. If it is genuine art—that is, service and not domination—I do not believe it. Art can be demonic. But the service of demons is also a kind of religion, admittedly somewhat questionable. Art can also come into conflict with particular ethical notions. But ethical notions are not religion. There is a more difficult case. Much art is permeated with a spirit which is not only in conflict with the ruling morality, that actually says nothing, but contradicts everything genuine and pure. Discrimination is here extraordinarily difficult. We do not have the right to force our own notions of honor and virtue, of what is fitting and what is not, upon the artist. But we do have the right to judge the work of art by its own standard, whether it is a genuine and pure work of art. If it is not, then we do not recognize it as art. Perhaps we can even condemn it as immoral; that is an ethical, often only a pedagogical, question. Let us take an example. Sensual art can very well be great art. Every art is sensual to a certain degree, and it is easy to see that in many arts the sensual is strongly emphasized. But art whose intention is to arouse the senses cannot be great art. On the contrary, the more this is its purpose, the more decidedly it deserts service for the sake of servility or slavery, the further it is from being art at all. Rubens was an artist; the illustrations in an indecent humor magazine are not art, no matter how well they are drawn. Between Boccaccio and Aristophanes and the pornographic novel lies all the difference in the world.

These difficulties confront us neither as pedagogical nor as ethical problems, but solely as questions of pure art.

In all the influences which we have studied, the "other" was revealed, not necessarily the wholly "other" of religion, but yet its expression, or at least the precondition for this expression. Then it is as though doors opened, as though perspective were spread before us, as though backgrounds came into view. Painting, sculpture, and rhetoric are nearer to the human content of religious experience. The other arts, especially music, renounce everything particular. The pictorial arts, whether they represent in marble, paint, or words, are therefore most suitable for the expression of the holy as it is revealed in concrete, historical religion. Music strives for the mystical, the indefinite. But it would be quite wrong to conclude that the arts, with the possible exception of music, can reproduce one or another positive religious experience. Of this they are incapable. Art cannot preach. It can be religious, or it can appear to be religious; but it can be neither Mohammedan nor Buddhist nor Christian. The *St. Matthew Passion* deals with Christian material, *Tristan and Isolde* with Buddhist material, but the one is not a Christian nor the other a Buddhist work. There is no Christian art, any more than there is a Christian science. There is only art which has stood before the holy, and this is as a service among men.

What is this service as a prerequisite for creation, which means real art, if not love?

Creation and love are correlates. Creation is not a stationary bringing-into-being, but the pledging of one's life for what is created. Thus Christianity has understood the word "creation." God created the world, not in the sense of an arbitrary act which he might just as well have left unperformed, but out of love, which is confirmed and revealed in Christ, the Mediator of creation. Every artist, even one who knows nothing of the Christian faith, can confirm that in the act of creation love is the element in which one's own life and the work of art are united. This is most strongly expressed in those forms of art which, from a superficial point of view, have nothing to do with religion. What a world of love for the tiniest detail lies in Balzac's *Comédie Humaine*, what a deeply penetrating affection for even the least and the most unlovable in Galsworthy's *The Forsyte Saga*, in (to name the greatest at once) Shakespeare's dramas. To forget one's self, to lose one's self to the subject of one's work, is to have arrived once more at that service which proved itself such a close bond between religion and art[342] (see also page 107). The love of the artist is different from that of the moral, the religious, man. One must not expect of the artist an extended hand, or even the desire to better his life. On the contrary, it sometimes seems as though the love of many great artists was exhausted in their work, so that there is none left over for their own lives. In spite of everything, the fact remains that genuine altruism, genuine love, genuine pity, are the driving forces of all great art. In that love meet life and work, the old world of human existence, and the new world of the work of art. For the work of art is a creation, and there is no creation without love. Thus, when we recognize in the "creation" of man features of the creation of God, it is also an incorporation of the love of man into the love of God, in which it rests.

THE WORLD OF ART   We said that the new world which art constructs is a creation, a second world, with its own power.

Art is related to a self-consistent, completely independent structure of reality which arises on the basis of a particular religious or nonreligious experience, but at once leaves this experience behind. A poem is not a piece of experience, even if it stands in a particular relationship to experience. It is rather a world newly constructed on the basis of the experience.[184] Out of experience, drenched with emotion, which even here is the womb of creation, a series of images must loose itself, viewed completely objectively; one's own character must transmigrate into completely alien figures, which obey a different law; the event must be completely removed from one's personal destiny. The transformation of subjective dependence into objective form is the true secret of the genuine poetic gift."[82] Even earlier, we discovered differences in the direction art takes, depending on whether distance from the subject or identification with it predominates. We may speak in general of "classic" and "romantic" art, but we must never connect these words with a historical concept. Bekker points out, for example, that Romantic music "extorted experience," while Bach, in spite of the gigantic nature of his music, could remain an upright citizen.* [184, 274]

For the artist, the dream is life; but it is a dream which lacks the arbitrary quality of the nightly dream life. The dream is an experience and is therefore not quite suited to comparison with the created work of art. We should do better to think of daydreams. Or perhaps even better, of that remarkable activity we go through when we wake from our dreams at night, and consciously interpreting, carry on the dream story. The world which then arises has come directly from the immediate dream experience, but it has meanwhile become something different; the creative spirit has taken possesion of the subject of the dream, has given it a particular meaning, extended it and omitted all arbitrary and fantastic portions. Seen from this standpoint, art, to use the language of Richard Wagner's Hans Sachs, is a *"Morgentraumdeutweise"* (a way of interpreting the morning dream).[343]

Only thus, in respect to its own realm, may one speak of independence of art. (I shall return to this point, but even now it is clear to us that this independence can never mean the domination of an abstract axiom of beauty and form.) That is why it is so foolish to demand "nature" from art and to condemn, for example, the opera or landscape architecture of the seventeenth century as "unnatural." It is equally foolish to demand "religion" of art. Every experience is expressed by art only mediately; it is "indicated," reconstructed. We have already seen that even the lyric poem is not an experience, but

* Cf. also, for example, the ancient and modern song. The ancient song goes its own way musically, having only a vague connection with the text; if necessary, it can also be used with other words. The modern song (Schubert, Schumann, Wolf) follows on the heels of the experience expressed in the words. The emphasis is correspondingly transferred from the melody to the harmony; the song becomes "romantic, emotional."

stands in an inner relationship to an experience, making possible the re-experiencing of a particular context of life, "not the real one, but that which the poet places in the mouth of an ideal person" (Wilhelm Dilthey). What binds art to religion is not its "proximity to experience," but its distance from experience. In this sense we must make our own the confession of Leonhardt in Schleiermacher's *Feast of Christmas*: "As a Christian, very unartistic, and as an artist, very un-Christian." Only the fact that both construct their own, different worlds out of the ground of all things, and that both religion and art seek to leave the boundaries of this world, binds them by nature. Artists and believers have both awakened and now interpret their dreams.

ABSOLUTISM   That other world, which has its own laws, gives both religion and art an absolutistic character. *De gustibus non est disputandum* (there can be no arguing about taste). That is not true. If it were, all opinions in the realm of art would be of equal value, along the lines of, "You find it beautiful, I find it ugly." Actually the reverse is true; every judgment in the realm of the beautiful is absolute and bears no discussion. Whoever defends the beauty of a particular work and says at the same time, "It could also be different"; indeed, whoever entertains even the least doubt as to the validity of his judgment knows no more what beauty is than a person knows what holiness is as long as he thinks that God might or might not exist. Neither in the realm of religion nor in the realm of art can "everyone reach heaven by his own road." Both the aesthetic and the religious demand is absolute. I am not convinced that there are aesthetic laws except in the heads of aestheticians. But there is one almighty aesthetic law: let there be beauty. And there is only a single judgment of art which seems to approach in its honorable pride that of the creator over his work: "Thus it is good."

Thus, religion and art are both extremely intolerant. It is surely no accident that there are nowhere so many quarrels as among believers and among artists. Following Voltaire, people have reminded us of the religious wars as an argument against religion. They have forgotten that man must be completely claimed by something so that he will be ready to die for it. People also die for art, although scarcely in a war.

But this intolerance simultaneously implies an amazing liberality. Though the possessors of a norm may argue, though the content of the norm may change, the norm itself always retains its validity. Everything beautiful, everything holy, is true. The norm is absolute; only the content changes daily. It has room for Rembrandt and Giotto, just as there is also a place in the sanctuary for the abysses of God's counsels and for the song of the angels. In this norm both Raphael and the drawings of the primitives have a place, just as in the sanctuary there is room for that piety which draws the delicate lines of dogma with a firm hand, and also for that other piety which constructs an impoverished image of a strange saint. Both art and religion can be approached only in catholic fashion.

Only then does one escape a relativism which limits religious values, and those of beauty, regionally and culturally.[193] Of course the meaning of a particular work of art only becomes clear when it is understood, and all human understanding is bound to a cultural domain. A Negro from Central Africa will probably understand little of Rembrandt; until recently, it seemed as though we were equally incapable of understanding Negro art. Now we are enthusiasts for Negro sculpture. It is difficult for us to understand the meaning of Asian music. Yet even here there is no unbridgeable gulf. Our understanding of the expression of the human spirit is always incomplete; it is simplified as soon as we belong to the same cultural domain, or when the same objective spirit moves within us, or when we speak and understand the same language. But the boundaries are always fluid. The art of yesterday is already no longer our own, unless we ourselves belong to yesterday. It is difficult to understand the Middle Ages, more difficult still to understand a Negro, but it is also difficult for a child to understand his father, for a neighbor to understand his neighbor.

PSYCHOLOGICAL PARALLELS   Religion and art spring from the depths of life; both strive for the distance which separates from life; both construct a new world. But the new world of art is only "other"; that of religion, on the contrary, wholly other. The means of bringing the holy to expression through the beautiful are only of use when beauty and holiness have grown strong in the same soul, when this soul can bear and work with the tension which has been created, when the one who says the penultimate word also says the ultimate.

A psychological parallel is offered by the relationship between the feeling of happiness and religious experience. Both are completely independent. A feeling of happiness can have causes completely different from those of "bliss" in the religious sense. It can occur, even with great intensity, as a result of extremely trivial causes. Proust gives a beautiful example: the feeling of happiness which comes over a young man on the occasion of the very simple experience of well-being caused by a cool, moist environment, is therefore simply euphoria, while the same feeling is absent during the immediately preceding experience of a "happy" love.[344] Religious experience and the experience of happiness are not always bound together by a logical relationship. Nevertheless, man is happy in the possession of his God, and he possesses God in his happiness. But while happiness always means "God," "God" is not always happiness. God is more; God is he who is always "more." Similarly, man is an artist only in the possession of his God. But whoever is in possession of his God is not thereby always an artist. For God is more than beauty. The logical relationship therefore does not always exist; when it does, we must find it with the aid of one of our "influences." But they can also be absent.

Thus we search for points of access where boundaries are usually found; boundaries, where points of access are usually found. One cannot say, Whoever has God, has beauty; but rather, There is also a beauty which has nothing to do with God. This does not detract from God's all-sufficiency. Nevertheless, whoever has beauty, has God, but there is also a possession of God which does not lead to beauty.

The possession of God in beauty can be latent; it can also come to light at any moment. As soon as something "of the total meaning of life" shines forth, the aesthetic experience has become a religious experience.[3] The same is true for ethical and for scientific experience. When we see how Molière's Harpagon is concerned with the care of his money, we are experiencing a brilliant comedy. But when the miser is rid of his money and screams in raving desperation, "Alas, my poor money, my truest companion—we are separated! Since I have you no longer, I have lost all support, all comfort, all confidence. I am done with; what is left for me in this world? I cannot live without you," we feel in this comedy, which transforms itself into a tragedy, the latent possession of God, the consciousness of the boundary of life, the nearness of death, of a very perverse but yet very deep humanity which prays to money as to a god, but at least prays. Harpagon in his possession is only absurd; Harpagon in his despair is infinitely greater than his entire environment of upstanding and generous men. He is great because he is small.

RESISTANCES   In summarizing theoretically the difficulties we have stumbled upon in our search for points of access, we can here speak of resistances which oppose religion on its path toward art.

We saw earlier that sensuality is falsely counted among them.

Religion and art are both limited to the sensual. The actual obstruction lies in lack of distance, autocracy (see page 255 ff.).

Whether the holy directs itself to humans or to art, it always meets the same obstruction of sin.

That is a large word, but it is also a splendid word. It is the word of the proud man who will not serve, the word of the fallen angel who now reigns, albeit over Hell. Yet we can say it without the emphasis of the sermon. Karl Jaspers speaks, in his *Psychology of World Views*, of "shells." These are firm shelters in which man can seek protection, to which he clings. They can be principles, convictions, dogmas, forms, ideals. But they are always resistances in a double sense. They give a man a foothold, so that he is not carried away. But the foothold is a "foothold in the finite." I am a completely different man if I call myself a counter-revolutionary or a Social Democrat than if I let myself drift about in the dismal sea of my half-baked political views. In the first case I have found a "shell," a complete collection of firm opinions in which I can seek shelter, to which I can cling. It bears me along and protects me from surprising accidents, but at the same time it protects me from the surprises of eternities, and it keeps me from progressing in the service of God, should he call me forth from my safe shell. I live more comfortably as a philosopher if I can say that I am a Neo-Kantian of the Marburg wing than if I continue with my own powerless philosophy. I am actually finished as an artist if I have discovered my own way of painting, my own "bent," to which I can adhere from that time on. As a religious man I feel secure as soon as I know that I am a "right-wing liberal" or "Biblical-Orthodox." Then I have made myself comfortable in my own little world and largely shut out storm and rain; but at the same time I have shut out the wind of the Spirit and the fertile rain of God. I can no longer serve, only obey.

Those are the resistances which lie on the path from the holy to the beautiful. Art always seeks the "foothold in the finite," the closed form. It must do so by its very nature. Formless art, art which has no style, is a creature of the imagination. Religion, too, is subject to form. It also has its shells, and there are all too many of them. But it knows that the "foothold in the finite" stands in inmost contradiction to its essence. Art, on the other hand, must demand this foothold as the goal of its perfection. A myth, a ritual, a dogma are "shells," and thus mean resistance, disobedience. Living religion knows this, and bears it as a cross; it confesses it as a sin. But a novel, a drama, a symphony, a painted picture are the more perfect the more they approach the ideal of the perfect form, beauty which rests in itself. When the longing for service and the demand for obedience drive the artist to make the extreme move of relinquishing his shells, yearning for "music, not tonal art," then there arises not a religious work of art, but the end of art itself. The artist yearns for heaven, and that is dangerous for artists.

But art can find the only form which religion can recognize, the form of God, creation. Religious art always arises when we recognize in the form of man the form of God, in the building of man, creation.

Thus Goethe speaks in a famous passage about Bach. He feels, when he hears Bach's music, "as though eternal harmony were entertaining itself, as may have taken place in God's bosom shortly before the Creation."[345]

Because art, however much it may strive for perfect form, still has service as its final goal, it would extinguish itself in this service if an act of God did not save it and make possible the visualizing of the form of God in what men create.

The artist builds himself a world; one speaks of the creations of art and of creative artists. Since Shaftsbury, the poet has been compared to God, or at least to Prometheus, ". . . under Jupiter. Like that highest artist or universal creative nature, he forms a whole, completely coherent and in itself well formed, with proper order and articulation of its parts."

And Schiller:

> *Wodurch gibt sich der Genius kund? Wodurch sich der Schöpfer*
> *kund gibt in der Natur, in dem unendlichen All.*

Whereby does the genius proclaim himself? Whereby the creator proclaims himself in nature, in the endless whole.

Conversely, God is a genius.[346] The Enlightenment and the Age of Genius are right, put in another way than they thought. The artist creates figures, but if he really succeeds, if his work is more than a "work," if it becomes a living creation, then it is not the "creative genius" which accomplishes this miracle, but the creator himself. And the artist is not the proud hero,

> *Hier sitz' ich,*
> *Forme Menschen nach meinem Bilde,*

Here I sit,
Forming men after my image,

but the humble servant, who with bated breath and trembling excitement recognizes in the work of his hands the image of God.

2   THE REPUBLIC OF

THE ARTS

Something more catches our attention here, where we have penetrated into the center of art and religion. Before we attempt to determine the last, worst, connection between the two, there arises the question of the relationship of the arts among themselves. We have already spoken about "art," about the world of art, and about the artist, but there are phenomena and facts which bring us once more to practical matters. We are of the opinion that the essence and goal of art are found in representation, in the image, in form, in the figure. But are there not arts which deny this? What is the position of music, for example,[347] and dance?

The art of the image is more than "pictorial art." It is powerful; it participates in the dance, the drama, architecture, poetry. In a building, image does not conflict with sound; in dance and drama, they meet imagery without coming to blows. But in true poetry, word, image, and sound are at war. Therefore, Kierkegaard declared the poetic art the highest, in a masterly analysis which I shall cite here *in toto*:

> If one pursues historically and dialectically the development of the aesthetic-beautiful, it becomes apparent that the direction in which one is going progresses from space to time, for which reason the entire perfection of art depends upon one's freeing one's self successively from space and going over to the laws of time. Therein lies the transition, and the significance of the transition, from sculpture to painting, to which Schelling already pointed. The element of music is time; but it does not exist in time, it sounds and falls silent at once, and exists only in the moment that it comes and vanishes. Of all the arts, poetry best validates the meaning of time, and for just

that reason it is the most perfect of all arts. It need not limit itself to the moment, neither in the sense of painting nor in that of music.[197]

Thus at the start we must examine more closely the relationship between music and verbal art. Whoever discusses art must be aware that he is discussing, not beautiful decoration, a pretty embellishment of life, but life itself. A flowery style may call works of art "flowers of culture," but they are that only to the extent that out of the flower a very real fruit develops. Art is itself culture; it is like the hard work of the man who makes the world arable, who makes it his own world. Just as the farmer brings the land "under cultivation," as the craftsman makes implements out of wood, stone, and similar materials which are at hand, as the man of science cultivates the kingdom of nature or the distant past or the activity of the human mind, so the artist re-creates the world around him; he makes it arable, brings it under cultivation. Thus it develops that a separation between artists and other workers is by no means as meaningful as is usually supposed. The Middle Ages made no difference between artist and artisan; and *logica* and *arithmetica*, together with music, were called *artes liberales*. In our own time man is becoming more conscious that all the sciences contain an element of art.

As far as music is concerned, the song of a bird, the rustling of leaves, or the roaring of a waterfall are far from being music. They await the artist who will "cultivate" them, who will, in his sovereignty, determine their rhythm and melody. Music, like every art and every culture, is an act of aggression. Man takes possession of what is given him and makes of it something that belongs to him. The same thing is true of music that Evers said in his superb discussion of Egyptian monumental architecture and sculpture: it is a mental instrument between man and the event, "through whose effect man takes possession of process."[190]

WORDS   Among the conquests of man belongs the word. Language is not a system of signals by which specific signs correspond in a previously agreed way to specific concepts. It no more rests on an agreement than our society rests upon a *contrat social*.

If we ask how the living word comes to be, and is differentiated from a cry, we come face to face with the image. A cry can express much, but only in connection with a specific situation, with specific gestures. The shouting at a football stadium might seem to a person who did not see the field like the howling of the damned in Hell, but to the viewer it indicates enthusiasm. A word calls forth an image: it is *mythos*, that is, word and image together. It creates an existence by placing one before our eyes. According to Genesis, when God had created the animals, he brought them to Adam to see what he would name them, and as he named them, so were their names. Therein lies the subjugation of objects through the word, and simultaneously the connection between things and the words which designate them. In words as they were originally spoken by man lives his confrontation with subjugated things: they create for him a new world.

Language is poetry. "At the beginning of human society, every author is of necessity a poet, for language itself is poetry," said Shelley.[348] Whoever speaks produces an effect; he changes things, he transforms them into something new. We are still conscious of this when we speak of the relief which confession of something brings. The matter remains exactly as it was before we spoke of it. Yet it has become completely different. Outside the moon is shining. Someone says, "Look, the moon!" That is not a deep poem, but it gives a name to the perception and the feeling which slumber in everyone. We who observe the moon now see it with other eyes. In our life it has become something with a name. With our word we have bounded a piece of the world, have conquered it.

The word is a creative force (see pages 122, 214) and speaking is a responsible task. Words receive even greater power when they are encased in a fixed and strict formula. A definite rhythm, a definite series of words, definite, necessary expressions make of the word a formula: *carmen*. Thus it is on the path to music; in fact, it is already music. Cadance, the fixed raising and lowering of pitch, rhyme or alliteration, "exalted tone" in which a formula is recited, all bring the word nearer to music. Thus the word is, in principle, self-annihilating.

To speak correctly is incredibly difficult. Whoever speaks finds himself continually in the position of the farmer who protects his land against the floods of water; from all sides music threatens to break in. He must call up with his words images which have clear and sharp contours. He may not be borne along by the musical stream, but he feels its undertow powerfully. Deep beneath his controlled speech, tone and rhythm roar and work; and so he recites, he drones, he sings without knowing it.

The Maori sings when he is moved inwardly. We have already forgotten that he is completely natural. When we are happy or angry with someone, we express ourselves by a high pitch, but a child dances and sings. A small girl I once saw on the street was dancing and jumping while she repeated over and over in a monotone, "Riekchen is dumb." Similarly the Botocude drones endlessly: "The chief has no fear."

Actually, it would be more correct to speak not of the undertow of music, but of the dance. I speak not only with my mouth, but with my whole being. The gesture belongs as part of it, even if we Northerners have kept it to the minimum. Posture analyses long ago indicated that speaking is a movement of the entire man, and Curt Sachs has shown convincingly that spoken, recitative song corresponds to dance "against the body," and melodic song to dance "with the body." Word and tone, but, above all, word and rhythm, belong together. The word, which is limitation and image, vanishes in sound and rhythm. The dance continues, movement banishing visibility. (Of course the dance, too, is visible; but that is not its essence. Dance does not have to be seen, but perceived, experienced by the dancer.) That is the unavoidable result of the union (more correctly, reunion) of word and tone. The word as image and limitation must be defeated; the little piece of reality which it separated and set up as a monument is dispersed in the great undifferentiated totality. Rhythm sweeps the word away and destroys it.

Thus it was not without good reason that the English Reformers gave instruction that in every church a Bible was to lie ready "to be read in an audible voice," for with the singing of Epistle and Gospel, as was the custom at that time, the words and their meanings hardly received their due. The natural reaction of the musically illiterate man to coloratura singing is absolutely negative. The endless, apparently meaningless repetition of the same words, the extension of syllables over countless notes, disturb him and seem absurd to him, because he starts from the unmusical but quite sensible assumption that the words are there to create an image. He does not see this image when the coloratura makes the words whirl like an autumn leaf in the wind. Now, there are two kinds of coloratura singing, the one to which the word is indifferent except as sound, and the other which attempts to reproduce the content of a word plastically through the coloratura. The unexcelled example of the latter sort is Bach's coloratura music. In his texts he comes to no rising or falling movement, no wave breaking and no sound of bells, no flight and no quick movement, without seizing the word which created these images, underscoring the image musically with a coloratura passage. Whoever, for example, has noted the way Bach treats the word "joy" musically, is forever cured of the madness that all coloratura singing is without meaning. [248, 349] Even so, the word and, above all, the context, suffer loss. Even in the recitative, the music which remains most true to the word, the word takes second place. Bach and Wagner, the two great declaimers of the history of music who pay homage to the majesty of the word with tone and rhythm as well, are examples of this. It is hardly possible to treat the word with more respect, to express its meaning more clearly, than in the recitatives of the *St. Matthew Passion* and in the mighty declamations of Wotan, Hans Sachs, or Gurnemanz. Nevertheless, any good actor reciting the texts of these masterpieces of music will place the accent differently. For he speaks, and his word is a word which represents in images, proof against all musical imperialism. After 1600, the text is given more importance in monody, the so-called concentrating style. Claudio Monteverdi's statement is famous: "The word is the master of harmony, and not its servant."[350] But this does not solve the problem; nor does equilibrium between word and music, even if this is the occasion of a rare harmony, in a lucky case such as that of Mozart. "The tune in the service of the word? Thus the lazy and incompetent solve the problem. The word in service of the tune—or the song which becomes word, that is genuine."[93] But this truth seldom becomes reality. I know few musical settings of words which are more impressive than Kundry's *"und lachte"* from *Parsifal*. Yet I can picture to myself a great tragedienne who can express more purely with a simply spoken word in the same situation the horrible picture of the woman who mocks what is holy. Unforgettable to anyone who has heard it is the last word of Bach's Christ: *"Eli, Eli, lama sabachtani."* But closer to the event, to the desolate victim, comes the simply spoken, "My God, my God, why hast Thou forsaken me?" when it is spoken by a minister who knows the meaning of worship, pronouncing it in the Communion Prayer without music, without even declaiming. Of course I do not mean that the latter is more beautiful or better; I only assert that the words cannot stand up to the music.

And yet the words must stand up to the music, battle with it, let themselves be suppressed. For there are moments when the words are not enough. It is like the well-known song by Klaus Groth, which Brahms set to music:

> *Wie Melodien zieht es*
> *Mir leise durch den Sinn,*
> *Wie Frühlingsblumen blüht es,*
> *Und schwebt wie Duft dahin.*

Doch kommt das Wort und fasst es
Und führt es vor das Aug',
Wie Nebelgrau erblasst es
Und schwindet wie ein Hauch.

A melody is lifting
A song within my ear—
Like perfume gently drifting
From flowers to me here.

Then comes the word and holds it
And brings it to the eye;
A fog of grey enfolds it,
It fades and starts to die.

The Church has the jubilus, the hallelujah, which threatens to lose its meaning in an endless chain of notes. Objections have often been made to these many notes. But Augustine knew better: "Whoever rejoices needs no words ... for our language is too poor for God; and if language cannot help you when you may not keep silent, what is left but to rejoice, to let your heart exult without words, since your unbounded joy does not allow itself to be hemmed in by a limited word?"[97, 351] It cannot be put more clearly: music breaks through the bars of words and seeks infinite space. Upon the jubilus follows the reaction of the word, the sequence, which writes under the many notes a new text in the rhythm of the jubilus, a *prosa* (*pro sequentia*). But the sequence, too, received independent importance, retaining its own sound within church music as a whole, but remaining in harmonic agreement with the mighty musical river which flows through the Church.

The word is the point of departure for music, nothing more; it determines the mood, and then is whirled away in the flood. That is true for every song and for every kind of music. It is especially true for Dionysiac music, for the rhythm which robs one of breath; for the gasping pauses in ecstatic sound, which rise from the edge of silence; for the music of which it is said, "unconscious, highest joy." Essentially it is true for all music.

MUSIC   Even in its simplest form, where it is only rhythm, music compellingly expresses something for which there are no words. We hear this in the drum rolls of primitive tribes; we hear it also in the exclusiveness of the obsessive rhythm in Ravel's quasi-primitive *Bolero*.

Music killed the words as soon as it was born. But what, then, does it express?

In endless repetition the doxology resounds in the church: *Gloria Patri et Filio et Spiritu Sancto, sicut erat in principio et nunc et semper et in saecula saeculorum. Amen.* Every time this expression occurs in the liturgy an indication of eternity is given us; everything particular, solitary, enters into the eternity of God. But there is another eternity than this, which is described in a sermon, in a poem. Here it is not spoken at all. Music does not speak.

Schering says: "The sensible hermeneut does not attempt to translate music into concepts or words, nor to be a prophet of what the composer was thinking here or there . . . that would be presumption or charlatanry." For music can express everything, if one means by "express" the same thing as when one is dealing with words. The mistake lies precisely in the fact that one thinks music should express something in the same way words do. One thinks it has to conjure up images. One should be able to get some idea from it, imagine something. Yet all music, both so-called absolute as well as dramatic music and program music (the difference is relative), differs from words by the fact that in it one can imagine nothing or everything, unless it is imitative. But even imitation of thunder or the song of a bird becomes musically interesting only when the natural phenomenon is forgotten. We have already seen that music is nothing but music, its own world; never does it tell anything of the so-called "reality of life." But it can be the expression of another reality, of which the world, too, is only a partial revelation (see page 248 f.). Music has no name. If nothing were written in our programs except *Allegro, Largo,* etc., we should basically be none the poorer. Everything else is literature. "Shake oil and water together as long as you will, the oil will finally rise to the surface. Try, however wise you are, to marry music to poetry, music, which comes from a lighter domain, will always rule as it wills," says Werfel in his *Verdi.* Brahms is right with his arrogant statement about the writers of texts, when he writes to Reinthaler in regard to *Hyperions Schicksalslied*: "For I say something that the poet does not say, and of course it would be better if what is lacking had been his main concern." He was concerned only with the musical conception, and this is not affected by the fact that Hölderlin's poem is a much greater work of art than Brahms's composition. Bach and Wagner are both great, because the one proceeds from a Christian theology, the other from a Romantic world view, and because with their music they destroyed all Christian and Romantic words.

To that extent old Hanslick is right: whoever sings, sings a song without words, whether he wants to or not.

Music is certainly not always, not even primarily, a matter of luxuriance and enthusiasm. It can be very clear and built on the basis of firm laws. It is the art of the order of relationships, and can be expressed in numbers. That is also true for harmony and counterpoint. The musical edifice can be sketched in terms of proportion, but words find no place within. They are at most the inscription written on the musical edifice, perhaps very useful and in itself even beautiful, yet not necessary. The building remains what it is, even if the inscription is missing.

CONFLICT   Therefore, the word opposes the power of music. In our time we find a remarkable expression of this resistance in the school of the great word-magician Stefan George, the poet who once more discovered the word in its original power:

> *Des sehers wort ist wenigen gemeinsam:*
> *Schon als die ersten kühnen wünsche kamen*
> *In einem seltnen reiche ernst und einsam*
> *Erfand er für die dinge eigne namen.*

> The seer's word is granted to him only.
> When daring wishes came in his possession
> In a peculiar kingdom, strange and lonely,
> He named all things with names, his own expression.

Among the members of this school, it is Karl Wolfskehl who takes the field passionately against the imperialism of music. Of course, he attacks music because it is incapable of representing: "the only expression of the soul whose clarity does not rest upon an image." Schopenhauer had praised music because of its freedom from time and space. Yet precisely therein lies its impotence, its religious imperfection: "But we know that the revelation of every domain of life, and the ultimately attainable miracles are limited to the domain itself. God must become man in order to be God to men. We cannot see an appearance of the eternal in time, a symbol, in an art which has its own absolute nature and thereby steps out of the basic artistic-human unity." The theological portion of our problem is announced here already. The limitation of the word is essential, because it is the precondition for visibility of the divine. In fact, an image, a building, a word can be symbols, but never a sound.

Let us follow Wolfskehl a moment longer: Music "does not arise from a forming principle . . . in it chaos is added to chaos, macrochaos to microchaos. Music has sweetness and melancholy, but also the energy and fervor of life not bound in a cosmos, its surge, its path, the insatiability of material neglected by forming forces, that which glows as *hyle*, boils up, totters, everything tired, ready for dissolution, everything greedy for downfall and uprising. Chaos is revealed in music, and finds in music a related chaos." Naturally, this attack is inspired by *Tristan* and not by *Figaro*. Naturally, it is unfair and incorrect. Naturally, music is not chaos, for even the music of Romanticism, "ready for dissolution," possesses a clear and firm structure. Nevertheless, Wolfskehl's statement does not derive from a caprice. That which "glows as *hyle*" is never absent from any music, not even from the clear forms of Mozart. For limitation by word and name, by image, is missing. This he has rightly recognized.

We can ignore the question of whether the conclusion reached by him and Nietzsche before him is correct, that all music is by nature Romantic: "There has never been a Classical music." Nietzsche sees in music a product of degeneration, a "late arrival of culture." Handel is, accordingly, the last echo of the dying Reformation; Mozart is the reverberation of the culture of Louis XIV and Racine; Beethoven is the musical decline of the Enlightenment.[208, 323] Of course, Wolfskehl agrees with this. Only when the iconomachy and theomachy of the Reformation had destroyed divine visibility could Bach "cause the Church to come roaring up as a structure of sound. . . let its shedding blood suffer on the organ." But his soul, which he thought was directed upward, was in reality turned backward.

We can let the matter rest here. For us, the most important part of this observation is not the philippic against Romanticism, which can be explained in large part as a very understandable reaction against Schopenhauer's theory (see page 245 f.). A religion of feeling finds all too easily a music of feeling. The portion of music which is voluptuous, which flows with emotion, is surely not what brings us nearest the divine. It is at most a numinous influence. Any premature identification of music and religion which bases itself on their obliteration of emotion we shall have to note with great caution, even when this is done with such fine enthusiasm as it was, for example, by the young Dilthey:

How like the blissful mystery of religion is music! This surging up and calming of emotions, this flood of stormy thoughts followed by their dreamy submersion, their soft fading! Where does the magic lie which gives to sound the power to proclaim all this? A mystery, as primeval as that of the union of sound and thought [but right here lies our difficulty], is that of sound and emotion. If we might only understand it, we might everywhere walk in the mystery![353]

With respect to the musical dissolution of emotions, Wolfskehl is quite right: "All creation is a making visible, all life is a becoming visible, every mystery of God an epiphany, an enlightenment for man." In every religion, limitation, naming, localization in myth, are essential. Music has no myth.

Of course, even Wolfskehl understands perfectly well that music is not merely a matter of emotion. But it is just this connection of fixed structure with luxuriant emotion which puts him in bad temper:

> Through the strictness of its logical formation, the consistency of its articulation, it is, though in itself fully irrational, subjected to the rules of abstract mentality, capable of being called an art, almost provable to be so, but at the same time ready and willing to satisfy all unbounded, all overly powerful, all indefinite drives. [Then he continues, almost filled with hate:] Foreign, alien it stands in the course of human activity as the youngest of the arts, feeling itself to be the heir of the others, for a century the undisputed mid-point in fact among us, practically the sum total of the artists' labor and enjoyment.

Here, too, the philippic is one-sided and incorrect; music appears as the youngest of the arts only to a person who views culture as something which grew out of the Renaissance; to all others, it is almost the oldest. And yet here again there is some truth: music is almost predictable, and yet capable of the infinite, while—and now I cite Wolfskehl for the last time—"Self-representation of language, self-representation of the body are the immovable, unenlargeable soul of art, sculpture, and poetry, their actual essence, whose foci, the image of God and the hymn, stand in the midst of all art."

Here we come to the weak point of his argument. There is an art which is even older than music, more universal and more intimately connected with the entire human life; it is dance. The dance is "self-representation of the body" and music simultaneously. It is the art of totality, which comprehends within itself all music, but at the same time living, moving image and form. The dance is the art which, "free" and "controlled" simultaneously, has a logical, almost predictable structure, and is visible at the same time. It is the art in which man uses all his functions, his soul and his body, his Logos and his rhythm, in which he not only plays, speaks, and sings, but also acts, performs. All the arts, above all, music, but also sculpture and certainly words, feel this attractive power of the dance, through which the image of God is carried in procession and the words of the hymn (in truth the embodiment of all art) resound through the vaults of the church.

That Wolfskehl could forget this derives from an error which he was not the only one to commit. All too often it is overlooked that art is a function of the whole man, not only of the part which enjoys looking upon beauty. Just as we have an emaciated, theoretical man in our modern world, we also have an aesthetic man. He is caricatured beautifully by Christian Morgenstern in one of his *Galgenlieder*:

> *Wenn ich sitze, will ich nicht*
> *Sitzen, wie mein Sitz-Fleisch möchte;*
> *Sondern wie mein Sitz-Geist sich,*
> *Sässe er, den Stuhl sich flöchte.*

> *Der jedoch bedarf nicht viel,*
> *Schätzt am Stuhl allein den Stil,*
> *Überlässt den Zweck des Möbels*
> *Ohne Grimm der Gier des Pöbels.*

> When I sit, I'm not contented
> Sitting as my flesh compels me.
> I would take the chair and bend it
> As my sitting-spirit tells me.

> This, however, has no guile,
> Valuing alone the style,
> Gladly to the masses quitting
> Things as practical as sitting.

Here the egotism of the artist is seen: the artist lives in a world of his own structure, and is blind and deaf to life. In his dramatic epilogue, "When We Dead Awaken," Ibsen drew an unforgettable figure of this sort in his sculptor Rubek. Nietzsche seeks the reason for this: "A man becomes an artist at the price of perceiving what all non-artists call 'form' as content, as 'the thing itself.' Thereby he belongs, of course, to a perverted world, for now he perceives all content, our lives included, as purely formal."[323] The artist truly builds himself another world, but if this does not receive its vital forces from the world which exists, everything becomes sterile, as Nietzsche with his formalism drifted from Wagner to Bizet.

Here are found the aesthete (whose features we find to a great extent also in Wolfskehl) and the scholastic. For in the scholastic doctrine of beauty as the reflection of truth, the reflection of order and the form of things, is contained too much of the calm of the observer, and too little of the holy seriousness and passionate life of the artist himself. Art is not a game, except in the sense of play that children and primitives take with such seriousness. Art is not a mirror, a reflection, but, like human life, partakes of the image of God. Thus we have so formulated the matter that both, art and life, participate in the wholly other reality, and there are connected (see page 276). Here we must let the proud self-awareness of art speak through the actor of Hofmannsthal: "For here upon the stage is reality, and everything else is metaphor and a game in a mirror."

The artist discovers basic forms of life. His word and his sound participate in the deepest reality of life. That is their religious value, which the aesthete never understands. It leads us into a self-created world, a complete world, in which word and music, image and sound, limitation and dissolution, have their place and their original unity.

THE HOLY WORD   By the holy word we mean the spoken word of myth, the tale of "Once upon a time . . ."; "In the beginning was . . ."; "And if they have not died . . ."; and "It is finished." We mean the word which aims at reality, which brings things to life before our eyes: the creative word. This word can deal with the past, the present, or the future; but it always brings reality into the midst of our lives, present, acute, clear, sharply defined. It can be related to the most trivial and the highest reality, but always it has power, creative power, something of the power of God (see page 119).

The poet knows that: "The poet does not deserve the name of creator, if God is not the creator," as Tasso says. God speaks, and something is. A part of that power is transferred to the speaker, the poet. Whoever can speak can create.

Here lies the enormous importance of the myth, in which we comprehend all words, poetic and scientific (which has not separated itself so far from the word of the poet as we often think), and even the theoretical word. Only *logica*, as a "liberal art" in the medieval sense, moves in the direction of mathematics and music, realms in which the contours are blurred, where relationship assumes the role of concrete reality. But primarily, myth is the active word, the word which acts and affects. Its highest form we find in the word of the Annunciation.[136]

HOLY SOUND   Sound does not know the word: music is without myth, without image, without appearance. Whoever speaks a word forms an image out of rock. The event stands still as a monument about which the speaker moves. That is the decisive thing about a word. When it has been spoken, the deed stands there. Whoever sings a note stands still himself, letting the world pass by in endless procession. Around him reality moves rhythmically.[199] It would be even more correct to say that in him, inside him, the world moves rhythmically. For he has no view of that world, and it does not become a comprehensible deed for him. He has banished it within him, robbed it of forms and contours, made it audible inwardly. The note has power, but this power does not make the sun stand still. It causes the "storm of the Horites" to resound without. Thus one can say with Goethe that architecture is "petrified music," or, more correctly, that music is moving architecture.

UNITY OF WORD AND MUSIC   Words and music have a common ground, and it is holy. Art is a means by which man subjugates life. In his art, the primal force of life is revealed to man; only in a work of art does life become reality, "grow out of him."

Words and music are nevertheless different realities; in word and image there reigns another order of things than in music. An image demands space; music demands time. Words and music are related to each other as a temple to a peal of bells, as altar to altar music, as liturgy to the Church year.

The man who builds a house, carves an image, speaks a word, thereby makes space visible. I cannot see space, but I can see a house or a picture. When I speak, basically I only mark off space. My word changes space into place, indeed, into a holy place. Not only because ever since the early days of humanity the delimitation of a space by deed or word has had a ritually religious character,[136] but also because the settling of man is also in fact a holy action, a laying hold of the infinite, a making visible of the invisible. Everyone who makes anything creates form. Whoever gives a name to what has been made or formed calls it forth, so to speak, from infinite space. He creates, and his creation is an analogy to the creation of God, who calls things by name that they may be.

As the word grasps the infinite and settles it in space, so music tries to settle it in time. "Settle" is here the wrong expression, for nothing can be settled in time. Here we find ourselves in another dimension. The musician creates a reality by reaching into the infinity of time and making the inaudible audible. Space becomes visible in image and word; time becomes audible in rhythm and melody. That, too, is a holy action. Not only because for earliest humanity rhythm and song were considered the essence of the holy, but because music is in actual fact a holy action, a "settling down," to use our wrong expression once more, of man in time. Music marks off time, makes of every arbitrary time that healing time which is God's time, the time of grace.

That is the holy ground of words and music. Here both are one, just as time and space are one. Something of this is revealed to us in the dance, that art in the primitive sense which is more deeply rooted in humanity than verbal art or music. In the dance, music and rhythm become visible, while the image dissolves in rhythm and sound. Therefore, dance is nearest to the basis of art, the bounded and defined, yet flexible and fluid. To a lesser degree, that is also true of those forms of art which have as a precondition an apparently impossible union of word and music: the hymn, the song, the music drama (which did not come into being with Wagner). Therefore, vocal music makes such a deep impression upon unprejudiced minds, revealing something of this holy basis.

Holiness is here given with life itself; it is born, so to speak. We think of Plato, who finds in conception and birth the beautiful and also the eternal in man. In time, this basis, this womb from which all life emerges, remains nearer than in space. The house, the picture, the word have received independent life. The symphony and song remain connected with the life of the mother. Nowhere do we find this expressed more beautifully and nobly than in the prelude to *Das Rheingold*, through the mighty pedal note on E flat under the rising waves of melody. It is as though we had found the way back to our origin, as though we were going beneath the primal waters of the ages.

In the service of the holy, too, the conflict between word and music is resolved, not in the sense that both lose their nature, but on the contrary; the word remains limiting, music enthusiastic. The conflict assumes another nature in the art of harmony. It would not occur to anyone listening to Mozart's music to demand precision in the words. Whoever observes the clearly defined figures of Homer by no means wishes for their dissolution in sound and music. The great artists of this harmony as a rule cannot be transposed. Verbal art cannot be made out of Mozart's music, nor can one set Homer or Dante to music.

Of course, music is not able to preach. It possesses no symbol, no myth. A sermon does not gain in clarity by being musically "illustrated" or meditated upon by the organ. But, nevertheless, we must sing during worship. We cannot do otherwise; in fact, we should have to sing the entire service except for the sermon. Otherwise, immovable verbal monuments arise.[354] In worship, word and music come together in the visualization of the sermon and the becoming audible of God's movement through time. The word pronounces and limits; music sings of the ineffable and undefinable. Music cannot preach, but it shares in the proclamation. For this is not performed by the spoken word alone, but also in the visualization of the sacrament. It also takes place through music. If that were not so, music would have to vanish from Christian worship. Calvin even wished it so. In music we can overhear an echo of the song of the angels. We cannot do without the myth, without clearly defined narrative of the act of God. But we cannot forget that when God created the world the morning stars sang happily and the angels greeted his creation with their song. The spoken word is absolutely indispensable, as is music. It is as in the sacrament: no sacrament without words, but also no sacrament without the elements, without the water of baptism, without the bread and without the wine. The spoken word is in no way superior, either to music or to other things which were created, and which, after man has wrested them from the depths of nature, are used by God in his grace for the *kerygma*. This takes place through nature and through culture, both of which belong to God's creation.

THE HIERARCHY OF THE ARTS   Let us now return to our question (see page 288) concerning the general relationship of the arts among themselves.

A hierarchy of the arts does not mean that a particular art is more valuable than the others. The glory of the sun is different from that of the moon. Every art has its own value. And every art has its own relationship to the holy. There is no art which guarantees the best expression of the holy or which stands nearer God than another. But there surely is a mid-point about which the arts can be ordered; this mid-point is the image.

Historically and phenomenologically viewed, dance is the original art. All arts are found within it in its undivided unity. The image, made dynamic through movement and countermovement, sings and speaks simultaneously, forms a circle and then a house. From the unity, the arts free themselves by turning to the image: undanced drama and rhetoric, painting, sculpture, and architecture. In this image, and it does not matter whether we are concerned with a verbal image or a painted or carved image, the holy action of art stands still, as though it were standing before God. Only one single art here goes its own way, and that is music. It is nothing but movement, and excludes the image. Word and music strive for each other, and occasionally, as though by a miracle, they find each other. But the word frees itself impatiently from the embrace of the notes, it is reminded of its nature as image and shakes off its tonal nature once more. On the other hand, music strives continually to subjugate the word, to whirl it along at its tempo and destroy it with its whirlwind. The arts developed out of the dance in the direction of the image; then in music the image dissolves once more, and all the arts meet again in a nameless, undifferentiated unity.

Here, then, the theological meaning of the hierarchy of the arts becomes clear. That theology which places the impersonal, the spiritual (in the sense of the immaterial) in the central position will attempt to follow the movement of the arts from the fixed center to music. Such an immanent, pantheistic, mystical theology will understand music as the essence of all arts and leave the image behind. Schopenhauer did this in masterful fashion. A theology, on the other hand, which thinks historically and transcendentally, which places the incarnation of God at the center, will seek the mid-point of the arts in the image. It will find a strong analogy between the undifferentiated primitive religion and the equally undifferentiated art of the dance. It will ascertain a similar analogy between the mysticism which once more breaks through all forms and boundaries, and music, which knows neither content nor boundaries. But for itself it will find the connection between beauty and holiness in the image; and, since God created man in his own image and walked the earth in the form of a man, this theology will be convinced that it cannot be a sinful pride to search for God's image in these forms of his creation.

3   THE IMAGE

OF GOD

With the image of God, we have arrived at theology. The times when it seemed that theology and art could have no understanding of each other are past. Artists no longer look down upon dogma, and theologians are at least willing to consider art as a problem. In Holland, admittedly, there still exists the semi-Puritan opinion of those who think that God would gladly see us despise his gifts. But in a period which is painfully aware that it is no longer able to raise itself to the biblical height, one can hardly share the attitude of Schopenhauer that biblical subjection, especially in the New Testament sense, is unsuitable for the pictorial arts.[172] It is clear that an art which loses God loses itself, and that art can never develop better than upon well-plowed and fertilized dogmatic ground: "For a Church, a firm doctrinal position is the necessary condition for the flowering of Christian art. It is hard to imagine what would have become of Protestant art if the doctrine of Protestantism had not previously been firmly established."[299, 355]

Therefore, we must investigate the theological premises and consequences of the criterion placed before us; namely, the recognition of the form of creation. We shall discover that the discussion of the image leads us into the midst of theological aesthetics, into the theological center of the arts. Every consideration of the theological position occupied by art must proceed from the image of God. Here lies a possibility for the holiness of beauty and the beauty of holiness.

A pictogram from Alaska represents a shaman herding deer. In this very primitive drawing one can see the movements of the shaman.[356] How is it possible that an image, a fixation of movable reality, moves? How can a picture live? Here the Laokoön problem is raised anew.

304

We may not seek the life of the image in any merely apparent movement. By pictorial fixation life is not killed; a new degree of life is attained. We could also say that the man who represents, kills living reality in order to awaken it to a new life. All represented life has died and is resurrected.

The ancient Egyptian tomb statues were overwhelmingly great art, yet, when they had once left the workshop of the sculptor, no mortal eye saw them any more, sealed as they usually were in subterranean tombs. How are we to understand that? The artist creates; he makes what is not into what is; he creates a living reality. But this reality is not objective and static, since it exists only within the cult, in the possibility of "forcing," as Evers calls it. "For just as a fluid which is to become a solid needs a particle about which its crystals can collect, so, in the belief of the Egyptians, everything that is to be present needs a firm place in tangible reality so that something can arise from it. The Egyptian must compress what is intangibly present and localize it somewhere, and must give it its name and its form, for without this active deed of man it would not stand ready for his forcing. As this compression of the present day, this providing with a name, the monument arises."[199]

Here we achieve deep insight. Things do not exist, at least man has no approach, if they are not represented. Only what is represented as an image in a second reality has existence. The second reality is that of a directive relationship to the cult.

If man wants to achieve a real relationship with what is, it must first "take place." It is not enough that it simply be there, that it happen. It must first be imagined or represented, in order to really exist. "The holy becomes valid only in the concrete situation of man." We can express the holy only when we can see it as an image. Conversely, we have access to the things of our life only when we understand them as symbols of the holy: fatherhood in the fatherhood of God, love in the love of God, beauty in the beauty of God. "All creatures are shadows, echoes, and pictures, are vestiges, likenesses, and masks."[136] There is no reality besides that which is consummated in an image. From this point the path leads us into the midst of theology, into the doctrine of the image of God.

PHENOMENOLOGICAL COMPONENT Now that we are speaking of the image of God, I need not busy myself with various abstract concepts which have been constructed about this concrete reality. I will, therefore, also say nothing about "points of contact" and similar hybrid, half-familiar, half-mathematical quantities which the devil may possibly need for his visits in heaven, but which only create confusion, where we are concerned, with the relationship between God and man. Bible and Church know nothing of either "contact" or "points." They speak concretely, massively, and honestly of the image of God.

What is an image? An image is something which can be seen and touched; it has firm contours and a particular nature. It is neither thought nor "idea," but harsh reality. But it is also not simply a thing, an object. It takes its nature from the fact that it tries to express, reproduce something, to be a likeness. An image is always an image "of" something, "representing" something, "meaning" something. If it does not do that, or if it does that no longer, then we do not speak of an image, but, at most, an ornament. The image is characterized by the fact that its reality coincides with another reality, with a "symbol," that is, coincides in the literal sense. Your portrait is not only a piece of canvas with paint, it is also a reality which in mysterious fashion coincides with your reality. For this mysterious coincidence we have the expression, "It resembles." By immersing ourselves in this expression, we can also understand the third quality of the image, that quality which was clearer to an earlier generation, and to the generation of the authors of the Bible, than it is to us. The relationship between both realities is neither accidentally nor purposely caused. The picture is not something arbitrary, but the essence of what is represented, its manifestation, its form of appearance. We are not concerned here with a curiosity from the history of religions, which would not concern ordinary mortals. We are concerned with the primitive expression of a deep truth. What does not appear before our eyes as an image we do not perceive within this world as powerful. We then say that it will have to be imagined, but actually this is just a turn of speech. In reality there is nothing for us of which we cannot make an image or likeness. The Second Commandment does not refer to one or another unimportant fancy, but to life itself, insofar as it is conscious, human life. In another place[136] I have called this peculiarity of our conscious life the "twofold experience of form." We experience things twice, first directly *in actu*, the second time in an image, as form; the first time as uninterpreted life, the second time as transformed life. Only what stands before our eyes as image, as form, as figure, has meaning for us, only that confronts us as power.

Therefore, a primitive man who treats an image as the reality it represents is not simply in error, but in sin, as we all sin because with conscience the transgression of the commandment was given us. Primitive man expresses it differently, but basically knows better what the concern is here than do we.

Now if the image is thus the concrete form, that is, the essence of a particular reality, then this is also true for the similarity of divine reality, for the image of God. Only when divine reality appears to us as an image can it mean something to us, does it have power over us. We know divine reality only as "symbol," that is, we know it only when it coincides with the represented reality of the image, when it has taken form in our reality. Divine reality must "take place" in this world, it must somewhere receive concrete contours, so that we can approach it and it can rule us. It must become "valid."

Everywhere in the world this "validity" is experienced in the wooden image, stone image, or verbal image; in any case, as image, as actual form. In the image, divine power becomes actual, it can be approached, and it approaches us. The image is not an arbitrary phenomenon, but a form in which and through which man can meet God.

Thus the temple is the image of the dwelling place of God, the manifestation of his presence. Of the many creatures of this world a few are singled out as "images of God," as bearers of his presence among men. These mediators can be images in the literal sense, but all other creatures are equal which, on whatever ground, appear to bear the "likeness" of God.

EXEGETICAL-HISTORICAL COMPONENT   If we now question ourselves as to what the Holy Scripture teaches of the image of God, on the one hand our task is made very easy, because we can limit ourselves almost exclusively to the text (Gen. 1:26,27); besides this there is almost nothing written about it in the Old Testament. The passages in the New Testament are dependent upon this basic text. On the other hand, precisely this isolation of the idea of the image of God creates difficulties for us, because thereby space is left for the most varied opinions. An extensive commentary on the text from Genesis would be out of place here. Therefore, I shall summarize briefly what seems most important to me.• [357, 358]

• According to Humbert, there is not much difference between *selem* and *demuth*. The latter "appears" somewhat less original than the former. Both are objects, not abstractions. "The author of Genesis 1:26 wants to express the fact that God makes man truly like the image, the palpable image of Elohim, his bodily appearance." But conversely: "God did not become flesh in man, but is only his physical archetype."

In the older creation story, God creates man out of the dust of the earth; he then breathes the breath of life into the form thus created. Thereby the man becomes a living soul; that is, a living, animated man. This does not mean that he receives a soul. Of dichotomy or trichotomy the Old Testament knows nothing. Even the "living soul," further, must die. The younger story of creation tells of the creation of man in a way which does not stand in contradiction to the one named above, but which places something else in the foreground. "Then God said, 'Let us make man in our image, after our likeness; and let them have dominion over the fish of the sea, and over the birds of the air, and over the cattle, and over all the earth, and over every creeping thing that creeps upon the earth.' So God created man in his own image, in the image of God he created him; male and female created he them." The general meaning of this text is unmistakable: it is the likeness between Elohim and the human creatures. Image *(selem)* and likeness *(demuth)* mean exactly the same thing: likeness, similar form.

The created thus resembles his creator. It is nevertheless important that God is here designated by the name Elohim. It has justly been pointed out that *"beselem Elohim"* may not be replaced by *"beselem Yahweh."* The old problem of the plural ("Let us make men") has not yet been solved for us, since the Genesis text does not speak of a similarity with Elohim creatures, as it says in Psalm 8:5: "Yet thou hast made him little less than God" (Elohim). Creation in the image of God in Genesis 1 is thus, in any case, a creation in the similarity of divine beings, in the image of beings from the divine realm. It is difficult to ascertain to what extent the author of this creation narrative identified Elohim and Yahweh, and we may by no means assert that he did not mean that man was created in similarity to his creator (the text is emphatic on this point), or that this creator is not the God of heaven and earth, the absolute God. But the use of the word "Elohim" does introduce a certain hesitance. When, later, Elohim receives a name, when the generic concept is replaced by the revealed name of God, it is Yahweh who proclaims the prohibition of images. Even later, in Deuteronomy, it is again Yahweh whose voice sounds from the midst of the darkness, and who has no form which could be viewed (Deut. 5:8; 4:12).

But this by no means detracts from the extremely concrete meaning of the Genesis text. The Old Testament may shrink from ascribing a form to God, and especially from bringing this into connection with the human form, so that God reveals himself in his name as soon as he appears among his people. The mention of the similarity of man to God may be limited to the less actual form of Elohim. All of this does not change the fact that man is made in the image of his creator, and that this is not metaphorical language, an apt thought, but a visible and tangible reality. We cannot interpret Genesis 1:26–27 without Genesis 5:3. For there it says, after we have once more been reminded of how God created man in the image of God, that this man, Adam, became the father of a son "after his own image." The expressions used in this verse are exactly the same as those in our text: *bidmutho* and *kesalmo*. The matter is here the human form. Adam's son is like his father, just as Adam is like his creator.

A generation like ours, which has been brought up in the doctrine of psychophysical dualism, or at least parallelism, finds it difficult to get used to the fact that this was unknown to the Old Testament. Neither in the Old Testament nor in the New Testament is man a soul which resides in a body, or a spirit which has the use of a body, but a living person, a "living soul." A biblical author never imagined that similarity could be anything but what in fact it is, that man looks like God. The question, Is this meant spiritually or corporally? has no meaning. If one wants to accommodate himself for a moment to this correct use of language, the answer must be: both spiritually and corporally.•

The consequences of the creation of man in the image of God are formulated no less concretely: man rules over the other creatures. The right to do so does not derive from his greater strength or ability, but from his special relationship with God. The fact of this relationship differentiates him from the animals and has the effect that he can and may rule them. In the same spirit, Psalm 8:5 says: "Yet thou hast made him a little less than God, and dost crown him with glory and honor. Thou has given him dominion over the works of thy hands." As God rules over the universe, so man rules over the earth and the fullness thereof. He rules "by the grace of God." Thereby the idea of the likeness of God has taken on concrete form. Man makes the world his world, and, as it says in Genesis 1:28, he fills the earth and subdues it. Man is here assigned his cultural task, not as contrast to the service of God, but as service of God, as this has become possible because the

---

• The remark of Köhler, that the addition "male and female created he them," prevents us from thinking of outward form, is all too formalistic. A son certainly can resemble his mother.

creature resembles the creator. Thus Psalm eight is a "cultural and faith-ful echo of the theologoumenon of Genesis."[358]

We might have reason here to speak with Paul de Lagarde of the most massive anthropomorphism. I shall not protest. We shall later see whether this anthropomorphism is a bogey or a blessing. But if the intention is to say that here God is very like man, then that is doubt-less correct to the degree that in the most concrete sense man is like God. God created man in such form that he would be like him. The nature of man is a likeness of God; here we must spiritualize nothing, nothing at all, since we are concerned with man, not with his "conscious-ness" or his "immortality" or the like. Genesis 9:6 must be so understood that reverence is not paid to man because of something that he is, but only because God created him after his image. Whoever spills human blood, his blood shall also be spilled by men, for God has made man his image. The only passage in which the idea of the image of God appears outside of Genesis is Sirach 17:3.

And now to the New Testament. In this regard, that is, anthro-pologically viewed, there is no difference between the Old and the New Testaments. The latter is just as "primitive" as the former. It is in no way influenced by Greek anthropology, which presupposes the separa-tion between body and soul. For pneuma is not spirit in contrast to body, but divine-holy in contrast to human-sinful life. The entire Platonic differentiation between body and soul is unbiblical. Far from being ashamed of the "primitiveness" of the idea of the image of God, we must return again to the simplicity and naïveté of the biblical use of lan-guage. We must not judge the Bible by Greek anthropology or by modern epistemology; on the contrary, we must develop our anthro-pology and epistemology from what revelation teaches us about our-selves.[359]

In the New Testament we find the idea of Genesis analyzed and worn out. Texts which simply repeat what was given in Genesis are James 3:9 ("With it [the tongue] we bless the Lord and Father, and with it we curse men, who are made in the likeness of God"); and I Corinthians 11:7 ("For a man ought not to cover his head, since he is the image and glory of God; but woman is the glory of man").[360] An extremely important extension is brought by the text Romans 8:29: "For those whom he foreknew he also predestined to be conformed to the image of his Son, in order that he might be the first-born among many brethren." Hereby the image idea is trans-ferred from God to Christ, and instead of being bound up with creation, is bound up with the new creation of man. The idea itself still remains the same, and here, too, it is concrete and realistic. Redeemed man receives the same form as the image of Christ (*Summorphous tes eikonos tou huiou autou*), and Christ he may even call his brother. This is the more eloquent, since here no general expressions are chosen for the divine, but God is named by the name under which he chose to reveal himself in this world: Christ. The God who actually comes into the human life is here no voice from the midst of the darkness, but a form, as in Deuteronomy. He possesses a visible form, that of the Son. And just as the significance of the first creation lay in our similarity to God, so in the second it lay in our similarity to Christ, God become flesh.

This, of course, presupposes that Christ was himself the likeness of God. We shall be like Christ, who is like God. We are the image of the image of God. In II Corinthians 4:4, Christ is called *eikon theou* (image of God); in Colossians 1:15, the *eikon* (image) of the invisible God, the first-born of all creatures. In Hebrews 1:3, other expressions are used, but with the same meaning, that the Son is "the glory of God, and bears the very stamp of his nature."• [361] But by far the most important passage is the great hymn in Philemon 2:5 ff.:

Have this mind among yourselves, which you have in Christ Jesus,
Who, though he was in the form of God,
Did not count equality with God
A thing to be grasped,
But emptied himself,
Taking the form of a servant, being born in the likeness of men
And being found in human form.•• [362]

This section is completely dominated by the contrast between *morphe theou* and *morphe doulou*. Christ has the form of God, but he gave it up and took on the form of a servant. Thus he fully and completely became man. Again the image-of-God idea is bound up most closely with the mystery of the Incarnation. This consists in

• H. Windisch points out parallels in Philo and the Wisdom of Solomon.
•• Verse 6 is the famous crux. Dibelius thinks two interpretations are possible: *harpagma poieisthai* or *hermaion (heurema) hegeisthai* can mean "count as easily obtained acquisition." Then the sense would be: Christ viewed his similarity with God not as something acquired to which he would thus hold fast, but on the contrary, something surrendered. The second possibility is the old interpretation of *harpagma* as theft. Christ did not steal divinity as did Adam or many of the spirits of the Gnostic systems. To me, the first possibility seems the more probable.

the fact that Christ gives up his equality in order to be equal to men. And when, at the end of the hymn, a name is given him which shall be above all other names, that happens because he did not desire it, not even equality with God, but wanted only to give. Compared with Genesis, everything here has changed. The second Creation has different presuppositions than the first. God does not create after his image, but discards his image. His revelation is his emptying, his incarnation. In Genesis, God creates man after his image and thereby achieves man. In Philippians, God gives up his own form in order to seek out man under his own form, the form of a slave or servant. Here is the heart of the Gospel.

But what has happened, that Paul speaks so differently from the redactor of Genesis? There is no answer in Holy Scripture, neither in Genesis nor elsewhere.• But the Church has developed with great assurance from the data of Scripture: the image of God in man is obscured, lost. Between Genesis 1 and Philippians 2 lies the Fall.

On this point the entire Church is in agreement. Something happened to the image of God, for something happened to creation. One cannot say, with an easy conscience, either of Adam, the fallen man, or of us, that we are images of God. One can only discover with fear and trembling that God wanted to make us into his image. At this point the Church begins. It can begin neither with creation nor with the image of God. I must begin with redemption and the figure of the servant, and from that point must find my way back to Creation and the image of God.

The Church has not always been able to say clearly where this path proceeded, nor has it always spoken clearly and unambiguously of the image of God. We who now must struggle for this understanding will certainly not hold this against it. The Church's hesitation and doubts are ours. They are very human. We found them already announced in the hesitation of all mankind about the image of God. We dare not recognize it, but we cannot do without it.

It is significant that the Eastern Church pictured the image of God as undistorted as possible, while the Western Church emphasized the shadows and privation much more. In this dichotomy is manifested an aporia which has never left the Church in peace, and

---

• The thesis of the darkening of the image of God through the Fall certainly cannot be developed directly out of Genesis. "The thesis of the Old Testament is clear and definite: the *imago dei* is an indispensable part of humanity, and no Fall changed anything about it.."[358] Thus only the Church can speak of a Fall.

which will never let it rest, because it is determined by the dichotomy of man himself. There is a turn of phrase which says that one cannot have one's cake and eat it, too. In regard to the image of God, the point is that in some manner this must be possible.

The fact that such a great portion of the argument which was conducted over the image of God had to remain fruitless was, if I am not mistaken, conditioned by two factors. First, this argument, which burst into flames over something concrete, a living reality, an image, was conducted with abstract concepts; a mystical datum was treated in a theoretical manner. Possibly this difficulty would have been overcome if a much worse mistake had not been made, a theological one; a beginning was made not with Christology, but with anthropology. This is seen in the fact that Irenaeus, Origen, Gregory of Nyssa, and others, like John Damascene later, differentiated between image and likeness, between *eikon* and *homoiosis*, *imago* and *similitudo*.

That this differentiation cannot be supported by the text of Genesis is not so important. Many a good point has been advanced with a wrongly interpreted text. But the differentiation itself is one of the most unfruitful attempts at a natural theology. Omitting the variations which occur, the heart of the matter is that the *imago dei* includes the universal human characteristics: human form, reason, freedom. These characteristics, in spite of the Fall, remained preserved. Adam, nevertheless, possessed in addition the *similitudo dei*, that is, moral equality with God, communion with him, and immortal life. These gifts were lost, and only through redemption can man attain them again. Origen even goes so far as to say: "God indeed made man after his own image, but not equal to him," which in any case contradicts Genesis. But even Irenaeus explains that the *similitudo* in the beginning was not perfect and never became so. By the Fall, man became subject to death, and thus the continued growth of the *similitudo* was prevented; man lost his communion with God and eternal life. Only Christ brought back with the *similitudo* eternal life and communion with God.[363]

Thus in all these considerations the image of God is divided into two parts: a man consists of a natural part, which remained spotless, and a spiritual part, which was lost to him. A Christian is therefore a human being like any other, but he has received something in addition. These considerations proceed from man in himself and explain his humanity as image of God. They do not proceed from Christ as *morphe theou.* They attempt to begin with man, and they consider it natural that he was created. Then they wish to ascend to perfect, prefected man. They overlook the fact that we cannot believe in a creation outside of Christ, that we cannot understand ourselves outside of Christ. They build a house with two stories. At the fire of the Fall, the lower remained whole. The upper was destroyed, but Christ rebuilt it.

Thus the further extension of the image of God is present. If we can differentiate between *imago* and *similitudo,* then the scholastic differentiation into *dona naturae* and *dona gratiae,* between what man has as a creature in any case and what was given him in addition (*superadditum*) but was immediately lost, lies near to hand. If one assumes that the human condition suffered when the *justitia originalis* was lost, one's life still becomes the opposite of a living image. The condition consists of a foundation of humanity, which remained rather undisturbed, beside what is added by grace. And because our condition today seems to agree with this dichotomy, one supposes it can also be found in Adam, who actually consisted of two men. The one fell, and the other still goes upright to this day, even if more or less shaken by what happened. This says too much in two respects: grace is irretrievably surrendered and seen as supernatural; "nature" is held too safe and incontrovertible, and it is forgotten that the Christian faith actually has no room for nature, but only for Creation, and that this creation as a whole is fallen.[364]

In other words, the Church has comprehended superbly that between Genesis and Philippians the Fall of Man must be proclaimed, but all too often it replaced this proclamation with the doctrine of man which had as little regard for the reality of the image of God as for the Fall. The image of God and the Fall are harsh realities, which cannot be transformed into characteristics, conditions, psychology, nature, or miracle. Of course we do not have the least right simply to accuse the Church of all this. She attempted to understand the relationship between the man of sin and the man of God; she tried to maintain the continuity between both and yet stress the weight of sin. We shall never be able to do anything different, and if we attempt to do so by different means, we shall possibly avoid the error of the ancient Church, but not without falling into new errors. For it is no accident that we find in Holy Scripture the concrete figures of the image of God, the Fall, and the Incarnation, but none for the loss of the image. Genesis 3 is not the continuation of Genesis 1, for there is no longer any talk there of the image of God. Nor later with the Incarnation, for it deals only with Christ as the image of God and the image of man. In between lies darkness, that darkness which does not remove the continuity, but makes of it an object of faith which can be grasped neither by a theory nor by mythical, concrete modes of expression. It is the darkness in which we live, and of which we therefore cannot speak, either in images or in concepts.

Before we continue with concepts, we shall turn to that branch of the Church which has always ranked the image far above the concept: the Church of the East. Here, in the icons, lives the doctrine of the image of God.• [225, 358] Of course, it can be objected that the connection is too strongly realized, the burden of sin weighs too lightly, the danger of an apotheosis of man is near, a theology which leads to the sacrament of the icon is so negligent of any anthropology that it has become complete theology, therefore running into the danger of ending, not in a heaven on earth, but in a dream world. . . . All that is completely true, and I am prepared to go the whole distance with the West, in the footsteps of Anselm, Luther, and Calvin. But we must not forget that perhaps nowhere else in the Church was the concrete reality of the image of God so seriously taken as in the East. Here we are apparently very far distant from Genesis, for it is not God in general, but the revealed God dwelling among us, Christ, whose form is like ours, so that we can feel safe in taking our own form as an expression of his. Or are we rather here on the right road, which lets us find our way back to Genesis? The doctrine of images of the East rests completely upon Christology. If we want to discover the doctrine of the image of God, we will in any case have to represent the divine. Then we shall not be allowed to forget "that God, in his revelation to man, has a face."

But let us return to Western dogma. There is not much more to be said. The differentiation already described between *imago* and *similitudo* remains in force, although under other names such as *imago substantialis* and *accidentalis*. It is well known that Luther left little or nothing of natural man, and his Church, too, ascribes nothing good to man. He was contradicted, of course, by the synergists, who by means of the old separation thought they could still expect something of man. Then again there was an extreme result, such as the view of Flacius, who thought the *imago dei* had been transformed by the Fall into an *imago satanae*. Thus one wavered between full loss of the *imago* and its de-

• The biblical idea of God has been much too strongly spiritualized. The Old Testament prophets opposed images of Yahweh, but by no means imagined him as a man (Isa. 6; Jer. 1:9; Amos 4:13; 9:1; Ezek. 1:26 f.).

formation; between total depravity of man and a little spark left within him.

It is no accident that the birth pangs of the Reformation went hand in hand with iconomachy and iconoclasm. Always when theology questions the image of God, the images are thought of, and vice versa. The proper exegesis of Genesis 1 always goes together with that of the Second Commandment. Thus we find in Reformed theology again and again the tendency to reduce man to nothing and to deny completely the possibility of God's assuming form among men. An Occamistic trait, which would like to destroy every connection between revelation and the world, between anthropology and theology, between the knowledge of God and knowledge of the world, can hardly be denied here. The Reformation occasionally goes to the opposite extreme from that of the Eastern Church, and threatens to lose all continuity and reduce the significance of man to a simple "being there."[365]

No less great is the danger of a dichotomy in Calvin. According to him, Adam, as the image of God, participated in divine wisdom, righteousness, virtue, holiness, and truth. But the Fall and man's ingratitude have extinguished the image of God within him. "Thus the image of God which he bore was extinguished; to the degree that he alienated himself from God through sin, he alienated himself from the bond with all those goods which one can share in, in him alone."[235] Although Calvin breaks radically with the differentiation between *imago* and *similitudo* (and a fortiori with the doctrine of the *donum superadditum*) and thus views the whole man as the image of God, he dares suddenly to say this image is radically extinguished. On this path he is followed by the Heidelberg Catechism, which contrasts to Creation in the image of God, "in true righteousness and holiness, so that man might rightly recognize God his creator and love him with all his heart and live with him in eternal blessedness," the fact that after the Fall man tends to hate God and his neighbor, that he is completely incapable of anything good and inclined toward everything evil, and that only a completely new beginning, a rebirth through the Spirit of God, could save him.[366] The Netherlands Confession also views "all of nature" as "distorted" from being the bearer of the image of God. Even if one must add that man has "retained small remnants" (*petites traces*), these only just suffice to deprive him of any innocence. Beyond this, Calvin dares to declare that the image of God was not destroyed, but only distorted: "Therefore, although we admit that the image of God is not fully displaced and destroyed in him, yet it has been so disfigured that only a gruesome distortion remains."[235, 367]

What, then, is left of the image of God in man? Not much, just enough to ascertain that he actually possesses nothing except godlessness and being worthy of damnation. But how is this related to our nature as creatures? Or has the Fall robbed us of even that? We find in the entire theology of the image of God the same hesitation which we already discovered in our phenomenological component, and which is related to every manifestation of God in form and image, going hand in hand with an inability to do without this image. The Eastern Church, in spite of strong opposition, retains the form. The Reformation destroys almost all forms so thoroughly that it often threatens to destroy the bond between God and man. The expression "God in flesh" has no meaning when nothing more remains of this "flesh"; then it shrinks back and discerns "small remnants." The "small remnants" are basically no better than the *imago* in opposition to the *similitudo*. In the second case, man goes with lowered head; in the first, he crawls and raises up his head out of the dust in order to see how badly off he is, yet continues to crawl. If it is true, as Dr. Koopmans says, that the word "flesh" in Reformed Protestantism has a less existential overtone than elsewhere,[368] then this threatens the central Christian idea of revelation, no less than the danger of an apotheosis. The incarnation of God presupposes a man. And a man is only man because he was created after the image of God. Thus Adam can sin; an animal does not sin. Thus can we be saved; everything else is not saved.

Here we can end this historical portion. After we have discovered that Schleiermacher introduces the image of God openly, as a proof of the impossibility of engaging in dogmatics with biblical expressions, we should prefer to forget that he transformed the *imago dei* into "consciousness of God," finding likeness insufficient, and bodily resemblance too anthropomorphic.[369] We should prefer to consider that Martin Kähler exhibited much more insight when he took the dominion over animals and the "coporeality" as "essential to the *imago dei*."[370]

DOGMATIC COMPONENT   If now in conclusion I try to formulate the points of view which are to lead us to the image of God from our consideration of the dogma of the creation, I am by no means doing so in an attempt to make a correction. Such an attempt would not only be stupid and arrogant, but also completely fruitless. Dogma is given us. Dogmatics remains a very uncertain affair. If we nevertheless retain it, we do so not in order to arrive at a more correct scientific knowledge. Scientific knowledge can be of value to us. But it is our goal to confess our creation and our creator with our entire being. This confession is only possible actually. Therefore, we must always begin from the beginning again.

Here, as everywhere, the beginning lies in Christ. The Creation is neither a pious opinion nor a plausible hypothesis, nor an obvious point of departure. It is a matter of faith. And faith begins solely with Christ, the Mediator of Creation. Thus we understand the image of God in man on the basis of the image of man in Christ. Only through the knowledge of Christ can we attain the knowledge of man. We can only point to ourselves and say "Behold the man," when we have first said, "*Ecce homo.*" In *The Epistle to the Romans,* Barth says that the image of the Son is the image of his death (Phil. 3:10). Through Christ, God enters the human world in the form of a slave, in the form of the crucified, in the form of him who was a worm and no man. Here lies our whole dogmatic question with both its equally necessary poles: God has an image in this world and of this world. He became flesh, and of the dust of the earth he created himself a form, a figure. The image is and remains an image, it is visible and tangible, it is not a spirit, not an idea; it does not participate in what we call "spirit," but no more in what we are accustomed to call "body"; it is a man. *Ecce homo.** At the other pole is the form of a servant. It is no apotheosis of man, no acme of his capabilities, no highest ideal, and certainly no divine spark or nucleus, which will soon unfold in its entire fullness. It is the bent and tortured figure of the Man of Sorrows, not a great man in the series of the "immortals," but scarcely even a man, and just for that reason the son of man and Son of God.

Let us now ask ourselves what significance attaches to the creation after the image of God. If we view it in connection with Pilate's judgment seat and Christ's cross, we must answer: as much as everything, as little as nothing. We must say both at once. Let us first see what our proposition does not say.

Creation after the image of God does not mean equality with God. We are not so now, nor were we so before the Fall; we are so according to neither our actual nor our essential existence. We are created after the image of God, but are not equal to God. We may probably assume that there is scarcely such a great difference between the Yahwist and the

* Newman: "Also through the fact of the incarnation it was taught us that material, as an essential component of us, is as capable of sanctification as is spirit."[371]

Priestly Code in Genesis; that in the one, God created man after His image, and in the other, causes him to be led astray by the words, "You shall be as God." The thought of being equal to God does not occur in the Holy Scriptures a single time in relation to man. Man is not "as God," and many of the "virtues" which were ascribed to him by the Church at once fall away, as his supposed immortality falls away. The Greek idea has here pushed aside the idea of Israel. Man is a mortal, a "living soul," which, since it lives, can also die. Equally miscarried is that doctrine of the divine spark, the scintilla, which so often inspired mysticism, and which believes in a divine principle, a germ in man. We find nothing of that in the Bible. We find only a similarity, but never God in man. We find only God in the man Christ. As soon as we speak of a divine spark, we have lost all Christology, which dissolves into anthropology. Christ then becomes a spark which burst into flame. The entire contrast between creator and creature vanishes.

And what does the principle of the *imago dei* say in place of this? It says to us primarily that man is the lord of creation. In most recent time, we have all too often taken this truth as a truth of culture. But it is a truth of faith, and points to the close connection between faith and culture. The place of man in creation, his self-differentiation from, and his dominion over, the animals is not a triumph of culture, nor a catastrophe (as we are often inclined to think today); it is, rather, a result of the creation of man after the image of God, "to have dominion over the fish of the sea," etc. The dominion of man, who subjects the world to himself and bends it according to his will, is no grounds for presumption. "Nothing more powerful than man," as the ancient poet sings, but nothing greater in self-denigration and despair, as today's bearer of dominion, technology, tries to suggest. It lies within God's purpose and is to be understood as his assignment. The cultural assignment of man, to conquer the seas and plow the fields, to clear trees and tame animals, is a command of God. Man is placed in the world by God, and entrusted with an assignment. The fact that he fell into sin makes this assignment enormously difficult, makes it unfulfillable, yet by no means frees him of the assignment.

In the second place, the principle of the image of God says to us that man has a possibility in respect to God. When Barth says that: "The possibility of faith, as is given to man in the reality of faith, can be understood only as lent to man by God, and lent exclusively for his use," that is self-evident, insofar as all gifts of the creator are, and remain, his property. I understand Barth's concern. "As soon as we try to understand it [the possibility] as somehow inherent in man, the other principle of human incapacity would have to be put in force again. We do not understand it as a possibility *inherent* in man." Nothing, nothing at all, belongs to me, but all is given by God. What we as creatures are and receive does not become our property which we can use as we like; therefore we speak of the creation of man, not his appearance or his development. But then we must take perfectly seriously the "similarity to God's form" which Barth ascribes to the created man. Otherwise, says Barth, we could not view man as the subject of faith, faith as his deed and experience. "Perception of the word of God could not take place if, in this word and this perception, there was not something in common between speaking God and listening man, an analogy, a similarity amid all the dissimilarity occasioned by the difference between man and God."[372]

In other words, if man is not similar to God, does not have the *morphe theou*, the one expression of the revelation vanishes. I ignore the question whether the formulation of the revelation as "hearing the word," peculiar to Dialectic Theology, is the correct one. I shall also leave undiscussed the fact that in the following passages Barth uses the abominable expression "point of contact." He replaces it immediately by "image of God," and we shall have to admit that Emil Brunner is right to hold, contrary to Barth, that this image does not mean the humanity and personality which remain to man. I am inclined to find him right when he discards the "exception of a residuum" and declares openly that the image of God is destroyed. It makes no sense to help one's self out after the old manner with dichotomies along the lines of the "remaining" and the "lost" image, or the "lost" image and its "residua." An image has no "residuum"; it is or it is not. What is inherent in man as a human being and what is not are anthropology's work of decision, nontheological anthropology, be it understood. Its results show a certain parallelism with theological anthropology. But we must never identify them. Theological anthropology never proceeds from man as a human being, but from the man of faith. The man as human being has inherent possibilities and other powers, but he does not have the image of God. If he is ever to receive it again, it needs nothing less than a new creation. And this, too, *qua talis*, can never refer only to portions. God creates us completely afresh, not half or three-quarters. Fallen man has no connection with God. If he had, he would not be fallen, he would only have stumbled.[372] The image of God for fallen man can mean only the image of Christ, the *morphe doulou*, that is, the death of the "natural" man, the resurrection of reconciled, redeemed, re-created man.

Only in this connection, furthermore, does theology have the right to speak of "nature." Nature in the theological sense can never be the given, simple existence which has come of itself, in a word, the "natural"; from all these concepts philosophical anthropology proceeds. In theology, "nature" means only fallen creation. Natural man is not man as he developed, but as he fell, or even less, man as he ought to be by his situation. He was robbed of his nature through the loss of the image of God—to express it with a paradox, denaturalized.[373]

I have gone a good part of the way with Barth, but I am not certain whether Barth will go the rest of the way with me. For now also the "similarity to the form of God" must be given full weight. What was given us at creation and then vanished is returned to us at the new creation, that is, the image of God. It is not an "idea," not a symbol after the manner of idealism,* not a norm, not an analogy, but an image. Not only phenomenology, but also biblical realism, warn us expressly of a distortion of image to a symbol, metaphor. Scholasticism understood this realism better than did idealism. The concern is the form, the stamp, the figure of God. Thus the concern is matter and spirit, for the concern is living reality, human reality. It is nowhere written that Adam in the state of innocence had no body. With similarity to God, with God's form, man receives his particular nature, body and soul, external and internal. Sin causes him to lose his nature together with this similarity. What is left we call "nature," that is, man without God, animals, and plants.

Therefore, I cannot agree with Noordmans, who in his sermon on the Creation as the giving of form sees only paganism, and will tolerate creation only as a critical principle.[375] I am afraid that with this critical

---

* A fine example of the idealistic understanding of the image as symbol is given by Paul Hofmann. God, he says, is the symbol of the meaning of life, the mystery of saying "I." And then: "It is hardly less 'correct' to say with the Bible, God created man after his image, than with Feuerbach that man created God after his image. For I-saying, freedom, continually creates man according to the symbol of God in which it is interpreted. It is the sense of 'freedom and of life' to want to create the image of God out of its will to self-realization."[374] In contrast, very realistically and powerfully, Karl Barth states: "Who and what the self-revealing God may otherwise be, one thing is sure, that according to the witness of the Bible in his revelation he has form, and just this possession of form is a self-disclosure. It is not possible for him, and it is too little for him, to be his own double in his revelation; double, insofar as his self-disclosure, his possession of form, is plainly not self-evident, but is an event."[372]

principle we shall sooner end up with idealism than with the realism of the Bible. Quite assuredly the Creation is separation, but only because it is a forming, a giving of shape, and vice versa. It would also be difficult to imagine what we should do with the word "image" if the Creation were only separation. The only thing left is to destroy it. The language of dialectics here blocks the path of the language of faith. The "point of contact" here reveals its true philosophical form. If we pursue this direction further, we shall ultimately find ourselves no longer in the dialectic of faith, but in the antinomian thought of theoretical reason. "A true idea of revelation knows neither a linear contact of God's actions with the cognitions of human reason and capabilities, nor a paradoxical, absolute opposition of God and world, time and eternity, which ultimately issues from reason."[376] In my opinion, we should do better to ignore in the future all argument over man *capax* or *non capax infiniti*. The revelation of Jesus Christ is not concerned with infinite man in contrast to finite man, but with the living, holy God in contrast to the sinner. It is not concerned with points of contact between two antinomies, that philosophy may search for, but with creation and new creation. It is not concerned with a tangent line, with a mathematical point, in which God and the world meet without extension, but with the form of God in creation and new creation.

I have not forgotten that Barth spoke of the possibility which was given man with the image of God, as a possibility of faith. The form which God gives with creation, which he restores at the new creation, is not a directly attainable, not a "natural" form. It is only concrete for faith, but not any the less concrete. Faith knows another reality than the empirical, but the reality of faith is not that of theory or of mathesis. It is by no means an idea; it is living reality. For faith is not an abstraction, but obedience. It is the duty which is laid upon us as bearers of the image of God. The dominion over the world comes to us from the King on the Cross, and is only exerted in the *morphe doulou*.

In this simple obedience lies what a secularized Christianity is wont to call its "cultural task," and concerning which it asks with alternating distaste and appetite to what degree it must or may be able to fulfill this task. This cultural task is in reality the obedience of faith, and it is fulfilled where we recognize the form of God's creation and adapt ourselves to it. Here we find the possibility and the reality of art, whose nature is form; but here we also find the possibility and the reality of the Christian life in the broadest sense of the word. It is the setting of faith in worship and liturgy, in the order of state and society, in the entire "service" which God demands of us, by desiring to become "of like form with the image of his Son."

This possibility and reality we call sacramental, whereby we indicate that it concerns neither an immediately accessible, empirically given reality, nor an abstract or idea. The concern is the image, not the symbol or the imagination. Two warnings are heard here. The first is that of mysticism, thoroughgoing mysticism, which seeks its God in emptiness, in the complete lack of images, its salvation in "coming away from the image," while it stumbles over all localization of God in the world. We hear its warning, and we hear it with respect. But it is not the voice which speaks to us out of Holy Scripture. It is not the voice which spoke from the Cross: It is finished. The second warning stands in the Second Commandment. It is the voice from the midst of the darkness, the voice which has no form: "Thou shalt make no image." This warning we hear, and we should like to obey it. We know that this commandment stands in the way of our life as expansion, as subjugation of the world, indeed in the way even of our becoming human.[47] We know that obedience costs us our life, as it cost the life of our Lord. We know that natural human life is nothing but the creation of images. We know the danger that threatens us, the taking of the image we have formed as the image of God which was given to us. It is the primal, and actually the only, sin: idolatry. We also know that it is written that we shall make no image, but not that no image may be given to us. And we know further that the entire life of faith consists solely of reverent recognition of this given image. As the Russian icon painter does not make a beautiful painting as a crown of human beauty, but, rather, discovers in awe the features of his Lord in the material which takes form under his hands. We spoke in another connection of these forbidden images as resistances, as shells in which man is happy to shut himself up, of that fixed form which must be the idea of every art (see pp. 186, 286 f.).

Here we come once again to that darkness which lies between Genesis and Philippians, between the creation and the new creation, those "dark streaks," as Noordmans once called them, that prevent us from viewing the creation directly from our sinful existence and from our existence sanctified by faith, the darkness that prevents us from drawing a continuous line from the creation to the Incarnation. We find the reality of the Fall. Nothing can be said about this. We cannot locate the dark streaks immediately in cosmology or anthropology, but we can think nothing, do nothing, which must not cut across these dark streaks. In Genesis, nothing is told us of the loss of the image of God. The whole biblical narrative from Genesis to Philippians nevertheless treats the history of this loss. If the image of God appears again, it has "neither form nor glory," but has emptied itself into the form of the man of sorrows.

Between the death of Christ on the cross and his Resurrection also lies the darkness. There, too, we humans cannot see with perspective, but that does not change the fact that everything which is God's has form. The new creation which begins with the Incarnation attains the Resurrection and is completed in the dividing, judging, but also building, forming work of the Creator Spiritus. In faith, man is "in the form of God," says Barth. He agrees with Thomas when the latter says: "But if the Christian faith instructs man about God, there arises in man a reflection of the divine wisdom." But he adds that this is no *analogia entis*, but an *analogia fidei*.[372] There is indeed no likeness external to faith. What does not come of faith is sin, is outside of God. There seems nevertheless to be no reason to set belief and being in opposition. Faith is not directed at an abstraction, but at that which is. It is not a mode of viewing which does not touch the nature of that which is, but it is a discovery of that which is after its true nature, as it is before God.

Therefore we do not believe that we are immortal, but that God has the power to rouse us from death, to renew our mortal flesh, to create us anew. The possibility which lies in the image of God does not mean a kind of capability, a talent which distinguishes man, but the possibility that God, who formed him of the dust of the earth, will give him a new form out of the same dust by causing his resurrection. "For if we have been united with him in a death like his, we shall certainly be united with him in a resurrection like his" (Rom. 6:5).[377]

Therefore we hold fast to the image of God. Man, as he is created, resembles God. Later we must cross all this out, because the image is destroyed, but that must not be. The true mode of human existence is that which resembles God. It seems to me that this is also Calvin's thought when he says very crassly that man "of himself is nothing more than depravity," and no less clearly that this is a depravity of something which was good: "We say that man on the path of nature degenerated into depravity, but that this depravity by no means lay in him by nature." • [235]

• To be the image of God belongs to man by nature, says Kreling.[378] True, if, in the first place, "nature" means creation and, in the second, "belong" does not mean "belong by right."

Through faith we hold fast to the image of God. We cannot command it, we cannot hold it. We can only share in it when we share in the image of God among us, in God in the image of man, in Jesus Christ, who emptied himself and took on the form of a servant. God "has a face," or as a member of the Confessional Church said: "The message that the word of God assumed earthly form in Jesus Christ compels every Christian, and especially the preacher of the Gospel, immediately to give this form his undivided attention. Whoever has heard the message of the incarnation of the Word can never again pass by this form, can never again want to conceive of Christianity as something formless." " 'Christianity' is the Christ," says Asmussen.[245] But this form is the form of the incognito, it is sacramental, it does not come without outward glory, it is always hidden form.

> Humbly I adore thee, Verity unseen,
> Who thy glory hidest 'neath these shadows mean;
>
> Jesus, whom now veiled, I by faith descry,
> What my soul doth thirst for, do not, Lord, deny,
> That thy face unveiled, I at last may see,
> With the blissful vision blest, my God, of thee.[230, 379]

Here we touch upon sacramental theology. For "sacrament" is nothing more than image, than "sign," through which that which is represented is made present. To go into this in more detail would be out of place here. We content ourselves with saying that the image of God among us is the Son, who has emptied himself of his majesty; he is the servant, the crucified, the resurrected, whom we may not touch. Therefore in art, as Maritain says, the *"moyens pauvres"* are better able to present his form than are the *"moyens riches."*[150] Therefore glory in its Christian meaning is found only in humiliation. *Ecce homo.*

The new man, the new creation of God, is "renewed in knowledge after the image of its creator" (Col. 3:10).[235] We have paid too little attention in theology to the Holy Spirit, the Creator Spiritus.* Through God's Spirit, all things came to be; God's Spirit creates them anew every day. He creates in, and from, sinful reality of "nature" the sacramental reality of faith. He makes us recognize God's creative form,

* Koopmans rightly says that the Reformation, in its sacramental doctrine, put the doctrine of the Holy Spirit once more in the foreground, which in the Middle Ages had almost been buried (*Oud-christl. Dogma*,[104]). But that is no reason to bring the Holy Spirit and sacrament into oppostion. On the contrary, it is the Holy Spirit which creates the new, sacramental reality.[368]

by making us be of like form to the image of the Son. The Holy Spirit gives us the continuity which we can neither see nor experience. In his creative work, the image of God from Genesis is identical with that from Philippians. He, the giver of life (*vivificans*), is one with the Father, Creator of heaven and earth (*factorem coeli et terrae*), and with the Son, through whom all things were made (*per quem omnia facta sunt*).[372]

We finally refer to the work of this spirit against those who are not able to see the doctrine of the image of God as anything more than a degraded anthropomorphism. From Xenophanes to Feuerbach and Paul de Lagarde, it has been asserted again and again that man made God after his image. It is remarkable that together with the very praiseworthy attempt to obey the Second Commandment and not create images autonomously, there is hidden behind this accusation again and again the denial of a living God. It is precisely among those who see in anthropomorphism a weakness or madness that the danger is clearly shown of the image becoming generalized, abstracted. In spite of the intention of serving God in spirit and in truth, one falls into the temptation of replacing God with the divine or with the universe. Whoever knows the sacramental reality of faith, created by the Holy Spirit, to him the accusation of anthropomorphism does not matter. He knows that he may present himself to God in human form because God himself assumed this form, as the word became flesh. Indeed, he will continue to long for the moment when the veil is torn away and the form of the king in majesty arises from the form of the servant. If there is a dogma which is eschatological from beginning to end, it is that of the image of God, which at the start we are no longer able to see, and at the end not yet, and which we all recognize behind the veil, in the sign of bread and wine. But this does not detract from the reality of the image of God. The Sacrament, the presence of the Lord in our midst, is in any eschatology another reality within ours, grace within nature. Here is the "strange mystery" of which Pascal spoke:

> He remained hidden behind the veil of nature, which hid him from us up to the incarnation; and when it was necessary for him to appear, he hid himself more deeply yet, by wrapping himself in humanity. He was much more easily recognizable when he was still invisible than when he made himself visible. And finally, when he wanted to fulfill the promise given his apostles, to remain with men until his final exaltation, then he decided, in the strangest and

darkest of all mysteries, namely in the forms of the Eucharist, to have his abode.[380]

This visibly invisible reality, this sacramental life in faith, this creation of the Spirit, is the image of God in our midst, within us. It is one who dies, who is emptied, but it is the reflection of God's glory and the mirror of his nature. Thus the doctrine of the image of God ultimately leads us to faith in God, not in the God of the philosophers, not in an *ens simplex et infinitum* (simple and infinite being), but in the living Lord, the Father who moves, who gave himself to the world in his only beloved Son, and set up his image among us in the form of the crucified.

That is also the answer to the "theology of the word." It would gladly have opposed word and image to each other, like word and sacrament. Does not the image possess color and sound in contrast to the simple, impoverished word? Is not fear of images, to which we pointed, a protest of the word against the glory of human culture? The answer must be that whoever says "image," at the same time says "word." The word is nothing else than the image: it defines, it forms, it gives color, it presents. But if it is taken in another sense, by seeking in the "theology of the word" a means of escaping the concrete reality of the world and concrete reality of revelation, one runs the danger of mistaking the revelation itself. One moves in the direction of idealism, seeking the nonsensual, but not the divine. The Word is the word become flesh, flesh of our flesh, of our sinful flesh. We do not speak of the crucified Word, but of the crucified man, of the form of the Man of Sorrows. The form newly created in Christ is the form of the cross, the form of death and humiliation, but nevertheless, form, the form of resurrected life and of glory.

The doctrine of the image of God includes the entire theological aesthetics or aesthetical theology. In the form of the crucified, humiliated and problematic, yet eternally worthy of worship, lies a judgment, but at the same time also a justification, for all human attempts at creating form. In his triumph lies also the possibility of the miracle which we can never attain, but which is given us as grace: the expression of the holy through the beautiful.

4   THE THEOLOGY OF

THE ARTS

If in this manner we seek the path from art to theology and from theology to art, we find a theology which we can comprehend in the following schema:

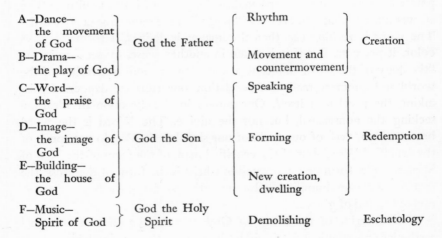

A—Dance— the movement of God		Rhythm	
B—Drama— the play of God	God the Father	Movement and countermovement	Creation
C—Word— the praise of God		Speaking	
D—Image— the image of God	God the Son	Forming	Redemption
E—Building— the house of God		New creation, dwelling	
F—Music— Spirit of God	God the Holy Spirit	Demolishing	Eschatology

We begin at the center:

D : THE IMAGE   Christian theology does not begin with God, but with Christ; not with creation, but with redemption. Only sorteriology has entrance to theology. Thus, at this point begins also the theology of the arts. Its center is the image, the fact that God represented himself. The central idea is therefore pictorial art. Of course, the representational element is missing in no art, just as Christology is missing in no portion of dogmatics. All art is representational art. So-called pictorial art is

328

so, nevertheless, in a very special sense. It is completely dominated by the form, by the shape. The further we go from the mid-point, the more it is blurred and disappearing: in art, it becomes music; in theology, it becomes mysticism. The mid-point lies between two extremes, between two eschata: creation and spirit. At the mid-point stands form, in which God represented himself, the form of the crucified.

Form is the central principle in both art and theology. Thus it was already in primitive culture. "It seems that a feeling for form is the beginning of wisdom, and since that can also be said, in a deeper sense, of the fear of God, the study of the fine arts and of religion in their earliest historical relationships would perhaps contribute something to bringing these two expressions into harmony."[10]

This also occurred to the philosophy of the Platonic school, which understood beauty as the reflection of the true (Plato), of order (Augustine), and of form (Thomas).[150]

In the image, the movement of God is brought to dynamic fixity. The image is not immobile; rather, it is petrified movement. The love of God, which set all things in motion by the force of its irresistible movement, came to a halt on Golgotha. Since that time there is a time and a place of salvation, a figure and a form. If we continue this movement autonomously, then we are carried along by ecstatic formlessness, the blissful denial of time and place which reigns in music and mysticism: nameless and infinite. Then we pass from the realm of the Son to the realm of the Spirit without recognizing that the Spirit proceeds from the Son. If we try to explore the ground and origin of the divine movement, we arrive at the creation, in the realm of the Father. We remember then that there can be no reality which does not exist as image, that creation and representation are closely related to each other. And we remember that we thought we always recognized in the "creations" of art the form of the creation. God created; that is, he formed. He created man after his image; he created all things through his love, which took on form in Christ, the archetype and mediator of creation.

We approach the creations of art, as we approach also God's creation, from redemption. This means that we view them as a portion and form of that great work of creation which God began in the crucified and resurrected Christ. We never know the creation immediately, as we know nature. What is given to us as the work of the merciful hands of God we know only through and as his newly creating love. In this world, which appears to the unbelieving eye as a piece of blind nature, lives and fights God's world, God's kingdom; and we can partake of it.

That kingdom is not of this world; it cannot be established. It is sacramental, a spiritual world in and behind the external world. And art, too, in which the form of creation can be recognized, bears this sacramental character.

C: THE WORD   If we return toward the creation and the realm of the Father, we arrive first at the word. As we have seen, the word is also image. That connects it with redemption. It is simultaneously sound, which calls for the image, which unites it with creation. We therefore speak of the inspiration which is an echo of divine inspiration.[150] The word which comes from God returns to him also in the form of praise. It directs itself also to human understanding. In theology this is the place of the sermon, which expounds the ineffable mystery of the love of God to men in comprehensible words. In verbal art (of course also in the other arts, but here centrally) lies, above all, the relationship of the artist to his—here we could blaspheme and say "public," which is almost as vile a curse as if a preacher spoke of his "public." The latter has a congregation. But what does the artist have? In German, one can speak of a Bach or Mozart congregation (*Bach oder Mozartgemeinde*), but everyone feels that this does not clear a path; it merely crosses a boundary. The organic position which art occupies in society is here once more put in question, and we can make no decision in this regard until we have found the position of art in relationship to God. Nothing is more fatal for art than a separation between public and people. The Russian, Konstantin Aksakov, says much that is true:

> The public orders thoughts and feelings from another shore; the people draws its life from the spring of the fatherland. The public speaks French; the people, Russian. The public eats forbidden food on fast days; the people fasts. The public sleeps; the people is already up and at work. The public despises the people; the people forgives the public. The public counts 150 years; the years of the people are not to be counted. The public is transitory; the people, eternal. The public includes the "whole world"; the people, the village congregation. The public and the people have epithets: among us, one speaks of the "favored public," but of the "Orthodox people."

"The public forward! The people back!" Such was the significant cry of a policeman.[231] Indeed, as soon as the preacher has found his congregation again, the artist his people, many questions in regard to Church and culture are solved.

B : THE DRAMA We go further back from the mid-point and arrive in the realm of the Father, at the creation. In it we see first the movement of God, which we find mixed with the movement of man in the drama. Time and place, which we discovered here, present themselves as the playing areas of God and man. The history of the world is the play of God and man, movement and countermovement of the protagonist and his opposite upon the earthly stage. All dramas created by writers and brought to life by actors are only a reflection of that great drama.

A : THE DANCE Finally we arrive at the ground of creation, the movement of God. Man dances because he is freed, mobilized by a moving power. In the most ancient, danced worship he follows this divine movement.

E : BUILDING The sacramental world is clearly manifested in a building. It is a bounded space, a delimitation of the playing area. Its model is the city of God. Art works here with great masses. It transforms great pieces of nature into a dwelling place. But form is lacking. Therefore, it can lose its holiness and become an empty shell. Of course, this danger threatens all arts, but it appears most clearly in architecture.

F : MUSIC This same danger is not small for music, the last art we have treated. Music does not work with masses, it occupies no space, and shape dissolves in it. In its most recent development, even its form threatens to vanish; endless melody tries to disperse every form in infinity.[93] I say this by no means as a criticism of music. That belongs to its nature. It represents eschatology in the theology of arts. We human beings can speak eschatologically only in terms of denial. We found this element in all the arts, but most evident in music. If the denial becomes simple negation of all form whatsoever, then it breaks not only the chains of words, but also those of music; then it becomes more and more like the theology which likewise denies every form, even the mysticism given by God. Just as every art has a musical component, so also every theology, every way of speaking of God, has a mystical component. If this becomes independent, then every theology becomes impossible, because all speaking ceases. Likewise, one is no longer able to hear perfectly musical music. Both theology and music lose their character of revelation, their connection with the ground of movement, and become immanent movement.

This need not be. Even the Hallelujah is a step from the comprehensible word to the incomprehensible, infinite melody. But at the same time it is the confession of the martyr:

Cecelia's dress is red, and at every blow the blood flows stronger,
Hear, louder at each blow, this voice, victorious over death,
Until at last, completely freed from the child who can no longer
   hold it back,
The joyous Hallelujah rises up in the inextinguishable sapphire.[157]

INDEPENDENCE AND INTERDEPENDENCE   Our time is full of yearning for the lost unity of life. Everywhere efforts are being made to replace the tangent planes with concentric circles. We have had our fill of limited "realms," and justly so. But this yearning must not tempt us to try to revive the primitive, nor even to erase the boundaries; least of all should we anticipate all that only exists in the eschatological sense, that is, through the grace of God. "Among primitive peoples, art and morality, as well as science, melt together with a confused and complex activity which one can call religious, but which in reality already contains the germ, the principle, of all the higher activities."[76] But we cannot restore this artificially. We can only recognize boundaries and points of access. The unity is a matter of faith. Art is not a province of life, still less, in the sense of the nineteenth century, a subdivision. Art participates in all of life, and all of life participates in it. Just as the whole of life, it has its origin elsewhere. This origin is hidden from our gaze. Therefore we need again and again the independence of art as a defense against the imperialism of scientific or dogmatic thought. The life stream of art does not flow into a fruitless and artificial seclusion: "Thus art strives to return to an undivided total life, seeking a new, a conscious, an articulated interdependence in which it, like all other realms of life, can simultaneously preserve and surrender its own nature."[236] We must constantly be aware that this striving is only a direction of life, not a goal attained. The goal attained is only conceivable in the beyond.

The recognition of the creation of God in the creation of the arts is analogous to the Platonic recognition in the reverse sense: it is a recognition in hope, not in fact. A complete unity of religion and art would be neither conceivable nor desirable, for both would have to be absolute. We have repeatedly stood at this boundary. Absolute religion is mysticism; it is without shape and without sound. Absolute art can neither be seen nor heard. True art is eschatological art, "music, no longer tonal art," the invisible image, the word falling silent, the dissolving dance, the building which is lost in the stretches of the infinite landscape. In silence, religion and art meet and interpenetrate. Religion and art are parallel lines which intersect only at infinity, and meet in God. If in spite of this we continue to speak of a renewed unity, of influences by which holiness and beauty can meet, of a point at which religion and art meet in our world, we mean a direction, a striving, a recognition, which ultimately must destroy itself.

POINT OF INTERSECTION   This point of intersection of religion and art we shall find where art turns to the absolute; where the wholly other is. For that was our definition of the holy. We have already seen that the holy by its very nature cannot approach the beautiful; the beautiful must instead betake itself to the holy (which, of course, does not mean that beauty gives up its rights in favor of those of the holy). But it is also true that the holy, equally by its own nature, already bears the beautiful within itself. Its meaning abolishes any other "meaning." It only remains to find the places where beauty passes over into holiness.

Thus we must tune our ears and sharpen our eyes for the beauty which confronts us with an absolute claim, for the beauty which appears in absolute majesty. We must listen to the word which is the Last Word, to the note which strives for the absoluteness of inaudibility; we must keep a lookout for the image which reminds us of the image and likeness of him whom we cannot see, for the movement which is conveyed by the rhythm of the stars, for the building which is the house of God. But we must also search within ourselves, to see whether we experience the beauty which is thus revealed to us as the wholly other. This we shall only know when beauty not only attracts us, but also repels us; not only enchants us, but also disturbs us in a way we never knew before. We seek in beauty both the friendly countenance of God and the terror of the Lord; we seek the Comforter who calls to us when we are weary and heavy-laden, but also the terrible one who repels us from himself with, "What have I to do with you?" At this point of intersection we seek, with the words of Rudolf Otto, that beauty which is both fascination and awe, which we approach with glad hope, but with trembling reverence.

The aesthetic form of life in itself, of course, brings edification and broadening, making us forget the ego for the sake of something differ-

ent, something higher. But only religion seeks the absolute and the
wholly other. Therefore only religious art is "one which causes the
ultimate sense of life to flow out into the play of richly related forms
of phantasy."³ The artist makes the depth of things resound:

> *Es haben aber die Dichter schon*
> *Und die Erbauer der königlichten Paläste*
> *Etwas geahnt vom Ordnen der Dinge,*
> *Der ungeheuren dumpfen Kräfte*
> *Vielfachen Mund, umhangen von Geheimnis,*
> *Liessen sie in Chorgesängen erschallen, wiesen ihm*
> *Gemessene Räume an, mit Wucht zu lasten,*
> *Empor zu drängen, Meere abzuhalten,*
> *Selbst urgewaltig wie die alten Meere.*

> But already the poets
> And the builders of the royal palaces
> Suspected something of the order of things,
> The enormous, dull forces'
> Multiple mouth, surrounded by mystery,
> They caused to resound with choral song, assigned it
> Measured space, to press with weight,
> To push toward heaven, to hold back seas,
> Powerful itself as the ancient seas.

But this order is not the fully real, the total order:

> *Was aber Paläste und die Gedichte;*
> *Traumhaftes Abbild des Wirklichen!*
> *Das Wirkliche fängt kein Gewebe ein:*
> *Den* GANZEN *Reigen anzuführen,*
> *Den wirklichen, begreift ihr dieses Amt?*

> For what are palaces, and what are poems;
> A dreamed reflection of what is real.
> No net can enclose what is real:
> To lead the round dance,
> The real dance, are you ready for this task?¹⁴⁷

HARMONY AS THE CREATION OF GOD   Upon the holy ground
we found harmony. We ascertained that it was achieved by men. Art
is nature and culture, and in both holiness is revealed. But it is also and

even primarily creature, the creation of God. Whoever believes this cannot view art as a birth from the primal womb; he cannot view it as a conquest of man. Of course, it is this, but by nature it is something else. The holy will of God also stands behind art.

This belief also shows us the reverse side of harmony: holiness means distance. Between the holy God and his creation yawns a mighty chasm. The "creation" of the artist is by no means a parallel to the creation of God. It is its dullest reflection, and is completely overwhelmed by the light of the life of God. Whoever truly serves beauty, serves God. But whoever serves God does not yet therefore serve beauty. God can destroy for his servant all beautiful words and sounds. The deepest, even the ultimate religious art, cannot exist before the face of God. In its highest forms of expression we feel a longing for a different image, a different song; for something which would be no longer "art." Whoever hears or uses many words feels an indescribable longing for the Word which is with God. Even in art, creator and creature confront each other as God confronts his image in man. Maritain expresses this clearly and beautifully when he says of God: "His and only his love calls forth the beauty of that which he loves, while our love is called forth by the beauty of that which we love."[150] Thus God's love is also wholly other than that of the artist. All came from God's love, even beauty. Our love, even if it devotes itself to a work of art, is only love returned.

Nevertheless, this is not said in order that we should have misgivings. There is creation. There is distance. There is incarnation. And there is proximity.

According to the Christian faith, he who created the heaven and the earth as a rule is the same who, as a servant, descended to earth:

> Behold, there lies in dingy stall
> Whose lordship rules above us all.

And if even here Maritain's statement holds true, that "no form of art, however perfect it may be, conceals beauty in the same way that the Virgin concealed the creator within her,"[150] yet we may believe that God gives us something of himself in art, in word and in sound. Through beauty we can share in his work of new creation. Perpendicular through nature and culture in its heathen holiness, the work of God's creation is erected, even in the work of art of men, which serves him. We may change the scholastic "*gratia naturam non tollit, sed perfecit*" (grace does not abolish nature, but perfects it) as follows: grace does not abolish nature, but creates it anew.

Therefore there is no "religious" art. Here Maritain warns us again: "If you want to make Christian art, be Christians, and seek to make a beautiful work, in which your entire heart lies; do not try to make it Christian." For genuine art is Christian: "Everywhere where art— whether Egyptian, Greek, or Chinese—has attained a certain level and a certain degree of purity, it is in expectation already Christian, because all spiritual radiance is the promise and image of the divine weighing out of the Gospel."[150]

There is an old Flemish verse about the bells' journey:

> Upon Maunday Thursday,
> The bells all go to Rome,
> Over hedges and treetops
> On Easter Eve they come home.

Thus the soul of the artist, during the period of Christ's Passion, undertakes a quiet pilgrimage to the holy place of God. Perhaps it hardly knows this. The builders of the great cathedrals did not think of "holiness"; they hardly thought of beauty, but, above all, of doing good work. "They believed, and, as they were, so they did. Their work revealed the truth of God, but without intention, and precisely because they did it without intention."[150]

God's holiness would destroy all art were it not at the same time for his grace, which deigns to reveal itself in beauty. Before the face of God, art is nothing and less than nothing (*ut palea*, like straw, said Thomas Aquinas). But this is the great paradox of faith, that before the face of God and from God's hand art receives simultaneously its life and its glory.

A METAPHYSICS OF ART?   Is what has been said sufficient to arrive at a metaphysics of art? I hardly think so. We shall remain phenomenologists. We do not want to forget that we have spoken only of experiences and phenomena. We shall let it rest at that. Logically viewed, we can call everything of the essence of art which we have related to the essence of religion "mere analogy." Thereby it becomes useless for metaphysics. Rudolf Otto warns justifiably of premature conclusions which, for example, might be drawn from the analogy of the musically and the religiously irrational; the one can be a "schema" of the other, whereby they by no means coincide.[2]

We have therefore not attempted to identify the metaphysical nature of art with the metaphysical nature of the world. Such attempts appear to us, furthermore, as not very fruitful. We have attempted only to illuminate the nature of art a bit more, as it is offered to us in experience and appearance. Further, we have shown how our gaze, going in all directions, makes us aware of the nature of religion, as it is presented to us in experience and learning. We do not say: Go along this path and you will arrive at the point where the two paths beginning here, those of beauty and holiness, cross. We do not believe that we shall find that path. But we say: Climb up upon this height and you will see how the paths of beauty and of holiness approach each other, growing distant, until finally, in the far distance, they can no longer be told apart. Thus we shall view this study, to use Kierkegaard's phrase, as "preliminary." We erect no ultimate truths, but remain modestly to one side. We believe we have noticed something there, and so we point it out.

We are in agreement with Schopenhauer, who says that music plays a special role in this work of pointing out (see page 245). But that it occupies a special position which differentiates it from the other arts, we cannot agree to. We can only repeat that every true work of art is in a sense religious. Every true work of art bears within itself the germ of self-abolishment. The lines yearn to be erased, the colors to pale. Every true art is experienced as the incarnation of what is further distant from us, and different.

A WORSHIP OF BEAUTY? We declined a metaphysics of art, because it is only a surrogate for something which art possesses in a world of the beyond. Here religion has its divine correlative in faith. But it does not coincide completely with faith, and it must not be confused with faith, though it is nevertheless rooted in faith. Religion as a human gesture derives its strength from faith, from the divine act. Still, there is nothing which could stand in the same relationship to art as faith does to religion. In other words: religion, in faith, becomes worship. Beauty, on the other hand, is served, but not worshiped. Wherever we find worship of beauty, we note at once that form and content are taken from the realm of religious belief. For example, the well-known lines of Jacques Perk:

> O Beauty, ever hallowed be thy name;
> Thy will be done, thy kingdom come in flame.
> No other god be honored next to thee.
> To see thee once and feel thee is enough,

> Though death at once our life's small candle snuff.
> What matter? Highest bliss was given us to see.

Shelley, too, who in his glorious lines in the "Hymn to Intellectual Beauty" fights against the forms of the old belief and can find no other forms for his worship:

> No voice from some sublimer world hath ever
>   To sage or poet these responses given—
>   Therefore the names of Daemon, Ghost, and Heaven,
> Remain the records of their vain endeavour,
> Frail spells—whose uttered charm might not avail to sever,
>   From all we hear and all we see,
>   Doubt, chance, and mutability.
> Thy light alone—like mist o'er mountains driven,
>   Or music by the night wind sent,
>   Thro' strings of some still instrument,
>   Or moonlight on a midnight stream,
> Gives grace and truth to life's unquiet dream.
>
> I vowed that I would dedicate my powers
>   To thee and thine—have I not kept the vow?
>   With beating heart and streaming eyes, even now
> I call the phantoms of a thousand hours
> Each from his voiceless grave; they have in visioned bowers
>   Of studious zeal or love's delight
>   Outwatched with me the envious night—
> They know that never joy illumed my brow
>   Unlinked with hope that thou wouldst free
>   This world from its dark slavery,
>   That thou O awful LOVELINESS,
> Wouldst give whate'er these words cannot express.
>
> The day becomes more solemn and serene
>   When noon is past—there is a harmony
>   In autumn, and a lustre in its sky,
> Which thro' the summer is not heard or seen,
> As if it could not be, as if it had not been!
>   Thus let thy power, which like the truth
>   Of nature on my passive youth
> Descended, to my onward life supply
>   Its calm—to one who worships thee,
>   And every form containing thee,

Whom, Spirit fair, thy spells did bind
To fear himself, and love all human kind.[381]

These verses, which keep renewing their moving effect, I have given in their entirety because they are typical of the turning from service of beauty to worship. The religious tone is unmistakable, that awe of the holy expressed by "awful loveliness." It is in the most moving prayer of a soul thirsting for beauty, that of Socrates, in the *Phaedrus:* "Dear Pan, thou and all the other gods of this place, oh, may ye grant to me to become beautiful within."[93] The longing for beauty is so deep in this most ugly of all men that the word "beautiful" here receives an extended meaning which it possessed more or less constantly in Greek. As soon as we pray to beauty or pray for beauty, it is clear to us that we have left the land of art and of beauty; simultaneously, we have left the land of religion. We stand in faith. Perhaps we stand just at the confluence of both rivers, there where both, which have been unable to come together, unite, and are now borne together to God in faith.

INCARNATION   We found religious art, where in the creation of the artist we recognized the lines and contours of God's creation. But is that possible?

Faith stands facing the creator. It worships him, for it comes from him. Religion is the human answer to faith. Art has no inherent faith. It possesses neither dogma nor metaphysics. Nevertheless, it is also an answer, and indeed to the same faith which religion answers.

Its word, like that of religion, needs image and form. In the human world of religion and art, one needs form in order to be able to exist. Is that possible? Is it possible without having the answer become a purely human word, without losing in the vagueness and impermanence of earthly lines the contours of the heavenly building?

It is possible, and it is clear to us in a very simple manner as soon as we discover in art something final and absolute, infinitely moving, and terrifying at the same time. We cannot prove it. But we can see it in connection with faith in God, the creator and father of Jesus Christ. It can and must be possible to recognize in the beautiful work of man the features of the work of God, since God himself gave to his earthly creation the features of his own image. It can and must be possible to praise the whole variety of the human world, the glorious multitude of forms of art and religion as revelation of the glory of God, if God himself gave himself to this human world, himself assumed form and moved as man among men. The Incarnation means our redemption, also in the sense that the world and our works in it need not be without meaning, but can be bearers of a divine revelation.

Thus, as phenomenologists, as men of the science of art and religion, we find points of access and boundaries. Thus, as religious men, we experience again and again the miracle of the blending of religion and art. As theologians, who can neither separate artifically the revelation in Christ and that apparently different one given us as revelation, nor desire to lose ourselves in the generality of an idea of God, we find the unity of art and religion where alone we know unity: in the doctrine of the Incarnation. As believers, we find the possibility of complete beauty in him in whom we find everything, in the divine figure, in the son of Mary, in the Son of God, who is the most beautiful. And, with the old folk song, we say:

> All the beauty
> Of heaven and earth
> Is contained in Thee alone.

BIBLIOGRAPHICAL NOTES

1. The following subsequent studies by van der Leeuw were utilized in whole or in part in preparation of the present edition.—*Trans.*
   Muziek en religie in verband met de verhouding van Woord en Toon. Amsterdam, 1934.
   Het beeld Gods. Amsterdam, 1939.
   "Dans en Beschaving." Bundel opstellen, aangeboden aan Prof. Dr. J. Huizinga ter gelegenheid van diens zeventigste verjaardag. Haarlem, 1942.
   Beeld van den mensch en beeld van God. De Gids: Sept. 1942.
2. OTTO, RUDOLF. *Das Heilige.* Breslau, 1927. English: *The Idea of the Holy.* Oxford, 1925.
3. SPRANGER, EDUARD. *Lebensformen.* Halle, 1925. English: *Types of Men; the Psychology and Ethics of Personality.* Halle, 1928.
4. VAN DER LEEUW, G. *"Über einige neuere Ergebnisse der psychologischen Forschung und ihre Anwendung auf die Geschichte, insonderheit die Religionsgeschichte." Studi e materiali della Storia di religioni* II. 1926.
   —— *"Strukturpsychologie und Theologie." Zeitschrift für Theologie und Kirche,* N. F. 9., 1928.
   —— *"Phänomenologie."* Article in *Die Religion in Geschichte und Gegenwart.*
   —— *Phänomenologie der Religion.* Tübingen, 1933. English: *Religion in Essence and Manifestation.* London, 1938.
5. —— *La Structure de la mentalité primitive.* Strasbourg-Paris, 1928.
   —— *De primitive Mensch en de Religie.* Groningen–Batavia, 1937.
   French: *L'homme primitif et la Religion.* Paris, 1940.
6. HUIZINGA, JOHAN. *Homo ludens.* Haarlem, 1938. English: *Homo Ludens.* London, 1949.
7. VAN DER LEEUW, G. *In den hemel is eenen dans.* Amsterdam, 1930.
   German: *In dem Himmel ist ein Tanz.* Berlin, 1930.
8. Goethe. *Maximen und Reflexionen.* Günther Müller, Stuttgart, 1944. English: *The Maxims and Reflections of Goethe.* New York, 1906.
9. SACHS, CURT. *Eine Weltgeschichte des Tanzes.* Berlin, 1938. English: *World History of the Dance.* New York, 1937.
10. MARETT, R. R. *Faith, Hope and Charity in Primitive Religion.* Oxford, 1932.
11. HORN, A. A., and ETHELREDA LEWIS. *The Ivory Coast.* Amsterdam, 1931.

────── *The Waters of Africa*. Amsterdam, 1932.

12. GRANET, MARCEL. *Danses et légendes de la Chine ancienne*. Paris. 1926.
13. PREUSS, K. TH. *"Der Unterbau des Dramas."* Lectures organized by the Warburg Library, 1927–28. Leipzig–Berlin, 1930.
14. ────── *Tod und Unsterblichkeit im Glauben der Naturvölker*. Tübingen, 1930.
15. LEENHARDT, M. *Gens de la Grande Terre*. Paris, 1937.
16. BLEEK, DOROTHEA F. *Rock Paintings in South Africa*. London, 1930.
17. TSUDZUMI, T. *Kunst Japans*. Leipzig, 1929.
18. BENEDICT, RUTH. *Patterns of Culture*. New York, 1934.
19. VAN LELYVELD, TH. B. *De javaansche danskunst*. Amsterdam, 1931. French: *La Danse dans le Théâtre Javanais*. Paris, 1931.
20. JANSSEN, JOHANNES. From *Jaarber. Ex Oriente Lux*, 7, 1940, p. 312.
21. DE GRUYTER, W. JOS. *Het Masker*. 's-Graveland, 1941.
    VAN DER LEEUW, G. *Beeld van den mensch en beeld van God*. (Cf. 1.)
22. DANZEL, THEODORE W. *Kultur und Religion des primitiven Menschen*. Stuttgart, 1924. (Cf. 9 and 88.)
23. LÉVY-BRUHL, LUCIEN. *Le Surnaturel et la Nature dans la Mentalité primitive*. Paris, 1931. English: *Primitives and the Supernatural*. New York, 1935.
24. Molière, *Le Bourgeois Gentilhomme*, Act I, Scene 2. New York, 1930. English: *The Would-be Gentleman*. London, 1926.
25. PANZER, MARIANNE. *Tanz und Recht*. Frankfurt, 1938.
26. CHAMBERS, SIR EDMUND K. *The medieval stage*. Oxford, 1903.
27. GRANET, M. *Fêtes et chansons anciennes de la Chine*. Paris, 1914. English: *Festivals and Songs of Ancient China*. New York, 1932.
    ────── *La civilisation Chinoise, la vie publique et la vie privée*. (*Evolution de l'humanité* No. 25.) Paris, 1929. English: *Chinese Civilization*. New York, 1930.
28. BRUNNER-TRAUT, EMMA. *Der Tanz im alten Ägypten*. Glückstadt–Hamburg–New York, 1938.
29. LUCIAN. *Von der Tanzkunst. Nach der Übersetzung von Wieland bearbeitet und ergänzt von Dr. Hanns Floerke*. Munich–Leipzig, 1911. English: *Lucian of Samosata*. London, 1820.
30. DANTE. *The Divine Comedy, Paradiso*.
31. VONDEL, JOOST VAN DEN. *Volled. en geïll. Tekstuitgave in tien deelen*. Part X. "Adam in Ballingschap." Amsterdam, 1940.
32. EURIPIDES. *Iphigeneia in Tauris*, 179. Trans. Gilbert Murray. Oxford, 1901.
33. VAN GRONINGEN, B. A. *"Van Poezie tot Proza"* (*Lecture, Ned. Klassiek Verbond, 1941*).
34. EURIPIDES. *The Trojan Women*. New York, 1915.
35. NYBERG, H. S. *Die Religionen des alten Iran*. Leipzig, 1938.
36. BARBET, P. *Quelques poésies de Fra Jacopone da Todi*. Paris, 1935.
37. JAMES, MONTAGUE R. *The Apocryphal New Testament, Acta Joannis*, 94–96. Oxford, 1924.
38. SANDYS, W. *Christmas Carols Ancient and Modern*. London, 1833.
39. MEAD, G. R. S. "The Sacred Dance of Jesus," *The Quest* II, 1910–1911.
40. MERKEL, G. F. *Die Mystik im Kulturleben der Völker*. Hamburg, 1940.
41. WOLTERS, FR. *Lobgesänge und Psalmen*, "Round Dance of Grace." Berlin, 1923.
42. BASILIUS. *Epist. ad Greg*. English: *Saint Basil, The Letters*. New York, 1926–34 (cf. 39).
43. VAN DUYSE, FLORIMOND. *Het oude nederlandse lied*, III. 1903–1907.

44. Van den Vondel, J. *Op. cit.*, Part IV. "*Altaergeheimenissen.*" Amsterdam, 1940.
45. Voltaire. "*L'hôte et l'hôtesse.*" *Divertissement 1776.* Complete works, Vol. XII, 1785.
46. Werumeus Buning, J. W. F. *De Wereld van den Dans.* Amsterdam, 1922.
47. Van der Leeuw, G. *Der Mensch und die Religion.* Basel, 1940.
48. Chesterton, G. K. *Chaucer.* London, 1932.
49. Strauch, Ph. "*Von der Sünde des Tanzens,*" Arch. f. Religionswissenschaft, 23 (1925), pp. 353 ff.
50. Kessels, M. F. *De Katholiek,* 142 (1912), pp. 286 ff.
51. Gougaud, L. "*La danse dans les églises,*" *Revue d'hist. eccl.,* XV (1914), p. 7.
52. Meinhof, Carl. *Afrikanische Märchen.* Jena, 1921.
53. Noack, F. "*Triumph und Triumphbogen.*" Lectures organized by the Warburg Library, 1925–26. Berlin, 1928.
54. Burckhardt, J. *Die Kultur der Renaissance in Italien,* II. Leipzig, 1919. English: *The Civilization of the Renaissance in Italy.* London, 1929.
55. De Rougemont, Denis. *Journal d'Allemagne.* Paris, 1938.
56. Junkers, H. "*Der Tanz der Mww und das butische Begräbnis im Alten Reich.*" mdaik 9 (1930), pp. 1 ff.
57. Stammler, Wolfgang. *Die Totentänze.* Leipzig o. J. (Cf. 122 and 160.)
58. Van der Ven, El. *Haags Maandblad* 13 (1930), p. 412.
59. Shakespeare. *A Midsummer Night's Dream.*
60. Knight, W. F. Jackson. *Cumaean Gates.* London, 1936.
61. Munich Ms. Number 6394, p. 164.
62. Drost, J. W. P. *Het Nederlandsche Kinderspel voor de zeventiende eeuw.* Den Haag, 1914.
   Van de Graft, C. Cath. *Volkskunde* 22 (1911), p. 46.
63. Cf. Meerdink, J. A. *Ariadne.* Wageningen, 1939.
64. Homer. *The Iliad.* Book XVIII, 590.
65. Müller, F. "Over de betekenis van het Labyrinth." *Med. Kon. Akad. v. Wetensch., Afd. Lett.* 78 B 1 (1934).
66. Verheyden, Prosper. "*De Maagdendans.*" *Hand. v. d. Mechelse Kring voor Oudheidkunde, Letteren en Kunst,* 27 (1922), p. 112.
67. Van Bakel, H. A. N. *Theol. Tijdschr.* 1932, p. 279. (For punishment because of dancing.) See also 66.
68. Pollman, Josephus. *Ons eigen Volkslied.* (Complete text.) Amsterdam, 1936.
   ——— "*Calvijn's Aesthetica.*" *Studiën-reeks* 4. 's-Hertogenbosch o. J.
69. *Een Kort Tractaetjen van de Dansen, tot dienst van de Eenvoudigen uyt de Latijnsche in Nederduytsche Tale overgeset.* t'Utrecht, 1644.
70. Reich, H. *Der Mimus.* Berlin, 1903.
71. Haskell, Arnold. *Ballet.* London, 1947.
72. Kees, H. *Der Opfertanz des ägyptischen Königs.* Leipzig, 1912.
73. Stählin, W. *Vom Sinn des Leibes.* Stuttgart o. J.
74. Van der Ven-ten Bensel, Elise. *De volksdans herleeft.* Middelburg o. J.
   Brom-Struick, Willemien. *Reidansen.* Rotterdam, 1940.
75. Tegethoff, Ernst. *Französische Volksmärchen.* Jena. 1923.
76. Lalo, C. "*L'art et la religion.*" *Revue philos.* 88 (1919).
77. Hugo, Victor. "*La contemplation d'aujourd'hui.*" Complete works. *Odes et Poésies Diverses* VI. Paris, 1928.
78. Farnell, L. R. *The cults of Greek states.* Oxford, 1896.
79. Plutarch. "On the E at Delphi," *Moralia.* London, 1936.

80. PINDAR. Fifth Pythian Ode. *The Extant Odes of Pindar*. New York, 1904.
81. VAN DER LEEUW, G. *Goden en menschen in Hellas*. Haarlem, 1927.
82. SPRANGER, E. *Psychologie des Jugendalters*. Leipzig, 1925.
83. NICHOLSON, REYNOLD A. *The Mystics of Islam*. London, 1914.
84. Cf. OESTERLEY, WILLIAM O. E. *The Sacred Dance*. Cambridge, 1923.
85. ARISTOPHANES. *The Frogs*. London, 1908.
86. VAN DER LEEUW, G. *Antieke Roepen Klaagliederen*. 's-Graveland, 1942.
87. LEIPOLDT, J. *Dionysos*. 1931.
88. OTTO, W. F. *Dionysos, Mythos und Kultus*. Frankfurt, 1933.
88a. VAN DER LEEUW, G. *De Godsdiensten der Wereld*. Amsterdam, 1948.
89. BACH, J. S. *Werke*. Vol. 38, *Orgelwerke*, Vol 3. Bach-Ges. Leipzig.
90. UTITZ, EMIL. *Der Künstler*. Stuttgart, 1925.
91. VOLKER, T. *Japansche Kunst*. The Hague, 1943.
92. HERTZ, WILHELM. *Die Sage von Parsival und dem Gral*. Breslau, 1882.
93. GHÉON, HENRI. *Promenades avec Mozart*. Paris, 1932. English: *In Search of Mozart*. New York, 1934.
94. EL TOUR, ANNA. From a program, *"Der Tanz im Lied."*
95. SHAKESPEARE. *Love's Labour's Lost*.
96. SINGER, SAMUEL. *Germanisch-romanisches Mittelalter*. Zürich–Leipzig, 1935.
97. VAN DER LEEUW, G., and H. P. BERNET KEMPERS. *Beknopte Geschiedenis van het Kerklied*. Groningen, 1948.
98. NILSSON, M. P. *Greek Popular Religion*. New York, 1940.
99. USENER, HERMANN. *Kleine Schriften IV*. Leipzig–Berlin, 1913.
100. VAN HUYEN, NGUYEN. *Les chants alternés des garçons et des filles en Annam*. Paris, 1933.
101. LÉVY-BRUHL, L. *La mythologie primitive*. Paris, 1935.
102. EURIPIDES. *Helen*. Cambridge, 1925.
103. MURRAY, G. *Aeschylus. The Creator of Tragedy*. Oxford, 1940.
104. BÖHL, F. M. TH. *"Mimus en Drama op het Babylonische Nieuwjaarsfeest." Stemmen des Tijds* 10 (1920–1921).
    ZIMMERN, HEINRICH. *Das babylonische Neujahrsfest*. Leipzig, 1926.
105. HIDDING, K. From *Tijdschr. v. Taal-, Land- en Volkenkunde* 73 (1933), p. 3.
106. MIC, C. *La commedia dell'arte*. Paris, 1927.
107. Cf. 88.
108. ALTHEM, FRANZ. *"Persona." Arch. f. Rel.wiss*. 27 (1929), pp. 48 ff.
109. DE GRUYTER, W. J. *Het Masker, ontstaan, betekenis, schoonheid*. 's-Graveland, 1941 (cf. 91).
110. SCHMALENBACH, HERMAN. *"Die Entstehung des Seelenbegriffes." Logos* 16 (1927), pp. 311–355.
111. VON FEUERBACH, ANSELM. *Ein Vermächtnis*. Henriette Feuerbach, Berlin o. J.
112. VON KLEIST, H. *Über das Marionettentheater*.
113. GOETHE. *"Das römische Karnaval," Italienische Reise*, III. English: *Goethe's Travels in Italy*. London, 1885 (cf. 261).
114. WALCH, JAN. *Ludwig Holbein als Blijspeldichter*. Groot Nederland, 1925. (A study of this motif from the *Thousand and One Nights* through the *Decameron* and Calderon to Holberg.)
115. SCHIRMER, WALTER. *Geschichte der englischen Literatur*. Halle, 1937.
116. BATHER, A. G. *"The Problem of the Bacchae," Journ. Hell. Stud.* 14 (1894) pp. 244 ff.
117. KERN, OTTO. *Eleusinische Beiträge*. Halle, 1908.
118. SETHE, KURT. *Dramatische Texte zu altägyptischen Mysterienspielen* I. Leipzig, 1928.

119. ——— *Die altägyptischen Pyramidentexte*. Leipzig, 1908–1910.
120. FRIEDRICH, JOHANNES. *Ras Shamra*. Leipzig, 1933.
    GASTER, TH. From *Studi e Materiali di Storia d. Rel*. 10 (1934).
121. VAN DER LEEUW, G. *Inleiding tot de phaenomenologie van den godsdienst*. Haarlem, 1948. German: *Einführung in die Phänomenologie der Religion*. Munich, 1925.
122. HASE, KARL B. *Das geistliche Schauspiel*. Leipzig, 1858. English: *Miracle Plays and Sacred Dramas*. London, 1880.
123. WIRTH, L. *Die Oster- und Passionsspiele bis zum 16. Jahrhundert*. Halle, 1889.
124. BRINKMAN, H. *Xenia Bonnensia*. 1929.
125. ALLEN AND SIKES. *The Homeric Hymns*. Oxford, 1904.
126. "The Chester Pageant of the Deluge." *Everyman and other Interludes*. London, 1909.
127. VAN WAESBERGE, P. SMITS. *Muziek en drama in de Middleleeuwen*. Amsterdam.
128. *Die Briefe der Liselotte von der Pfalz, Herzogin von Orléans. St. Cloud, 17. Juni 1693*. Holland. Bibliothek d. literarischen Vereins, 7 vols. Stuttgart, 1843–1881.
129. AUGUSTINE. *The City of God*.
130. LIVY. *The Annals of the Roman People*, 7, 2.
131. ALTHEIM, F. *Römische Religionsgeschichte* II. Berlin–Leipzig, 1932.
132. *The Works of the Emperor Julian*. New York, 1913–23.
133. QUASTEN, J. *"Musik und Gesang in den Kulturen der heidnischen Antike und christlichen Frühzeit." Liturgiegeschichtl. Quellen und Forchungen*, Vol. 25. Münster, 1930.
134. BOISSIER, GASTON. *La fin du Paganisme*. Paris, 1891.
135. USENER, H. *Vorträge und Aufsätze*. Leipzig, 1914.
136. VAN DER LEEUW, G. *Phänomenologie der Religion*. Tübingen, 1933.
137. VAN DER LEEUW, G. *Liturgiek?* Nijkerk, 1946.
138. GOETHE. *Das Jahrmarktfest zu Plundersweilern*.
139. LAGERLÖF, SELMA. *Antikrists mirakler*. Stockholm, 1946. English: *The Miracles of Antichrist*. Boston, 1899.
140. GÜNTHER, E. *Calderón und seine Werke* II. Freiburg, 1888.
141. ROHDE, ERWIN. *Psyche*. Tübingen, 1910. English: *Psyche; the Cult of Souls and Belief in Immortality Among the Greeks*. New York, 1925.
142. NIETZSCHE. *Die Geburt der Tragödie. Ges. Werke, Musarionausgabe*, Vol. III. Munich, 1928. English: *The Birth of Tragedy*. Garden City, N. Y., 1956.
143. SIMMEL, GEORGE. *"Zur Philosophie des Schauspielers." Logos* 9 (1920–1921), p. 359.
    NAEFF, TOP. *Willem Royaards. De Toneelkunstenaar in zijn tijd*. Den Haag, 1947.
144. REINHARDT, E. A. *Das Leben der Eleonora Duse*. Berlin, 1934.
145. SHAKESPEARE. *Hamlet*, II, 2.
146. CHESTERTON, G. K. *The Secret of Father Brown*. London, 1927.
147. VON HOFMANNSTHAL, HUGO. *Die Gedichte und kleinen Dramen*. Leipzig, 1922.
148. BJÖRNSON, BJÖRNSTJERNE. *Fiskerjenten*. Copenhagen, 1900–1902. English: *The Fisher Maiden*. New York, 1882. (This contains a fine apologia for the theater, and an accurate comparison of the dangers of the actor with those of the pastor.)
149. VAN DER LEEUW, G. *"Bouwmeester Solness." Omhoog, N. R.* (1922).
150. MARITAIN, JACQUES. *Art et Scolastique*. Paris, 1927. English: *Art and Scholasticism*. New York, 1930 (cf. 137).

151. SCHLEIERMACHER, F. E. D. *Praktische Theologie nach den Grundsätzen der Evangelischen Kirche dargestellt.* Berlin, 1850.
152. WILL, ROBERT. *Le Culte.* Paris, 1929.
153. MAYER, A. L. "*Renaissance, Humanismus und Liturgie.*" *Jahrbuch f. Liturgiewiss.* 14 (1938), pp. 131 ff.
154. LÉVY-BRUHL, L. *L'Expérience mystique et les Symboles chez les primitifs.* Paris, 1938.
155. NIETZSCHE. *Ecce Homo.* Musarionausgabe, Vol. XXI. Munich, 1928. English: *Ecce Homo.* New York, 1930.
156. BUYTENDIJK, F. J. J. *Het spel van mensch en dier.* Amsterdam.
157. CLAUDEL, PAUL. *Feuilles de Saints.* Paris, 1925.
158. THURNWALD, R. "*Psychologie des primitiven Menschen.*" *Handbuch der vergleichenden Psychologie* I, 2. Publ. Gustav Kafka, Munich: Reinhardt, 1922.
159. SCHNEIDER, M. From Preuss-Thurnwald: *Lehrbuch der Völkerkunde.* Stuttgart, 1939.
160. HUIZINGA, J. *Herfsttij der Middeleeuwen.* Haarlem, 1919. English: *The Waning of the Middle Ages.* London, 1924.
161. KRAMERS, J. H. *De taal van den Koran.* Leiden, 1940.
162. PORTENGEN, A. J. "*L'Influence des Tabous dans l'ancienne littérature germanique.*" *Revue Antropol.* 36 (1925).
163. WERNER, HEINZ. *Einführung in die Entwicklungspsychologie.* Leipzig, 1926. English: *Comparative Psychology of Mental Development.* New York, 1940.
164. KÜHNEMANN, EUGEN. *Herder.* Munich, 1927.
165. ARNOLD, MATTHEW. *Essays in Criticism,* Vol. II. London, 1935.
166. HUGO, VICTOR. *L'Homme qui Rit.* Complete works, Romans XIII. Paris, 1928. English: *The Man Who Laughs.* New York, 1889.
167. RENOUVIER, C. B. *Victor Hugo le Philosophe.* Paris, 1926.
168. DIELS, HERMANN. *Die Fragmente der Vorsokratiker,* Vol. II. Berlin, 1912.
169. BETHE, E. *Homer* I. Leipzig, 1914.
170. THOMAS, ADOLPHE V. "*L'Anthropologie du Geste, d'après Marcel Jousse.*" *Revue Antropol.* 51 (1941).
171. *Goethes Briefe an Frau von Stein,* Goethe's letters to Frau von Stein, Aug. 8, 1776. Frankfort, 1883–85.
172. SCHOPENHAUER. *Die Welt als Wille und Vorstellung.* Wiesbaden, 1949. English: *The World as Will and Idea.* London, 1907–09.
173. WIEGRÄBE, P. *Religionskundl. Beiblatt Marburg,* Sept. 3, 1934.
174. HUGO, VICTOR. *Préface de Cromwell.* Complete works, Drames 1. Paris, 1928.
175. PREUSS, K. TH. *Die geistige Kultur der Naturvölker.* Leipzig, 1914.
176. ADRIANI, N. *Het animistisch Heidendom als godsdienst.* Den Haag.
177. VAN GRONINGEN, B. A. *Vrijheid en gebondenheid in den Griekschen literairen vorm.* Med. Kon. Ned. Ak. v. Wet. Afd. Lett. N. R. I, 11 (1938).
178. BENÉT, STEPHEN VINCENT. *John Brown's Body.* Garden City, N. Y., 1928.
179. JOLLES, ANDRÉ. *Einfache Formen.* Halle, 1930.
180. PLATO. *Phaedrus.*
181. IBSEN, HENRIK. *Når vi døde vågner.* Copenhagen-Berlin, 1899. English: *When We Dead Awaken.* New York, 1900.
182. GEORGE, S. "*König und Harfner.*" *Der Siebente Ring.* Berlin, 1920. English: from *The Works of Stefan George.* Chapel Hill, North Carolina, 1949.
183. DILTHEY, W. *Gesammelte Schriften* VII. Leipzig, 1927.
184. MÜLLER, GÜNTHER. *Geschichte des deutschen Liedes vom Zeitalter des Barock bis zur Gegenwart.* Munich, 1925.
185. HASPELS, G. F. *Onze literatuur en onze Evangelieprediking.* Nijmwegen, 1898.

186. GOETHE. *Tages- und Jahreshefte*, 1801. English: *Annals*. New York, 1901.
187. VAN DER LEEUW, G., and P. J. ENK. *Horatius in dezen tijd. Horatius als dichter en levenskunstenaar*. Groningen, 1925.
188. VAN DER LEEUW, G. "Stefan George." *Stemmen des Tijds* 23 (1934).
189. VERWEY, A. *Mijn verhouding tot Stefan George*. Santpoort, 1934. German: *Mein Verhältnis zu Stefan George*. Strassbourg, 1936.
190. GOETHE. *Gespräch mit Eckermann*, Jan. 4, 1827. From *Goethes Gespräch*, Vol. III. Leipzig, 1909–11. English: *Conversations of Goethe with Eckermann and Soret*. London, 1892.
191. VAN DER LEEUW, G. *Uren met Novalis*. Baarn.
192. RIBOT, THEODULE A. *Psychologie des sentiments*. Paris, 1917. English: *The Psychology of the Emotions*. New York, 1897.
193. KONRAD, J. *Religion und Kunst*. Tübingen, 1929.
194. MANN, THOMAS. *Tonio Kröger*. Berlin, 1925. English: New York, 1931.
195. AUGUSTINE. *Confessions*.
196. VAN EYCK, P. N. *Verzen 1940–41*.
197. KIERKEGAARD, SØREN. *Enten—Eller* II. Copenhagen, 1920. English: *Either/Or*. Princeton, 1944.
198. ASTLEY, H. J. D. "Primitive Art and Magic." *Hibbert Journal* 18 (1930).
199. EVERS, H. G. *Staat aus dem Stein* I. Munich, 1929.
200. PRINZHORN, H. *Bildnerei der Geisteskranken*. Berlin, 1923.
201. SCHÄFER, H. *Äggyptische und heutige Kunst*. Berlin–Leipzig, 1928.
202. PONGS, H. *Das Bild in der Dichtung* I. Marburg, 1927.
203. KNUTTEL, G. *Over chineesche en japansche kunst*. Amsterdam.
204. ERDMANN, KURT. "Zur Deutung der iranischen Felsreliefs." *Forsch. u. Fortschritte* 18 (July 20, and Aug. 1, 1942).
205. KLEIWEG DE ZWAAN, J. P. *Paläolithische Kunst in Europa* I. Amsterdam, 1929.
206. SCHMALENBACH, H. "Die Entstehung des Seelenbegriffes." *Logos* 16, 1927.
207. Casel, Odo. "Älteste christliche Kunst und Christusmysterium." *Jahrbuch f. Rel.-wiss.* 12 (1932) p. 44.
208. NIETZSCHE. *Menschliches allzu Menschliches* II. Musarionausgabe, Vol. IX. Munich, 1928. English: *Human, all too human*. Chicago, 1908.
209. Cf. OBBINK, H. TH. "Jahwebilder." *Zeitschr. f. d. Altt. Wiss.* 1929.
210. FICK, RICH. "Die buddhistische Kultur und das Erbe Alexanders des Grossen." *Morgenland* 25. Leipzig, 1933.
211. LIN YUTANG. *My Country and My People*. London–Toronto, 1939.
212. *Le Visage du Christ*. Introduction, Pierre Mornand; preface, François Mauriac. Paris, 1908.
213. VISSE, W. J. A. *Die Entwicklung des Christusbildes in Literatur und Kunst in der frühchristlichen und frühbyzantinischen Zeit*. Bonn, 1934.
214. WILL, R. "Essai d'Iconographie chrétienne." *Revue d'hist. et de Philos. rel.* 400.
215. *The Life of Christ by Chinese Artists*. Westminster, 1940.
216. GEFFCKEN, JOHANNES. "Der Bilderstreit im Altertum." *Arch. f. Rel. Wiss.* 19 (1919), p. 308.
217. WILKEN, G. A. *Verspreide Geschriften* III. 's-Gravenhage, 1912.
218. VISCHER, FRIEDRICH THEODOR. *Ästhetik, oder Wissenschaft des Schönen*, par. 67. Munich, 1922.
219. MEHLIS, G. *Die Mystik*. Munich.
220. NILSSON, M. P. *Den Grekiska Religionens Historia*. Stockholm, 1921. English: *A History of Greek Religion*. Oxford, 1925.

221. TILLICH, PAUL. *Die religiöse Lage der Gegenwart.* Berlin, 1926. English: *The Religious Situation.* New York, 1932.
222. VAN DER LEEUW, G. *Achnaton.* Amsterdam, 1927.
223. TANKARD, ELAINE. "The curve in Amarnah-Art." *Journal of Egypt. Arch.* 18 (1932), p. 49.
224. HOLL, KARL. *"Die Entstehung der Bilderwand in der griechischen Kirche."* *Arch. f. Rel.wiss.* 9 (1906).
225. BOULGAKOFF, S. *L'orthodoxie.* Paris, 1932. English: *The Orthodox Church.* London, 1935.
226. VAN DER LEEUW, G. *Het beeld Gods.* Amsterdam, 1939.
227. LESKOV, N. Complete works, Vol. IV. Munich.
228. HACKEL, A. *Das altrussische Heiligenbild. Die Ikone.* Nijmegen, 1936.
229. KOCH, LUKAS. O. B. *"Zur Theologie der Christusikone."* *Bened. Monatsschrift* 19 (1937); 20 (1938).
230. CASEL, O. *Glaube, Gnosis, Mysterium.* Munich, 1941.
231. NEMITZ, FR. *Die Kunst Russlands.* Berlin, 1940.
232. Cf. MOWINCKEL, S. *"Wann wurde der Jahwäkultus in Jerusalem offiziell bildlos?"* *Acta Orient.* 8 (1930).
233. *The History of Herodotus.* London, 1933.
234. PLUTARCH. "Numa," *Parallel Lives.*
235. CALVIN. *Institutes of the Christian Religion.* Philadelphia, 1936.
236. UTITZ, E. *Ästhetik.* Berlin, 1923.
237. Cf. FAUST, AUG. *"Der dichterische Ausdruck mystischer Religiosität bei Rainer Maria Rilke."* Logos 11 (1923).
238. VAN DER LEEUW, G. *"Phénoménologie de l'âme."* *Revue d'hist. et de phil. rel.* 1930.
239. RILKE, RAINER MARIA. *Stundenbuch* I. Leipzig, 1912.
240. MARITAIN, JACQUES. *Religion et Culture.* Paris, 1930. English: *Religion and Culture.* London, 1931.
241. *"Een liedeken van vrage ende antwoord."* *Een lietboecken, tracterende van den Offer des Heeren 1563.* Bibl. ref. neerl. II, 1904.
242. ERASMUS. *Praise of Folly.* Princeton, 1941.
243. HUYGENS, CONSTANTIJN. *De gedichten* (Worp) II. Groningen, 1893. *Op. de doorschoten kerck te Groll.*
244. Cf. VAN DEN BRINK, J. N. BAKHUIZEN, and J. LINDEBOOM. *Handboek der Kerkgeschiedenis* I. 's-Gravenhage, 1942.
245. ASMUSSEN, HANS. *Die Lehre vom Gottesdienst.* Munich, 1937.
246. BALZAC. *"Le Chef d'Oeuvre Inconnu."* *Études Philosophiques* XVII. Paris, 1837. English: *Christ in Flanders, and other Stories.* New York, 1931.
247. KERN, O. *Die Religion der Griechen* II. Berlin, 1935.
248. CHESTERTON, G. K. *The Everlasting Man.* London, 1925.
249. SCHLEIERMACHER, F. E. D. *Reden über die Religion.* Leipzig, 1924. English: *On Religion; Speeches to its Cultured Despisers.* London, 1893.
250. GUNDOLF, FRIEDRICH. *Goethe.* Berlin, 1925.
251. RÖMER, ALFRED. *"Musik und Religion"* (*Zur Erlebnisfähigkeit des Primaners*). *Zeitschr. f. Religionspsychologie* III (1930).
252. FRAENGER, W. *Matthis Grünewald in seinen Werken.* Berlin, 1936.
253. JASPERS, KARL. *Psychologie der Weltanschauungen.* Berlin, 1922.
254. JEREMIAS, ALFRED. *Handbuch der altorientalischen Geisteskultur.* Leipzig, 1913.
255. HAMANN, RICHARD. *"Kunst und Können."* Logos 22 (1933).
256. BRENTANO, F. FUNCK. *Le Moyen Age.* Paris, 1922. English: *The Middle Ages.* London, 1922.

257. DEGENER, F. SCHMIDT. *Phoenix.* Amsterdam, 1942.
258. OZINGA, M. D. *Protestantsche kerken hier te lande gesticht.* Amsterdam, 1929.
259. VAN DEN BRINK, J. N. BAKHUIZEN. *Protestantsche Kerkbouw.* Arnhem, 1946.
260. *Kerkbouw. Ontwerpen van de studiekring Eredienst en Kerkbouw.* Arnhem, 1943.
261. WUNDT, WILHELM. *Völkerpsychologie,* III. Leipzig, 1919.
262. VON BISSING, FRIEDRICH WILHELM. "Das Re-Heiligtum des Königs Ne-Usr-Re." Vol. I: BORCHARDT LUDWIG. *Der Bau.* Leipzig, 1905.
263. SCHÄFER, H. *Die Leistung der ägyptischen Kunst.* Leipzig, 1929.
    DE BUCK, A. *De Zegepraal van het Licht.* Amsterdam, 1930.
    VAN DER LEEUW, G. *De godsdienst van het oude Egypte.* Den Haag, 1944.
    KROM, N. J. *Bara Boedoer.* Amsterdam, 1930. English: *Barabudur, Archaeological Description.* The Hague, 1927.
264. BORCHARDT, LUDWIG. *Das Grabdenkmal des Königs Sa-Hu-Re.* 1910–1913.
265. ERDMANN, K. *Das iranische Feuerheiligtum.* Leipzig, 1941.
266. PAUSANIAS. *Description of Greece.* New York, 1918–35.
267. IBSEN. *Bygmester Solness.* Complete works. Vol. 9. Copenhagen, 1898–1902. English: *The Master Builder.* New York, 1893.
268. WORRINGER, W. *Formprobleme der Gotik.* Munich, 1927. English: *Form-Problems of the Gothic.* New York, 1920.
269. OLDENBERG, HERMANN. *Das Mahabharata.* Göttingen, 1922.
270. OTTO, RUDOLF. *Aufsätze das Numinose betreffend.* Gotha-Stuttgart, 1923.
271. VAN STOCKUM, C., and J. VAN DAM. *Geschichte der deutschen Literatur,* Vol. II. Groningen-Djakarta, 1954.
272. MOLIÈRE, M. J. GRANPRÉ. "*Delft en het nieuwe bouwen.*" *Katholiek Bouwblad.*
273. CLAUDEL, PAUL. "*L'architecte.*" *Feuilles de Saints.* Paris, 1925.
274. BEKKER, P. *Musikgeschichte als Geschichte der musikalischen Formwandlungen.* Stuttgart, 1926. French: *La Musique; les Transformations des Formes Musicales depuis l'Antiquité jusqu'à nos Jours.* Paris, 1929.
275. NIETZSCHE. *Die fröhliche Wissenschaft.* Musarionausgabe, Vol. XII. Munich, 1928. English: *The Joyful Wisdom.* London, 1918.
276. HEINITZ, W. "Instrumentenkunde." E. Bücken, *Handbuch der Musikwissenschaft.* Potsdam, 1928–29.
277. WALPOLE, A. S. *Early Latin Hymns.* London, 1922.
278. DE GOEJE, C. H. "De Oayana-Indianen." *Bijdr. Taal-, Landen Volkenk. v. Ned. Indie* 100.
279. KRUYT, ALB. "*De fluit in Indonesie.*" *Tijdschr. Ind. Taal-, Land-, en Volkenk.* 78 (1938).
280. COMBARIEU, JULES. *La Musique et la Magie.* Paris, 1909.
281. HEILER, FRIEDRICH. *Der Katholizismus.* Munich, 1923.
282. VAN WAESBERGHE, JOS. SMITS. *Gregoriaansche musiek en haar plaats in den katholieken eeredienst.*
283. PARSCH, PIUS, and ROB. KRAMREITER. *Neue Kirchenkunst im Geist der Liturgie.* Vienna–Klosterneuburg, 1939.
284. VAN DER LEEUW, G. *Bach's Matthaeuspassion.* Amsterdam, 1947.
285. ────── *Bach's Johannespassion.* Amsterdam, 1945.
286. WILL, ROB. "La liturgie Luthérienne." *Revue d'hist. et de Philos. relig.* 7 (1927).
287. KAT, A. J. M. *Studie enuitvoering van de klassieke polyphonie.* Bilthoven, 1939.
288. *Lustgarten neuer teutscher Gesänge. Paletti, Galliarden und Intraden mit vier, fünf und acht Stimmen.* Nuremberg, 1601.

289. BURDACH, KONRAD. *Vorspiel* I, 1. Halle, 1925.
290. DEVOLUY, P. *Le Psautier Huguenot.* Paris, 1928.
291. WECKERLIN, JEAN B. T. *La chanson populaire.* Paris, 1886.
292. VAN DER LEEUW, G., and ANTH. VAN DER HORST. *Bach's Hoogmis.* Amsterdam, 1941.
293. BRUNING, EL., O.F.M. *De kerkelijke volkszang.* Bilthoven, 1938.
294. BUSONI, FERRUCCIO. *Entwurf einer neuen Aesthetik der Tonkunst.* Leipzig. English: *Sketch of a New Aesthetic of Music.* New York, 1911.
295. BEKKER, P. *Beethoven.* Leipzig, 1911. English: *Beethoven.* New York, 1925.
296. BERTHOLET, A. *Buddhismus im Abendland der Gegenwart.* Tübingen, 1928.
297. PLATO. *Laws.*
298. HUYGENS, C. *Gebruyk of Ongebruyk van 't Orgel.* SCHOUTEN, H. *Onze oude Orgels.* Baarn. BOUMANN, A. *Orgels in Nederland.* Amsterdam, 1943.
299. POLLMANN, J. *Calvijn's Aesthetiek.* 's-Hertogenbosch.
300. BALFOORT, D. J. *Het muziekleven in Nederland in de 17e en 18e eeuw.* Amsterdam, 1938.
301. KOMTER-KUIPERS, A. *Adr. Valerius, Nederlandsche Gedenck Clanck.* Amsterdam, 1942. cf. 234.
302. BAENSCH, O. *Aufbau und Sinn des Chorfinale in Beethovens Neunter Sinfonie.* Leipzig, 1930.
303. BRENTANO, CLEMENS. *Abendständchen.*
304. HESSE, HERMANN. *Der Steppenwolf.* Berlin, 1938. English: *Steppenwolf.* New York, 1929.
305. MAIURI, AM. *La ville dei misteri.* Rome, 1949.
306. GILBERT, WILL G. In *Studiën*, December, 1940.
——— In *De wereld der muziek*, June, 1942.
307. HÖWELER, C. *"Humor in de Muziek." Muziek en Religie*, 42 (1929).
308. MAUCLAIR, CAMILLE. *Essais sur l'émotion musicale*, Vol. II: *Religion de la musique.* Paris, 1909.
309. MENSCHING, G. *Das heilige Schweigen.* Giessen, 1926.
310. VOIGT, WOLDMAR, *Die Kirchenkantaten Joh. Seb. Bachs.* Leipzig, 1923.
311. HAAS, HANS. "Aufführungspraxis der Musik." E. Bücken, *Handbuch der Musikwissenschaft.* Potsdam, 1930 to 1932.
312. BLUME, FR. *"Die evangelische Kirchenmusik."* E. Bücken, *Handbuch der Musikwissenschaft.* Potsdam, 1931–34.
313. BESCH, H. *J. S. Bach, Frömmigkeit und Glaube.* I. Gütersloh, 1938.
314. NIETZSCHE. *Zur Genealogie der Moral.* Musarionausgabe, Vol. XV. Munich, 1928. English: *The Genealogy of Morals.* Garden City, N. Y., 1956.
315. WAGNER, RICHARD. *Beethoven.* Cologne, 1944. English: *Beethoven.* New York, 1883.
316. HEIM, KARL. *Glaubensgewissheit.* Leipzig, 1923.
317. BIE, OSKAR. *Die Oper.* Berlin, 1920.
318. HOFFMANN, E. T. A. *Fantastische Studiën in Callots Manier, Kreisleriana. Der Musikfeind.* Complete works. Berlin–Leipzig–Vienna–Stuttgart, 1912. French: *Kreisleriane.* Paris, 1931.
319. PAUL, JEAN (J. P. F. Richter). *Die Weihnachtsfeier.* Complete works. Berlin, 1826–1838.
320. HACKMANN, H. *Chineesche Wijsgeeren*, Vol. I. Amsterdam, 1930. German: *Chineesische Philosophie.* Munich, 1927.
321. GATZ, FELIX M. *Musikästhetik in ihren Hauptrichtungen.* Stuttgart, 1929.
322. HANSLICK, EDWARD. *Vom Musikalisch-Schönen.* Leipzig, 1865. English: *The Beautiful in Music.* London, 1891.

323. NIETZSCHE. *Der Wille zur Macht*, 840. Musarionausgabe, Vol. XIX. Munich, 1928.
324. SCHERING, A. in *Kongress f. Aesth*. 1913, report p. 490.
325. WACH, J. *Das Verstehen* II. Tübingen, 1929.
326. ROLLAND, ROMAIN. *Jean Christophe; La Fin du voyage*. Paris, 1924. English: *Jean Christophe; Journey's End*. New York, 1913.
327. RUTTERS, HERMAN. "J. S. Bach's *'Die Kunst der Fuge.'* " *Alg. Weekblad voor Christendom en Cultuur* 7 (1931), No. 25.
328. HAPGOOD, ISABEL F. *Service Book of the Holy Orthodox-Catholic Apostolic Church*. New York, 1922.
329. PETERSON, E. *Das Buch von den Engeln*. Leipzig, 1935.
       WAGENVOORT, H. *"De Horatii carminis saec. compositione."* *Mnemosyne* 3, p. iv. 1936.
       TÄSCHNER, FR. *Orient. Stimmen zum Erlösungsgedanken*. Leipzig, 1936.
       GUTHRIE, W. K. C. "Orpheus and Greek Religion." London, 1935.
330. WHITMAN, WALT. *Leaves of Grass*. Brooklyn, New York, 1885.
331. PETERSON, E. *Zeuge der Wahrheit*. Leipzig, 1937.
332. LEHMANN, MAX. *Untersuchungen zur mystischen Terminologie Richard Rolles*. Jena, 1936.
333. MICHELANGELO. *Sonnets and Madrigals of Michelangelo Buonarroti*. Cambridge, 1900.
334. THURNWALD, R. *Zeitschr. f. Aesthetik und allg. Kunstwissenschaft* XIX, 349.
335. BAUDELAIRE. *"La Beauté." Petits poèmes en prose*. Paris, 1917. English: *The Flowers of Evil*. New York, 1955.
336. SCHLEGEL, FRIEDRICH. *Fragmente 46. Seine prosaischen Jugendschriften 1794 bis 1802*. J. Minor: Vienna, 1906. 2 volumes.
337. GEBHARDT, CARL. *Kantstudien* 32, 1927 (Spinoza issue).
338. VAN DEYSSEL, LODEWIJK. *Verzamelde Opstellen*. Amsterdam, 1899.
339. KANT. *Kritik der Urteilskraft*. Kants Gesammelte Schriften, Königl. Preuss. Akademie d. Wissenschaften, Vol. V. English: *Kant's Critique of Judgment*. London, 1931.
340. SPOERRI, TH. *Die Götter des Abendlandes*.
341. BANDINELLI, BIANCHI. *Kunst der Antike und neuzeitliche Kritik*. Groningen, 1931.
342. DANE, CLEMENCE. *Broome Stages*. Garden City, N. Y., 1931.
343. DILTHEY, W. *Das Erlebnis und die Dichtung*. Leipzig, 1913.
344. PROUST, MARCEL. *A l'Ombre des Jeunes Filles en Fleurs*. Paris, 1947. English: *Within a Budding Grove*. New York, 1930.
       RÜMKE, H. C. *Phaenomenologische en klinisch-psychiatrische Studie over Geluksgevoel*. Leiden, 1923.
345. GOETHE. From *Briefwechsel zwischen Goethe und Zelter in den Jahren 1796 bis 1832*. Vol. IV. Berlin, 1833–34. Letter of 1827. English: *Goethe's Letters to Zelter*. London, 1887.
346. WALZEL, OSKAR F. *Das Prometheussymbol von Shaftesbury zu Goethe*. Munich, 1932.
347. REESER, EDUARD. *De muziek in de gemeenschap der kunsten*. Utrecht, 1947.
348. SHELLEY. *Defence of Poetry*.
349. SCHWEITZER, A. *J. S. Bach, le musicien-poète*. Leipzig, 1905. English: *J. S. Bach*. London, 1923.
       PIRRO, ANDRÉ. *L' Esthétique de J. S. Bach*. Paris, 1907.
350. HAAS, R. *Die Musik des Barock*. E. Bücken, Handbuch der Musikwissenschaften. Potsdam, 1928.

351. MIGNE (Publisher): Paris. *Patrologia latina* 37, 1272; 36, 283.
    AIGRAIN, RENÉ. *La musique religieuse*. Paris, 1929. English: *Religious Music*.
    London, 1931.
    JOHNER, P. D. *Neue Schule des Gregorianischen Choralgesangs*. Regensburg,
    1929. English: *A New School of Gregorian Chant*. New York, 1908.

352. VON ARSENIEW, NIK. In *Arch. f. Rel. Gesch.* 22 (1923–24), pp. 266 ff.

353. *Der junge Dilthey: Ein Lebensbild in Briefen und Tagebüchern 1852 bis
    1870*. Compiled by Clara Misch. Leipzig, 1933.

354. "Kerkmuziek," *Handboek voor den Eeredienst in de Ned. Herv. Kerk*. Rotter-
    dam, 1934.

355. MUSCULUS, PAUL R. "*La Prière des mains.*" *L'Église réformée et l'art*.

356. MALLERY, GARRICK. "Picture-writing of the American Indians." *10th Annual of
    the Bureau of Ethnology*. 1888–89. Smithsonian Institution: Washington, 1893.

357. Cf. the commentaries of Holzinger, 1898; Gunkel, 1910; Procksch, 1913;
    Böhl, 1930.
    L. KÖHLER, *Theologie des Alten Testaments*. Tübingen, 1936. Cf. 358.

358. HUMBERT, P. "Etudes sur le récit du paradis et de la chute dans la Genèse."
    Mem. de l'univ. de Neuchâtel XIV (1940).

359. VAN DER LEEUW, G. "*Psychologie en Wereldbeschouwing of de oorsprong der
    moderne psychologie in een misverstand.*" *Geref. Psych. Studievereeniging*,
    1942.

360. LIETZMANN, HANS. *An die Korinther I–II*. Tübingen, 1931.

361. WINDISCH, H. *Der Hebräerbrief*. Tübingen, 1931.

362. DIBELIUS, MARTIN. *Handbuch zum Neuen Testament* 11. 1937.

363. VON HARNACK, ADOLF. *Dogmengeschichte* I. Tübingen, 1905. English: *History
    of Dogma*. London, 1896–99.

364. LOOFS. *Leitfaden zum Studium der Dogmengeschichte*. Halle, 1906. 21:3; 43:3.
    Hutterus redivivus, 80.

365. AALDERS, W. J. "Het vraagstuk natuurlijk-bovennatuurlijk door moralisten
    bezien." *Med. Kon. Ned. Akad. v. Wetensch.*, afd. Lett. N. R. 2,4 (1939).

366. Questions 6 and 8 of the Heidelberg Catechism.

367. Netherlands Confession, Article 14.

368. KOOPMANS, J. *Het oud-kerkelijk dogma in de Reformatie*. Wageningen, 1938.

369. SCHLEIERMACHER, F. E. D. *Der Christliche Glaube nach den Grundsätzen der
    Evangelischen Kirche im Zusammenhange dargestellt*. Halle. English: *The
    Christian Faith*. Edinburgh, 1928.

370. KÄHLER, MARTIN. *Die Wissenschaft der christlichen Lehre*. Leipzig, 1893.
    BRUNNER, EMIL. *Gott und Mensch*. Tübingen, 1930.

371. PRZYWARA, ERICH. *A Newman Synthesis*. London, 1930.

372. BARTH, KARL. *Kirchliche Dogmatik* I, 1. Munich, 1932. English: *Dogmatics*.

373. PICARD, MAX. *Die Grenzen der Physiognomik*. Erlenbach–Zurich–Leipzig, 1937.

374. HOFMANN, PAUL. *Sinn und Geschichte*. Munich, 1937.

375. NOORDMANS, O. *Herschepping*. Zeist, 1934.

376. WOLF, HANNA. *Der lebendige Gott. Nathan Söderbloms Beitrag zur Offen-
    barungsfrage*. Emsdetten, 1938.

377. VAN DER LEEUW, G. *Onsterfelijkheid of Opstanding?* Assen, 1947.

378. KRELING. *Katholische Encyclopaedie* 4, 1933.

379. *The Hymnal 1940*, number 204. After Thomas Aquinas.

380. PASCAL. *Lettre à Mlle de Roannez* II. Paris, 1881.

381. SHELLEY. *Hymn to Intellectual Beauty*.

INDEX

Akhenaten, 172
Algazi, L., 61
Andersen, Hans Christian, 130
Anderson, Marian, 234
Apollo (Manticles), 187(n.)
Aristophanes, 279
Art of the Fugue (Bach), 226, 259, 260
Assunta (Titian), 170
Austen, Jane, 129

Bacchae (Euripides), 91
Bach, 32, 66, 242, 286, 291, 330; *Art of the Fugue*, 226, 259, 260; *Christmas Oratorio*, 221, 234, 237; *Fantasia and Fugue in G Minor*, 207; *Mass in B Minor*, xii, 236, 237, 243, 250; *Toccata and Fugue in D Minor*, 207; *St. Matthew Passion*, 218, 230, 233, 235, 237, 238, 239, 279, 292; *The Well-Tempered Clavier*, 232
Balzac, *Comédie Humaine*, 88, 280; *The Unknown Work of Art*, 187
Barth, Karl, *Epistle to the Romans*, 318, 319
Baudelaire, 136
Beethoven, 60; *Coriolanus Overture*, 255; *Eroica*, 249, 255; *Fidelio*, 105, 248; Fifth Symphony, 236, 255; Ninth Symphony, 59, 66, 237, 243, 254; *Pastoral*, 255; *Quartets*, 226;

Seventh Symphony, 66; Violin Concerto, 236
Beham, Sebald, 21, 34
Benedict, Ruth, 20
Birth of Tragedy from the Spirit of Music, The (Nietzsche), 247
Bizet (Nietzsche letter), 258(n.)
Boccaccio, 130, 279
Bolero (Ravel), 293
Breughel, 34
Broome Stages (Dane), 107
Bruckner, Anton, 207; Third Symphony, 232

Calderón, *Mysteries of the Mass*, 105
Canons of Hippolytus, 227
Caplet, André, *Les Prières*, 234
Cato, M. Porcius, *On Agriculture*, 40
Chaucer, 130
Chesterton, G. K., 33, 35, 36
Chopin, Frederic, *Préludes*, 270
Christ (Michelangelo), 170
Christmas Oratorio (Bach), 221, 234, 237
Christ with the Crown of Thorns (Dürer), 190
Cicero, 29
Comédie Humaine (Balzac), 88, 280
Coriolanus Overture (Beethoven), 255
Coronation Mass (Mozart), 70
Creation, The (Haydn), 235

353

Crucifixion of the Isenheim Altar (Grünewald), 190

Dane, Clemence, *Broome Stages*, 107
Dante, 302; *La Vita Nuova*, 244; *Paradiso*, 22, 144; *Purgatorio*, 41
Das Bild Christi im Wandel der Zeiten (Preuss), 166
Das Rheingold (Wagner), 301
Da Todi, Jacopone, *Laude*, 26
Da Vinci, Leonardo, vi, 32
Die Meistersinger (Wagner), 54, 248, 267
Don Giovanni (Mozart), 23
Duncan, Isadora, 56, 70
Dürer, Albrecht, *Christ with the Crown of Thorns*, 190; *Sudarium of St. Veronica*, 192

Eighth Symphony (Mahler), 207
Einführung in die Phänomenologie der Religion (van der Leeuw), v
Epistle to the Romans (Barth), 318, 319
Erasmus, 184
Eroica (Beethoven), 249, 255
Euripides, 23; *Bacchae*, 91
"Evening Song" (Tersteegen), 141

Fantasia and Fugue in G Minor (Bach), 207
Feast of Christmas (Schleiermacher), 282
Fidelio (Beethoven), 105, 248
Fifth Symphony (Beethoven), 236, 255
"First Love Song of a Young Girl" (Mörike), 120
Forsyte Saga, The (Galsworthy), 280
Fra Angelico, *The Last Judgment*, 68
Frazer, *The Golden Bough*, 81
"From Heaven High I Come to You" (Luther), 220

Galgenlieder (Morgenstern), 298

Galsworthy, John, *The Forsyte Saga*, 280; *Salta Pro Nobis*, 71
Gautier, Théophile, 179
George, Stefan, 122, 134, 143, 146, 295; *The Seventh Ring*, 145
Gerhardt, Paul, "O Welt, sieh hier dein Leben," 220
Gezelle, Guido, 137, 144, 146
Giotto, 181, 283
Goethe, vi, 12, 125, 132, 136, 140, 141, 286
Golden Bough, The (Frazer), 81
Gorter, Herman, *Mei*, 140, 247(n.)
Götterdämmerung (Wagner), 235
Grünewald, Matthis, *Crucifixion of the Isenheim Altar*, 190

Hamlet (Shakespeare), 92, 95
Handel, 32, 221; *Israel in Egypt*, 219; *The Messiah*, 219
Hauptmann, Gerhart, 53
Haydn, *The Creation*, 235; *The Seasons*, 246
Heine, Heinrich, *Travel Sketches*, 200
Heraclitus, 177
Hermes (Praxiteles), 170
Herodotus, 177
Holbein, *Dance of Death*, 19
Hölderlin, vi, 143, 146, 294
Homer, 133, 143, 301, 302
Horace, 143
Horn, A. A. ("Trader Horn"), 15
Hugo, Victor, 122, 126
Huizinga, Johan, 12, 21
Hundred-Gulden Note, The (Rembrandt), 191
"Hymn to Intellectual Beauty" (Shelley), 338

Ibsen, 53, 108; *Paa Viddeme*, 134; "When We Dead Awaken," 298
"In Memory of the Actor Mitterwurzer" (Hugo von Hofmannstahl), 106, 107, 299
"Invitation to the Dance" (Weber), 34

Israel in Egypt (Handel), 219

Jaspers, Karl, *Psychology of World Views*, 285
Jean Christophe (Rolland), 259
Jooss Ballet, 13, 74

Karoline (Schleiermacher), 249
Kierkegaard, 156, 288, 337
King Lear (Shakespeare), 92, 95, 105

Laokoön (Lessing), 155, 156
Last Judgment, The (Fra Angelico), 68
Last Judgment, The (Michelangelo), 192
Laude (Da Todi), 26
La Vita Nuova (Dante), 244
Laws (Plato), 228
Leskov, Nikolai, *The Sealed Angel*, 174
Les Prières (Caplet), 234
Lessing, Gotthold, *Laokoön*, 155, 156
Le Visage du Christ, Introduction to (Mornand), 166
Lied von der Erde (Mahler), 238
Lin Yutang, 166
"Litany" (Schubert), 270
Love's Labour's Lost (Shakespeare), 92
Lucian, 18, 22, 29, 48
Lucifer (van den Vondel), 140
Luther, "From Heaven High I Come to You," 220

Magic Flute, The (Mozart), 233, 243, 244, 270
Mahler, Gustav, 58, 142; Eighth Symphony, 207; *Lied von der Erde*, 238
Mallarmé, Stéphane, 278
Mann, Thomas, 149; *Tonio Kröger*, 273
Manticles, *Apollo*, 187(n.)
Maritain, Jacques, 183, 325, 335

Marriage of Figaro, The (Mozart), 233, 244, 257, 296
Mass in B Minor (Bach), xii, 236, 237, 243
Mayfart, Johann Mathäus, Jerusalem hymn, 69
Mei (Gorter), 140, 247(n.)
Messiah, The (Handel), 219
Michelangelo, vi; *Christ*, 170; *The Last Judgment*, 192
Milton, John, 146
Molière, 20, 284
Monteverdi, Claudio, 292
Morgenstern, Christian, *Galgenlieder*, 298
Mörike, "First Love Song of a Young Girl," 120
Mornand, Pierre, *Le Visage du Christ*, Introduction to, 166
Mozart, 60, 61, 301, 330; *Coronation Mass*, 70; *Don Giovanni*, 23; *The Magic Flute*, 233, 243, 244, 270; *The Marriage of Figaro*, 233, 244, 257, 296; *Requiem*, 244
Mysteries of the Mass (Calderón), 105

Nietzsche, 134, 258(n.), 296, 298, 299; *The Birth of Tragedy from the Spirit of Music*, 247; *Zarathustra*, 146, 148
Ninth Symphony (Beethoven), 59, 66, 237, 243, 254
Novalis, 146

Obrecht, 221
On Agriculture (Cato), 40
Othello (Shakespeare), 92
Otto, Rudolf, 4
"*O Welt, sieh hier dein Leben*" (Gerhardt), 220

Paa Viddeme (Ibsen), 134
Palestrina, 221
Paradiso (Dante), 22, 144
Parsifal (Wagner), 54, 230, 292
Pastoral (Beethoven), 255

Phaedrus, 339
Phänomenologie der Religion (van der Leeuw), v, vi
Phidias, 163
Pindar, 143
Plato, 132; Laws, 228
Praxiteles, 163; Hermes, 170
Préludes (Chopin), 270
Preuss, Hans, 22; Das Bild Christi im Wandel der Zeiten, 166
Proust, Marcel, 131

Quartets (Beethoven), 226

Racine, 278, 296
Raphael, 167, 278, 283
Ravel, Bolero, 293
Rembrandt, xi, 181, 278, 283; The Hundred-Gulden Note, 191; Simeon in the Temple, 191
Requiem (Mozart), 244
Requiem (Verdi), 240
Rilke, Rainer Maria, 181, 186
Robeson, Paul, 234
Rolland, Romain, Jean Christophe, 259
Rossetti, Sister Helen, 222
Rousseau, 136
Rubens, 167

Sachs, Curt, 14, 19, 22, 26, 32, 291
St. Matthew Passion (Bach) 218, 230, 233, 235, 237, 238, 239, 279, 292
Saint-Saéns, Third Symphony, 236
Salta Pro Nobis (Galsworthy), 71
Schiller, 286; "Song of the Bell," 214
Schleiermacher, Feast of Christmas, 282; Karoline, 249
Schopenhauer, 125, 245, 296, 303, 337
Schubert, Franz, 142; "Litany," 270
Sealed Angel, The (Leskov), 174
Seasons, The (Haydn), 246
Seventh Ring, The (George), 145
Seventh Symphony (Beethoven), 66
Shakespeare, 77, 146, 278; Hamlet, 92, 95; King Lear, 92, 95, 105; Love's Labour's Lost, 92; Othello, 92; The Taming of the Shrew, 92; Timon of Athens, 92
Shelley, Percy Bysshe, 147, 290; "Hymn to Intellectual Beauty," 338
Sibylline Books, 228
Siegfried (Wagner), 161
Simeon in the Temple (Rembrandt), 191
Sistine Madonna, 170
Sister Helen (Rossetti), 222
"Song of the Bell" (Schiller), 214
Spranger, Eduard, 4
Sudarium of St. Veronica (Dürer), 192

Taming of the Shrew, The (Shakespeare), 92
Tannhäuser (Wagner), 53, 54, 270
Tersteegen, 146; "Evening Song," 141
Timon of Athens (Shakespeare), 92
Third Symphony (Bruckner), 232
Third Symphony (Saint-Saéns), 236
Titian, Assunta, 170
Toccata and Fugue in D Minor (Bach), 207
Tolstoi, 136
Tonio Kröger (Mann), 273
Travel Sketches (Heine), 200
Tristan und Isolde (Wagner), 238, 258, 279, 296

Unknown Work of Art, The (Balzac), 187

Van den Vondel, Joost, 22, 30, 146; Lucifer, 140
Van der Leeuw, Gerardus, Einführung in die Phänomenologie der Religion, v; Phänomenologie der Religion, v, vi
Van Eyck, 137, 150, 188
Van St. Aldegonde, "Apologia of the Dance," 52
Venus of Willendorf, 162
Verdi, Requiem, 240
Verdi (Werfel), 272, 294

Veronese, Paolo, 167, 178

Verwey, Albert, 145, 147

Village Magistrate, 172

Violin Concerto (Beethoven), 236

Voltaire, 282

Von Hofmannsthal, Hugo, "In Memory of the Actor Mitterwurzer," 106, 107, 299

Wagner, Richard, *Das Rheingold*, 301; *Die Meistersinger*, 54, 248, 267; *Götterdämmerung*, 235; *Parsifal*, 54, 230, 292; *Siegfried*, 161;

Tannhäuser, 53, 54, 270; *Tristan und Isolde*, 238, 258(n.), 279, 296

Weber, "Invitation to the Dance," 34

Well-Tempered Clavier, The (Bach), 232

Werfel, Franz, *Verdi*, 272, 294

"When We Dead Awaken" (Ibsen), 298

Wolfskehl, Karl, 295, 296, 297

Would-be Gentleman, The (Molière), 20

Xenophanes, 132

Zarathustra (Nietzsche), 146, 148